Modern Time Series Forecasting with Python

Explore industry-ready time series forecasting using modern machine learning and deep learning

Manu Joseph

BIRMINGHAM—MUMBAI

Modern Time Series Forecasting with Python

Publishing Product Manager: Dhruv Kataria

Senior Editors: Roshan Ravikumar, Tazeen Shaikh

Content Development Editor: Shreya Moharir

Technical Editor: Devanshi Ayare

Copy Editor: Safis Editing

Project Coordinator: Farheen Fathima

Proofreader: Safis Editing

Indexer: Subalakshmi Govindhan

Production Designer: Alishon Mendonca

Marketing Coordinator: Shifa Ansari

First published: November 2022

Production reference: 1181122

Published by Packt Publishing Ltd.

Livery Place

35 Livery Street

Birmingham

B3 2PB, UK.

ISBN 978-1-80324-680-2

www.packt.com

For my son, Zane,

For his boundless curiosity,

For his endless questions,

And for his innocent love of learning.

(All great qualities for adults who read this book as well.)

Contributors

About the author

Manu Joseph is a self-made data scientist with more than a decade of experience working with many Fortune 500 companies, enabling digital and AI transformations, specifically in machine learning-based demand forecasting. He is considered an expert, thought leader, and strong voice in the world of time series forecasting. Currently, Manu leads applied research at Thoucentric, where he advances research by bringing cutting-edge AI technologies to the industry. He is also an active open source contributor and has developed an open source library—PyTorch Tabular—which makes deep learning for tabular data easy and accessible. Originally from Thiruvananthapuram, India, Manu currently resides in Bengaluru, India, with his wife and son.

About the reviewers

Dr. Julien Siebert is currently working as a researcher at the Fraunhofer **Institute for Experimental Software Engineering** (**IESE**), in Kaiserslautern, Germany. He studied engineering sciences and AI and obtained a PhD in computer science on the topic of modeling and simulation of complex systems. After several years of research both in computer science and theoretical physics, Dr. Julien Siebert worked as a data scientist for an e-commerce fashion company. Since 2018, he has been working at the intersection between software engineering and data science.

Gerzson David Boros is the owner and CEO of Data Science Europe and a senior data scientist who has been involved in data science for more than 10 years. He has an MSc and is a candidate for an MBA. In the last 5 years, he and his team have made business proposals for 100 different executives and worked on more than 30 different projects on the topic of data science and artificial intelligence. His motto is "*Social responsibility is also achievable with the help of data.*"

Table of Contents

3

Analyzing and Visualizing Time Series Data   49

4

Setting a Strong Baseline Forecast   77

Part 2 – Machine Learning for Time Series   105

5

Time Series Forecasting as Regression   107

6

Feature Engineering for Time Series Forecasting   121

9

Ensembling and Stacking   203

10

Global Forecasting Models   225

Part 3 – Deep Learning for Time Series   259

11

Introduction to Deep Learning   261

Part 4 – Mechanics of Forecasting   453

17

Multi-Step Forecasting   455

18

Evaluating Forecasts – Forecast Metrics   469

19

Evaluating Forecasts – Validation Strategies   491

Index   505

Other Books You May Enjoy   522

Preface

Mankind has always sought the ability to predict the future. Since the earliest civilizations, people have tried to predict the future. Shamans, oracles, and prophets used anything ranging from astrology and palmistry to numerology to satisfy the human need to see into the future. In the last century, with the developments in IT, the mantle of predicting the future landed on data analysts and data scientists. And how do we predict the future? It's not by examining the lines and creases on our hands or the positions of the stars anymore but by using data that has been generated in the past. And instead of prophecies, we now have forecasts.

Time, being the fourth dimension in our world, makes all the data generated in the world time series data. All the data that is generated in the real world has an element of time associated with it. Whether the temporal aspect is relevant to the problem or not is another question altogether. However, to be more concrete and immediate, we can find time series forecasting use cases in many industries, such as retail, energy, healthcare, and finance. We might want to know how many units of a particular product are to be dispatched to a particular store, or we might want to know how much electricity is to be produced to meet demand.

In this book, using a real-world dataset, you will learn how to handle and visualize time series data using `pandas` and `plotly`, generate baseline forecasts using `darts`, and use machine learning and deep learning for forecasting, using popular Python libraries such as `scikit-learn` and `PyTorch`. We conclude the book with a few chapters that cover seldom-touched aspects, such as multi-step forecasting, forecast metrics and cross validation for time series.

The book will enable you to build real-world time series forecasting systems that scale to millions of time series by mastering and applying modern concepts in machine learning and deep learning.

Who this book is for

The book is ideal for data scientists, data analysts, machine learning engineers and Python developers who want to build industry-ready time series models. Since the book explains most concepts from the ground up, basic proficiency in Python is all you need. A prior understanding of machine learning or forecasting would help speed up the learning. For seasoned practitioners in machine learning and forecasting, the book has a lot to offer in terms of advanced techniques and traversing the latest research frontiers in time series forecasting.

What this book covers

Chapter 1, Introducing Time Series, is all about introducing you to the world of time series. We lay down a definition of time series and talk about how it is related to a **Data Generating Process** (**DGP**). We will also talk about the limits of forecasting and talk about what we cannot forecast, and then we finish off the chapter by laying down some terminology that will help you understand the rest of the book.

Chapter 2, Acquiring and Processing Time Series Data, covers how you can process time series data. You will understand how different forms of time series data can be represented in a tabular form. You will learn different date-time-related functionalities in pandas and learn how to fill in missing data using techniques suited for time series. Finally, using a real-world dataset, you will go through a step-by-step journey in processing time series data using pandas.

Chapter 3, Analyzing and Visualizing Time Series Data, furthers your introduction to time series by learning how to visualize and analyze time series. You will learn different visualizations that are commonly used for time series data and then learn how to go one level deeper by decomposing time series into its components. To wrap it up, you will also look at ways to identify and treat outliers in time series data.

Chapter 4, Setting a Strong Baseline Forecast, gets right to the topic of time series forecasting as we use tried and tested methods from econometrics, such as *ARIMA* and *exponential smoothing*, to generate strong baselines. These efficient forecasting methods will provide strong baselines so that we can go beyond these classical techniques and learn modern techniques, such as machine learning. You will also get an introduction to another key topic – assessing forecastability using techniques such as *spectral entropy* and *coefficient of variation*.

Chapter 5, Time Series Forecasting as Regression, starts our journey into using machine learning for forecasting. A short introduction to machine learning lays down the foundations of what is to come in the next chapters. You will also understand, conceptually, how we can cast a time series problem as a regression problem so that we can use machine learning for it. To close off the chapter, we tease you with the possibility of global forecasting models.

Chapter 6, Feature Engineering for Time Series Forecasting, shifts gear into a more practical lesson. Using a real-world dataset, you will learn about different feature engineering techniques, such as *lag features*, *rolling features*, and *Fourier terms*, which help us formulate a time series problem as a regression problem.

Chapter 7, Target Transformations for Time Series Forecasting, continues the practice of exploring different target transformations to accommodate non-stationarity in time series. You will learn techniques such as the *augmented Dickey–Fuller test* and *Mann–Kendall test* to identify and treat non-stationarity.

Chapter 8, Forecasting Time Series with Machine Learning Models, continues from where the last chapter left off to start training machine learning models on the dataset we have been working on. Using the standard code framework present in the book, you will train models such as *linear regression*, *random forest*, and *gradient-boosted decision trees* on our dataset.

Chapter 9, Ensembling and Stacking, takes a step back and explores how we can use multiple forecasts and combine them to create a better forecast. You will explore popular techniques such as *best fit,* different versions of the *hill-climbing algorithm, simulated annealing,* and *stacking* to combine the different forecasts we have generated to get a better one.

Chapter 10, Global Forecasting Models, concludes your guided journey into machine learning-enabled forecasting to an exciting and new paradigm – global forecasting models. You will learn how to use global forecasting models and industry-proven techniques to improve their performance, which finally lets you develop scalable and efficient machine learning forecasting systems for thousands of time series.

Chapter 11, Introduction to Deep Learning, we switch tracks and start with a specific type of machine learning – deep learning. In this chapter, we lay the foundations of deep learning by looking at different topics such as *representation learning, linear transformations, activation functions,* and *gradient descent.*

Chapter 12, Building Blocks of Deep Learning for Time Series, continues the journey into deep learning by making it specific to time series. Keeping in mind the compositionality of deep learning systems, you will learn about different building blocks with which you can construct a deep learning architecture. The chapter starts off by establishing the *encoder-decoder architecture* and then talks about different blocks such as *feed forward networks, recurrent neural networks,* and *convolutional neural networks.*

Chapter 13, Common Modeling Patterns for Time Series, strengthens the encoder-decoder architecture that you saw in the previous chapter by showing you a few concrete and common patterns in which you can arrange building blocks to generate forecasts. This is a hands-on chapter where you will be creating forecasts using deep learning-based *tabular regression* and different *sequence-to-sequence models.*

Chapter 14, Attention and Transformers for Time Series, covers the contemporary topic of using attention to improve deep learning models. The chapter starts off by talking about a generalized attention model with which you will learn different types of attention schemes, such as *scaled dot product* and *additive.* You will also tweak the sequence-to-sequence models from the previous chapter to include attention and then train those models to generate a forecast. The chapter then talks about *transformer* models, which is a deep learning architecture that relies solely on attention, and then you will use that to generate forecasts as well.

Chapter 15, Strategies for Global Deep Learning Forecasting Models, tackles yet another important aspect of deep learning-based forecasting. Although the book talked about global forecasting models earlier, there are some differences in how it is implemented for deep learning models. In this chapter, you will learn how to implement global deep learning models and techniques on how to make those models better. You will also see them working in the hands-on section, where we will be generating forecasts using the real-world dataset we have been working with.

Chapter 16, Specialized Deep Learning Architectures for Forecasting, concludes your journey into deep learning-based time series forecasting by talking about a few popular, specialized deep learning architectures for time series forecasting. Using the concepts and building blocks you have learned through the previous chapters, this chapter takes you to the cutting edge of research and exposes the leading state-of-the-art models in time series forecasting such as *N-BEATS, N-HiTS, Informer, Autoformer*, and *Temporal Fusion Transformer*. In addition to understanding them, you will also learn how to use these models to generate forecasts using a real-world dataset.

Chapter 17, Multi-Step Forecasting, tackles the rarely talked about but highly relevant topic of multi-step forecasting. You will learn about different strategies for generating forecasts for more than one time step into the future, such as *Recursive, Direct, DirRec, RecJoint*, and *Rectify*. The book also talks about the merits and demerits of each of them and helps you choose the right strategy for your problem.

Chapter 18, Evaluating Forecasts – Forecast Metrics, traverses yet another topic that is rarely talked about and rife with controversy, with many opinions from different quarters. You will learn about different ways to measure the goodness of a forecast and through experiments, which you can run, expose the strengths and weaknesses of different metrics. The chapter concludes by laying down some guidelines that can help you choose the correct metric for your problem.

Chapter 19, Evaluating Forecasts – Validation Strategies, concludes the evaluation of forecasts and the book by talking about different validation strategies we can use for time series. You will learn different validation strategies such as hold-out, cross-validation, and their variations. The chapter also touches upon aspects to keep in mind while designing validation strategies for global settings as well. At the conclusion of the chapter, you will come across a few guidelines for choosing your validation strategies and answers to questions such as *can we use cross-validation for time series?*

To get the most out of this book

You should have basic familiarity with Python programming, as the entire code that we use for the practical sections is in `Python`. Familiarity with major libraries in Python, such as `pandas` and `scikit-learn`, are not essential (because the book covers some basics) but will help you get through the book much faster. Familiarity with `PyTorch`, the framework the book uses for deep learning, is also not essential but would accelerate your learning by many folds. Any of the software requirements shouldn't stop you because, in today's internet-enabled world, the only thing that is standing between you and a world of knowledge is the search bar in your favorite search engine.

Another key aspect to get the most out of this book is to run the associated notebooks as you go along the lessons. Also, feel free to experiment with different variations that the book doesn't go into. That is a surefire way to internalize what's being talked about in the book. And for that, we need to set up an environment, as you'll see in the following section.

Setting up an environment

The easiest way to set up an environment is by using Anaconda, a distribution of Python for scientific computing. You can use Miniconda, a minimal installer for Conda, as well if you do not want the pre-installed packages that come with Anaconda:

1. **Install Anaconda/Miniconda**: Anaconda can be installed from `https://www.anaconda.com/products/distribution`. Depending on your operating system, choose the corresponding file and follow the instructions. Alternatively, you can install Miniconda from here: `https://docs.conda.io/en/latest/miniconda.html#latest-miniconda-installer-links`.

2. **Open conda prompt**: To open Anaconda Prompt (or Terminal on Linux or macOS), do the following:

    - **Windows**: Open the Anaconda Prompt (**Start | Anaconda Prompt**)

    - **macOS**: Open Launchpad and then open Terminal. Type `conda activate`.

    - **Linux**: Open Terminal. Type `conda activate`.

3. **Navigate to the downloaded code**: Use operating system-specific commands to navigate to the folder where you have downloaded the code. For instance, in Windows, use `cd`.

4. **Install the environment**: Using the `anaconda_env.yml` file that is included, install the environment:

    ```
    conda env create -f anaconda_env.yml
    ```

    This creates a new environment under the name `modern_ts` and will install all the required libraries in the environment. This can take a while.

5. **Checking the installation**: We can check whether all the libraries required for the book are installed properly by executing a script in the downloaded code folder:

    ```
    python test_installation.py
    ```

6. **Activating the environment and running notebooks**: Every time you want to run the notebooks, first activate the environment using the `conda activate modern_ts` command and then use the Jupyter Notebook (`jupyter notebook`) or JupyterLab (`jupyter lab`), according to your preference.

Download the data

You are going to be using a single dataset throughout the book. The book uses the *London Smart Meters dataset* from Kaggle for this purpose. Therefore, if you don't have an account with Kaggle, please go ahead and create one: `https://www.kaggle.com/account/login?phase=startRegisterTab`.

There are two ways you can download the data-automated and manual.

For the automated way, we need to download a key from Kaggle. Let's do that first (if you are going to choose the manual way, you can skip this):

1. Click on your profile picture in the top-right corner of Kaggle.
2. Select **Account**, and find the section for **API**.
3. Click the **Create New API Token** button. A file with the name `kaggle.json` will be downloaded.
4. Copy the file and place it in the `api_keys` folder in the downloaded code folder.

Now that we have `kaggle.json` downloaded and placed in the right folder, let's look at the two methods to download data:

Method one – automated download

1. Activate the environment using `conda activate modern_ts`.
2. Run the provided script from the `root` directory of the downloaded code:

```
python scripts/download_data.py
```

That's it. Now, just wait for the script to finish downloading, unzip it, and organize the files in the expected format.

Method two – manual download

3. Go to `https://www.kaggle.com/jeanmidev/smart-meters-in-london` and download the dataset.
4. Unzip the contents to `data/london_smart_meters`.
5. Unzip `hhblock_dataset` to get the raw files we want to work with.
6. Make sure the unzipped files are in the expected folder structure (see the next section).

Now that you have downloaded the data, we need to make sure it is arranged in the following folder structure. The automated download does it automatically, but with the manual download, this structure needs to be created. To avoid ambiguity, the expected folder structure can be found as follows:

```
data
├── london_smart_meters
│   ├── hhblock_dataset
│   │   ├── hhblock_dataset
│   │   │   ├── block_0.csv
│   │   │   ├── block_1.csv
│   │   │   ├── ...
```

```
|    |              ├── block_109.csv
|── acorn_details.csv
├── informations_households.csv
├── uk_bank_holidays.csv
├── weather_daily_darksky.csv
├── weather_hourly_darksky.csv
```

There can be additional files as part of the extraction process. You can remove them without impacting anything. There is a helpful script that checks this structure.

```
python test_data_download.py
```

If you are using the digital version of this book, we advise you to type the code yourself or access the code from the book's GitHub repository. Doing so will help you avoid any potential errors related to the copying and pasting of code.

The code that is provided along with the book is in no way a library but more of a guide for you to start experimenting on. The amount of learning you can derive from the book and code is directly proportional to how much you experiment with the code and stray outside your comfort zone. So, go ahead and start experimenting and putting the skills you pick up in the book to good use.

Download the example code files

You can download the example code files for this book from GitHub at `https://github.com/PacktPublishing/Modern-Time-Series-Forecasting-with-Python`. If there's an update to the code, it will be updated in the GitHub repository.

We also have other code bundles from our rich catalog of books and videos available at `https://github.com/PacktPublishing/`. Check them out!

Download the color images

We also provide a PDF file that has color images of the screenshots and diagrams used in this book. You can download it here: `https://packt.link/5NVrW`.

Conventions used

There are a number of text conventions used throughout this book.

`Code in text`: Indicates code words in text, database table names, folder names, filenames, file extensions, pathnames, dummy URLs, user input, and Twitter handles. Here is an example: "`statsmodels.tsa.seasonal` has a function called `seasonal_decompose`."

A block of code is set as follows:

```
#Does not support missing values, so using imputed ts instead
res = seasonal_decompose(ts, period=7*48, model="additive",
extrapolate_trend="freq")
```

Any command-line input or output is written as follows:

```
conda env create -f anaconda_env.yml
```

Bold: Indicates a new term, an important word, or words that you see onscreen. For instance, words in menus or dialog boxes appear in **bold**. Here is an example: "But if you look at the **Time Elapsed** column, it stands out."

> **Tips or important notes**
> Appear like this.

Get in touch

Feedback from our readers is always welcome.

General feedback: If you have questions about any aspect of this book, email us at customercare@ packtpub.com and mention the book title in the subject of your message.

Errata: Although we have taken every care to ensure the accuracy of our content, mistakes do happen. If you have found a mistake in this book, we would be grateful if you would report this to us. Please visit www.packtpub.com/support/errata and fill in the form.

Piracy: If you come across any illegal copies of our works in any form on the internet, we would be grateful if you would provide us with the location address or website name. Please contact us at copyright@packt.com with a link to the material.

If you are interested in becoming an author: If there is a topic that you have expertise in and you are interested in either writing or contributing to a book, please visit authors.packtpub.com.

Share Your Thoughts

Once you've read *Modern Time Series Forecasting with Python*, we'd love to hear your thoughts! Scan the QR code below to go straight to the Amazon review page for this book and share your feedback.

https://packt.link/r/1-803-24680-4

Your review is important to us and the tech community and will help us make sure we're delivering excellent quality content.

Download a free PDF copy of this book

Thanks for purchasing this book!

Do you like to read on the go but are unable to carry your print books everywhere?

Is your eBook purchase not compatible with the device of your choice?

Don't worry, now with every Packt book you get a DRM-free PDF version of that book at no cost.

Read anywhere, any place, on any device. Search, copy, and paste code from your favorite technical books directly into your application.

The perks don't stop there, you can get exclusive access to discounts, newsletters, and great free content in your inbox daily

Follow these simple steps to get the benefits:

1. Scan the QR code or visit the link below

https://packt.link/free-ebook/9781803246802

2. Submit your proof of purchase
3. That's it! We'll send your free PDF and other benefits to your email directly

Part 1 –
Getting Familiar with
Time Series

We dip our toes into time series forecasting by understanding what a time series is, how to process and manipulate time series data, and how to analyze and visualize time series data. This part also covers classical time series forecasting methods, such as ARIMA, to serve as strong baselines.

This part comprises the following chapters:

- *Chapter 1, Introducing Time Series*
- *Chapter 2, Acquiring and Processing Time Series Data*
- *Chapter 3, Analyzing and Visualizing Time Series Data*
- *Chapter 4, Setting a Strong Baseline Forecast*

1

Introducing Time Series

Welcome to *Advanced Time Series Analysis Using Python*! This book is intended for data scientists or **machine learning** (**ML**) engineers who want to level up their time series analysis skills by learning new and advanced techniques from the ML world. **Time series analysis** is something that is commonly overlooked in regular ML books, courses, and so on. They typically start with classification, touch upon regression, and then move on. But it is also something that is immensely valuable and ubiquitous in business. As long as time is one of the four dimensions in the world we live in, time series data is all-pervasive.

Analyzing time series data unlocks a lot of value for a business. Time series analysis isn't new—it's been around since the 1920s and 1930s. But in the current age of data, the time series that are collected by businesses are growing larger and wider by the minute. Combined with an explosion in the quantum of data collected and the renewed interest in ML, the landscape of time series analysis also changed considerably. This book attempts to take you beyond classical statistical methods such as **AutoRegressive Integrated Moving Average** (**ARIMA**) and introduce to you the latest techniques from the ML world in time series analysis.

We are going to start with the basics and quickly scale up to more complex topics. In this chapter, we're going to cover the following main topics:

- What is a time series?
- Data-generating process (DGP)
- What can we forecast?
- Forecasting terminology and notation

Technical requirements

You will need to set up the **Anaconda** environment following the instructions in the *Preface* of the book to get a working environment with all the packages and datasets required for the code in this book.

The associated code for the chapter can be found at `https://github.com/PacktPublishing/Modern-Time-Series-Forecasting-with-Python-/tree/main/notebooks/Chapter01`.

What is a time series?

To keep it simple, a **time series** is a set of observations taken sequentially in time. The focus is on the word *time*. If we keep taking the same observation at different points in time, we will get a time series. For example, if you keep recording the number of bars of chocolate you have in a month, you'll end up with a time series of your chocolate consumption. Suppose you are recording your weight at the beginning of every month. You get another time series of your weight. Is there any relation between the two time series? Most likely, yeah. But we can analyze that scientifically by the end of this book.

A few other examples of time series are the weekly closing price of a stock that you follow, daily rainfall or snow in your city, or hourly readings of your heartbeat from your smartwatch.

Types of time series

There are two types of time series data, as outlined here:

- **Regular time series**: This is the most common type of time series where we have observations coming in at regular intervals of time, such as every hour or every month.

- **Irregular time series**: There are a few time series where we do not have observations at a regular interval of time. For example, consider we have a sequence of readings from lab tests of a patient. We see an observation in the time series only when the patient heads to the clinic and carries out the lab test, and this may not happen in regular intervals of time.

> **Important note**
> This book only focuses on regular time series, which are evenly spaced in time. Irregular time series are slightly more advanced and require specialized techniques to handle them. A couple of survey papers on the topic is a good way to get started on irregular time series and you can find them in the *Further reading* section of this chapter.

Main areas of application for time series analysis

There are broadly three important areas of application for time series analysis, outlined as follows:

- **Time series forecasting**: Predicting the future values of a time series, given the past values—for example, predict the next day's temperature using the last 5 years of temperature data.

- **Time series classification**: Sometimes, instead of predicting the future value of the time series, we may also want to predict an action based on past values. For example, given a history of an **electroencephalogram** (**EEG**; tracking electrical activity in the brain) or an **electrocardiogram** (**EKG**; tracking electrical activity in the heart), we need to predict whether the result of an EEG or an EKG is normal or abnormal.

- **Interpretation and causality**: Understand the whats and whys of the time series based on the past values, understand the interrelationships among several related time series, or derive causal inference based on time series data.

> **Important note**
>
> The focus of this book is predominantly on *time series forecasting*, but the techniques that you learn will help you approach *time series classification* problems also, with minimal change in the approach. *Interpretation* is also addressed, although only briefly, but *causality* is an area that this book does not address because it warrants a whole different approach.

Now that we have an overview of the time series landscape, let's build a mental model on how time series data is generated.

Data-generating process (DGP)

We saw that time series data is a collection of observations made sequentially along the time dimension. Any time series is, in turn, generated by some kind of *mechanism*. For example, time series data of daily shipments of your favorite chocolate from the manufacturing plant is affected by a lot of factors such as the time of the year, the holiday season, the availability of cocoa, the uptime of the machines working on the plant, and so on. In statistics, this underlying process that generated the time series is referred to as the **DGP**. Often, time series data is generated by a stochastic process.

If we had complete and perfect knowledge of reality, all we must do is put this DGP together in a mathematical form and you will get the most accurate forecast possible. But sadly, nobody has complete and perfect knowledge of reality. So, what we try to do is approximate the DGP, mathematically, as much as possible so that our imitation of the DGP gives us the best possible forecast (or any other output we want from the analysis). This imitation is called a **model** that provides a useful approximation to the DGP.

But we must remember that the model is not the DGP, but a representation of some essential aspects of reality. For example, let's consider an aerial view of Bengaluru and a map of Bengaluru, as represented here:

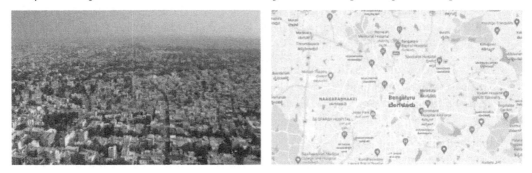

Figure 1.1 – An aerial view of Bengaluru (left) and a map of Bengaluru (right)

The map of Bengaluru is certainly useful—we can use it to go from point A to point B. But a map of Bengaluru is not the same as a photo of Bengaluru. It doesn't showcase the bustling nightlife or the insufferable traffic. A map is just a model that represents some useful features of a location, such as roads and places. The following diagram might help us internalize the concept and remember it:

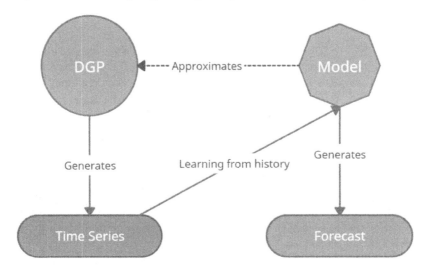

Figure 1.2 – DGP, model, and time series

Naturally, the next question would be this: *Do we have a useful model?* Every model is unrealistic. As we saw already, a map of Bengaluru does not perfectly represent Bengaluru. But if our purpose is to navigate Bengaluru, then a map is a very useful model. What if we want to understand the culture? A map doesn't give you a flavor of that. So, now, the same model that was useful is utterly useless in the new context.

Different kinds of models are required in different situations and for different objectives. For example, the best model for forecasting may not be the same as the best model to make a causal inference.

We can use the concept of DGPs to generate multiple synthetic time series, of varying degrees of complexity.

Generating synthetic time series

Let's take a look at a few practical examples where we can generate a few time series using a set of fundamental building blocks. You can get creative and mix and match any of these components, or even add them together to generate a time series of arbitrary complexity.

White and red noise

An extreme case of a stochastic process that generates a time series is a **white noise** process. It has a sequence of random numbers with zero mean and constant standard deviation. This is also one of the most popular assumptions of noise in a time series.

Let's see how we can generate such a time series and plot it, as follows:

```
# Generate the time axis with sequential numbers upto 200
time = np.arange(200)
# Sample 200 hundred random values
values = np.random.randn(200)*100
plot_time_series(time, values, "White Noise")
```

Here is the output:

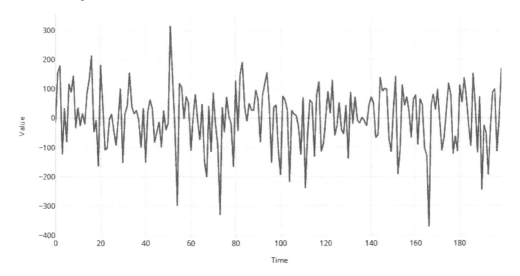

Figure 1.3 – White noise process

Red noise, on the other hand, has zero mean and constant variance but is serially correlated in time. This serial correlation or redness is parameterized by a correlation coefficient *r*, such that:

$$x_{j+1} = r \cdot x_j + (1 - r^2)^{\frac{1}{2}} \cdot w$$

where *w* is a random sample from a white noise distribution.

Let's see how we can generate that, as follows:

```
# Setting the correlation coefficient
r = 0.4
# Generate the time axis
time = np.arange(200)
# Generate white noise
white_noise = np.random.randn(200)*100
# Create Red Noise by introducing correlation between
subsequent values in the white noise
values = np.zeros(200)
for i, v in enumerate(white_noise):
    if i==0:
        values[i] = v
    else:
        values[i] = r*values[i-1]+ np.sqrt((1-np.power(r,2)))
*v
plot_time_series(time, values, "Red Noise Process")
```

Here is the output:

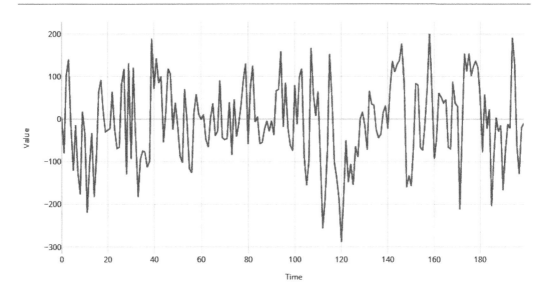

Figure 1.4 – Red noise process

Cyclical or seasonal signals

Among the most common signals you see in time series are seasonal or cyclical signals. Therefore, you can introduce seasonality into your generated series in a few ways.

Let's take the help of a very useful library to generate the rest of the time series—TimeSynth. For more information, refer to https://github.com/TimeSynth/TimeSynth.

This is a very useful library to generate time series. It has all kinds of DGPs that you can mix and match and create authentic synthetic time series.

> **Important note**
> For the exact code and usage, please refer to the associated Jupyter notebooks.

Let's see how we can use a sinusoidal function to create cyclicity. There is a helpful function in TimeSynth called generate_timeseries that helps us combine signals and generate time series. Have a look at the following code snippet:

```
#Sinusoidal Signal with Amplitude=1.5 & Frequency=0.25
signal_1 =ts.signals.Sinusoidal(amplitude=1.5, frequency=0.25)
#Sinusoidal Signal with Amplitude=1 & Frequency=0. 5
signal_2 = ts.signals.Sinusoidal(amplitude=1, frequency=0.5)
#Generating the time series
```

```
samples_1, regular_time_samples, signals_1, errors_1 =
generate_timeseries(signal=signal_1)

samples_2, regular_time_samples, signals_2, errors_2 =
generate_timeseries(signal=signal_2)

plot_time_series(regular_time_samples,
                 [samples_1, samples_2],
                 "Sinusoidal Waves",
                 legends=["Amplitude = 1.5 | Frequency = 0.25",
"Amplitude = 1 | Frequency = 0.5"])
```

Here is the output:

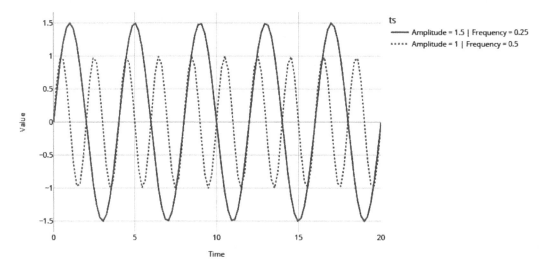

Figure 1.5 – Sinusoidal waves

Note the two sinusoidal waves are different with respect to the frequency (how fast the time series crosses zero) and amplitude (how far away from zero the time series travels).

TimeSynth also has another signal called PseudoPeriodic. This is like the Sinusoidal class, but the frequency and amplitude itself has some stochasticity. We can see in the following code snippet that this is more realistic than the vanilla sine and cosine waves from the Sinusoidal class:

```
# PseudoPeriodic signal with Amplitude=1 & Frequency=0.25
signal = ts.signals.PseudoPeriodic(amplitude=1, frequency=0.25)
#Generating Timeseries
samples, regular_time_samples, signals, errors = generate_
timeseries(signal=signal)
```

```
plot_time_series(regular_time_samples,
                 samples,
                 "Pseudo Periodic")
```

Here is the output:

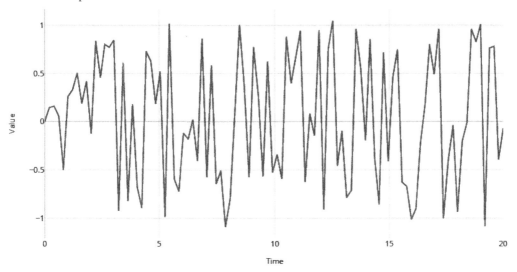

Figure 1.6 – Pseudo-periodic signal

Autoregressive signals

Another very popular signal in the real world is an **autoregressive (AR) signal**. We will go into this in more detail in *Chapter 4, Setting a Strong Baseline Forecast*, but for now, an AR signal refers to when the value of a time series for the current timestep is dependent on the values of the time series in the previous timesteps. This serial correlation is a key property of the AR signal, and it is parametrized by a few parameters, outlined as follows:

- Order of serial correlation—or, in other words, the number of previous timesteps the signal is dependent on

- Coefficients to combine the previous timesteps

Let's see how we can generate an AR signal and see what it looks like, as follows:

```
# Autoregressive signal with parameters 1.5 and -0.75
# y(t) = 1.5*y(t-1) - 0.75*y(t-2)
signal=ts.signals.AutoRegressive(ar_param=[1.5, -0.75])
#Generate Timeseries
```

```
samples, regular_time_samples, signals, errors = generate_
timeseries(signal=signal)
plot_time_series(regular_time_samples,
                 samples,
                 "Auto Regressive")
```

Here is the output:

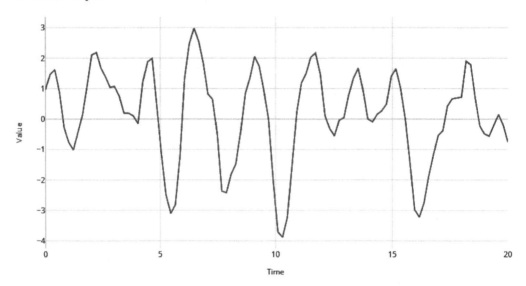

Figure 1.7 – AR signal

Mix and match

There are many more components you can use to create your DGP and thereby generate a time series, but let's quickly look at how we can combine the components we have already seen to generate a realistic time series.

Let's use a pseudo-periodic signal with white noise and combine it with an AR signal, as follows:

```
#Generating Pseudo Periodic Signal
pseudo_samples, regular_time_samples, _, _ = generate_
timeseries(signal=ts.signals.PseudoPeriodic(amplitude=1,
frequency=0.25), noise=ts.noise.GaussianNoise(std=0.3))
# Generating an Autoregressive Signal
ar_samples, regular_time_samples, _, _ = generate_
timeseries(signal=ts.signals.AutoRegressive(ar_param=[1.5,
-0.75]))
```

```
# Combining the two signals using a mathematical equation
ts = pseudo_samples*2+ar_samples
plot_time_series(regular_time_samples,
                 ts,
                 "Pseudo Periodic with AutoRegression and White
Noise")
```

Here is the output:

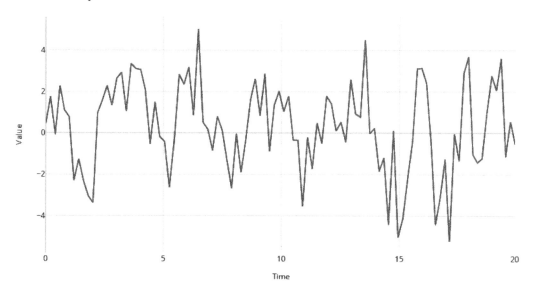

Figure 1.8 – Pseudo-periodic signal with AR and white noise

Stationary and non-stationary time series

In time series, **stationarity** is of great significance and is a key assumption in many modeling approaches. Ironically, many (if not most) real-world time series are non-stationary. So, let's understand what a stationary time series is from a layman's point of view.

There are multiple ways to look at stationarity, but one of the clearest and most intuitive ways is to think of the probability distribution or the data distribution of a time series. We call a time series stationary when the probability distribution remains the same at every point in time. In other words, if you pick different windows in time, the data distribution across all those windows should be the same.

A standard Gaussian distribution is defined by two parameters—the mean and the standard deviation. So, there are two ways the stationarity assumption can be broken, as outlined here:

- Change in mean over time
- Change in variance over time

Let's look at these assumptions in detail and understand them better.

Change in mean over time

This is the most popular way a non-stationary time series presents itself. If there is an upward/downward trend in the time series, the mean across two windows of time would not be the same.

Another way non-stationarity manifests itself is in the form of seasonality. Suppose we are looking at the time series of average temperature measurements in a month for the last 5 years. From our experience, we know that temperature peaks during summer and falls in winter. So, when we take the mean temperature of winter and mean temperature of summer, they will be different.

Let's generate a time series with trend and seasonality and see how it manifests, as follows:

```
# Sinusoidal Signal with Amplitude=1 & Frequency=0.25
signal=ts.signals.Sinusoidal(amplitude=1, frequency=0.25)
# White Noise with standard deviation = 0.3
noise=ts.noise.GaussianNoise(std=0.3)
# Generate the time series
sinusoidal_samples, regular_time_samples, _, _ = generate_
timeseries(signal=signal, noise=noise)
# Regular_time_samples is a linear increasing time axis and can
be used as a trend
trend = regular_time_samples*0.4
# Combining the signal and trend
ts = sinusoidal_samples+trend
plot_time_series(regular_time_samples,
                 ts,
                 "Sinusoidal with Trend and White Noise")
```

Here is the output:

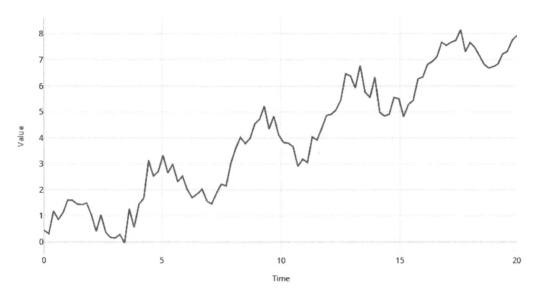

Figure 1.9 – Sinusoidal signal with trend and white noise

If you examine the time series in *Figure 1.9*, you will be able to see a definite trend and the seasonality, which together make the mean of the data distribution change wildly across different windows of time.

Change in variance over time

Non-stationarity can also present itself in the fluctuating variance of a time series. If the time series starts off with low variance and as time progresses, the variance keeps getting bigger and bigger, we have a non-stationary time series. In statistics, there is a scary name for this phenomenon—**heteroscedasticity**.

This book just tries to give you intuition about stationary versus non-stationary time series. There is a lot of statistical theory and depth in this discussion that we are skipping over to keep our focus on the practical aspects of time series.

Armed with the mental model of the DGP, we are at the right place to think about another important question: *What can we forecast?*

What can we forecast?

Before we move ahead, there is another aspect of time series forecasting that we have to understand—
the predictability of a time series. The most basic assumption when we forecast a time series is that the future depends on the past. But not all time series are equally predictable.

Let's take a look at a few examples and try to rank these in order of predictability (from easiest to hardest), as follows:

- High tide next Monday

- Lottery numbers next Sunday

- The stock price of Tesla next Friday

Intuitively, it is very easy for us to rank them. High tide next Monday is going to be the easiest to predict because it is so predictable, the lottery numbers are going to be very hard to predict because these are pretty much random, and the stock price of Tesla next Friday is going to be difficult to predict, but not impossible.

> **Note**
>
> However, for people thinking that they can forecast stock prices with the awesome techniques covered in the book and get rich, that won't happen. Although it is worthy of a lengthy discussion, we can summarize the key points in a short paragraph.
>
> Share prices are not a function of their past values but an anticipation of their future values, and this thereby violates our first assumption while forecasting. And if that is not bad enough, financial stock prices typically have a very low signal-to-noise ratio. The final wrench in the process is the **efficient-market hypothesis** (**EMH**). This seemingly innocent hypothesis proclaims that all known information about a stock price is already factored into the price of the stock. The implication of the hypothesis is that if you can forecast accurately, many others will also be able to do that, and thereby the market price of the stock already reflects the change in price that this forecast brought about.

Coming back to the topic at hand—predictability—three main factors form a mental model for this, as follows:

- **Understanding the DGP**: The better you understand the DGP, the higher the predictability of a time series.

- **Amount of data**: The more data you have, the better your predictability is.

- **Adequately repeating pattern**: For any mathematical model to work well, there should be an adequately repeating pattern in your time series. The more repeatable the pattern is, the better your predictability is.

Even though you have a mental model of how to think about predictability, we will look at more concrete ways of assessing the predictability of time series in *Chapter 3*, *Analyzing and Visualizing Time Series Data*, but the key takeaway is that not all time series are equally predictable.

In order to fully follow the discussion in the coming chapters, we need to establish a standard notation and get updated on terminology that is specific to time series analysis.

Forecasting terminology

There are a few terminologies that will help you follow the book as well as other literature on time series. These are described in more detail here:

- **Forecasting**

  Forecasting is the prediction of future values of a time series using the known past values of the time series and/or some other related variables. This is very similar to prediction in ML where we use a model to predict unseen data.

- **Multivariate forecasting**

  Multivariate time series consist of more than one time series variable that is not only dependent on its past values but also has some dependency on the other variables. For example, a set of macroeconomic indicators such as **gross domestic product** (**GDP**), inflation, and so on of a particular country can be considered as a multivariate time series. The aim of multivariate forecasting is to come up with a model that captures the interrelationship between the different variables along with its relationship with its past and forecast all the time series together in the future.

- **Explanatory forecasting**

  In addition to the past values of a time series, we might use some other information to predict the future values of a time series. For example, for predicting retail store sales, information regarding promotional offers (both historical and future ones) is usually helpful. This type of forecasting, which uses information other than its own history, is called explanatory forecasting.

- **Backtesting**

  Setting aside a validation set from your training data to evaluate your models is a practice that is common in the ML world. Backtesting is the time series equivalent of validation, whereby you use the history to evaluate a trained model. We will cover the different ways of doing validation and cross-validation for time series data later.

- **In-sample and out-sample**

  Again, drawing parallels with ML, in-sample refers to training data and out-sample refers to unseen or testing data. When you hear in-sample metrics, this is referring to metrics calculated on training data, and out-sample metrics is referring to metrics calculated on testing data.

- **Exogenous and endogenous variables**

    Exogenous variables are parallel time series variables that are not modeled directly for output but used to help us model the time series that we are interested in. Typically, exogenous variables are not affected by other variables in the system. Endogenous variables are variables that are affected by other variables in the system. A purely endogenous variable is a variable that is entirely dependent on the other variables in the system. Relaxing the strict assumptions a bit, we can consider the target variable as the endogenous variable and the explanatory regressors we include in the model as exogenous variables.

- **Forecast combination**

    Forecast combinations in the time series world are similar to ensembling from the ML world. It is a process by which we combine multiple forecasts by using some function, either learned or heuristic-based, such as a simple average of three forecast models.

There are a lot more terms specific to time series, some of which we will be covering throughout the book. But to start with a basic familiarity in the field, these terms should be enough.

Summary

We had our first dip into time series as we understood the different types of time series, looked at how a DGP generates a time series, and saw how we can think about the important question: *How well can we forecast a time series?* We also had a quick review of the terminology and notation required to understand the rest of the book. In the next chapter, we will be getting our hands dirty and will learn how to work with time series data, how to preprocess a time series, how to handle missing data and outliers, and so on. If you have not set up the environment yet, take a break and put some time into doing that.

Further reading

- *A Survey on Principles, Models and Methods for Learning from Irregularly Sampled Time Series: From Discretization to Attention and Invariance* by S.N. Shukla and B.M. Marlin (2020): https:// arxiv.org/abs/2012.00168

- *Learning from Irregularly-Sampled Time Series: A Missing Data Perspective* by S.C. Li and B.M. Marlin (2020), ICML: https://arxiv.org/abs/2008.07599

2

Acquiring and Processing Time Series Data

In the previous chapter, we learned what a time series is and established a few standard notations and terminologies. Now, let's switch tracks from theory to practice. In this chapter, we are going to get our hands dirty and start working with data. Although we said time series data is everywhere, we are still yet to get our hands dirty with a few time series datasets. We are going to start working on the dataset we have chosen to work on throughout this book, process it in the right way, and learn about a few techniques for dealing with missing values.

In this chapter, we will cover the following topics:

- Understanding the time series dataset
- pandas datetime operations, indexing, and slicing – a refresher
- Handling missing data
- Mapping additional information
- Saving and loading files to disk
- Handling longer periods of missing data

Technical requirements

You will need to set up the Anaconda environment following the instructions in the *Preface* of the book to get a working environment with all the packages and datasets required for the code in this book.

The code for this chapter can be found at `https://github.com/PacktPublishing/Modern-Time-Series-Forecasting-with-Python-/tree/main/notebooks/Chapter02`.

Handling time series data is like handling other tabular datasets, but with a focus on the temporal dimension. As with any tabular dataset, pandas is perfectly equipped to handle time series data as well.

Let's start getting our hands dirty and work through a dataset from the beginning. We are going to use the *London Smart Meters* dataset throughout this book. If you have not downloaded the data already as part of the environment setup, go to the *Preface* and do that now.

Understanding the time series dataset

This is the key first step in any new dataset you come across, even before **Exploratory Data Analysis** (**EDA**), which we will be covering in *Chapter 3, Analyzing and Visualizing Time Series Data*. Understanding where the data is coming from, the data generating process behind it, and the source domain is essential to having a good understanding of the dataset.

London Data Store, a free and open data-sharing portal, provided this dataset, which was collected and enriched by Jean-Michel D and uploaded on Kaggle.

The dataset contains energy consumption readings for a sample of 5,567 London households that took part in the UK Power Networks-led Low Carbon London project between November 2011 and February 2014. Readings were taken at half-hourly intervals. Some metadata about the households is also available as part of the dataset. Let's look at what metadata is available as part of the dataset:

- CACI UK segmented the UK's population into demographic types, called Acorn. For each household in the data, we have the corresponding Acorn classification. The Acorn classes (Lavish Lifestyles, City Sophisticates, Student Life, and so on) are grouped into parent classes (Affluent Achievers, Rising Prosperity, Financially Stretched, and so on). A full list of Acorn classes can be found in *Table 2.1*. The complete documentation detailing each class is available at `https://acorn.caci.co.uk/downloads/Acorn-User-guide.pdf`.

- The dataset contains two groups of customers – one group who was subjected to **dynamic time-of-use** (**dToU**) energy prices throughout 2013, and another group who were on flat-rate tariffs. The tariff prices for the dToU were given a day ahead via the Smart Meter IHD or via text message.

- Jean-Michel D also enriched the dataset with weather and UK bank holidays data.

The following table shows the Acorn classes:

ACORN Group	ACORN Class
Affluent Achievers	A—Lavish Lifestyles
	B—Executive Wealth
	C—Mature Money
Rising Prosperity	D—City Sophisticates
	E—Career Climbers
Comfortable Communities	F—Countryside Communities
	G—Successful Suburbs
	H—Steady Neighborhoods
	I—Comfortable Seniors
	J—Starting Out
Financially Stretched	K—Student Life
	L—Modest Means
	M—Striving Families
	N—Poorer Pensioners
Urban Adversity	O—Young Hardship
	P—Struggling Estates
	Q—Difficult Circumstances

Table 2.1 – ACORN classification

Important note

The Kaggle dataset also preprocesses the time series data daily and combines all the separate files. Here, we will ignore those files and start with the raw files, which can be found in the `hhblock_dataset` folder. Learning to work with the raw files is an integral part of working with real-world datasets in the industry.

Preparing a data model

Once we understand where the data is coming from, we can look at the data, understand the information present in the different files, and figure out a mental model of how to relate the different files. You may call it old school, but Microsoft Excel is an excellent tool for gaining this first-level understanding. If the file is too big to open in Excel, we can also read it in Python and save a sample of the data to an Excel file and open it. However, keep in mind that Excel sometimes messes with the format of the data, especially dates, so we need to take care to not save the file and write back the formatting changes Excel made. If you are allergic to Excel, you can do it in Python as well, albeit with a lot more keystrokes. The purpose of this exercise is to *see* what the different data files contain, explore the relationship between the different files, and so on. We can make this more formal and explicit by drawing a data model, similar to the one shown in the following diagram:

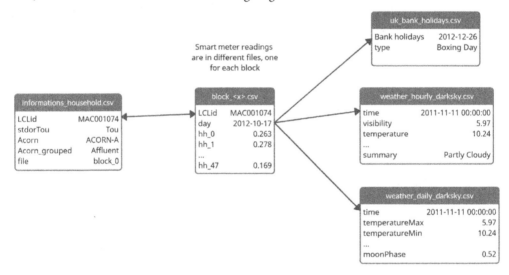

Figure 2.1 – Data model of the London Smart Meters dataset

The data model is more for us to understand the data rather than any data engineering purpose. Therefore, it only contains bare-minimum information, such as the key columns on the left and the sample data on the right. We also have arrows connecting different files, with keys used to link the files.

Let's look at a few key column names and their meanings:

- LCLid: The unique consumer ID for a household
- stdorTou: Whether the household has dToU or standard
- Acorn: The ACORN class
- Acorn_grouped: The ACORN group
- file: The block number

Each LCLid has a unique time series attached to it. The time series file is formatted in a slightly tricky format – each day, there will be 48 observations at a half-hourly frequency in the columns of the file.

> **Notebook alert**
>
> To follow along with the complete code, use the `01 - Pandas Refresher & Missing Values Treatment.ipynb` notebook in the `chapter01` folder.

Before we start working with our dataset, there are a few concepts we need to establish. One of them is a concept in pandas DataFrames, which is of utmost importance – the pandas datetime properties and index. Let's quickly look at a few pandas concepts that will be useful.

> **Important note**
>
> If you are familiar with the datetime manipulations in pandas, feel free to skip ahead to the next section.

pandas datetime operations, indexing, and slicing – a refresher

Instead of using our dataset, which is slightly complex, let's pick an easy, well-formatted stock exchange price dataset from the UCI Machine Learning Repository and look at the functionality of pandas:

```
df = pd.read_excel("https://archive.ics.uci.edu/ml/machine-
learning-databases/00247/data_akbilgic.xlsx", skiprows=1)
```

The DataFrame that we read looks as follows:

	date	ISE	ISE.1	SP	DAX	FTSE	NIKKEI	BOVESPA	EU	EM
0	2009-01-05	0.035754	0.038376	-0.004679	0.002193	0.003894	0.000000	0.031190	0.012698	0.028524
1	2009-01-06	0.025426	0.031813	0.007787	0.008455	0.012866	0.004162	0.018920	0.011341	0.008773
2	2009-01-07	-0.028862	-0.026353	-0.030469	-0.017833	-0.028735	0.017293	-0.035899	-0.017073	-0.020015
3	2009-01-08	-0.062208	-0.084716	0.003391	-0.011726	-0.000466	-0.040061	0.028283	-0.005561	-0.019424
4	2009-01-09	0.009860	0.009658	-0.021533	-0.019873	-0.012710	-0.004474	-0.009764	-0.010989	-0.007802

Figure 2.2 – The DataFrame with stock exchange prices

Now that we have read the DataFrame, let's start manipulating it.

Converting the date columns into pd.Timestamp/DatetimeIndex

First, we must convert the date column (which may not always be parsed as dates automatically by pandas) into pandas datetime. For that, pandas has a handy function called pd.to_datetime. It infers the datetime format automatically and converts the input into a pd.Timestamp, if the input is a string, or into a DatetimeIndex if the input is a list of strings. So, if we pass a single date as a string, pd.to_datetime converts it into pd.Timestamp, while if we pass a list of dates, it converts it into DatetimeIndex:

```
>>> pd.to_datetime("13-4-1987").strftime("%d, %B %Y")
'13, April 1987'
```

Now, let's look at a case where the automatic parsing fails. The date is January 4, 1987. Let's see what happens when we pass the string to the function:

```
>>> pd.to_datetime("4-1-1987").strftime("%d, %B %Y")
'01, April 1987'
```

Well, that wasn't expected, right? But if you think about it, anyone can make that mistake because we are not telling the computer whether the month or the day comes first, and pandas assumes the month comes first. Let's rectify that:

```
>>> pd.to_datetime("4-1-1987", dayfirst=True).strftime("%d, %B %Y")
'04, January 1987'
```

Another case where automatic date parsing fails is when the date string is in a non-standard form. In that case, we can provide a strftime formatted string to help pandas parse the dates correctly:

```
>>> pd.to_datetime("4|1|1987", format="%d|%m|%Y").strftime("%d, %B %Y")
'04, January 1987'
```

A full list of strftime conventions can be found at https://strftime.org/.

> **Practitioner's tip**
>
> Because of the wide variety of data formats, pandas may infer the time incorrectly. While reading a file, pandas will try to parse the dates automatically and create an error. There are many ways we can control this behavior: we can use the `parse_dates` flag to turn off date parsing, the `date_parser` argument to pass in a custom date parser, and `year_first` and `day_first` to easily denote two popular formats of dates.
>
> Out of all these options, I prefer to use `parse_dates=False` in both `pd.read_csv` and `pd.read_excel` to make sure pandas is not parsing the data automatically. After that, you can convert the date using the `format` parameter, which lets you explicitly set the date format of the column using `strftime` conventions. There are two other parameters in `pd.to_datetime` that will also make inferring dates less error-prone – `yearfirst` and `dayfirst`. If you don't provide an explicit date format, at least provide one of these.

Now, let's convert the date column in our stock prices dataset into datetime:

```
df['date'] = pd.to_datetime(df['date'], yearfirst=True)
```

Now, the `'date'` column, dtype, should be either `datetime64[ns]` or `<M8[ns]`, which are both pandas/NumPy native datetime formats. But why do we need to do this?

It's because of the wide range of additional functionalities this unlocks. The traditional `min()` and `max()` functions will start working because pandas knows it is a datetime column:

```
>>> df.date.min(),df.date.max()
(Timestamp('2009-01-05 00:00:00'), Timestamp('2011-02-22
00:00:00'))
```

Let's look at a few cool features the datetime format gives us.

Using the .dt accessor and datetime properties

Since the column is now in date format, all the semantic information that is encoded in the date can be used through pandas datetime properties. We can access many datetime properties, such as `month`, `day_of_week`, `day_of_year`, and so on, using the `.dt` accessor:

```
>>> print(f"""
    Date: {df.date.iloc[0]}
    Day of year: {df.date.dt.day_of_year.iloc[0]}
    Day of week: {df.date.dt.dayofweek.iloc[0]}
    Week of Year: {df.date.dt.weekofyear.iloc[0]}
    Month: {df.date.dt.month.iloc[0]}
    Month Name: {df.date.dt.month_name().iloc[0]}
```

```
      Quarter: {df.date.dt.quarter.iloc[0]}
      Year: {df.date.dt.year.iloc[0]}
      ISO Week: {df.date.dt.isocalendar().week.iloc[0]}
      """)
Date: 2009-01-05 00:00:00
Day of year: 5
Day of week: 0
Week of Year: 2
Month: 1
Month Name: January
Quarter: 1
Year: 2009
ISO Week: 2
```

As of pandas 1.1.0, `week_of_year` has been deprecated because of the inconsistencies it produces at the end/start of the year. Instead, the ISO Calendar standards (which are commonly used in government and business) have been adopted and we can access the ISO calendar to get the ISO weeks.

Slicing and indexing

The real fun starts when we make the date column the index of the DataFrame. By doing this, you can use all the fancy slicing operations that pandas supports but on the datetime axis. Let's take a look at few of them:

```
# Setting the index as the datetime column
df.set_index("date", inplace=True)
# Select all data after 2010-01-04(including)
df["2010-01-04":]
# Select all data between 2010-01-04 and 2010-02-06(not
including)
df["2010-01-04": "2010-02-06"]
# Select data 2010 and before
df[: "2010"]
# Select data between 2010-01 and 2010-06(both including)
df["2010-01": "2010-06"]
```

In addition to the semantic information and intelligent indexing and slicing, pandas also provides tools for creating and manipulating date sequences.

Creating date sequences and managing date offsets

If you are familiar with `range` in Python and `np.arange` in NumPy, then you will know they help us create `integer/float` sequences by providing a start point and an end point. pandas has something similar for datetime – `pd.date_range`. The function accepts start and end dates, along with a frequency (daily or monthly, and so on) and creates the sequence of dates in between. Let's look at a couple of ways of creating a sequence of dates:

```
# Specifying start and end dates with frequency
pd.date_range(start="2018-01-20", end="2018-01-23", freq="D").
astype(str).tolist()
# Output: ['2018-01-20', '2018-01-21', '2018-01-22', '2018-01-
23']
```

```
# Specifying start and number of periods to generate in the
given frequency
pd.date_range(start="2018-01-20", periods=4, freq="D").
astype(str).tolist()
# Output: ['2018-01-20', '2018-01-21', '2018-01-22', '2018-01-
23']
```

```
# Generating a date sequence with every 2 days
pd.date_range(start="2018-01-20", periods=4, freq="2D").
astype(str).tolist()
# Output: ['2018-01-20', '2018-01-22', '2018-01-24', '2018-01-
26']
```

```
# Generating a date sequence every month. By default it starts
with Month end
pd.date_range(start="2018-01-20", periods=4, freq="M").
astype(str).tolist()
# Output: ['2018-01-31', '2018-02-28', '2018-03-31', '2018-04-
30']
```

```
# Generating a date sequence every month, but month start
pd.date_range(start="2018-01-20", periods=4, freq="MS").
astype(str).tolist()
# Output: ['2018-02-01', '2018-03-01', '2018-04-01', '2018-05-
01']
```

We can also add or subtract days, months, and other values to/from dates using `pd.TimeDelta`:

```
# Add four days to the date range
(pd.date_range(start="2018-01-20", end="2018-01-23", freq="D")
+ pd.Timedelta(4, unit="D")).astype(str).tolist()
# Output: ['2018-01-24', '2018-01-25', '2018-01-26', '2018-01-
27']
```

```
# Add four weeks to the date range
(pd.date_range(start="2018-01-20", end="2018-01-23", freq="D")
+ pd.Timedelta(4, unit="W")).astype(str).tolist()
# Output: ['2018-02-17', '2018-02-18', '2018-02-19', '2018-02-
20']
```

There are a lot of these aliases in pandas, including `W`, `W-MON`, `MS`, and others. The full list can be found at `https://pandas.pydata.org/docs/user_guide/timeseries.html#timeseries-offset-aliases`.

In this section, we looked at a few useful features and operations we can perform on datetime indices and know how to manipulate DataFrames with datetime columns. Now, let's review a few techniques we can use to deal with missing data.

Handling missing data

While dealing with large datasets in the wild, you are bound to encounter missing data. If it is not part of the time series, it may be part of the additional information you collect and map. Before we jump the gun and fill it with a mean value or drop those rows, let's think about a few aspects:

- The first consideration should be whether the missing data we are worried about is missing or not. For that, we need to think about the **Data Generating Process (DGP)** (the process that is generating the time series). As an example, let's look at sales at a local supermarket. You have been given the **point-of-sale (POS)** transactions for the last 2 years and you are processing the data into a time series. While analyzing the data, you found that there are a few products where there aren't any transactions for a few days. Now, what you need to think about is whether the missing data is missing or whether there is some information that this missingness is giving you. If you don't have any transactions for a particular product for a day, it will appear as missing data while you are processing it, even though it is not missing. What that tells us you that there were no sales for that item, and that you should fill such missing data with zeros.

- Now, what if you see that, every Sunday, the data is missing – that is, there is a pattern to the missingness. This becomes tricky because how you fill in such gaps depends on the model that you intend to use. If you fill in such gaps with zeros, a model that looks at the immediate past to predict the future will predict inaccurate results on Monday. However, if you tell the model that the previous day was Sunday, then the model still can learn to tell the difference.

- Lastly, what if you see zero sales on one of the best-selling products that always gets sold? This can happen because of something such as a POS machine malfunction, a data entry mistake, or an out-of-stock situation. These types of missing values can be imputed with a few techniques.

Let's look at an Air Quality dataset published by the ACT Government, Canberra, Australia under the CC by Attribution 4.0 International License (`https://www.data.act.gov.au/Environment/Air-Quality-Monitoring-Data/94a5-zqnn`) and see how we can impute such values using pandas (there are more sophisticated techniques available, all of which will be covered later in this chapter).

> **Practitioner's tip**
>
> When reading data using a method such as `read_csv`, pandas provides a few handy ways to handle missing values. pandas treats many values such as `#N/A`, `null`, and so on as `NaN` by default. We can control this list of allowable `NaN` values using the `na_values` and `keep_default_na` parameters.

We have chosen region **Monash** and **PM2.5** readings and introduced some missing values, as shown in the following diagram:

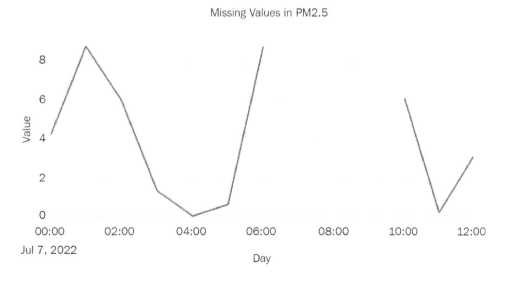

Figure 2.3 – Missing values in the Air Quality dataset

Now, let's look at a few simple techniques we can use to fill the missing values:

- **Last Observation Carried Forward or Forward Fill**: This imputation technique takes the last observed value and uses that to fill all the missing values until it finds the next observation. It is also called forward fill. We can do this like so:

```
df['pm2_5_1_hr'].ffill()
```

- **Next Observation Carried Backward of Backward Fill**: This imputation technique takes the next observation and backtracks to fill in all the missing values with this value. This is also called backward fill. Let's see how we can do this in pandas:

```
df['pm2_5_1_hr'].bfill()
```

- **Mean Value Fill**: This imputation technique is also pretty simple. We calculate the mean of the entire series and wherever we find missing values, we fill it with the mean value:

```
df['pm2_5_1_hr'].fillna(df['pm2_5_1_hr'].mean())
```

Let's plot the imputed lines we get from using these three techniques:

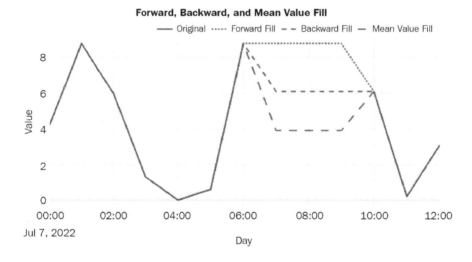

Figure 2.4 – Imputed missing values using forward, backward, and mean value fill

Another family of imputation techniques covers interpolation:

- **Linear Interpolation**: Linear interpolation is just like drawing a line between the two observed points and filling the missing values so that they lie on this line. This is how we do it:

```
df['pm2_5_1_hr'].interpolate(method="linear")
```

- **Nearest Interpolation**: This is intuitively like a combination of the forward and backward fill. For each missing value, the closest observed value is found and is used to fill in the missing value:

```
df['pm2_5_1_hr'].interpolate(method="nearest")
```

Let's plot the two interpolated lines:

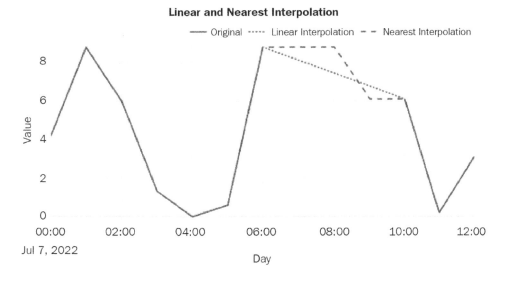

Figure 2.5 – Imputed missing values using linear and nearest interpolation

There are a few non-linear interpolation techniques as well:

- **Spline, Polynomial, and Other Interpolations**: In addition to linear interpolation, pandas also supports non-linear interpolation techniques that call a SciPy routine at the backend. Spline and polynomial interpolations are similar. They fit a spline/polynomial of a given order to the data and use that to fill in missing values. While using `spline` or `polynomial` as the method in `interpolate`, we should always provide `order` as well. The higher the order, the more flexible the function that is used will be to fit the observed points. Let's see how we can use spline and polynomial interpolation:

```
df['pm2_5_1_hr'].interpolate(method="spline", order=2)
df['pm2_5_1_hr'].interpolate(method="polynomial",
order=5)
```

Let's plot these two non-linear interpolation techniques:

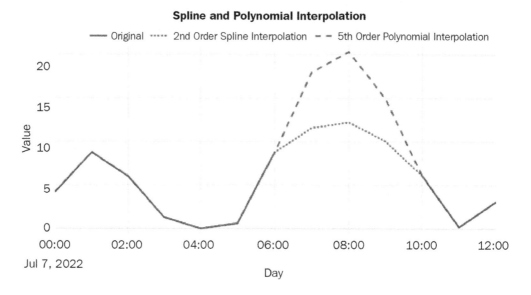

Figure 2.6 – Imputed missing values using spline and polynomial interpolation

For a complete list of interpolation techniques supported by `interpolate`, go to `https://pandas.pydata.org/pandas-docs/stable/reference/api/pandas.Series.interpolate.html` and `https://docs.scipy.org/doc/scipy/reference/generated/scipy.interpolate.interp1d.html#scipy.interpolate.interp1d`.

Now that we are more comfortable with the way pandas manages datetime, let's go back to our dataset and convert the data into a more manageable form.

> **Notebook alert**
>
> To follow along with the complete code for pre-processing, use the `02 - Preprocessing London Smart Meter Dataset.ipynb` notebook in the `chapter01` folder.

Converting the half-hourly block-level data (hhblock) into time series data

Before we start processing, let's understand a few general categories of information we will find in a time series dataset:

- **Time Series Identifiers**: These are identifiers for a particular time series. It can be a name, an ID, or any other unique feature – for example, the SKU name or the ID of a retail sales dataset or the consumer ID in the energy dataset that we are working with are all time series identifiers.

- **Metadata or Static Features**: This information does not vary with time. An example of this is the ACORN classification of the household in our dataset.

- **Time-Varying Features**: This information varies with time – for example, the weather information. For each point in time, we have a different value for weather, unlike the Acorn classification.

Next. Let's discuss formatting of a dataset.

Compact, expanded, and wide forms of data

There are many ways to format a time series dataset, especially a dataset with many related time series, like the one we have now. Apart from the standard terminology of **wide** data, we can also look at two non-standard ways of formatting time series data. Although there is no standard nomenclature for those, we will refer to them as **compact** and **expanded** in this book.

Compact form data is when any particular time series occupies only a single row in the pandas DataFrame – that is, the time dimension is managed as an array within a DataFrame row. The time series identifiers and the metadata occupy the columns with scalar values and then the time series values; other time-varying features occupy the columns with an array. Two additional columns are included to extrapolate time – `start_datetime` and frequency. If we know the start datetime and the frequency of the time series, we can easily construct the time and recover the time series from the DataFrame. This only works for regularly sampled time series. The advantage is that the DataFrames take up much less memory and are easy and faster to work with:

LCLid	start_timestamp	frequency	energy_consumption	series_length
MAC000002	2012-10-13	30min	[0.263, 0.2689999999999999, 0.275, 0.256, 0.21...	24144
MAC000246	2011-12-04	30min	[0.175, 0.098, 0.144, 0.065, 0.071, 0.037, 0.0...	39216
MAC000450	2012-03-23	30min	[0.337, 1.426, 0.996, 0.971, 0.994, 0.952, 0.8...	33936
MAC001074	2012-05-09	30min	[0.18, 0.086, 0.106, 0.173, 0.146, 0.223, 0.21...	31680
MAC003223	2012-09-18	30min	[0.076, 0.079, 0.123, 0.109, 0.051, 0.069, 0.0...	25344

Figure 2.7 – Compact form data

The expanded form is when the time series is expanded along the rows of a DataFrame. If there are *n* steps in the time series, it occupies *n* rows in the DataFrame. The time series identifiers and the metadata get repeated along all the rows. The time-varying features also get expanded along the rows. And instead of the start date and frequency, we have the datetime as a column:

LCLid	energy_consumption	series_length	timestamp	frequency
MAC000002	0.263	24144	2012-10-13 00:00:00	30min
MAC000002	0.269	24144	2012-10-13 00:30:00	30min
MAC000002	0.275	24144	2012-10-13 01:00:00	30min
MAC000002	0.256	24144	2012-10-13 01:30:00	30min
MAC000002	0.211	24144	2012-10-13 02:00:00	30min

Figure 2.8 – Expanded form data

If the compact form had a time series identifier as the key, the time series identifier and the datetime column would be combined and become the key.

Wide-format data is more common in traditional time series literature. It can be considered a legacy format, which is limiting in many ways. Do you remember the stock data we saw earlier (*Figure 2.2*)? We have the date as an index or as one of the columns and the different time series as different columns of the DataFrame. As the number of time series increases, they become wider and wider, hence the name. This data format does not allow us to include any metadata about the time series. For instance, in our data, we have information about whether a particular household is under standard or dynamic pricing. There is no way for us to include such metadata in the wide format. From an operational perspective, the wide format also does not play well with relational databases because we have to keep adding columns to the table when we get new time series. We won't be using this format in this book.

Enforcing regular intervals in time series

One of the first things you should check and correct is whether the regularly sampled time series data that you have has equal intervals of time. In practice, even regularly sampled time series have some samples missing in between because of some data collection error or some other peculiar way data is collected. So, while working with the data, we will make sure we enforce regular intervals in the time series.

> **Best practice**
> While working with datasets with multiple time series, it is best practice to check the end dates of all the time series. If they are not uniform, we can align them with the latest date across all the time series in the dataset.

In our smart meters dataset, some `LCLid` columns end much earlier than the rest. Maybe the household opted out of the program, or they moved out and left the house empty; the reason could be anything. However, we need to handle that while we enforce regular intervals.

We will learn how to convert the dataset into a time series format in the next section. The code for this process can be found in the `02 - Preprocessing London Smart Meter Dataset. ipynb` notebook.

Converting the London Smart Meters dataset into a time series format

For each dataset that you come across, the steps you would have to take to convert it into either a compact or expanded form would be different. It depends on how the original data is structured. Here, we will look at how the London Smart Meters dataset can be transformed so that we can transfer those learnings to other datasets.

There are two steps we need to do before we can start processing the data into either compact or expanded form:

1. **Find the Global End Date**: We must find the maximum date across all the block files so that we know the global end date of the time series.

2. **Basic Preprocessing**: If you remember how `hhblock_dataset` is structured, you will remember that each row had a date and that along the columns, we have half-hourly blocks. We need to reshape that into a long form, where each row has a date and a single half-hourly block. It's easier to handle that way.

Now, let's define separate functions for converting the data into compact and expanded forms and `apply` that function to each of the `LCLid` columns. We will do this for each `LCLid` separately since the start date for each `LCLid` is different.

Expanded form

The function for converting into expanded form does the following:

1. Finds the start date.
2. Create a standard DataFrame using the start date and the global end date.
3. Left merges the DataFrame for `LCLid` to the standard DataFrame, leaving the missing data as `np.nan`.
4. Returns the merged DataFrame.

Once we have all the `LCLid` DataFrames, we must perform a couple of additional steps to complete the expanded form processing:

1. Concatenate all the DataFrames into a single DataFrame.

2. Create a column called offset, which is the numerical representation of the half-hour blocks; for example, `hh_3` → 3.

3. Create a timestamp by adding a 30-minute offset to the day and dropping the unnecessary columns.

For one block, this representation takes up ~47 MB of memory.

Compact form

The function for converting into compact form does the following:

1. Finds the start date and time series identifiers.

2. Creates a standard DataFrame using the start date and the global end date.

3. Left merges the DataFrame for `LCLid` to the standard DataFrame, leaving the missing data as `np.nan`.

4. Sorts the values on the date.

5. Returns the time series array, along with the time series identifier, start date, and the length of the time series.

Once we have this information for each `LCLid`, we can compile it into a DataFrame and add `30min` as the frequency.

For one block, this representation takes up only ~0.002 MB of memory.

We are going to use the compact form because it is easy to work with and much less resource hungry.

Mapping additional information

From the data model that we prepared earlier, we know that there are three key files that we have to map: *Household Information*, *Weather*, and *Bank Holidays*.

The `informations_households.csv` file contains metadata about the household. There are static features that are not dependent on time. For this, we just need to left merge `informations_households.csv` to the compact form based on `LCLid`, which is the time series identifier.

Best practice

While doing a pandas merge, one of the most common and unexpected outcomes is that the number of rows before and after the operation is not the same (even if you are doing a left merge). This typically happens because there are duplicates in the keys on which you are merging. As a best practice, you can use the `validate` parameter in the pandas merge, which takes in inputs such as `one_to_one` and `many_to_one` so that this check is done while merging and will throw an error if the assumption is not met. For more information, go to `https://pandas.pydata.org/docs/reference/api/pandas.merge.html`.

Bank Holidays and Weather, on the other hand, are time-varying features and should be dealt with accordingly. The most important aspect to keep in mind is that while we map this information, it should perfectly align with the time series that we have already stored as an array.

`uk_bank_holidays.csv` is a file that contains the dates of the holidays and the kind of holiday. The holiday information is quite important here because the energy consumption patterns would be different on a holiday when the family members are at home spending time with each other or watching television, and so on. Follow these steps to process this file:

1. Convert the date column into the datetime format and set it as the index of the DataFrame.

2. Using the `resample` function we saw earlier, we must ensure that the index is resampled every 30 minutes, which is the frequency of the times series.

3. Forward fill the holidays within a day and fill in the rest of the NaN values with NO_HOLIDAY.

Now, we have converted the holiday file into a DataFrame that has a row for each 30-minute interval. On each row, we have a column that specifies whether that day was a holiday or not.

`weather_hourly_darksky.csv` is a file that is, once again, at the daily frequency. We need to downsample it to a 30-minute frequency because the data that we need to map to this is at a half-hourly frequency. If we don't do this, the weather will only be mapped to the hourly timestamps, leaving the half-hourly timestamps empty.

The steps we must follow to process this file are also similar to the way we processed holidays:

1. Convert the date column into the datetime format and set it as the index of the DataFrame.

2. Using the `resample function`, we must ensure that the index is resampled every 30 minutes, which is the frequency of the times series.

3. Forward fill the weather features to fill the missing values that were created while resampling.

Now that you have made sure the alignment between the time series and the time-varying features is ensured, you can loop over each of the time series and extract the weather and bank holiday array before storing it in the corresponding row of the DataFrame.

Saving and loading files to disk

The fully merged DataFrame in its compact form takes up only ~10 MB. But saving this file requires a little bit of engineering. If we try to save the file in CSV format, it will not work because of the way we have stored arrays in pandas columns (since the data is in its compact form). We can save it in `pickle` or `parquet` format, or any of the binary forms of file storage. This can work, depending on the size of the RAM available in our machines. Although the fully merged DataFrame is just ~10 MB, saving it in `pickle` format will make the size explode to ~15 GB.

What we can do is save this as a text file while making a few tweaks to accommodate the column names, column types, and other metadata that is required to read the file back into memory. The resulting file size on disk still comes out to ~15 GB but since we are doing it as an I/O operation, we are not keeping all that data in our memory. We call this the time series (`.ts`) format. The functions for saving a compact form in `.ts` format, reading the `.ts` format, and converting the compact form into expanded form are available in this book's GitHub repository under `src/data_utils.py`.

If you don't need to store all of the DataFrame in a single file, you can split it into multiple chunks and save them individually in a binary format, such as `parquet`. For our datasets, let's follow this route and split the whole DataFrame into chunks of blocks and save them as `parquet` files. This is the best route for us because of a few reasons:

- It leverages the compression that comes with the format
- It reads in parts of the whole data for quick iteration and experimentation
- The data types are retained between the read and write operations, leading to less ambiguity

Now that we have processed the dataset and stored it on disk, let's read it back into memory and look at a few more techniques to handle missing data.

Handling longer periods of missing data

We saw some techniques for handling missing data earlier – forward and backward filling, interpolation, and so on. Those techniques usually work if there are one or two missing data points. But if a large section of data is missing, then these simple techniques fall short.

> **Notebook alert**
>
> To follow along with the complete code for missing data imputation, use the `03 - Handling Missing Data (Long Gaps).ipynb` notebook in the `chapter02` folder.

Let's read blocks 0-7 `parquet` from memory:

```
block_df = pd.read_parquet("data/london_smart_meters/
preprocessed/london_smart_meters_merged_block_0-7.parquet")
```

The data that we have saved is in compact form. We need to convert it into expanded form because it is easier to work with time series data in that form. Since we only need a subset of the time series (for faster demonstration purposes), we are just extracting one block from these seven blocks. To convert compact form into expanded form, we can use a helpful function in `src/utils/data_utils.py` called `compact_to_expanded`:

```
#Converting to expanded form
exp_block_df = compact_to_expanded(block_df[block_
df.file=="block_7"], timeseries_col = 'energy_consumption',
static_cols = ["frequency", "series_length", "stdorToU",
"Acorn", "Acorn_grouped", "file"],
time_varying_cols = ['holidays', 'visibility', 'windBearing',
'temperature', 'dewPoint',
        'pressure', 'apparentTemperature', 'windSpeed',
'precipType', 'icon',
        'humidity', 'summary'],
ts_identifier = "LCLid")
```

One of the best ways to visualize the missing data in a group of related time series is by using a very helpful package called `missingno`:

```
# Pivot the data to set the index as the datetime and the
different time series along the columns
plot_df = pd.pivot_table(exp_block_df, index="timestamp",
columns="LCLid", values="energy_consumption")
# Generate Plot. Since we have a datetime index, we can mention
the frequency to decide what do we want on the X axis
msno.matrix(plot_df, freq="M")
```

The preceding code produces the following output:

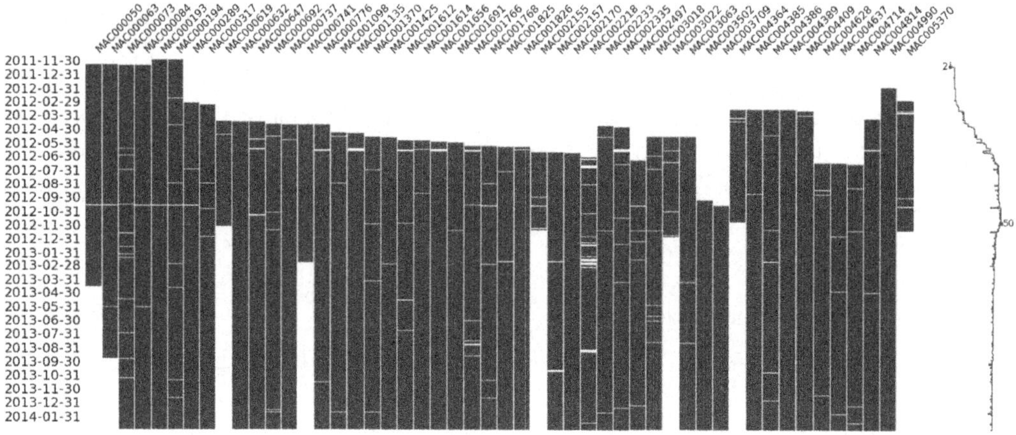

Figure 2.9 – Visualization of the missing data in block 7

> **Important note**
>
> Only attempt the `missingno` visualization on related time series where there are less than 25 time series. If you have a dataset that contains thousands of time series (such as in our full dataset), applying this visualization will give us an illegible plot and a frozen computer.

This visualization tells us a lot of things at a single glance. The *Y*-axis contains the dates that we are plotting the visualization for, while the *X*-axis contains the columns, which in this case are the different households. We know that all the time series are not perfectly aligned – that is, not all of them start at the same time and end at the same time. The big white gaps we can see at the beginning of many of the time series show that data collection for those consumers started later than the others. We can also see that a few time series finish earlier than the rest, which means either they stopped being consumers or the measurement phase stopped. There are also a few smaller white lines in many time series, which are real missing values. We can also notice a sparkline to the right, which is a compact representation of the number of missing columns for each row. If there are no missing values (all time series have some value), then the sparkline would be at the far right. Finally, if there are a lot of missing values, the line will be to the left.

Just because there are missing values, we are not going to fill/impute them because the decision of whether to impute missing data or not comes later in the workflow. For some models, we do not need to do the imputation, while for others, we do. There are multiple ways of imputing missing data and which one to choose is another decision we cannot make beforehand.

So, for now, let's pick one LCLid and dig deeper. We already know that there are some missing values between 2012-09-30 and 2012-10-31. Let's visualize that period:

```
# Taking a single time series from the block
ts_df = exp_block_df[exp_block_df.LCLid=="MAC000193"].set_
index("timestamp")
msno.matrix(ts_df["2012-09-30": "2012-10-31"], freq="D")
```

The preceding code produces the following output:

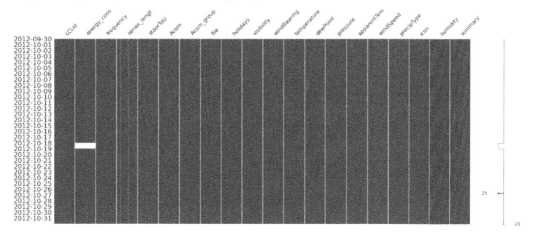

Figure 2.10 – Visualization of missing data of MAC000193 between 2012-09-30 and 2012-10-31

Here, we can see that the missing data is really between 2012-10-18 and 2012-10-19. Normally, we would go ahead and impute the missing data in this period, but since we are looking at this with an academic lens, we will take a slightly different route. Let's introduce an artificial missing data section and see how the different techniques we are going to look at impute the missing data:

```
# The dates between which we are nulling out the time series
window = slice("2012-10-07", "2012-10-08")
# Creating a new column and artificially creating missing
values
ts_df['energy_consumption_missing'] = ts_df.energy_consumption
ts_df.loc[window, "energy_consumption_missing"] = np.nan
```

Now, let's plot the missing area in the time series:

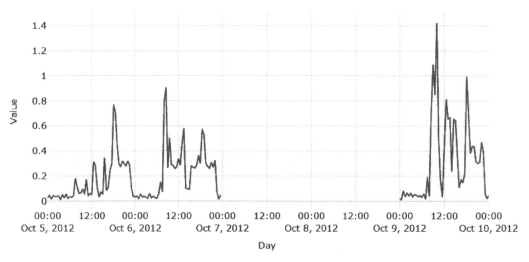

Figure 2.11 – The energy consumption of MAC000193 between 2012-10-05 and 2012-10-10

We are missing 2 whole days of energy consumption readings, which means there are 96 missing data points (half-hourly). If we use one of the techniques we saw earlier, such as interpolation, we will see that it will mostly be a straight line because none of the methods are complex enough to capture the pattern over a long time.

There are a few techniques that we can use to fill in such large missing gaps in data. We will cover these now.

Imputing with the previous day

Since this is a half-hourly time series of energy consumption, it stands to reason that there might be a pattern that is repeating day after day. The energy consumption between 9:00 A.M. and 10:00 A.M. might be higher as everybody gets ready to go to the office and a slump during the day when most houses may be empty. So, the simplest way to fill in the missing data would be to use the last day energy readings so that the energy reading at 10:00 A.M. 2012-10-18 can be filled with the energy reading at 10:00 A.M. 2012-10-17:

```
#Shifting 48 steps to get previous day
ts_df["prev_day"] = ts_df['energy_consumption'].shift(48)
#Using the shifted column to fill missing
ts_df['prev_day_imputed'] =  ts_df['energy_consumption_
missing']
```

```
ts_df.loc[null_mask,"prev_day_imputed"] = ts_df.loc[null_
mask,"prev_day"]
mae = mean_absolute_error(ts_df.loc[window, "prev_day_
imputed"], ts_df.loc[window, "energy_consumption"])
```

Let's see what the imputation looks like:

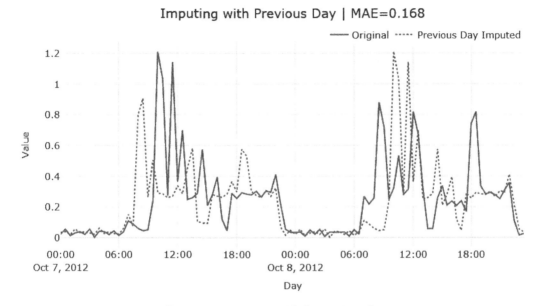

Figure 2.12 – Imputing with the previous day

While this looks better, this is also very brittle. When we are copying the previous day, we are also assuming that any kind of variation or anomalous behavior is also repeated. We can already see that the patterns for the day before and the day after are not the same.

Hourly average profile

A better approach would be to calculate an hourly profile from the data – the mean consumption for every hour – and use the average to fill the missing data:

```
#Create a column with the Hour from timestamp
ts_df["hour"] = ts_df.index.hour
#Calculate hourly average consumption
hourly_profile = ts_df.groupby(['hour'])['energy_consumption'].
mean().reset_index()
hourly_profile.rename(columns={"energy_consumption": "hourly_
```

```
profile"}, inplace=True)
#Saving the index because it gets lost in merge
idx = ts_df.index
#Merge the hourly profile dataframe to ts dataframe
ts_df = ts_df.merge(hourly_profile, on=['hour'], how='left',
validate="many_to_one")
ts_df.index = idx


#Using the hourly profile to fill missing
ts_df['hourly_profile_imputed'] = ts_df['energy_consumption_
missing']
ts_df.loc[null_mask,"hourly_profile_imputed"] = ts_df.loc[null_
mask,"hourly_profile"]
mae = mean_absolute_error(ts_df.loc[window, "hourly_profile_
imputed"], ts_df.loc[window, "energy_consumption"])
```

Let's see if this is better:

Imputing with Hourly Profile | MAE=0.121

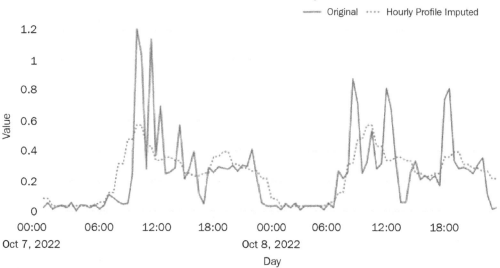

Figure 2.13 – Imputing with an hourly profile

This is giving us a much more generalized curve that does not have the spikes that we saw for the individual days. The hourly ups and downs have also been captured as per our expectations. The **mean absolute error** (**MAE**) is also lower than before.

The hourly average for each weekday

We can further refine this rule by introducing a specific profile for each weekday. It stands to reason that the usage pattern on a weekday is not going to be the same on a weekend. Hence, we can calculate the average hourly consumption for each weekday separately so that we have one profile for Monday, another for Tuesday, and so on:

```python
#Create a column with the weekday from timestamp
ts_df["weekday"] = ts_df.index.weekday
#Calculate weekday-hourly average consumption
day_hourly_profile = ts_df.groupby(['weekday','hour'])['energy_
consumption'].mean().reset_index()
day_hourly_profile.rename(columns={"energy_consumption": "day_
hourly_profile"}, inplace=True)
#Saving the index because it gets lost in merge
idx = ts_df.index
#Merge the day-hourly profile dataframe to ts dataframe
ts_df = ts_df.merge(day_hourly_profile, on=['weekday', 'hour'],
how='left', validate="many_to_one")
ts_df.index = idx


#Using the day-hourly profile to fill missing
ts_df['day_hourly_profile_imputed'] = ts_df['energy_
consumption_missing']
ts_df.loc[null_mask,"day_hourly_profile_imputed"] = ts_
df.loc[null_mask,"day_hourly_profile"]
mae = mean_absolute_error(ts_df.loc[window, "day_hourly_
profile_imputed"], ts_df.loc[window, "energy_consumption"])
```

Let's see what this looks like:

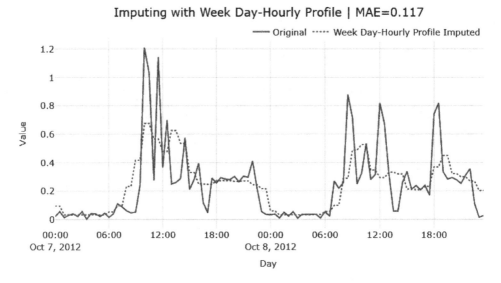

Figure 2.14 – Imputing the hourly average for each weekday

This looks very similar to the other one, but this is because the day we are imputing is a weekday and the weekday profiles are similar. The MAE is also lower than the day profile. The weekend profile is slightly different, which you can see in the associated Jupyter Notebook.

Seasonal interpolation

Although calculating seasonal profiles and using them to impute works well, there are instances, especially when there is a trend in the time series, where such a simple technique falls short. The simple seasonal profile doesn't capture the trend at all and ignores it completely. For such cases, we can do the following:

1. Calculate the seasonal profile, similar to how we calculated the averages earlier.

2. Subtract the seasonal profile and apply any of the interpolation techniques we saw earlier.

3. Add the seasonal profile back to the interpolated series.

This process has been implemented in this book's GitHub repository in the `src/imputation/interpolation.py` file. We can use it as follows:

```
from src.imputation.interpolation import SeasonalInterpolation
# Seasonal interpolation using 48*7 as the seasonal period.
recovered_matrix_seas_interp_weekday_half_hour =
SeasonalInterpolation(seasonal_period=48*7,decomposition_
```

```
strategy="additive", interpolation_strategy="spline",
interpolation_args={"order":3}, min_value=0).fit_transform(ts_
df.energy_consumption_missing.values.reshape(-1,1))
ts_df['seas_interp_weekday_half_hour_imputed'] = recovered_
matrix_seas_interp_weekday_half_hour
```

The key parameter here is `seasonal_period`, which tells the algorithm to look for patterns that repeat every `seasonal_period`. If we mention `seasonal_period=48`, it will look for patterns that repeat every 48 data points. In our case, they are after each day (because we have 48 half-hour timesteps in a day). In addition to this, we need to specify what kind of interpolation we need to perform.

> **Additional information**
>
> Internally, we use something called seasonal decomposition (`statsmodels.tsa.seasonal.seasonal_decompose`), which will be covered in *Chapter 3, Analyzing and Visualizing Time Series Data*, to isolate the seasonality component.

Here, we have done seasonal interpolation using 48 (half-hourly) and 48*7 (weekday to half-hourly) and plotted the resulting imputation:

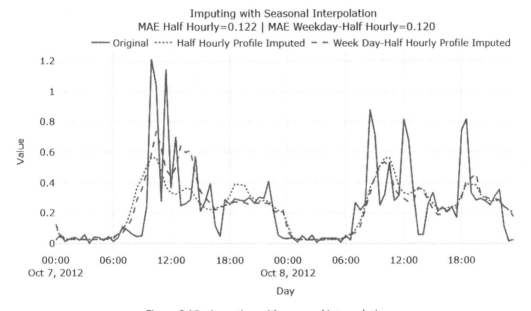

Figure 2.15 – Imputing with seasonal interpolation

Here, we can see that both have captured the seasonality patterns, but the half-hourly profile every weekday has captured the peaks in the first day better, so they have a lower MAE. There is no improvement in terms of hourly averages, mostly because there is no strong increasing or decreasing patterns in the time series.

With this, we have come to the end of this chapter. We are now officially into the nitty-gritty of juggling time series data, cleaning it, and processing it. Congratulations on finishing this chapter!

Summary

After a short refresher on pandas DataFrames, especially on the datetime manipulations and simple techniques for handling missing data, we learned about the two forms of storing and working with time series data – compact and expanded. With all this knowledge, we took our raw dataset and built a pipeline to convert it into compact form. If you have run the accompanying notebook, you should have the preprocessed dataset saved on disk. We also had an in-depth look at some techniques for handling long gaps of missing data.

Now that we have the processed datasets, in the next chapter, we will learn how to visualize and analyze a time series dataset.

3

Analyzing and Visualizing Time Series Data

In the previous chapter, we learned where to obtain time series datasets, as well as how to manipulate time series data using `pandas`, handle missing values, and so on. Now that we have the processed time series data, it's time to understand the dataset, which data scientists call **Exploratory Data Analysis** (**EDA**). It is a process by which the data scientist analyzes the data by looking at aggregate statistics, feature distributions, visualizations, and so on to try and uncover patterns in the data that they can leverage in modeling. In this chapter, we will look at a couple of ways to analyze a time series dataset, a few specific techniques that are tailor-made for time series, and review some of the visualization techniques for time series data.

In this chapter, we will cover the following topics:

- Components of a time series
- Visualizing time series data
- Decomposing a time series
- Detecting and treating outliers

Technical requirements

You will need to set up the Anaconda environment following the instructions in the *Preface* of the book to get a working environment with all the packages and datasets required for the code in this book.

You will need to run `02 - Preprocessing London Smart Meter Dataset.ipynb` notebook from `Chapter02` folder.

The code for this chapter can be found at `https://github.com/PacktPublishing/Modern-Time-Series-Forecasting-with-Python-/tree/main/notebooks/Chapter03`.

Components of a time series

Before we start analyzing and visualizing time series, we need to understand the structure of a time series. Any time series can contain some or all of the following components:

- **Trend**
- **Seasonal**
- **Cyclical**
- **Irregular**

These components can be mixed in different ways, but two very commonly assumed ways are *additive* (*Y = Trend + Seasonal + Cyclical + Irregular*) and *multiplicative* (*Y = Trend * Seasonal * Cyclical * Irregular*).

The trend component

The **trend** is a long-term change in the mean of a time series. It is the smooth and steady movement of a time series in a particular direction. When the time series moves upward, we say there is an *upward or increasing trend*, while when it moves downward, we say there is a *downward or decreasing trend*. At the time of writing, if we think about the revenue of Tesla over the years, as shown in the following figure, we can see that it has been increasing consistently for the last few years:

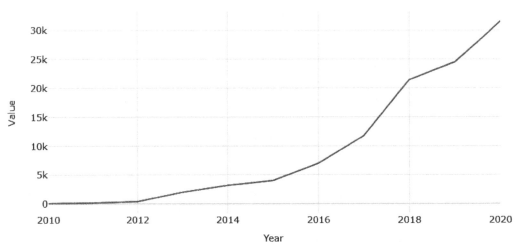

Figure 3.1 – Tesla's revenue in millions of USD

Looking at the preceding figure, we can say that Tesla's revenue is having an increasing trend. The trend doesn't need to be linear; it can also be non-linear.

The seasonal component

When a time series exhibits regular, repetitive, up-and-down fluctuations, we call that **seasonality**. For instance, retail sales typically shoot up during the holidays, specifically Christmas in western countries. Similarly, electricity consumption peaks during the summer months in the tropics and the winter months in colder countries. In all these examples, you can see a specific up-and-down pattern repeating every year. Another example is sunspots, as shown in the following figure:

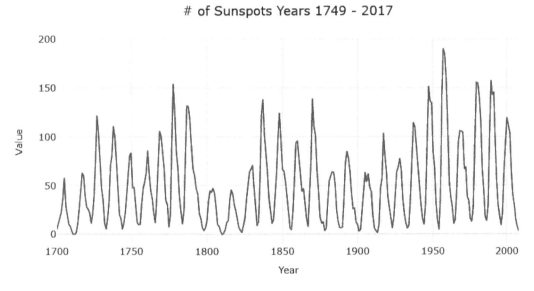

Figure 3.2 – Number of sunspots from 1749 to 2017

As you can see, sunspots peak every 11 years.

The cyclical component

The **cyclical** component is often confused with seasonality, but it stands apart due to a very subtle difference. Like seasonality, the cyclical component also exhibits a similar up-and-down pattern around the trend line, but instead of repeating the pattern every period, the cyclical component is irregular. A good example of this is economic recession, which happens over a 10-year cycle. However, this doesn't happen like clockwork; sometimes, it can be fewer or more than every 10 years.

The irregular component

This component is left after removing the trends, seasonality, and cyclicity from a time series. Traditionally, this component is considered *unpredictable* and is also called the *residual* or *error term*. In common classical statistics-based models, the point of any "model" is to capture all the other components to the point that the only part that is not captured is the irregular component. In modern machine learning, we do not consider this component entirely unpredictable. We try to capture this component, or parts of it, by using exogenous variables. For instance, the irregular component of retail sales may be explained as the different promotional activities they run. When we have this additional information, the "unpredictable" component starts to become predictable again. But no matter how many additional variables you add to the model, there will always be some component, which is the true irregular component (or true error), that is left behind.

Now that we know what the different components of a time series are, let's see how we can visualize them.

Visualizing time series data

In *Chapter 2, Acquiring and Processing Time Series Data*, we learned how to prepare a data model as a first step toward analyzing a new dataset. If preparing a data model is like approaching someone you like and making that first contact, then EDA is like dating that person. At this point, you have the dataset, and you are trying to get to know them, trying to figure out what makes them tick, what the person likes and dislikes, and so on.

EDA often employs visualization techniques to uncover patterns, spot anomalies, form and test hypotheses, and so on. Spending some time understanding your dataset will help you a lot when you are trying to squeeze out every last bit of performance from the models. You may understand what sort of features you must create, or what kind of modeling techniques should be applied, and so on.

In this chapter, we will cover a few visualization techniques that are well suited for time series datasets.

> **Notebook alert**
>
> To follow along with the complete code for visualizing time series, use the `01-Visualizing Time Series.ipynb` notebook in the `chapter03` folder.

Line charts

This is the most basic and common visualization that is used for understanding a time series. We just plot the time on the *X*-axis and the time series value on the *Y*-axis. Let's see what it looks like if we plot one of the households from our dataset:

Energy Consumption for MAC000193

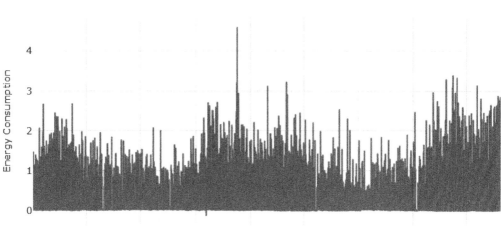

Figure 3.3 – Line plot of household MAC000193

When you have a long time series with high variation, as we have, the line plot can get a bit chaotic. One of the options to get a macroview of the time series in terms of trends and movement is to plot a smoothed version of the time series. Let's see what a rolling monthly average of the time series look like:

Rolling Monthly Average Energy Consumption for MAC000193

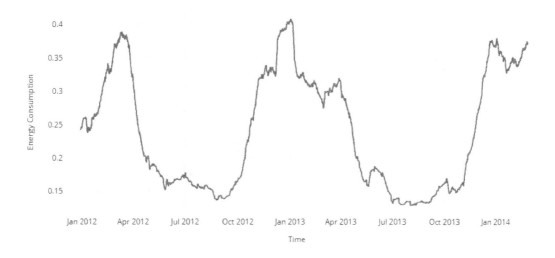

Figure 3.4 – Rolling monthly average energy consumption of household MAC000193

We can see the macro patterns much more clearly now. The seasonality is clear – the series peaks in winter and troughs during summer. And if you think about it critically, it makes sense. This is London we are talking about, and the energy consumption would be higher during the winter because of lower temperatures and subsequent heating system usage. For a household in the tropics, for example, the pattern may be reversed, with the peaks coming in summer when air conditioners come into play.

Another use for the line chart is to visualize two or more time series together and investigate any correlations between them. In our case, let's try plotting the temperature along with the energy consumption and see if the hypothesis we have about temperature influencing energy consumption holds good:

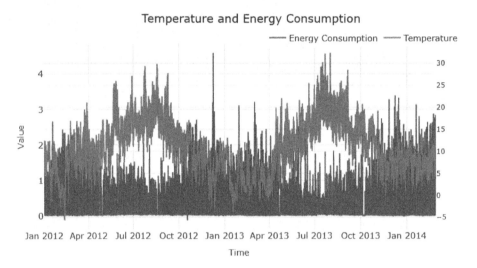

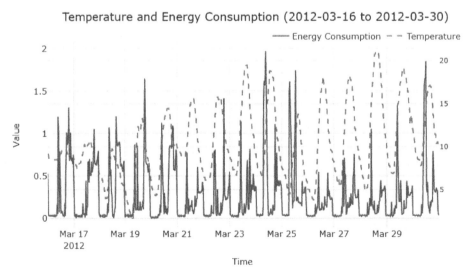

Figure 3.5 – Temperature and energy consumption (zoomed-in plot at the bottom)

Here, we can see a clear negative correlation in yearly resolution between energy consumption and temperature. Winters show higher energy consumption on a macro scale. We can also see the daily patterns that are loosely correlated with temperature, but maybe because of other factors such as people coming back home after work and so on.

There are a few other visualizations that are more suited to bringing out seasonality in a time series. Let's take a look.

Seasonal plots

A **seasonal plot** is very similar to a line plot, but the key difference here is that the X-axis denotes the "seasons", the Y-axis denotes the time series value, and the different seasonal cycles are represented in different colors or line types. For instance, the yearly seasonality at a monthly resolution can be depicted with months on the X-axis and different years in different colors.

Let's see what this looks like for our household in question. Here, we have plotted the average monthly energy consumption across multiple years:

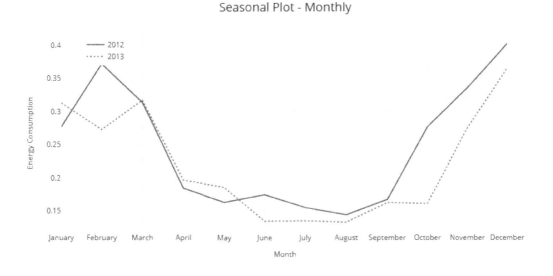

Figure 3.6 – Seasonal plot at a monthly resolution

We can instantly see the appeal in this visualization because it lets us visualize the seasonality pattern easily. We can see that the consumption goes down in the summer months and we can also see that it happens consistently across multiple years. In the 2 years that we have data for, we can see that in October, the behavior in 2013 slightly deviated from 2012. Maybe there is something else that can help us explain this difference – what about temperature? We can also plot the seasonal plots with another variable of interest, such as the temperature:

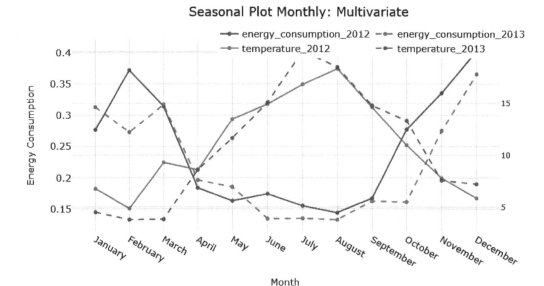

Figure 3.7 – Seasonal plot at a monthly resolution (energy consumption versus temperature)

Notice October? In October 2013, the temperature stayed warmer for 1 month more, hence why the energy consumption pattern was slightly different from last year.

We can plot these kinds of plots at other resolutions as well, such as hourly seasonality. But when there are too many seasonal cycles to be plotted, it increases visual clutter. An alternative to a seasonal plot is a seasonal box plot.

Seasonal box plots

Instead of plotting the different seasonal cycles in different colors or line types, we can represent them as a box plot. This instantly clears up the clutter in the plot. The additional benefit you get from this representation is that it lets us understand the variability across seasonal cycles:

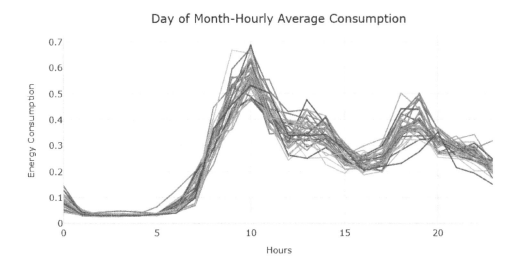

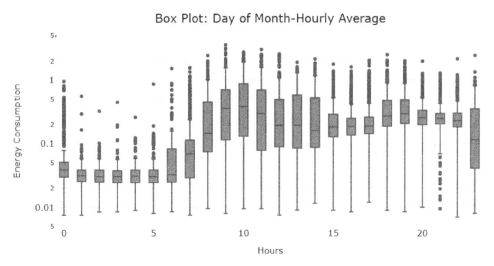

Figure 3.8 – Seasonal plot (top) and seasonal box plot (bottom) at an hourly resolution

Here, we can see that the seasonal plot at this resolution is too cluttered to make out the pattern and the variation across seasonal cycles. However, the seasonal box plot is much more informative. The horizontal line in the box tells us about the median, the box is the **interquartile range** (**IQR**), and the points that are marked are the outliers. By looking at the medians, we can see that the peak consumption occurs from 9 A.M. onward. But the variability is also higher from 9 A.M. If you plot separate box plots for each week, for example, you will see that the patterns are slightly different on Sundays (additional visualizations are in the associated notebook).

However, there is another visualization that lets you inspect these patterns along two dimensions.

Calendar heatmaps

Instead of having separate box plots or separate line charts for each week of the day, it would be useful if we could condense that information into a single plot. This is where **calendar heatmaps** come in. A calendar heatmap uses colored cells in a rectangular block to represent the information. Along the two sides of the rectangle, we can find two separate granularities of time, such as month and year. In each intersection, the cell is colored relative to the value of the time series at that intersection.

Let's look at the hourly average energy consumption across the different weekdays in a calendar heatmap:

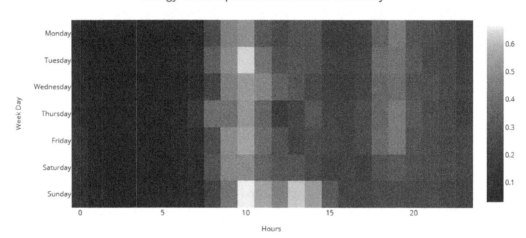

Figure 3.9 – A calendar heatmap for energy consumption

From the color scale on the right, we know that lighter colors mean higher values. We can see how Monday to Saturday have similar peaks – that is, once in the morning and once in the evening. However, Sunday has a slightly different pattern, with higher consumption throughout the day.

So far, we've reviewed a lot of visualizations that can bring out seasonality. Now, let's look at a visualization for inspecting autocorrelation.

Autocorrelation plot

If correlation indicates the strength and direction of the linear relationship between two variables, autocorrelation is the correlation between the values of a time series in successive periods. Most time series have a heavy dependence on the value in the previous period, and this is a critical component in a lot of the forecasting models we will be seeing as well. Something such as ARIMA (which we will briefly look at in *Chapter 4, Setting a Strong Baseline Forecast*) is built on autocorrelation. So, it's always helpful to just visualize and understand how strong the dependence on previous time steps is.

This is where **autocorrelation plots** come in handy. In such plots, we have the different lags (*t-1*, *t-2*, *t-3*, and so on) on the *X*-axis and the correlations between *t* and the different lags on the *Y*-axis. In addition to autocorrelation, we can also look at **partial autocorrelation**, which is very similar to autocorrelation but with one key difference: partial autocorrelation removes any indirect correlation that may be present before presenting the correlations. Let's look at an example to understand this. If *t* is the current time step, let's assume *t-1* is highly correlated to *t*. So, by extending this logic, *t-2* will be highly correlated with *t-1* and because of this correlation, the autocorrelation between *t* and *t-2* would be high. However, partial autocorrelation corrects this and extracts the correlation, which can be purely attributed to *t-2* and *t*.

One thing we need to keep in mind is that the autocorrelation and partial autocorrelation analysis works best if the time series is stationary (we will talk about stationarity in detail in *Chapter 6, Feature Engineering for Time Series Forecasting*).

> **Best practice**
>
> There are many ways of making a series stationary, but a quick and dirty way is to use seasonal decomposition and just pick the residuals. It should be devoid of trends and seasonality, which are the major drivers of non-stationarity in a time series. But as we will see later in this book, this is not a foolproof method of making a series stationary in the truest sense.

Now, let's see what these plots look like for our household from the dataset (after making it stationary):

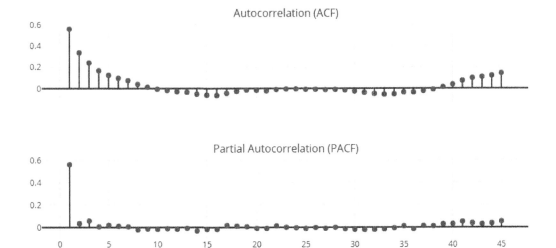

Figure 3.10 – Autocorrelation and partial autocorrelation plots

Here, we can see that the first lag (*t-1*) has the most influence and that its influence quickly drops down to close to zero in the partial autocorrelation plot. This means that the energy consumption of a day is highly correlated with the energy consumption the day before.

With that, we've looked at the different components of a time series and learned how to visualize a few of them. Now, let's see how we can decompose a time series into its components.

Decomposing a time series

Seasonal decomposition is the process by which we deconstruct a time series into its components – typically, trend, seasonality, and residuals. The general approach for decomposing a time series is as follows:

1. **Detrending**: Here, we estimate the **trend component** (which is the smooth change in the time series) and remove it from the time series, giving us a **detrended time series**.

2. **Deseasonalizing**: Here, we estimate the seasonality component from the detrended time series. After removing the seasonal component, what is left is the residual.

Let's discuss them in detail.

Detrending

Detrending can be done in a few different ways. Two popular ways of doing it are by using **moving averages** and **locally estimated scatterplot smoothing (LOESS) regression**.

Moving averages

One of the easiest ways of estimating trends is by using a moving average along the time series. It can be seen as a window that is moved along the time series in steps, and at each step, the average of all the values in the window is recorded. This moving average is a smoothed-out time series and helps us estimate the slow change in time series, which is the trend. The downside is that the technique is quite noisy. Even after smoothing out a time series using this technique, the extracted trend will not be smooth; it will be noisy. The noise should ideally reside with the residuals and not the trend (see the trend line shown in *Figure 3.11*).

LOESS

The **LOESS** algorithm, which is also called *locally weighted polynomial regression*, was developed by Bill Cleveland through the 70s to the 90s. It is a non-parametric method that is used to fit a smooth curve onto a noisy signal. We use an ordinal variable that moves between the time series as the independent variable and the time series signal as the dependent variable. For each value in the ordinal variable, the algorithm uses a fraction of the closest points and estimates a smoothed trend using only those points in a weighted regression. The weights in the weighted regression are the closest points to the point in question. This is given the highest weight and it decays as we move farther away from it. This gives us a very effective tool for modeling the smooth changes in the time series (trend).

Deseasonalizing

The seasonality component can also be estimated in a few different ways. The two most popular ways of doing this are by using period-adjusted averages or a Fourier series.

Period adjusted averages

This is a pretty simple technique wherein we calculate a seasonality index for each period in the expected cycle by taking the average values of all such periods over all the cycles. To make that clear, let's look at a monthly time series where we expect an annual seasonality in this time series. So, the up-and-down pattern would complete a full cycle in 12 months, or the seasonality period is 12. In other words, every 12 points in the time series have similar seasonal components. So, we take the average of all January values as the period-adjusted average for January. In the same way, we calculate the period average for all 12 months. At the end of the exercise, we have 12 period averages, and we can also calculate an *average* period average. Now, we can make these period averages into an index by either subtracting the average of all period averages from each of the period averages (for additive) or dividing the average of all period averages from each of the period averages (multiplicative).

Fourier series

In the late 1700s, Joseph Fourier, a mathematician and physicist, while studying heat flow, realized something profound – *any* periodic function can be broken down into a simple series of sine and cosine waves. Let's dwell on that for a minute. Any periodic function, no matter the shape, curve, or absence of it, or how wildly it oscillates around the axis, can be broken down into a series of sine and cosine waves.

> **Additional information**
>
> For the more mathematically inclined, the original theory proposes to decompose any periodic function into an integral of exponentials. Using Euler's identity, $e^{iy} = cos(y) + i \cdot sin(y)$, we can consider them as a summation of sine and cosine waves. The *Further reading* section contains a few resources if you want to delve deeper and explore related concepts, such as the Fourier transform.

It is this property that we use to extract seasonality from a time series because seasonality is a periodic function, and any periodic function can be approximated by a combination of sine and cosine waves. The sine-cosine form of a Fourier series is as follows:

$$s_{N(x)} = \frac{a_0}{2} + \Sigma_{n=1}^{N} \left(a_n \cdot cos \left(\frac{2\pi}{P} \cdot n \cdot x \right) + b_n \cdot sin \left(\frac{2\pi}{P} \cdot n \cdot x \right) \right)$$

Here, S_N is the N-term approximation of the signal, S. Theoretically, when N is infinite, the resulting approximation is equal to the original signal. P is the maximum length of the cycle.

We can use this Fourier series, or a few terms from the Fourier series, to model our seasonality. In our application, P is the maximum length of the cycle we are trying to model. For instance, for a yearly seasonality for monthly data, the maximum length of the cycle (P) is 12. x would be an ordinal variable that increases from 1 to P. In this example, x would be $1, 2, 3, \ldots 12$. Now, with these terms, all that is left to do is find a_n and b_n, which we can do by regressing on the signal.

We've seen that with the right combination of Fourier terms, we can replicate any signal. But the question is, should we? What we want to learn from data is a generalized seasonality profile that does well with unseen data as well. So, we use N as a hyperparameter to extract as complex a signal as we want from the data.

This is a good time to brush up on your trigonometry and remember what sine and cosine waves look like. The first Fourier term ($n=1$) is your age-old sine and cosine waves, which complete one full cycle in the maximum cycle length (P). As we increase n, we get sine and cosine waves that have multiple cycles in the maximum cycle length (P). This can be seen in the following figure:

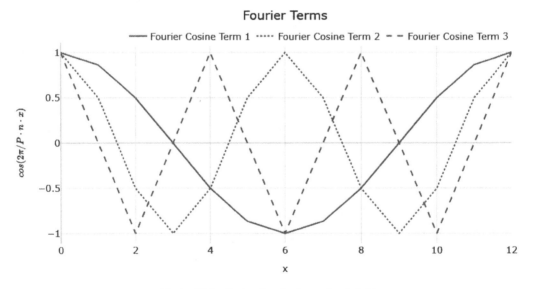

Figure 3.11 – Cosine Fourier terms (n=1, 2, 3)

The sine and cosine waves are complementary to each other, as shown in the following figure:

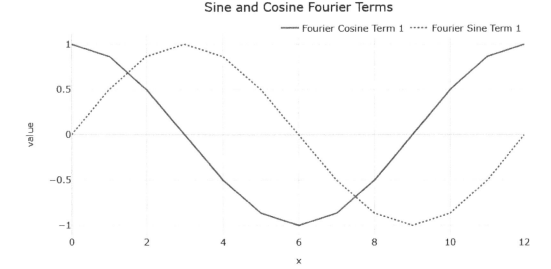

Figure 3.12 – Sine and cosine Fourier terms (n=1)

Now, let's see how we can use this in practice.

Implementations

> **Notebook alert**
>
> To follow along with the complete code for decomposing time series, use the `02-Decomposing Time Series.ipynb` notebook in the `chapter03` folder.

There are four implementations that we will cover here in the following subsections.

seasonal_decompose from statsmodel

`statsmodels.tsa.seasonal` has a function called `seasonal_decompose`. This is an implementation that uses moving averages for the trend component and period-adjusted averages for the seasonal component. It supports both additive and multiplicative modes of decomposition. However, it doesn't tolerate missing values. Let's see how we can use it:

```
#Does not support missing values, so using imputed ts instead
res = seasonal_decompose(ts, period=7*48, model="additive",
extrapolate_trend="freq")
```

A few key parameters to keep in mind are as follows:

- `period` is the seasonal period you expect the pattern to repeat.
- `model` takes `additive` or `multiplicative` as arguments to determine the type of decomposition.
- `filt` takes in an array that is used as the weights in the moving average (convolution, to be specific). It can also be used to define the window over which we need our moving average. We can increase it to smooth out the trend component to some extent.
- `extrapolate_trend` is a parameter that we can use to extend the trend component to both sides to avoid the missing values that are generated when applying the moving average filter.
- `two_sided` is a parameter that lets us define how the moving averages are calculated. If `True`, which it is by default, the moving average is calculated using the past as well as future values because the window for the moving average is centered. If `False`, it only uses past values to calculate the moving average.

Let's see how well we have been able to decompose one of the time series in our datasets. We used `period=7*48` to capture a weekday-hourly profile and `filt=np.repeat(1/(30*48), 30*48)` to make the moving average over 30 days with uniform weights:

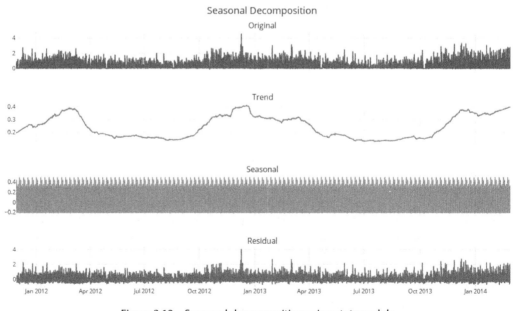

Figure 3.13 – Seasonal decomposition using statsmodels

We can't see the seasonal pattern because it's too small in the grand scale of the plot. The associated notebook has zoomed-in plots to help you understand the seasonal pattern. Even with a large window (for example, 20 days) of smoothing, the trend still has some noise in it. We may be able to reduce this a bit more by increasing the window, but there is a better alternative, as we will see now.

Seasonality and trend decomposition using LOESS (STL)

As we saw earlier, LOESS is much more suited for trend estimation. **Seasonality and trend decomposition using LOESS (STL)** is an implementation that uses LOESS for trend estimation and period averages for seasonality. Although `statsmodels` has an implementation, we have reimplemented it for better performance and flexibility. This implementation can be found in this book's GitHub repository under `src.decomposition.seasonal.py`. It expects a pandas DataFrame or series with a datetime index as an input. Let's see how we can use this:

```
stl = STL(seasonality_period=7*48, model = "additive")
res_new = stl.fit(ts_df.energy_consumption)
```

The key parameters here are as follows:

- `seasonality_period` is the seasonal period you expect the pattern to repeat.

- `model` takes `additive` or `multiplicative` as arguments to determine the type of decomposition.

- `lo_frac` is the fraction of the data that will be used to fit the LOESS regression.

- `lo_delta` is the fractional distance within which we use a linear interpolation instead of weighted regression. Using a non-zero `lo_delta` significantly decreases computation time.

Let's see what this decomposition looks like. Here, we used `seasonality_period=7*48` to capture a weekday-hourly profile:

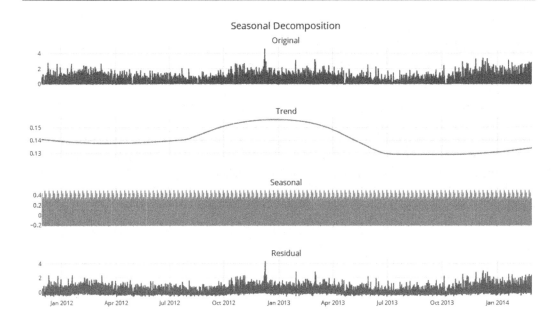

Figure 3.14 – STL decomposition

Let's also look at the decomposition for just 1 month to see the extracted seasonality patterns clearer:

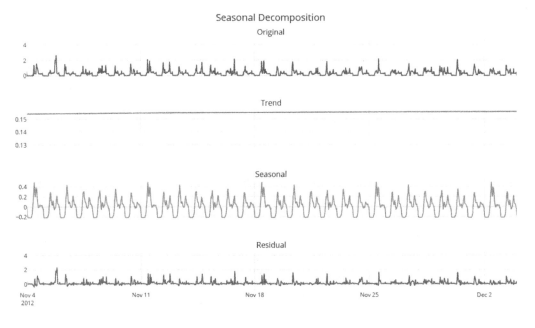

Figure 3.15 – STL decomposition (zoomed-in for a month)

The trend is smooth enough now and seasonality has also been captured. Here, we can clearly see the hourly peaks and valleys and the higher peaks on weekends. But since we are relying on averages to derive the seasonality, it is also highly influenced by outliers. A few very high or very low values in the time series will skew your seasonality profile that's been derived from period averages. Another disadvantage of this technique is that the "goodness" of the seasonality that's been extracted suffers when the difference between the resolution of the data and the expected seasonality cycle is greater. For instance, when extracting a yearly seasonality on daily or sub-daily data, this would make the extracted seasonality very noisy. This technique will also not work if you have less than two cycles of the expected seasonality – for instance, if we want to extract a yearly seasonality, but we have less than 2 years of data.

Fourier decomposition

We can find the Python implementation for decomposing a time series using Fourier terms in `src.decomposition.seasonal.py`. It uses LOESS for trend detection and Fourier terms for seasonality extraction. There are two ways we can use it. First, we can specify `seasonality_period` as one of the `pandas` datetime properties (such as `hour`, `week_of_day`, and so on):

```
stl = FourierDecomposition(seasonality_period="hour", model =
"additive", n_fourier_terms=5)
res_new = stl.fit(pd.Series(ts.squeeze(), index=ts_df.index))
```

Alternatively, we can create any custom seasonality array that's the same length as the time series that has an ordinal representation of the seasonality. If it is an annual seasonality of daily data, the array would have a minimum value of 1 and a maximum value of 365 as it increases by one every day of the year:

```
#Making a custom seasonality term
ts_df["dayofweek"] = ts_df.index.dayofweek
ts_df["hour"] = ts_df.index.hour
#Creating a sorted unique combination df
map_df = ts_df[["dayofweek","hour"]].drop_duplicates().sort_
values(["dayofweek", "hour"])
# Assigning an ordinal variable to capture the order
map_df["map"] = np.arange(1, len(map_df)+1)
# mapping the ordinal mapping back to the original df and
getting the seasonality array
seasonality = ts_df.merge(map_df, on=["dayofweek","hour"],
how='left', validate="many_to_one")['map']
stl = FourierDecomposition(model = "additive", n_fourier_
terms=50)
res_new = stl.fit(pd.Series(ts, index=ts_df.index),
seasonality=seasonality)
```

The key parameters that are involved in this process are as follows:

- `seasonality_period` is the seasonality to be extracted from the *datetime index*. pandas datetime properties such as `week_of_day`, `month`, and so on can be used to specify the most prominent seasonality. If left set to `None`, you need to provide the seasonality array while calling `fit`.

- `model` takes `additive` or `multiplicative` as arguments to determine the type of decomposition.

- `n_fourier_terms` determines the number of Fourier terms to be used to extract the seasonality. The more we increase this parameter, the more complex the seasonality that is extracted from the data.

- `lo_frac` is the fraction of the data that will be used to fit the LOESS regression.

- `lo_delta` is the fractional distance within which we use linear interpolation instead of weighted regression. Using a non-zero `lo_delta` significantly decreases computation time.

Let's see the zoomed-in plot for the decomposition using `FourierDecomposition`:

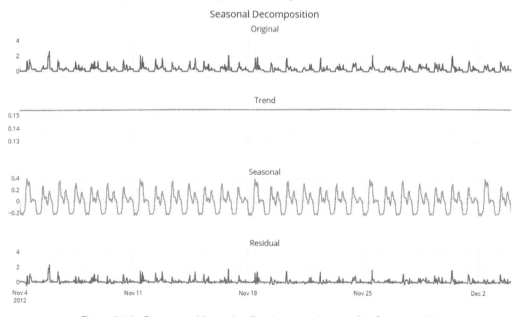

Figure 3.16 – Decomposition using Fourier terms (zoomed-in for a month)

The trend is going to be the same as the STL one because we are using LOESS here as well. The seasonality profile may be slightly different and robust to outliers because we are doing regularized regression using the Fourier terms on the signal. Another advantage is that we have decoupled the resolution of the data and the expected seasonality. Now, extracting a yearly seasonality on sub-daily data is not as challenging as with period averages.

So far, we have only seen techniques that extract one seasonality per series; mostly, we extract the major seasonality. So, what do we do when we have multiple seasonal patterns?

Multiple seasonality decomposition using LOESS (MSTL)

Time series with high-frequency data (such as daily, hourly, or minutely data) are prone to exhibit multiple seasonal patterns. For instance, there may be an hourly seasonality pattern, a weekly seasonality pattern, and a yearly seasonality pattern. But if we extract only the dominant pattern and leave the rest to residuals, we are not doing justice to the decomposition. Kasun Bandara et al. proposed an extension of STL decomposition for multiple seasonality, known as **multiple seasonal-trend decomposition using LOESS (MSTL)**, and a corresponding implementation is present in the R ecosystem. A very similar implementation in Python can be found in `src.decomposition.seasonal.py`. In addition to MSTL, the implementation extracts multiple seasonality using Fourier terms.

> **Reference check**
>
> The research paper by Kasun Bandara et al. is cited in the *References* section as reference *1*.

Let's look at an example of how we can use this:

```
stl = MultiSeasonalDecomposition(seasonal_
model="fourier",seasonality_periods=["day_of_year", "day_of_
week", "hour"], model = "additive", n_fourier_terms=10)
res_new = stl.fit(pd.Series(ts, index=ts_df.index))
```

The key parameters here are as follows:

- `seasonality_periods` is the list of expected seasonalities. For STL, it is a list of seasonal periods, while for `FourierDecomposition`, it is a list of strings that denotes `pandas` datetime properties.

- `seasonality_model` takes `fourier` or `averages` as arguments to determine the type of seasonality decomposition.

- `model` takes `additive` or `multiplicative` as arguments to determine the type of decomposition.

- `n_fourier_terms` determines the number of Fourier terms to be used to extract the seasonality. As we increase this parameter, the more complex the seasonality that is extracted from the data.

- `lo_frac` is the fraction of the data that will be used to fit the LOESS regression.

- `lo_delta` is the fractional distance within which we use linear interpolation instead of weighted regression. Using a non-zero `lo_delta` significantly decreases computation time.

Let's see what the decomposition looks like when using Fourier decomposition:

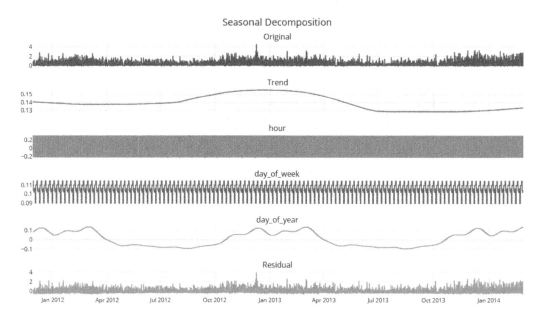

Figure 3.17 – Multiple seasonality decomposition using Fourier terms

Here, we can see that the `day_of_week` seasonality has been extracted. To see the `day_of_week` and `hour` seasonal components, we need to zoom in a bit:

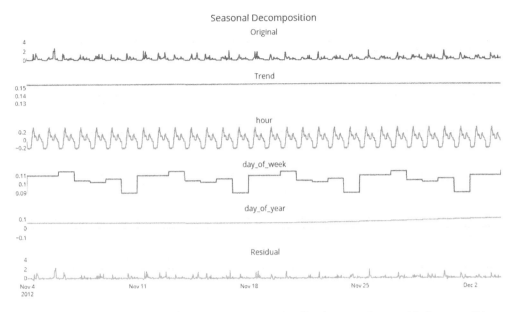

Figure 3.18 – Multiple seasonality decomposition using Fourier terms (zoomed-in for a month)

Here, we can observe that the hour seasonality has been extracted well and that it has also isolated the day_of_week seasonal component, which peaks on weekends. The **discrete step** nature of the day_of_week seasonal component is because the frequency of the data is half-hourly, and for 48 data points, day_of_week will be the same.

We have summarized the four techniques we've covered in the following table:

Implementation	Trend	Seasonal	Supports Multiple Seasonality?	Supports Missing?
seasonal_decompose (statsmodels)	Moving Averages	Period-Adjusted Averages	No	No
STL	LOESS	Period-Adjusted Averages	No	Yes
FourierDecomposition	LOESS	Fourier Terms	No	No
MultiSeasonalDecomposition	LOESS	Period-Adjusted Averages / Fourier Terms	Yes	No

Table 3.1 – Different seasonal decomposition techniques

Now, let's understand and analyze a time series dataset.

Detecting and treating outliers

An **outlier**, as its name suggests, is an observation that lies at an abnormal distance from the rest of the observations. If we are looking at a **data generating process (DGP)** as a stochastic process that generates the time series, the outliers are the points that have the least probability of being generated from the DGP. This can be for many reasons, including faulty measurement equipment, incorrect data entry, and black-swan events, to name a few. Being able to detect such outliers and *treat* them may help your forecasting model understand the data better.

Outlier/anomaly detection is a specialized field itself in time series, but in this book, we are going to restrict ourselves to simpler techniques of identifying and treating outliers. This is because our main aim is not to detect outliers, but to clean the data for our forecasting models to perform better. If you want to learn more about anomaly detection, head over to the *Further reading* section for a few resources to get started.

Now, let's look at a few techniques for identifying outliers.

> **Notebook alert**
>
> To follow along with the complete code for detecting outliers, use the `03-Outlier Detection.ipynb` notebook in the `chapter03` folder.

Standard deviation

This is a rule of thumb that almost everyone who has worked with data for some time would have heard of – if μ is the mean of the time series and σ is the standard deviation, then anything that falls beyond $\mu \pm 3\sigma$ is an **outlier**. The underlying theory is deeply rooted in statistics. If we assume that the values of the time series follow a normal distribution (which is a symmetrical distribution with very desirable properties), using probability theory, we can derive that 68% of the area under the normal distribution lies within one standard deviation on either side of the mean, about 95% of the area within two standard deviations, and about 99% of the area within three standard deviations. So, when we make the bounds as three standard deviations (by using the rule of thumb), what we are saying is that if any observation whose probability of belonging to the probability distribution is less than 1%, then they are an outlier. Moving slightly to more practical issues, this cutoff of three standard deviations is in no way sacrosanct. We need to try out different values of this multiple and determine the right multiple by subjectively evaluating the results we get. The higher the multiple is, the fewer outliers there will be.

For highly seasonal data, the naïve way of applying the rule to the raw time series will not work well. In such cases, we must deseasonalize the data using any of the techniques we discussed earlier and then apply the outliers to the residuals. If we don't do that, we may flag a seasonal peak as an outlier, which is not what we want.

Another key assumption here is the normal distribution. However, in reality, a lot of the time series we come across may not be normal and hence the rule will lose its theoretical guarantees fast.

Interquartile range (IQR)

Another very similar technique is using the IQR instead of the standard deviation to define the bounds beyond which we mark the observations as outliers. IQR is the difference between the 3rd quartile (or the 75th percentile or 0.75 quantile) and the 1st quartile (or the 25th percentile or 0.25 quantile). The upper and lower bounds are defined as follows:

- *Upper bound = Q3 + n x IQR*
- *Lower bound = Q1 - n x IQR*

Here, *IQR = Q3-Q2*, and *n* is the multiple of IQRs that determines the width of the acceptable area.

For datasets where we observe high occurrences of outliers and wild variations, this is slightly more robust than the standard deviation. This is because the standard deviation and the mean are highly influenced by individual points in the dataset. If 2 σ was the rule of thumb in the earlier method, here, it is 1.5 times the IQR. This also ties back to the same normal distribution assumption, and 1.5 times the IQR is equivalent to ~3 σ (2.7 σ to be exact). The point about deseasonalizing before applying the rule applies here as well. It applies to all the techniques we will see here.

Isolation Forest

Isolation Forest is an unsupervised anomaly detection algorithm based on decision trees. A typical anomaly detection algorithm models the *normal* points and profiles outliers as any points that do not fit the *normal*. But Isolation Forest takes a different path and models the outliers directly. It does this by creating a forest of decision trees by randomly splitting the feature space. This technique works on the assumption that the outlier points fall in the outer periphery and are easier to fall into a leaf node of a tree. Therefore, you can find the outliers in short branches, whereas normal points, which are closer together, will require longer branches. The "anomaly score" of any point is determined by the depth of the tree to be traversed before reaching that particular point. scikit-learn has an implementation of the algorithm under `sklearn.ensemble.IsolationForest`. Apart from the standard parameters for decision trees, the key parameter here is contamination. It is set to `auto` by default but can be set to any value between 0 and 0.5. This parameter specifies what percentage of the dataset you expect to be anomalous. But one thing we have to keep in mind is that `IsolationForest` does not consider time at all and just highlights values that fall *outside the norm*.

Extreme studentized deviate (ESD) and seasonal ESD (S-ESD)

This statistics-based technique is more sophisticated than the basic $\pm$ σ technique, but still uses the same assumption of normality. It is based on another statistical test, called Grubbs's Test, which is used to find a *single outlier* in a normally distributed dataset. ESD iteratively uses Grubbs's test by identifying and removing an outlier at each step. It also adjusts the critical value based on the number of points left. For a more detailed understanding of the test, go to the *Further reading* section, where we have provided a couple of resources about ESD and S-ESD. In 2017, Hochenbaum et al. from Twitter Research proposed to use the generalized ESD with deseasonalization as a method of detecting outliers for time series.

We have adapted an existing implementation of the algorithm for our use case, and it is available in this book's GitHub repository. While all the other methods leave it to the user to determine the right level of outliers by tweaking a few parameters, S-ESD only takes in an upper bound on the number of expected outliers and then identifies the outliers independently. For instance, we set the upper bound to 800 and the algorithm identified ~400 outliers in the data we are working with.

> **Reference check**
>
> The research paper by Hochenbaum et al. is cited in the *References* section as reference *2*.

Let's see how the outliers were detected using all the techniques we have reviewed:

	# of Outliers	% of Outliers
3SD	802	2.12%
2SD on Residuals	728	1.92%
4IQR	747	1.97%
4SD on Residuals	468	1.24%
Isolation Forest	364	0.96%
Isolation Forest on Residuals	359	0.95%
ESD	420	1.11%
S-ESD	424	1.12%

Figure 3.19 – Outliers detected using different techniques

Now that we've learned how to detect outliers, let's talk about how we can treat them and clean the dataset.

Treating outliers

The first question that we must answer is whether or not we should correct the outliers we have identified. The statistical tests that identify outliers automatically should go through another level of human verification. If we blindly "treat" outliers, we might be chopping off a valuable pattern that will help us forecast the time series. If you are only forecasting a handful of time series, then it still makes sense to look at the outliers and anchor them to reality by looking at the causes for such outliers.

But when you have thousands of time series, a human can't inspect all the outliers, so we will have to resort to automated techniques. A common practice is to replace an outlier with a heuristic such as the maximum, minimum, 75th percentile, and so on. A better method is to consider the outliers as missing data and use any of the techniques we discussed earlier to impute the outliers.

One thing we must keep in mind is that outlier correction is not a necessary step in forecasting, especially when using modern methods such as machine learning or deep learning. Whether we do outlier correction or not is something we have to experiment with and figure out.

Well done! This was a pretty busy chapter, with a lot of concepts and code, so congratulations on finishing it. Feel free to head back and revise a few topics as needed.

Summary

In this chapter, we learned about the key components of a time series and familiarized ourselves with terms such as trend, seasonality, and so on. We also reviewed a few time series-specific visualization techniques that will come in handy during EDA. Then, we learned about techniques that let you decompose a time series into its components and saw techniques for detecting outliers in the data. Finally, we learned how to treat the identified outliers. Now, you are all set to start forecasting the time series, which we will start in the next chapter.

References

The following are the references for this chapter:

1. Kasun Bandara and Rob J Hyndman and Christoph Bergmeir. (2021). *MSTL: A Seasonal-Trend Decomposition Algorithm for Time Series with Multiple Seasonal Patterns.* arXiv:2107.13462 [stat.AP]. `https://arxiv.org/abs/2107.13462`.

2. Hochenbaum, J., Vallis, O., & Kejariwal, A. (2017). *Automatic Anomaly Detection in the Cloud Via Statistical Learning.* ArXiv, abs/1704.07706. `https://arxiv.org/abs/1704.07706`.

Further reading

To learn more about the topics that were covered in this chapter, take a look at the following resources:

*   Fourier Series: `https://www.setzeus.com/public-blog-post/the-fourier-series`.

*   Fourier Series from Khan Academy: `https://www.youtube.com/watch?v=UKHBWzoOKsY`.

*   Fourier Transform - `https://betterexplained.com/articles/an-interactive-guide-to-the-fourier-transform/`.

- Ane Blázquez-García, Angel Conde, Usue Mori, and Jose A. Lozano. (2021). *A Review on Outlier/Anomaly Detection in Time Series Data.* arXiv:2002.04236. `https://arxiv.org/abs/2002.04236`.

- Braei, M., & Wagner, S. (2020). *Anomaly Detection in Univariate Time-series: A Survey on the State-of-the-Art.* ArXiv, abs/2004.00433. `https://arxiv.org/abs/2004.00433`.

- Generalized ESD Test for Outliers: `https://www.itl.nist.gov/div898/handbook/eda/section3/eda35h3.htm`.

4

Setting a Strong
Baseline Forecast

In the previous chapter, we saw some techniques we can use to understand **time series data**, do some **Exploratory Data Analysis** (**EDA**), and so on. But now, let's get to the crux of the matter – **time series forecasting**. The point of understanding the dataset and looking at patterns, seasonality, and so on was to make the job of forecasting that series easier. And with any machine learning exercise, one of the first things we need to establish before going further is a **baseline**.

A baseline is a simple model that provides reasonable results without requiring a lot of time to come up with them. Many people think of baselines as something that is derived from common sense, such as an average or some rule of thumb. But as a best practice, a baseline can be as sophisticated as we want it to be, so long as it is quickly and easily implemented. Any further progress we want to make will be in terms of the performance of this baseline.

In this chapter, we will look at a few classical techniques that can be used as baselines, and a strong baseline at that. Some may feel that the forecasting techniques we will be discussing in this chapter shouldn't be baselines, but we are keeping them in here because these techniques have stood the test of time – and for good reason. They are also very mature and can be applied with very little effort, thanks to the awesome open source libraries that implement them. There can be many types of problems/datasets where it is difficult to beat the baseline techniques we will discuss in this chapter, and in those cases, there is no shame in just sticking to one of these baseline techniques.

In this chapter, we will cover the following topics:

- Setting up a test harness
- Generating strong baseline forecasts
- Assessing the forecastability of a time series

Technical requirements

You will need to set up the **Anaconda** environment following the instructions in the *Preface* of the book to get a working environment with all the packages and datasets required for the code in this book.

To run the notebooks for this chapter, you need to run the `02-Preprocessing London Smart Meter Dataset.ipynb` preprocessing notebook from `Chapter02`.

The code for this chapter can be found at `https://github.com/PacktPublishing/Modern-Time-Series-Forecasting-with-Python-/tree/main/notebooks/Chapter04`.

Setting up a test harness

Before we start forecasting and setting up baselines, we need to set up a **test harness**. In software testing, a test harness is a collection of code and the inputs that have been configured to test a program under various situations. In terms of machine learning, a test harness is a set of code and data that can be used to evaluate algorithms. It is important to set up a test harness so that we can evaluate all future algorithms in a standard and quick way.

The first thing we need is **holdout (test)** and **validation** datasets.

Creating holdout (test) and validation datasets

As a standard practice, in machine learning, we set aside two parts of the dataset, name them *validation data* and *test data*, and don't use them at all to train the model. The validation data is used in the modeling process to assess the quality of the model. To select between different model classes, tune the hyperparameters, perform feature selection, and so on, we need a dataset. Test data is like the final test of your chosen model. It tells you how well your model is doing in unseen data. If validation data is like the mid-term exams, the test data is your final exam.

In regular regression or classification, we usually sample a few records at random and set them aside. But while dealing with time series, we need to respect the temporal aspect of the dataset. Therefore, a best practice is to set aside the latest part of the dataset as the test data. Another rule of thumb is to set equal-sized validation and test datasets so that the key modeling decisions we make based on the validation data are as close as possible to the test data. The dataset that we introduced in *Chapter 2, Acquiring and Processing Time Series Data* (the London Smart Energy dataset), contains the energy consumption readings of households in London from November 2011 to February 2014. So, we are going to put aside January 2014 as the validation data and February 2014 as the test data.

Let's open 01-Setting up Experiment Harness.ipynb from the chapter04 folder and run it. In the notebook, we must create the train-test split both before and after filling the missing values with SeasonalInterpolation and save them accordingly. Once the notebook finishes running, you will have created the following files in the preprocessed folder with the 2014 data saved separately:

- selected_blocks_train.parquet
- selected_blocks_val.parquet
- selected_blocks_test.parquet
- selected_blocks_train_missing_imputed.parquet
- selected_blocks_val_missing_imputed.parquet
- selected_blocks_test_missing_imputed.parquet

Now that we have a fixed dataset that can be used to fairly evaluate multiple algorithms, we need a way to evaluate the different forecasts.

Choosing an evaluation metric

In machine learning, we have a handful of metrics that can be used to measure continuous outputs, mainly **Mean Absolute Error** (**MAE**) and **Mean Squared Error** (**MSE**). But in the time series forecasting realm, there are scores of metrics with no real consensus on which ones to use. One of the reasons for this overwhelming number of metrics is that no one metric measures every characteristic of a forecast. Therefore, we have a whole chapter devoted to this topic (*Chapter 18, Evaluating Forecasts – Forecast Metrics*). For now, we will just review a few metrics, all of which we are going to use to measure the forecasts. We are just going to consider them at face value:

- **Mean Absolute Error** (**MAE**): MAE is a very simple metric. It is the average of the unsigned error between the forecast at timestep $t(f_t)$ and the observed value at time $t(y_t)$. The formula is as follows:

$$MAE = \frac{1}{N \times L} \times \sum_{i}^{N} \sum_{j}^{L} |f_{i,j} - y_{i,j}|$$

  Here, N is the number of time series, L is the length of time series (in this case, the length of the test period), and f and y are the forecast and observed values, respectively.

- **Mean Squared Error** (**MSE**): MSE is the average of the squared error between the forecast (f_t) and observed (y_t) values:

$$MSE = \frac{1}{N \times L} \times \sum_{i}^{N} \sum_{j}^{L} (f_{i,j} - y_{i,j})^2$$

- **Mean Absolute Scaled Error (MASE)**: MASE is slightly more complicated than MSE or MAE but gives us a slightly better measure to overcome the scale-dependent nature of the previous two measures. If we have multiple time series with different average values, MAE and MSE will show higher errors for the high-value time series as opposed to the low-valued time series. MASE overcomes this by scaling the errors based on the in-sample MAE from the **naïve forecasting method** (which is one of the most basic forecasts possible; we will review it later in this chapter). Intuitively, MASE gives us the measure of how much better our forecast is as compared to the naïve forecast:

$$MASE = \frac{\frac{1}{L} \times \Sigma_i^L |f_i - y_i|}{\frac{1}{L-1} \times \Sigma_{j=2}^L |y_j - y_{j-1}|}$$

- **Forecast Bias (FB)**: This is a metric with slightly different aspects from the other metrics we've seen. While the other metrics help assess the *correctness* of the forecast, irrespective of the direction of the error, forecast bias lets us understand the overall *bias* in the model. Forecast bias is a metric that helps us understand whether the forecast is continuously over- or under-forecasting. We calculate forecast bias as the difference between the sum of the forecast and the sum of the observed values, expressed as a percentage over the sum of all actuals:

$$FB = \frac{\Sigma_i^N \Sigma_j^L f_{i,j} - \Sigma_i^N \Sigma_j^L y_{i,j}}{\Sigma_i^N \Sigma_j^L y_{i,j}}$$

Now, our test harness is ready. We also know how to evaluate and compare forecasts that have been generated from different models on a single, fixed holdout dataset with a set of predetermined metrics. Now, it's time to start forecasting.

Generating strong baseline forecasts

Time series forecasting has been around since the early 1920s, and through the years, many brilliant people have come up with different models, some statistical and some heuristic-based. I refer to them collectively as **classical statistical models** or **econometrics models**, although they are not strictly statistical/econometric.

In this section, we are going to review a few such models that can form really strong baselines when we want to try modern techniques in forecasting. As an exercise, we are going to use an excellent open source library for time series forecasting – darts (https://github.com/unit8co/darts). The 02-Baseline Forecasts using darts.ipynb notebook contains the code for this section so that you can follow along.

Before we start looking at forecasting techniques, let's quickly understand how to use the darts library to generate the forecasts. We are going to pick one consumer from the dataset and try out all the baseline techniques on the validation dataset one by one.

The first thing we need to do is select the consumer we want using the unique ID for each customer, the LCLid column (from the expanded form of data), and set the timestamp as the index of the DataFrame:

```
ts_train = train_df.loc[train_df.LCLid=="MAC000193",
["timestamp","energy_consumption"]].set_index("timestamp")
ts_test = val_df.loc[val_df.LCLid=="MAC000193",
["timestamp","energy_consumption"]].set_index("timestamp")
```

Now that we have a single time series, we need to put it into a data structure that the darts library expects – a TimeSeries data structure, which is native to darts. TimeSeries can be built easily using a few factory methods:

- From a pandas DataFrame using TimeSeries.from_dataframe()
- From a separate array of time index and observed values using TimeSeries.from_times_and_values()
- From a numpy array using TimeSeries.from_values()
- From a pandas series using TimeSeries.from_series()
- From a CSV file using TimeSeries.from_csv()

In our case, since we have the time series as a pandas series, we can just use the from_series() method:

```
ts_train = TimeSeries.from_series(ts_train)
ts_test = TimeSeries.from_series(ts_test)
```

Once we have the TimeSeries data structure, we can just initialize the model and call .fit and .predict to get the forecast:

```
model = <initialize the model>
model.fit(ts_train)
y_pred = model.predict(len(ts_test))
```

When we call .predict, we have to tell the model how long into the future we have to predict. This is called the horizon of the forecast. In our case, we need to predict our test period, which we can easily do by just taking the length of the ts_test array.

We can also calculate the metrics we discussed earlier in the test harness easily:

```
mae(actual_series = ts_test, pred_series = y_pred)
mse(actual_series = ts_test, pred_series = y_pred)
# For MASE calculation, the training set is also needed
mase(actual_series = ts_test, pred_series = y_pred,
```

```
insample=ts_train)
# Forecast Bias is not part of darts, but an own implementation
available in src.utils.ts_utils
forecast_bias(actual_series = ts_test, pred_series = y_pred)
```

For ease of experimentation, we have encapsulated all of this into a handy function, `eval_model`, in the notebook. This returns the predictions and the calculated metrics in a dictionary.

Now, let's start looking at a few very simple methods of forecasting.

Naïve forecast

A naïve forecast is as simple as you can get. The forecast is just the last/most recent observation in a time series. If the latest observation in a time series is 10, then the forecast for all future timesteps is 10. This can be implemented as follows using the `NaiveSeasonal` class in `darts`:

```
from darts.models import NaiveSeasonal
naive_model = NaiveSeasonal(K=1)
```

Once we have initialized the model, we can call our helpful `eval_model` function in the notebook to run and record the forecast and metrics.

Let's visualize the forecast we just generated:

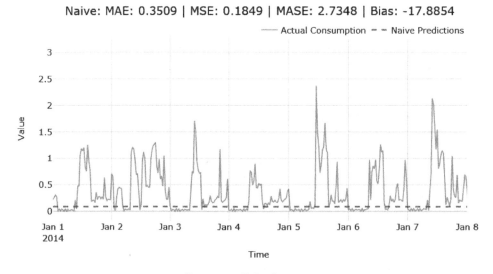

Figure 4.1 – Naïve forecast

Here, we can see that the forecast is a straight line and completely ignores any pattern in the series. This is by far the simplest way to forecast, hence why it is naïve. Now, let's look at another simple method.

Moving average forecast

While a naïve forecast memorizes the most recent past, it also memorizes the noise at any timestep. **A moving average forecast** is another simple method that tries to overcome the pure memorization of the naïve method. Instead of taking the latest observation, it takes the mean of the latest *n* steps as the forecast. Moving average is not one of the models present in `darts`, but we have implemented a darts-compatible model in this book's GitHub repository in the `chapter04` folder:

```
from src.forecasting.baselines import NaiveMovingAverage
#Taking a moving average over 48 timesteps, i.e, one day
naive_model = NaiveMovingAverage(window=48)
```

Let's look at the forecast we generated:

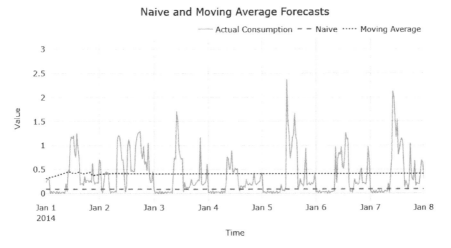

Figure 4.2 – Moving average forecast

This forecast is also almost a straight line. Now, let's look at another simple method, but one that considers seasonality as well.

Seasonal naive forecast

A seasonal naive forecast is a twist on the simple naive method. Whereas in the naive method, we took the last observation (Y_{t-1}), in seasonal naïve, we take the Y_{t-k} observation. So, we look back *k* steps for each forecast. This enables the algorithm to mimic the last seasonality cycle. For instance, if we set `k=48*7`, we will be able to mimic the latest seasonal weekly cycle. This method is implemented in darts and we can use it like so:

```
from darts.models import NaiveSeasonal
naive_model = NaiveSeasonal(K=48*7)
```

Let's see what this forecast looks like:

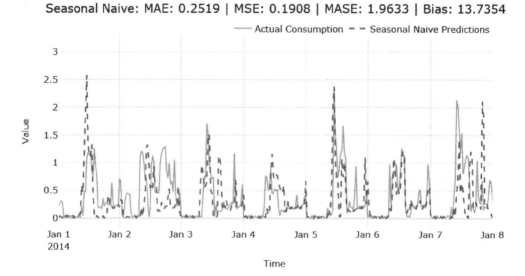

Figure 4.3 – Seasonal naïve forecast

Here, we can see that the forecast is trying to mimic the seasonality pattern. However, it's not very accurate because it is blindly following the last seasonal cycle.

Now that we've looked at a few simple methods, let's look at a few statistical models.

Exponential smoothing (ETS)

Exponential smoothing (**ETS**) is one of the most popular methods for generating forecasts. It has been around since the late 1950s and has proved its mettle and stood the test of time. There are a few different variants of ETS – **single exponential smoothing, double exponential smoothing, Holt-Winters' seasonal smoothing**, and so on. But all of them have one key idea that has been used in different ways. In the naïve method, we were just using the latest observation, which is like saying only the most recent data point in history matters and no data point before that matters. On the other hand, the moving average method considers the last n observations to be equally important and takes the mean of them.

ETS combines both these intuitions and says that all the history is important, but the recent history is more important. Therefore, the forecast is generated using a weighted average where the weights decrease exponentially as we move farther into the history:

$$f_t = \alpha \cdot y_{t-1} + \alpha \cdot (1 - \alpha) \cdot y_{t-2} + \alpha \cdot (1 - \alpha)^2 \cdot y_{t-3} + \cdots$$

Here, $0 \leq \alpha \leq 1$ is the smoothing parameter that lets us decide how fast or slow the weights should decay, y_t is the actuals at timestep t, and f_t is the forecast at timestep t.

Simple exponential smoothing (**SES**) is when you simply apply this smoothing procedure to the history. This is more suited for time series that have no trends or seasonality, and the forecast is going to be a flat line. The forecast is generated using the following formula:

Forecast Equation	$f_t = \alpha y_{t-1} + (1 - \alpha)f_{t-1}$

Double exponential smoothing (**DES**) extends the smoothing idea to model trends as well. It has two smoothing equations – one for the level and the other for the trend. Once you have the estimate of the level and trend, you can combine them. This forecast is not necessarily flat because the estimated trend is used to extrapolate it into the future. The forecast is generated according to the following formula:

Forecast Equation	$f_{t+h} = l_t + h \cdot b_t$
Level Equation	$l_t = \alpha \cdot y_t + (1 - \alpha) \cdot (l_{t-1} + b_{t-1})$
Trend Equation	$b_t = \beta \cdot (l_t - l_{t-1}) + (1 - \beta) \cdot b_{t-1}$

First, we estimate the level (l_t) using the *Level Equation* with the available observations. Then, we estimate the trend using the *Trend Equation*. Finally, to get the forecast, we combine l_t and b_t using the *Forecast Equation*.

Researchers have found empirical evidence that this kind of constant extrapolation can result in over-forecasts over the long-term forecast. This is because, in the real world, time series data doesn't increase at a constant rate forever. Motivated by this, an addition to this has also been introduced that dampens the trend by a factor of $0 < \phi < 1$, such that when $\phi = 1$, there is no damping, and it is identical to double exponential smoothing.

Triple exponential smoothing or **Holt -Winters** (**HW**) takes this one step forward by including another smoothing term to model the seasonality. This has three parameters (α, β, γ) for the smoothing and uses a seasonality period (m) as input parameters. You can also choose between additive or multiplicative seasonality. The forecast equations for the additive model are as follows:

Forecast Equation	$f_{t+h} = l_t + h \cdot b_t + s_{t+h-m(k+1)}$
Level Equation	$l_t = \alpha \cdot y_t - s\_\{t - m\} + (1 - \alpha) \cdot (l_{t-1} + b_{t-1})$
Trend Equation	$b_t = \beta \cdot (l_t - l_{t-1}) + (1 - \beta) \cdot b_{t-1}$
Seasonality Equation	$s_t = \gamma(y_t - l_{t-1} - b_{t-1}) + (1 - \gamma)s_{t-m}$

These formulae are also used like in the double exponential case. Instead of estimating level and trend, we estimate level, trend, and seasonality separately.

The family of exponential smoothing methods is not limited to the three that we just discussed. A way to think about the different models is in terms of the trend and seasonal components of these models. The trend can either be no trend, additive, or additive damped. The seasonality can be no seasonality, additive, or multiplicative. Every combination of these parameters is a different technique in the family, as shown in the following table:

Trend component	Seasonal component		
	N (None)	A (Additive)	M (Multiplicative)
N (None)	*Simple Exponential Smoothing*	-	-
A (Additive)	*Double Exponential Smoothing*	*Additive Holt-Winters*	*Multiplicative Holt-Winters*
Ad (Additive damped)	*Damped Double Exponential Smoothing*	-	*Damped Holt-Winters*

Table 4.1 – Exponential smoothing family

This entire family of methods has been wrapped in a single implementation from `statsmodels` under `statsmodels.tsa.holtwinters.ExponentialSmoothing`. The `darts` library has a wrapper implementation around the `statsmodels` implementation to make it work in the standardized way we have adopted in this chapter. Let's see how we can initialize the ETS model in `darts`:

```
from darts.models import ExponentialSmoothing
from darts.utils.utils import ModelMode, SeasonalityMode
ets_model = ExponentialSmoothing(trend=ModelMode.ADDITIVE,
damped=True, seasonal=SeasonalityMode.ADDITIVE, seasonal_
periods=48*7)
```

The key parameters are `trend`, `damped`, `seasonal`, and `seasonal_periods`. They help you decide what kind of model you want to fit the data.

Let's see what the forecast that we generated using ETS looks like:

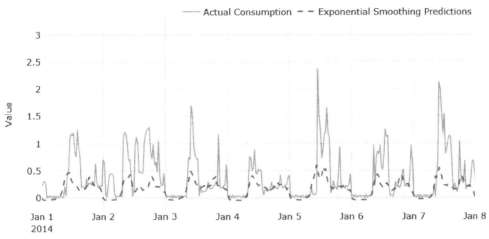

Figure 4.4 – Exponential smoothing forecast

The forecast has captured the seasonality but has failed to capture the peaks. But we can see the improvement in MAE already.

Now, let's look at one of the most popular forecasting methods out there.

ARIMA

Autoregressive Integrated Moving Average (ARIMA) models are the other class of methods that, like ETS, have stood the test of time and are one of the most popular classical methods of forecasting. The ETS family of methods is modeled around trend and seasonality, while ARIMA relies on **autocorrelation** (the correlation of y_t with y_{t-1}, y_{t-2}, and so on).

The simplest in the family are the $AR(p)$ models, which use **linear regression** with p previous timesteps or, in other words, p lags. Mathematically, it can be written as follows:

$$y_t = c + \phi_1 y_{t-1} + \phi_2 y_{t-2} + \cdots \phi_p y_{t-p} + \epsilon_t$$

Here, c is the intercept and ϵ_t is the noise or error at timestep t.

The next in the family are $MA(q)$ models, in which instead of past observed values, we use the past q errors in the forecast (which is assumed to be pure white noise) to come up with a forecast:

$$y_t = c + \theta_1 \epsilon_{t-1} + \theta_2 \epsilon_{t-2} + \cdots \theta_q \epsilon_{t-q}$$

Here, ϵ is white noise and c is the intercept.

This is not typically used on its own but in conjunction with AR(p) models, which makes the next one on our list *ARMA(p,q)* models. ARMA models are defined as $y_t = AR(p) + MA(q)$.

In all the ARIMA models, there is one underlying assumption – the *time series is stationary* (we talked about stationarity in *Chapter 1, Introducing Time Series*, and will elaborate on this in *Chapter 6, Feature Engineering for Time Series Forecasting*). There are many ways to make the series stationary but taking the difference of successive values is one such technique. This is known as **differencing**. Sometimes, we need to do differencing once, while other times, we have to perform successive differencing before the time series becomes stationary. The number of times we do the differencing operation is called the *order of differencing*. The I in ARIMA, and the final piece of the puzzle, stands for *Integrated*. It defines the order of differencing we need to do before the series becomes stationary and is denoted by *d*.

So, the complete *ARIMA(p,d,q)* model says that we do *d*th order of differencing and then consider the last *p* terms in an autoregressive manner, and then include the last *q* moving average terms to come up with the forecast.

The ARIMA models we have discussed so far only handle non-seasonal time series. But using the same concepts we discussed, but on a seasonal cycle, we get **Seasonal ARIMA**. *p*, *d*, and *q* are slightly tweaked so that they work on the seasonal period, *m*. To differentiate them from the normal *p*, *d*, and *q*, we call the seasonal values *P*, *D*, and *Q*. For instance, if *p* meant taking the last *p* lags, *P* means taking the last *P* seasonal lags. If p_1 is y_{t-1}, P_1 would be y_{t-m}. Similarly, *D* means the order of seasonal differencing.

Picking the right *p*, *d*, and *q* and *P*, *D*, and *Q* values is not very intuitive, and we will have to resort to statistical tests to find them. However, this becomes a bit impractical when you are forecasting many time series. An automatic way of iterating through the different parameters and finding the best *p*, *d*, and *q*, and *P*, *D*, and *Q* values for the data is called **Auto ARIMA**. In Python, `pmdarima` is a library that has implemented this, and the `darts` library, once again, has a wrapper around it to make our work easy. `darts` also has a normal ARIMA implementation that is a wrapper around `statsmodels.tsa.arima.model.ARIMA`.

Practical considerations

Although ARIMA and Auto ARIMA can give you good-performing models in many cases, they can be quite slow when you have long seasonal periods and a long time series. In our case, where we have almost 27k observations in the history, ARIMA becomes very slow and a memory hog. Even when using just the latest 8,000 observations, a single ARIMA fit takes around 6 minutes. Letting go of the seasonal parameters brings down the runtime drastically, but for a seasonal time series such as energy consumption, it doesn't make sense. Auto ARIMA includes many such fits to identify the best parameters and therefore becomes impractical for long time series datasets. Almost all the implementations in the Python ecosystem suffer from this drawback except for `statsforecast` (`https://github.com/Nixtla/statsforecast`). At the time of writing, the new library has just been released, but it shows a lot of promise in having a fast implementation of `ARIMA` and `AutoARIMA`.

Let's see how we can apply ARIMA and AutoARIMA using darts:

```
#ARIMA model by specifying parameters
arima_model = ARIMA(p=2, d=1, q=1, seasonal_order=(1, 1, 1,
48))
```

```
#AutoARIMA model by specifying max limits for parameters and
letting the algorithm find the best ones
auto_arima_model = AutoARIMA(max_p=5, max_q=3, m=48,
seasonal=True)
```

For the entire list of parameters for AutoARIMA, head over to the pmdarima documentation at https://alkaline-ml.com/pmdarima/modules/generated/pmdarima.arima.AutoARIMA.html.

Let's see what the ETS and ARIMA forecasts look like for the households we were experimenting with:

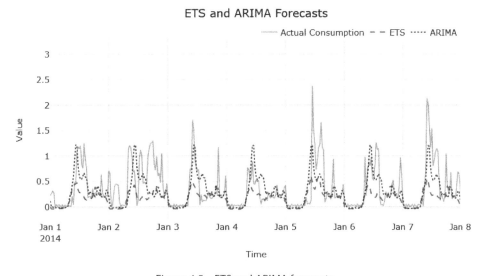

Figure 4.5 – ETS and ARIMA forecasts

The ARIMA forecast has captured the seasonality and the peaks better than ETS and it reflects in a lower MAE score.

Now, let's look at another method – the Theta Forecast.

Theta Forecast

The **Theta Forecast** was the top-performing submission in the M3 forecasting competition that was held in 2002. The method relies on a parameter, θ, that amplifies or smooths the local curvature of a time series, depending on the value chosen. Using θ, we smooth or amplify the original time series.

These smoothed lines are called **theta lines**. V. Assimakopoulos and K. Nikolopoulos proposed this method as a decomposition approach to forecasting. Although in theory any number of theta lines can be used, the originally proposed method used two theta lines, $=0$ and $=2$, and took an average of the forecast of the two theta lines as the final forecast.

Side note

The M-competitions are forecasting competitions organized by Spyros Makridakis, a leading forecasting researcher. They typically curate a dataset of time series, lay down the metrics with which the forecasts will be evaluated, and open these competitions to researchers all around the world to get the best forecast possible. These competitions are considered to be some of the biggest and most popular time series forecasting competitions in the world. At the time of writing, five such competitions have already been completed and the sixth one has been announced: `https://mofc.unic.ac.cy/the-m6-competition/`.

In 2002, Rob Hyndman et al. simplified the Theta method and showed that we can use ETS with a drift term to get equivalent results to the original Theta method, which is what is adapted into most of the implementations of the method that exist today. The major steps that are involved in the Theta Forecast (which is implemented in `darts`) are as follows:

1. Check for seasonality and use `statsmodels.tsa.seasonal.seasonal_decompose` to extract seasonality if the series is seasonal. This step creates a new deseasonalized time series, y_{new}.

2. Use SES on the deseasonalized time series, y_{new}, and retrieve the estimated smoothing parameter, α.

3. Fit a linear trend on $(1 - \theta) \times y_{new}$ and retrieve the estimated coefficient, b_θ.

4. $y_{t+H} = SES_{t+H} + b_\theta \times T_{t+H}$, where SES_{t+H} is the SET forecast for timesteps t to $t+H$ and T_{t+H} is an array denoting time, $[t, t+1, t+2, \dots t+H]$.

5. Reseasonalize if the data was deseasonalized in the beginning.

Let's see how we can use it practically:

```
theta_model = Theta(theta=3, seasonality_period=48*7, season_
mode=SeasonalityMode.ADDITIVE)
```

The key parameters here are as follows:

*   `theta`: This functions as a dampening of the trend and is not to be confused with θ in the context of theta lines. The implementation takes $\theta = 0$ and $\theta = 2$ as a fixed configuration. The higher the theta value, the higher the dampening of the trend.

*   `season_mode` and `seasonality_period`: These parameters are used for the initial seasonal decomposition. If left empty, the implementation automatically tests for seasonality and deseasonalizes the time series automatically. It is recommended to set these parameters with our domain knowledge if we know them.

Let's visualize the forecast we just generated using the Theta Forecast:

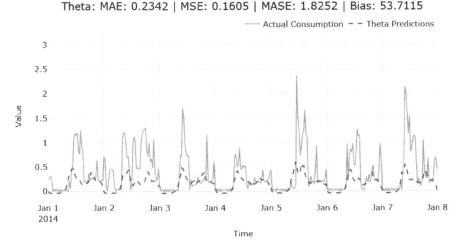

Figure 4.6 – The Theta Forecast

> **Reference check**
>
> The research paper in which V. Assimakopoulos and K. Nikolopoulos proposed the Theta method is cited as reference *1* in the *References* section, while subsequent simplification by Rob Hyndman is cited as reference *2*.

Fast Fourier Transform forecast

We used a Fourier series in *Chapter 3, Analyzing and Visualizing Time Series Data*, to decompose seasonality. Fourier Transform is a very related concept.

Fourier Transform decomposes a time series, which is in the time domain, to temporal frequencies, which is in the frequency domain. It breaks apart a time series and returns the information about the frequency of all the sine (or cosine) waves that constitute the time series. The period of a sine wave is the time it takes to perform one complete cycle, while the frequency of a sine wave is as follows:

$$\frac{1}{period}$$

This is the number of complete cycles that can happen upon every unit of time. Therefore, by knowing the frequencies of all the sine waves of a time series, we can reconstruct the time series perfectly, allowing a seamless transition from the frequency domain to the time domain.

The following diagram shows what Fourier Transform strives to do. The time series, which is in the time domain, is split into several frequencies in the frequency domain so that when we add all of those frequencies to the time domain, we get the original time series:

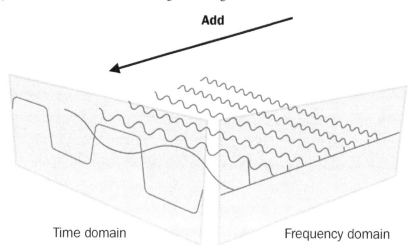

Figure 4.7 – Fourier Transform

The theory is quite beautiful and if you want to know more, go to the *Further reading* section. But for now, let's take it at face value and move on.

For sequences that are evenly spaced, **Discrete Fourier Transform** is applicable, which does away with the integral and makes it into a summation. However, this is also very slow to compute. Fortunately, there is an algorithm called **Fast Fourier Transform (FFT)** that makes it computationally feasible. Coupled with this, there is an **Inverse Fast Fourier Transform (IFFT)** to go back to the time domain.

While FFT will let us reconstruct the time series exactly, that is not something we want when we are forecasting. We only want to capture the signal in the time series and exclude the noise. Therefore, we can filter out noise by choosing a few prominent frequencies from FFT and only use this smaller set in IFFT. Since FFT needs the time series to be detrended, we must apply a detrending step before the FFT step and add the trend once we have reconstructed the time series.

This is implemented in `darts`, and we can use the implementation shown here:

```
fft_model = FFT(nr_freqs_to_keep=35, trend="poly", trend_poly_
degree=2)
```

The `nr_freqs_to_keep` and `trend` hyperparameters must be tweaked to get the best forecast possible.

Let's see what the FFT forecast looks like:

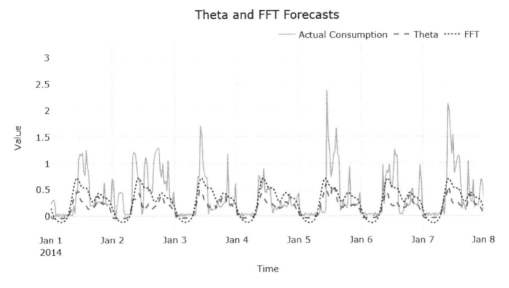

Figure 4.8 – FFT forecast

Again, the seasonality pattern has been replicated, although it is not capturing the peaks in the forecast. Let's also take a look at how the different metrics that we chose did for each of these forecasts for the household we were experimenting with (from the notebook):

Algorithm	MAE	MSE	MASE	Forecast Bias	Time Elapsed
Naive	0.305	0.249	2.380	74.34%	0.045541
Moving Average Forecast	0.351	0.185	2.735	-17.89%	0.096654
Seasonal Naive Forecast	0.252	0.191	1.963	13.74%	0.055316
Exponential Smoothing	0.233	0.159	1.813	52.45%	29.352878
ARIMA	0.203	0.107	1.639	24.00%	319.322491
Theta	0.234	0.160	1.825	53.71%	0.268956
FFT	0.239	0.120	1.860	23.15%	0.592196

Figure 4.9 – Summary of all the baseline algorithms

Out of all the baseline algorithms we tried, ARIMA is performing the best on both MAE as well as MSE. But if you look at the **Time Elapsed** column, it stands out. Even after taking only the latest 8,000 observations to train, it took much more time than the other baseline algorithms. The next best from MAE and MSE are Theta, EST, and FFT, out of which Theta and FFT are orders of magnitude faster than EST.

So, we can take these two algorithms as our baseline and run them on all 399 households in the dataset (both validation and test) we've chosen (the code for this is available in the `02-Baseline Forecasts using darts.ipynb` notebook).

Evaluating the baseline forecasts

Since we have the baseline forecasts generated from Theta as well as FFT, we should also evaluate these forecasts. The aggregate metrics for all the selected households for both these methods are as follows:

	Algorithm	MAE	MSE	meanMASE	Forecast Bias
Validation	FFT	0.206	0.128	2.179	16.73%
	Theta	0.282	0.245	2.274	11.80%

	Algorithm	MAE	MSE	meanMASE	Forecast Bias
Test	FFT	0.198	0.113	2.014	8.54%
	Theta	0.226	0.139	1.913	7.64%

Figure 4.10 – The aggregate metrics of all the selected households (both validation and test)

It looks like FFT is performing much better in all three metrics. We also have these metrics calculated at a household level. Let's look at the distribution of these metrics in the validation dataset for all the selected households:

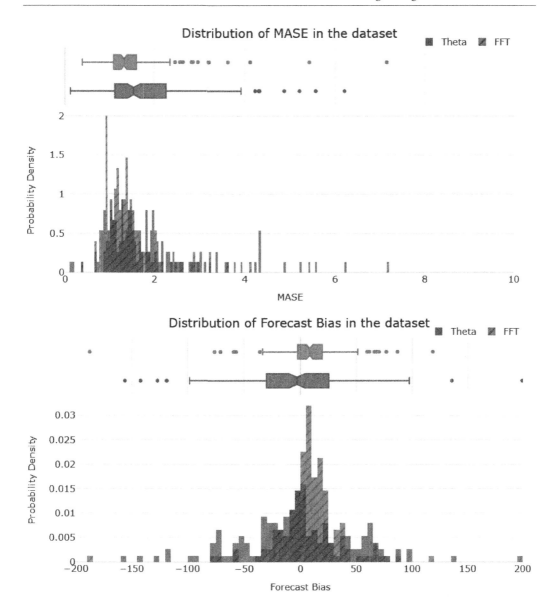

Figure 4.11 – The distribution of MASE and forecast bias of the baseline forecast in the validation dataset

The MASE histogram of FFT seems to have a smaller spread than Theta. FFT also has a lower median MASE than Theta. We can see a similar pattern for forecast bias as well, with the forecast bias of FFT centered around zero and much less spread.

Back in *Chapter 1, Introducing Time Series*, we saw why every time series is not equally predictable and saw three factors to help us think about the issue – understanding the Data Generating Process (DGP), the amount of data, and adequately repeating the pattern. In most cases, the first two are pretty easy to evaluate, but the third one requires some analysis. Although the performance of baseline methods gives us some idea about how predictable any time series is, they still are model-dependent. So, instead of measuring how well a time series is forecastable, we might be better measuring how well the chosen model can approximate the time series. This is where a few techniques that are more fundamental (relying on the statistical properties of a time series) come in.

Assessing the forecastability of a time series

Although there are many statistical measures that we can use to assess the predictability of a time series, we will just look at a few that are easier to understand and practical when dealing with large time series datasets. The associated notebook (`02-Forecastability.ipynb`) contains the code to follow along.

Coefficient of Variation (CoV)

The **Coefficient of Variation (CoV)** relies on the intuition that the more variability that you find in a time series, the harder it is to predict it. And how do we measure variability in a random variable? **Standard deviation**.

In many real-world time series, the variation we see in the time series is dependent on the scale of the time series. Let's imagine that there are two retail products, *A* and *B*. *A* has a mean monthly sale of 15, while *B* has 50. If we look at a few real-world examples like this, we will see that if *A* and *B* have the same standard deviation, *B*, which has a higher mean, is much more forecastable than *A*. To accommodate this phenomenon and to make sure we bring all the time series in a dataset to a common scale, we can use the CoV:

$$CoV_n = \frac{\sigma_n}{\mu_n}$$

Here, σ_n is the standard deviation and μ_n is the mean of the time series, *n*.

The CoV is the relative dispersion of data points around the mean, which is much better than looking at the pure standard deviation.

The larger the value for the CoV, the worse the predictability of the time series. There is no hard cutoff, but a value of 0.49 is considered a rule of thumb to separate time series that are relatively easier to forecast from the hard ones. But depending on the general *hardness* of the dataset, we can tweak this cutoff. Something I have found useful is to plot a histogram of CoV values in a dataset and derive cutoffs based on that.

Even though the CoV is widely used in the industry, it suffers from a few key issues:

- It doesn't consider seasonality. A sine or cosine wave will have a higher CoV than a horizontal line, but we know both are equally predictable.

- It doesn't consider the trend. A linear trend will make a series have a higher CoV, but we know it is equally predictable like a horizontal line is.

- It doesn't handle negative values in the time series. If you have negative values, it makes the mean smaller, thereby inflating the CoV.

To overcome these shortcomings, we propose another derived measure.

Residual variability (RV)

The thought behind residual variability (**RV**) is to try and measure the same kind of variability that we were trying to capture with the CoV but without the shortcomings. I was brainstorming on ways to avoid the problems of using the CoV, typically the seasonality issue, and was applying the CoV to the residuals after seasonal decomposition. It was then I realized that the residuals would have a few negative values and that the CoV wouldn't work well. Stefan de Kok, who is a thought leader in demand forecasting and probabilistic forecasting, suggested using the mean of the original actuals, which worked.

To calculate RV, you must perform the following steps:

1. Perform seasonal decomposition.
2. Calculate the standard deviation of the residuals or the irregular component.
3. Divide the standard deviation by the mean of the original observed values (before decomposition).

The key assumption here is that seasonality and trend are components that can be predicted. Therefore, our assessment of the predictability of a time series should only look at the variability of the residuals. But we cannot use CoV on the residuals because the residuals can have negative and positive values, so the mean of the residuals loses the interpretation of the level of the series and tends to zero. When residuals tend to zero, the CoV measure tends to infinity because of the division by mean. Therefore, we use the mean of the original series as the scaling factor.

Let's see how we can calculate RV for all the time series in our dataset (which are in a compact form):

```
block_df["rv"] = block_df.progress_apply(lambda x: calc_norm_
sd(x['residuals'],x['energy_consumption']), axis=1)
```

In this section, we looked at two measures that are based on the standard deviation of the time series. Now, let's look at assessing the forecastability of a time series.

Entropy-based measures

Entropy is a ubiquitous term in science. We see it popping up in Physics, quantum mechanics, social sciences, and information theory. And everywhere, it is used to talk about a measure of chaos or lack of predictability in a system. The entropy we are most interested in now is the one from Information Theory. Information Theory involves quantifying, storing, and communicating digital information.

Claude E. Shannon presented the qualitative and quantitative model of communication as a statistical process in his seminal paper *A Mathematical Theory of Communication*. While the paper introduced a lot of ideas, some of the concepts that are relevant to us are Information Entropy and the concept of a *bit* – a fundamental unit of measurement of information.

> **Reference check**
>
> *A Mathematical Theory of Communication* by Claude E. Shannon is cited as reference 3 in the *References* section.

The theory in itself is quite a lot to cover, but to summarize the key bits of information, take a look at the following short glossary:

- Information is nothing but a sequence of *symbols*, which can be transmitted from the *receiver* to the *sender* through a medium, which is called a *channel*. For instance, when we are texting somebody, the sequence of symbols are the letters/words of the language in which we are texting; the channel is the electronic medium.

- *Entropy* can be thought of as the amount of *uncertainty* or *surprise* in a sequence of symbols given some distribution of the symbols.

- A *bit*, as we mentioned earlier, is a unit of information and is a binary digit. It can either be 0 or 1.

Now, if we were to transfer 1 bit of information, it would reduce the uncertainty of the receiver by 2. To understand this better, let's consider a coin toss. We toss the coin in the air, and as it is spinning through the air, we don't know whether it is going to be heads or tails. But we know it is going to be one of these two. When the coin hits the ground and finally comes to rest, we find that it is heads. We can represent whether the coin toss is heads or tails with 1 bit of information (0 for heads and 1 for tails). So, the information that was passed to us when the coin fell reduced the possible outcomes from two to one (heads). This transfer was possible with 1 bit of information.

In Information Theory, the entropy of a discrete random variable is the average level of *information*, *surprise*, or *uncertainty* inherent in the variable's possible outcomes. In more technical parlance, it is the expected number of bits required for the best possible encoding scheme of the information present in the random variable.

> **Additional reading**
>
> If you want to intuitively understand entropy, cross-entropy, Kullback-Leibler divergence, and so on, head over to the *Further reading* section. There are a couple of links to blogs (one of which is my own) where we try to lay down the intuition behind these metrics).

Entropy is formally defined as follows:

$$H(X) = -\sum_{i=1}^{n} P(x_i) \cdot logP(x_i)$$

Here, X is the discrete random variable with possible outcomes, and $x_1, x_2, \ldots, x_n$. Each of those outcomes has a probability of occurring, which is denoted by and $P(x_1), P(x_2), \ldots, P(x_n)$.

To develop some intuition around this, we can think that the more spread out a probability distribution is, the more chaos is in the distribution, and thus more entropy. Let's quickly check this in code:

```
# Creating an array with a well balanced probability
distribution
flat = np.array([0.1,0.2, 0.3,0.2, 0.2])
# Calculating Entropy
print((-np.log2(flat)* flat).sum())
>> 2.2464393446710154
# Creating an array with a peak in probability
sharp = np.array([0.1,0.6, 0.1,0.1, 0.1])
# Calculating Entropy
print((-np.log2(sharp)* sharp).sum())
>> 1.7709505944546688
```

Here, we can see that the probability distribution that spread its mass has higher entropy.

In the context of a time series, n is the total number of time series observations, and $P(x_i)$ is the probability for each symbol of the time series alphabet. A sharp distribution means that the time series values are concentrated on a small area and should be easier to predict. On the other hand, a wide or flat distribution means that the time series value can be equally likely across a wider range of values and hence is difficult to predict.

If we have two time series – one containing the result of a coin toss and the other containing the result of a dice throw – the dice throw would have any output between one and six, whereas the coin toss would be either zero or one. The coin toss time series would have lower entropy and be easier to predict than the dice throw time series.

But since time series is typically continuous, and entropy requires a discrete random variable, we can resort to a few strategies to convert the continuous time series into a discrete one. Many strategies, such as quantization or binning, can be applied, which leads to a myriad of complexity measures. Let's review one such measure that is useful and practical.

Spectral entropy

To calculate the entropy of a time series, we need to discretize the time series. One way to do that is by using FFT and **power spectral density (PSD)**. This discretization of the continuous time series is used to calculate spectral entropy.

We learned what Fourier Transform is earlier in this chapter and used it to generate a baseline forecast. But using FFT, we can also estimate a quantity called power spectral density. This answers the question, *How much of the signal is at a particular frequency?* There are many ways of estimating power spectral density from a time series, but one of the easiest ways is by using the **Welch method**, which is a non-parametric method based on Discrete Fourier Transform. This is also implemented as a handy function with the `periodogram(x)` signature in `scipy`.

The returned *PSD* will have a length equal to the number of frequencies estimated, but these are densities and not well-defined probabilities. So, we need to normalize *PSD* to be between zero and one:

$$nPSD_i = \frac{PSD_i}{\sum_{j=1}^{F} PSD_j}$$

Here, *F* is the number of frequencies that are part of the returned power spectrum density.

Now that we have the probabilities, we can just plug this into the entropy formula and arrive at the spectral entropy:

$$H_{s(X)} = -\sum_{i=1}^{n} nPSD_i \cdot log(nPSD_i)$$

When we introduced **entropy-based measures**, we saw that the more spread out the probability mass of a distribution is, the higher the entropy is. In this context, the more frequencies across which the spectral density is spread, the higher the spectral entropy. So, a higher spectral entropy means the time series is more complex and therefore more difficult to forecast.

Since FFT has an assumption of stationarity, it is recommended that we make the series stationary before using spectral entropy as a metric. We can even apply this metric to a detrended and deseasonalized time series, which we can refer to as **residual spectral entropy**. This book's GitHub repository contains an implementation of spectral entropy under `src.forecastability.entropy.spectral_entropy`. This implementation also has a parameter, `transform_stationary`, which, if set to `True`, will detrend the series before we apply spectral entropy. Let's see how we can calculate spectral entropy for our dataset:

```
from src.forecastability.entropy import spectral_entropy
block_df["spectral_entropy"] = block_df.energy_consumption.
```

```
progress_apply(lambda x: spectral_entropy(x, transform_
stationary=True))
block_df["residual_spectral_entropy"] = block_df.residuals.
progress_apply(spectral_entropy)
```

There are other entropy-based measures such as approximate entropy and sample entropy, but we will not cover those in this book. They are more computationally intensive and don't tend to work for time series that contain fewer than 200 values. If you are interested in learning more about these measures, head over to the *Further reading* section.

Another metric that takes a slightly different path is the Kaboudan metric.

Kaboudan metric

In 1999, Kaboudan defined a metric for time series predictability, calling it the η-metric. The idea behind it is very simple. If we block -shuffle a time series, we are essentially destroying the information in the time series. **Block shuffling** is the process of dividing the time series into blocks and then shuffling those blocks. So, if we calculate the **sum of squared errors** (**SSE**) of a forecast that's been trained on a time series and then contrast it with the SSE of a forecast trained on a shuffled time series, we can infer the predictability of the time series. The formula to calculate this is as follows:

$$\eta = 1 - \frac{SSE_Y}{SSE_S}$$

Here, SSE_Y is the SSE of the forecast that was generated from the original time series, while SSE_S is the SSE of the forecast that was generated from the block-shuffled series.

If the time series contains some predictable signals, SSE_Y would be lower than SSE_S and η would approach zero. This is because there was some information or patterns that were broken due to the block shuffling. On the other hand, if a series is just white noise (which is unpredictable by definition) there would be hardly any difference between SSE_Y and SSE_S, and η would approach one.

In 2002, Duan investigated this metric and suggested some modifications in his thesis. One of the problems he identified, especially in long time series, is that the η values are found in a narrow band around 1 and suggested a slight modification to the formula. We call this the **modified Kaboudan metric**. The measure on the lower side is also clipped to zero. Sometimes, the metric can go below zero because SSE_S is lower than SSE_Y, which is because the series is unpredictable and, by pure chance, block shuffling made the SSE lower:

$$\eta_{modified} = 1 - \sqrt{\frac{SSE_Y}{SSE_S}}$$

> **Reference check**
>
> The research paper that proposed the Kaboudan metric is cited as reference *4* in the *References* section. The subsequent modification that Duan suggested is cited as reference *5*.

This modified version, as well as the original, has been implemented in this book's GitHub repository.

There is no restriction on the forecasting model you use to generate the forecast, which makes it a bit more flexible. Ideally, we can choose one of the classical statistical methods that is fast enough to be applied to the whole dataset. But this also makes the Kaboudan metric dependent on the model, and the limitations of the model are inherent in the metric. The metric measures a combination of how difficult a series is to forecast and how difficult it is for the model to forecast the series.

Again, both metrics are implemented in this book's GitHub repository. Let's see how we can use them:

```
from src.forecastability.kaboudan import kaboudan_metric,
modified_kaboudan_metric
model = Theta(theta=3, seasonality_period=48*7, season_
mode=SeasonalityMode.ADDITIVE)
block_df["kaboudan_metric"] = [kaboudan_metric(r[0],
model=model, block_size=5, backtesting_start=0.5, n_folds=1)
for r in tqdm(zip(*block_df[["energy_consumption"]].to_
dict("list").values()), total=len(block_df))]
block_df["modified_kaboudan_metric"] = [modified_kaboudan_
metric(r[0], model=model, block_size=5, backtesting_start=0.5,
n_folds=1) for r in tqdm(zip(*block_df[["energy_consumption"]].
to_dict("list").values()), total=len(block_df))]
```

Although there are many more metrics we can use for this purpose, the metrics we just reviewed for assessing forecastability cover a lot of the popular use cases and should be more than enough to gauge any time series dataset in regards to the difficulty of forecasting it. We can use these metrics to compare onetime series with another time series or to profile a whole set of related time series in a dataset with another dataset for benchmarking purposes.

Additional reading

If you want to delve a little deeper and analyze the behavior of these metrics, how similar they are to each other, and how effective they are in measuring forecastability, go to the end of the 03-Forecastability.ipynb notebook. We compute rank correlations among these metrics to understand how similar these metrics are. We can also find rank correlations with the computed metrics from the best performing baseline method to understand how well these metrics did in estimating the forecastability of a time series. I strongly encourage you to play around with the notebook and understand the differences between the different metrics. Pick a few time series and check how the different metrics give you slightly different interpretations.

Congratulations on generating your baseline forecasts – the first set of forecasts we have generated using this book! Feel free to head over to the notebooks and play around with the parameters of the methods and see how forecasts change. It'll help you develop an intuition around what the baseline methods are doing. If you are interested in learning more about how to make these baseline methods better, head over to the *Further reading* section, where we have provided a link to the paper *The Wisdom of the Data: Getting the Most Out of Univariate Time Series Forecasting*, by F. Petropoulos and E. Spiliotis.

Summary

And with this, we have come to the end of *Section 1, Getting Familiar with Time Series*. We have come a long way from just understanding what a time series is to generating competitive baseline forecasts. Along the way, we learned how to handle missing values and outliers and how to manipulate time series data using pandas. We used all those skills on a real-world dataset regarding energy consumption. We also looked at ways to visualize and decompose time series. In this chapter, we set up a test harness, learned how to use the `darts` library to generate a baseline forecast, and looked at a few metrics that can be used to understand the forecastability of a time series. For some of you, this may be a refresher, and we hope this chapter added some value in terms of some subtleties and practical considerations. For the rest of you, we hope you are in a good place, foundationally, to start venturing into modern techniques using machine learning in the next section of the book.

In the next chapter, we will discuss the basics of machine learning and delve into time series forecasting.

References

The following references were provided in this chapter:

1. Assimakopoulos, Vassilis and Nikolopoulos, K.. (2000). *The theta model: A decomposition approach to forecasting*. International Journal of Forecasting. 16. 521-530. `https://www.researchgate.net/publication/223049702_The_theta_model_A_decomposition_approach_to_forecasting`.

2. Rob J. Hyndman, Baki Billah. (2003). *Unmasking the Theta method*. International Journal of Forecasting. 19. 287-290. `https://robjhyndman.com/papers/Theta.pdf`.

3. Shannon, C.E. (1948), *A Mathematical Theory of Communication*. Bell System Technical Journal, 27: 379-423. `https://people.math.harvard.edu/~ctm/home/text/others/shannon/entropy/entropy.pdf`.

4. Kaboudan, M. (1999). *A measure of time series' predictability using genetic programming applied to stock returns*. Journal of Forecasting, 18, 345-357: `http://www.aiecon.org/conference/efmaci2004/pdf/GP_Basics_paper.pdf`.

5. Duan, M. (2002). *TIME SERIES PREDICTABILITY*: `https://citeseerx.ist.psu.edu/viewdoc/download?doi=10.1.1.68.1898&rep=rep1&type=pdf`.

Further reading

To learn more about the topics that were covered in this chapter, take a look at the following resources:

- *Information Theory and Entropy*, by Manu Joseph: `https://deep-and-shallow.com/2020/01/09/deep-learning-and-information-theory/`.

- *Visual Information*, by Chris Olah: `https://colah.github.io/posts/2015-09-Visual-Information`.

- Fourier Transform: `https://betterexplained.com/articles/an-interactive-guide-to-the-fourier-transform/`.

- *Fourier Transform* by 3blue1brown – a visual introduction: `https://www.youtube.com/watch?v=spUNpyF58BY&vl=en`.

- *Understanding Fourier Transform by Example*, by Richie Vink: `https://www.ritchievink.com/blog/2017/04/23/understanding-the-fourier-transform-by-example/`.

- Delgado-Bonal A, Marshak A. *Approximate Entropy and Sample Entropy: A Comprehensive Tutorial*. Entropy. 2019; 21(6):541: `https://www.mdpi.com/1099-4300/21/6/541`.

- Yentes, J.M., Hunt, N., Schmid, K.K. et al. *The Appropriate Use of Approximate Entropy and Sample Entropy with Short Data Sets*. Ann Biomed Eng 41, 349–365 (2013): `https://doi.org/10.1007/s10439-012-0668-3`

- Ponce-Flores M, Frausto-Solís J, Santamaría-Bonfil G, Pérez-Ortega J, González-Barbosa JJ. *Time Series Complexities and Their Relationship to Forecasting Performance*. Entropy. 2020; 22(1):89. `https://www.mdpi.com/1099-4300/22/1/89`

- Petropoulos F, Spiliotis E. *The Wisdom of the Data: Getting the Most Out of Univariate Time Series Forecasting*. Forecasting. 2021; 3(3):478-497. `https://doi.org/10.3390/forecast3030029`

Part 2 –
Machine Learning for
Time Series

In this part, we will be looking at ways of applying modern machine learning techniques for time series forecasting. This part also covers powerful forecast combination methods and the exciting new paradigm of global models. By the end of this part, you will be able to set up a modeling pipeline using modern machine learning techniques for time series forecasting.

This part comprises the following chapters:

- *Chapter 5, Time Series Forecasting as Regression*

- *Chapter 6, Feature Engineering for Time Series Forecasting*

- *Chapter 7, Target Transformations for Time Series Forecasting*

- *Chapter 8, Forecasting Time Series with Machine Learning Models*

- *Chapter 9, Ensembling and Stacking*

- *Chapter 10, Global Forecasting Models*

Time Series Forecasting as Regression

In the previous part of the book, we have developed a fundamental understanding of time series and equipped ourselves with tools and techniques to analyze and visualize time series and even generate our first baseline forecasts. We have mainly covered classical and statistical techniques in this book so far. Let's now dip our toes into modern **machine learning** and learn how we can leverage this comparatively newer field for **time series forecasting**. Machine learning is a field that has grown in leaps and bounds in recent times, and being able to leverage these newer techniques for time series forecasting is a skill that will be invaluable in today's world.

In this chapter, we will be covering these main topics:

- Understanding the basics of machine learning
- Time series forecasting as regression
- Local versus global models

Understanding the basics of machine learning

Before we get started with using machine learning for time series, let's spend some time establishing what machine learning is and setting up a framework to demonstrate what it does (if you are already very comfortable with machine learning, feel free to skip ahead, or just stay with us and refresh the concepts). In 1959, Arthur Samuel defined machine learning as a *"field of study that gives computers the ability to learn without being explicitly programmed."* Traditionally, programming has been a paradigm under which we know a set of rules/logic to perform an action, and that action is performed on the given data to get the output that we want. But, machine learning flipped this on its head. In machine learning, we start with data and the output, and we ask the computer to tell us about the rules with which the desired output can be achieved from the data: `

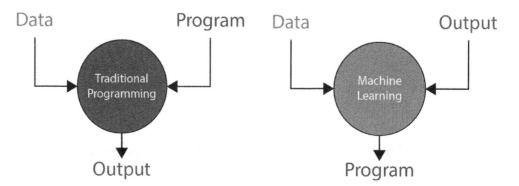

Figure 5.1 – Traditional programming versus machine learning

There are many kinds of problem settings in machine learning, such as supervised learning, unsupervised learning, self-supervised learning, and so on, but we will stick to supervised learning, which is the most popular one and the most applicable one to the contents of this book.

Let's start our discussion small and slowly build up to the whole schematic, which encapsulates most of the key components of a supervised machine learning problem:

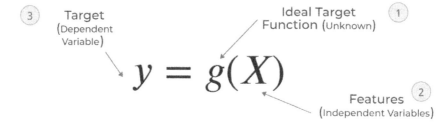

Figure 5.2 – Supervised machine learning schematic, part 1 – the ideal function

As we already discussed, what we want from machine learning is to *learn* from the data and come up with a set of rules/logic. The closest analogy in mathematics for logic/rules is a function, which takes in an input (here, data) and provides an output. Mathematically, it can be written as follows:

$$y = g(X)$$

where X is the set of features and g is the **ideal target function** (denoted by **1** in *Figure 5.2*) that maps the X input (denoted by **2** in the schematic) to the target (ideal) output, y (denoted by **3** in the schematic). The ideal target function is largely an unknown function, similar to the **data generating process** (**DGP**) we saw in *Chapter 1, Introducing Time Series*, which is not in our control.

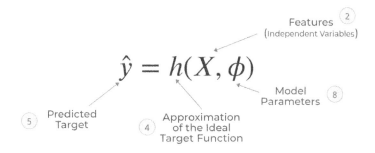

Figure 5.3 – Supervised machine learning schematic, part 2 – the learned approximation

But, we want the computer to *learn* this ideal target function. This approximation of the ideal target function is denoted by another function, h (**4** in the schematic), which takes in the same set of features, X, and outputs a predicted target, $\hat{y}$ (**5** in the schematic). Φ are the parameters of the h function (or model parameters):

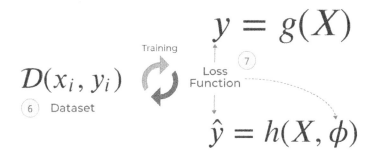

Figure 5.4 – Supervised machine learning schematic, part 3 – putting it all together

Now, how do we find this approximation h function and its parameters, Φ? With the dataset of examples (**6** in the schematic). The supervised machine learning problem works on the premise that we are able to collect a set of examples that shows the features, X, and the corresponding target, y, which is also referred to as *labels* in literature. It is from this set of examples (the dataset) that the computer *learns* the approximation function, h, and the optimal model parameters, Φ. In the preceding diagram, the only real unknown entity is the ideal target function, g. So, we can use the training dataset, D, to get predicted targets for every sample in the dataset. We already know the ideal target for all the examples. We need a way to compare the ideal targets and predicted targets, and this is where the loss function (**7** in the schematic) comes in. This loss function tells us how far away from the real truth we are with the approximated function, h.

Although h can be any function, it is typically chosen from a set of a well-known class of functions, $\mathcal{H}$. $\mathcal{H}$ is the finite set of functions that can be fit to the data. This class of functions is what we colloquially call **models**. For instance, h can be chosen from all the linear functions or all the tree-based functions, and so on. Choosing an h from $\mathcal{H}$ is done by a combination of hyperparameters (which the modeler specifies) and the model parameter, which is learned from data.

Now, all that is left is to run through the different functions so that we find the best approximation function, *h*, which gives us the lowest loss. This is an optimization process that we call **training**.

Let's also take a look at a few key concepts, which will be important in all our discussions ahead.

Supervised machine learning tasks

Machine learning can be used to solve a wide variety of tasks such as **regression, classification**, and **recommendation**. But, since classification and regression are the most popular classes of problems, we will spend just a little bit of time reviewing what they are.

The difference between classification and regression tasks is very simple. In the machine learning schematic (*Figure 5.2*), we talked about *y*, the target. This target can be either a real-valued number or a class of items. For instance, we could be predicting the stock price for next week or we could just predict whether the stock was going to go up or down. In the first case, we are predicting a real-valued number, which is called **regression**. In the other case, we are predicting one out of two classes (*up* or *down*), and this is called **classification**.

Overfitting and underfitting

The biggest challenge in machine learning systems is that the model we trained must perform well on a new and unseen dataset. The ability of a machine learning model to do that is called the **generalization capability** of the model. The training process in a machine learning setup is akin to mathematical optimization, with one subtle difference. The aim of mathematical optimization is to arrive at the global maxima in the provided dataset. But in machine learning, the aim is to achieve low test error by using the training error as a proxy. How well a machine learning model is doing on training error and testing error is closely related to the concepts of overfitting and underfitting. Let's use an example to understand these terms.

The learning process of a machine learning model has many parallels to how humans learn. Suppose three students, *A*, *B*, and *C*, are studying for an examination. *A* is a slacker and went clubbing the night before. *B* decided to double down and memorize the textbook end to end. And, *C* paid attention in class and understood the topics up for the examination.

As expected, *A* flunked the examination, *C* got the highest score, and *B* did OK.

A flunked the examination because they didn't learn enough. This happens to machine learning models as well when they don't learn enough patterns, and this is called **underfitting**. This is characterized by high training errors and high test errors.

B didn't score as highly as expected; after all, they did memorize the whole text, word for word. But many questions in the examination weren't directly from the textbook and *B* wasn't able to answer them correctly. In other words, the questions in the examination were *new and unseen*. And because *B* memorized everything but didn't make an effort to understand the underlying concepts, *B* wasn't able to *generalize* the knowledge they had to new questions. This situation, in machine learning, is called **overfitting**. This is typically characterized by a big delta in training and test errors. Typically, we will see very low training errors and high test errors.

The third student, C, learned the right way and understood the underlying concepts and because of that, was able to *generalize* to *new and unseen* questions. This is the ideal state for a machine learning model, as well. This is characterized by reasonably low test errors and a small delta between training and test errors.

We just saw the two greatest challenges in machine learning. Now, let's also look at a few ways we have that can be used to tackle these challenges.

There is a close relationship between the **capacity** of a model and underfitting or overfitting. A model's capacity is its ability to be flexible enough to fit a wide variety of functions. Models with low capacity may struggle to fit the training data, leading to underfitting. Models with high capacity may overfit by memorizing the training data too much. Just to develop an intuition around this concept of capacity, let's look at an example. When we move from linear regression to polynomial regression, we are adding more capacity to the model. Instead of fitting just straight lines, we are letting the model fit curved lines as well. Machine learning models generally do well when their capacity is appropriate for the learning problem at hand.

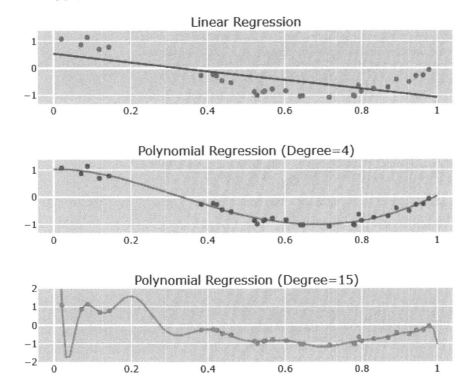

Figure 5.5 – Underfitting versus overfitting

Figure 5.5 shows a very popular case to illustrate overfitting and underfitting. We create a few random points using a known function and try to learn that by using those data samples. We can see that the linear regression, which is one of the simplest models, has underfitted the data by drawing a straight line through those points. Polynomial regression is linear regression, but with some higher-order features. For now, you can consider the move from linear regression to polynomial regression with higher degrees as increasing the capacity of the model. So, when we use a degree of 4, we see that the learned function fits the data well and matches our ideal function. But if we keep increasing the capacity of the model and reach *degree = 15*, we see that the learned function is still passing through the training samples, but has learned a very different function, overfitting to the training data. Finding the optimal capacity to learn a generalizable function is one of the core challenges of machine learning.

While capacity is one aspect of the model, another aspect is **regularization**. Even with the same capacity, there are multiple functions a model can choose from the hypothesis space of all functions. With regularization, we try to give preference to a set of functions in the hypothesis space over the others. While all these functions are valid functions that can be chosen, we nudge the optimization process in such a way that we end up with a kind of function toward which we have a preference. Although regularization is a general term used to refer to any kind of constraint we place on the learning process to reduce the complexity of the learned function, more commonly, it is used in the form of a weight decay. Let's take an example of linear regression, which is when we fit a straight line to the input features by learning a weight associated with each feature.

A linear regression model can be written mathematically as follows:

$$\hat{y} = c + \sum_{i=1}^{N} w_i \times x_i$$

Here, N is the number of features, c is the intercept, x_i is the ith feature, and w_i is the weight associated with the ith feature. We estimate the right weight (L) by considering this as an optimization problem that minimizes the error between $\hat{y}$ and y (real output).

Now, with regularization, we add an additional term to L, which forces the weights to become smaller. Commonly, this is done using an *l1* or *l2* regularizer. An *l1* regularizer is when you add the sum of squared weights to L:

$$L + \lambda \sum_{i=1}^{N} w_i^2$$

where λ is the regularization coefficient that determines how strongly we penalize the weights. An *l2* regularizer is when you add the sum of absolute weights to L:

$$L + \lambda \sum_{i=1}^{N} |w_i|^2$$

In both cases, we are enforcing a preference for smaller weights over larger weights because it keeps the function from relying too much on any one feature from the ones used in the machine learning model. Regularization is an entire topic unto itself and if you want to learn more, head over to the *Further reading* section for a few resources on regularization.

Another really effective way to reduce overfitting is to simply train the model with more data. With a larger dataset, the chances of the model overfitting become less because of the sheer variety that can be captured in a large dataset.

Now, how do we tune the knobs to strike a balance between underfitting and overfitting? Let's look at it in the following section.

Hyperparameters and validation sets

Almost all machine learning models have a few hyperparameters associated with them. **Hyperparameters** are parameters of the model that are not learned from data but rather are set before the start of training. For instance, the weight of the regularization is a hyperparameter. Most hyperparameters either help us control the capacity of the model or apply regularization to the model. By controlling either capacity or regularization or both, we can travel the frontier between underfitting and overfitting models and arrive at a model that is *just right*.

But since these hyperparameters have to be set outside of the algorithm, how do we estimate the best hyperparameters? Although it is not part of the core *learning process*, we learn the hyperparameters also from the data. But if we just use the training data to learn the hyperparameters, it will just choose the maximum possible model capacity, which results in overfitting. This is where we need a **validation set**, a part of the data that the training process does not have access to. But when the dataset is small (not hundreds of thousands of samples), the performance on a single validation set doesn't guarantee a fair evaluation. In such cases, we rely on **cross-validation**. The general trick is to repeat the training and evaluation procedure on different subsets of the original dataset. A common way of doing this is called **k-fold cross validation**, when the original dataset is divided into *k* equal, non-overlapping, and random subsets, and each subset is evaluated after training on all the other subsets. We have provided a link in the *Further reading* section if you want to read up about cross-validation techniques. Later in the book, we will also be covering this topic, but from the time series perspective, which has a few differences from the standard way of doing cross-validation.

> **Suggested reading**
>
> Although we have touched the surface of machine learning in the book, there is a lot more, and to truly appreciate the rest of the book better, we suggest gaining more understanding of machine learning. We suggest starting with *Machine Learning* by *Stanford (Andrew Ng)* – `https://www.coursera.org/learn/machine-learning`. If you are in a hurry, the *Machine Learning Crash Course* by *Google* is also a good starting point – `https://developers.google.com/machine-learning/crash-course/ml-intro`.

Now that we have a basic understanding of machine learning, let's start looking at how we can use it to do time series forecasting.

Time series forecasting as regression

A time series, as we saw in *Chapter 1, Introducing Time Series*, is a set of observations taken sequentially in time. And typically, time series forecasting is about trying to predict what these observations will be in the future. Given a sequence of observations of arbitrary length of history, we predict the future to an arbitrary horizon.

We saw that regression, or machine learning to predict a continuous variable, works on a dataset of examples, and each example is a set of input features and targets. We can see that regression, which is tasked with predicting a single output provided with a set of inputs, is fundamentally incompatible with forecasting, where we are given a set of historical values and asked to predict the future values. This fundamental incompatibility between the time series and machine learning regression paradigms is why we cannot use regression for time series forecasting directly.

Moreover, time series forecasting, by definition, is an extrapolation problem, whereas regression, most of the time, is an interpolation one. Extrapolation is typically harder to solve using data-driven methods. Another key assumption in regression problems is that the samples used for training are **independent and identically distributed** (**IID**). But time series break that assumption as well because subsequent observations in a time series display considerable dependence.

However, to use the wide variety of techniques from machine learning, we need to cast time series forecasting as a regression. Thankfully, there are ways to convert a time series into a regression and get over the IID assumption by introducing some memory to the machine learning model through some features. Let's see how it can be done.

Time delay embedding

We talked about the ARIMA model in *Chapter 4, Setting a Strong Baseline Forecast*, and saw how it is an autoregressive model. We can use the same concept to convert a time series problem into a regression one. Let's use the following diagram to make the concept clear:

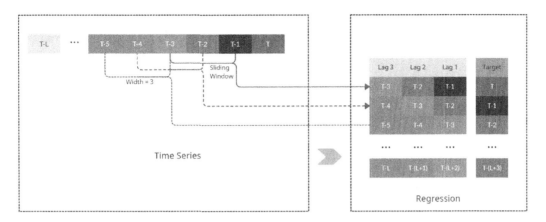

Figure 5.6 – Time series to regression conversion using a sliding window

Let's assume we have a time series with time steps, Y_L. Consider we are at time t, and we have a time series of the length of history as L. So, our time series will look something like in the diagram with y_t as the latest observation in the time series, and y_{t-1}, y_{t-2}, and so on as we move backward in time.

In an ideal world, each observation in Y_L should be conditioned on all the previous observations when we forecast. But, it is not practical because L can be arbitrarily long. We often restrict the forecasting function to use only the most recent M observations of the series, where $M < L$. These are called finite memory models or **Markov models** and M is called the order of autoregression, memory size, or the receptive field.

Therefore, in time delay embedding, we assume a window of arbitrary length $M < L$ and extract fixed-length subsequences from the time series by sliding the window over the length of the time series.

In the diagram, we have taken a sliding window with a memory size of 3. So, the first subsequence we can extract (if we are starting from the most recent and working backward) is $y_{t-3}, y_{t-2}, y_{t-1}$. And y_t is the observation that comes right after the subsequence. This becomes our first example in the dataset (row 1 in the table in the diagram). Now, we slide the window one time step to the left (backward in time) and extract the new subsequence, $y_{t-4}, y_{t-3}, y_{t-2}$. The corresponding target would become y_{t-1}. We repeat this process as we move back to the beginning of the time series, and at each step of the sliding window, we add one more example to the dataset.

At the end of it, we have an aligned dataset with a fixed vector size of features (which will be equal to the window size) and a single target, which is what a typical machine learning dataset looks like.

Now that we have a table with three features, let's also assign semantic meaning to the three features. If we look at the right-most column in the table in the diagram, we can see that the time step present in the column is always one time step behind the target. We call it **Lag 1**. The second column from the right is always two time steps behind the target, and this is called **Lag 2**. Generalizing this, the feature that has observations that are *n* time steps behind the target, we call **Lag n**.

This transformation from time series to regression using **time-delay embedding** encodes the autoregressive structure of a time series in a way that can be utilized by standard regression frameworks. Another way we can think about using regression for time series forecasting is to perform **regression on time**.

Temporal embedding

If we rely on previous observations in autoregressive models, we rely on the concept of time for temporal embedding models. The core idea is that we forget the autoregressive nature of the time series and assume that any value in the time series is only dependent on time. We derive features that capture time, the passage of time, periodicity of time, and so on, from the timestamps associated with the time series, and then we use these features to predict the target using a regression model. There are many ways to do this, from simply aligning a monotonically and uniformly increasing numerical column that captures the passage of time to sophisticated **Fourier** terms to capture the periodic components in time. We will talk about those techniques in detail in *Chapter 6, Feature Engineering for Time Series Forecasting*.

Before we wind up the chapter, let's also talk about a key concept that is gaining ground steadily in the time series forecasting space. A large part of this book embraces this new paradigm of forecasting.

Global forecasting models – a paradigm shift

Traditionally, each time series was treated in isolation. Because of that, traditional forecasting has always looked at the history of a single time series alone in fitting a forecasting function. But recently, because of the ease of collecting data in today's digital-first world, many companies have started collecting large amounts of time series from similar sources, or related time series.

For example, retailers such as Walmart collect data on sales of millions of products across thousands of stores. Companies such as Uber or Lyft collect the demand for rides from all the zones in a city. In the energy sector, energy consumption data is collected across all consumers. All these sets of time series have shared behavior and are hence called **related time series**.

We can consider that all the time series in a related time series come from separate **data generating processes (DGPs)**, and thereby model them all separately. We call these the **local** models of forecasting. An alternative to this approach is to assume that all the time series are coming from a single DGP. Instead of fitting a separate forecast function for each time series individually, we fit a single forecast function to all the related time series. This approach has been called **global** or **cross-learning** in literature.

Reference check

The terminology *global* was introduced by *David Salinas et al.* in the *DeepAR* paper (reference number 1) and *Cross-learning* by *Slawek Smyl* (reference number 2).

We saw earlier that having more data will lead to lower chances of overfitting and, therefore, lower generalization error (the difference between training and testing errors). This is exactly one of the shortcomings of the local approach. Traditionally, time series are not very long, and in many cases, it is difficult and time-consuming to collect more data as well. Fitting a machine learning model (with all its expressiveness) on small data is prone to overfitting. This is why time series models that enforce strong priors were used to forecast such time series, traditionally. But these strong priors, which restrict the fitting of traditional time series models, can also lead to a form of underfitting and limit accuracy.

Strong and expressive data-driven models, as in machine learning, require a larger amount of data to have a model that generalizes to new and unseen data. A time series, by definition, is tied to time, and sometimes, collecting more data means waiting for months or years and that is not desirable. So, if we cannot increase the *length* of the time-series dataset, we can increase the *width* of the time series dataset. If we add multiple time series to the dataset, we increase the width of the dataset, and there by increase the amount of data the model is getting trained with. *Figure 5.7* shows the concept of increasing the width of a time series dataset visually:

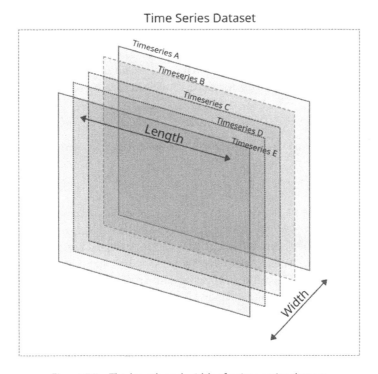

Figure 5.7 – The length and width of a time series dataset

This works in favor of machine learning models because with higher flexibility in fitting a forecast function and the addition of more data to work with, the machine learning model can learn a more complex forecast function than traditional time series models, which are typically shared between the related time series, in a completely data-driven way.

Another shortcoming of the local approach revolves around scalability. In the case of Walmart we mentioned earlier, there are millions of time series that need to be forecasted and it is not possible to have human oversight on all these models. If we think about this from an engineering perspective, training and maintaining millions of models in a production system would give any engineer a nightmare. But under the global approach, we only train a single model for all these time series, which drastically reduces the number of models we need to maintain and yet can generate all the required forecasts.

This new paradigm of forecasting has gained traction and has consistently been shown to improve the local approaches in multiple time series competitions, mostly in datasets of related time series. In Kaggle competitions, such as *Rossman Store Sales* (2015), *Wikipedia WebTraffic Time Series Forecasting* (2017), *Corporación Favorita Grocery Sales Forecasting* (2018), and *M5 Competition* (2020), the winning entries were all global models—either machine learning or deep learning or a combination of both. The *Intermarché Forecasting Competition* (2021) also had global models as the winning submissions. Links to these competitions are provided in the *Further reading* section.

Although we have many empirical findings where the global models have outperformed local models for related time series, global models are still a relatively new area of research. *Montero-Manson and Hyndman* (2020) showed a few very interesting results and showed that any local method can be approximated by a global model with required complexity, and the most interesting finding they put forward is that the global model will perform better, even with unrelated time series. We will talk more about global models and strategies for global models in *Chapter 10, Global Forecasting Models*.

> **Reference check**
>
> The *Montero-Manson and Hyndman* (2020) research paper is cited in *References* under reference number 3.

Summary

We have started our journey beyond baseline forecasting methods and dipped our toes into the world of machine learning. After a brief refresher on machine learning, where we looked at key concepts such as overfitting, underfitting, regularization, and so on, we saw how we can convert a time series forecasting problem into a regression problem from the machine learning world. We also developed a conceptual understanding of different embeddings, such as time delay embedding and temporal embedding, which can be used to convert a time series problem into a regression problem. To wrap things up, we also learned about a new paradigm in time series forecasting – global models – and contrasted them with local models on a conceptual level. In the next few chapters, we will start putting these concepts into practice, and see techniques for feature engineering, and strategies for global models.

References

Following are the references that we used in this chapter:

1. David Salinas, Valentin Flunkert, Jan Gasthaus, Tim Januschowski (2020). *DeepAR: Probabilistic forecasting with autoregressive recurrent networks*. International Journal of Forecasting. 36-3. 1181-1191: `https://doi.org/10.1016/j.ijforecast.2019.07.001`

2. Slawek Smyl (2020). *A hybrid method of exponential smoothing and recurrent neural networks for time series forecasting*. International Journal of Forecasting. 36-1: 75-85 `https://doi.org/10.1016/j.ijforecast.2019.03.017`

3. Montero-Manso, P., Hyndman, R.J.. (2020), *Principles and algorithms for forecasting groups of time series: Locality and globality*. arXiv:2008.00444[cs.LG]: `https://arxiv.org/abs/2008.00444`

Further reading

You can check out the following resources for further reading:

- *Regularization for Sparsity from Google Machine Learning Crash Course*: `https://developers.google.com/machine-learning/crash-course/regularization-for-sparsity/l1-regularization`

- *L1 and L2 Regularization from Foundations of Machine Learning, Bloomberg ML EDU*: `https://www.youtube.com/watch?v=d6XDOS4btck`

- *Cross-validation: evaluating estimator performance from scikit-learn*: `https://scikit-learn.org/stable/modules/cross_validation.html`

- *Rossmann Store Sales*: `https://www.kaggle.com/c/rossmann-store-sales`

- *Web Traffic Time Series Forecasting* – `https://www.kaggle.com/c/web-traffic-time-series-forecasting`

- *Corporación Favorita Grocery Sales Forecasting* – `https://www.kaggle.com/c/favorita-grocery-sales-forecasting`

- *M5 Forecasting – Accuracy* – `https://www.kaggle.com/c/m5-forecasting-accuracy`

6

Feature Engineering for Time Series Forecasting

In the previous chapter, we started looking at **machine learning** (**ML**) as a tool to solve the problem of **time series forecasting**. We also talked about a few techniques such as **time delay embedding** and **temporal embedding**, which cast time series forecasting problems as classical regression problems from the ML paradigm. In this chapter, we'll look at those techniques in detail and go through them in a practical sense using the dataset we have been working with throughout this book.

In this chapter, we will cover the following topics:

- Feature engineering
- Avoiding data leakage
- Setting a forecast horizon
- Time delay embedding
- Temporal embedding

Technical requirements

You will need to set up the Anaconda environment following the instructions in the *Preface* of the book to get a working environment with all the packages and datasets required for the code in this book.

You will need to run these notebooks:

- `02-Preprocessing London Smart Meter Dataset.ipynb` from Chapter02
- `01-Setting up Experiment Harness.ipynb` from Chapter04

The code for this chapter can be found at `https://github.com/PacktPublishing/Modern-Time-Series-Forecasting-with-Python-/tree/main/notebooks/Chapter06`.

Feature engineering

Feature engineering, as the name suggests, is the process of engineering features from the data, mostly using domain knowledge, to make the learning process smoother and more efficient. In a typical ML setting, engineering good features is essential to get good performance from any ML model. Feature engineering is a highly subjective part of ML where each problem at hand has a different path – one that is hand-crafted to that problem.

When we are casting a time series problem as a regression problem, there are a few standard techniques that we can apply. This is a key step in the process because how well an ML model acquires an understanding of *time* is dependent on how well we engineer features to capture *time*. The baseline methods we covered in *Chapter 4, Setting a Strong Baseline Forecast*, are the methods that are created for the specific use case of time series forecasting and because of that, the temporal aspect of the problem is built into those models. For instance, ARIMA doesn't need any feature engineering to understand time because it is built into the model. But a standard regression model has no explicit understanding of time, so we need to create good features to embed the temporal aspect of the problem.

In the previous chapter (*Chapter 5, Time Series Forecasting as Regression*), we talked about two main ideas to encode time into the regression framework: **time delay embedding** and **temporal embedding**. Although we touched on these concepts at a high level, it is time to dig deeper and see them in action.

> **Notebook alert**
>
> To follow along with the complete code, use the `01-Feature Engineering.ipynb` notebook in the `chapter06` folder.

We have already split the dataset that we were working on into train, validation, and test datasets. But since we are generating features that are based on previous observations, operationally, it is better when we have the train, validation, and test datasets combined. It will be clearer why shortly, but for now, let's take it on faith and move ahead. Now, let's go ahead and combine the two datasets:

```
# Reading the missing value imputed and train test split data
train_df = pd.read_parquet(preprocessed / "selected_blocks_
train_missing_imputed.parquet")
val_df = pd.read_parquet(preprocessed / "selected_blocks_val_
missing_imputed.parquet")
test_df = pd.read_parquet(preprocessed / "selected_blocks_test_
missing_imputed.parquet")
```

```
#Adding train, validation and test tags to distinguish them
before combining
train_df['type'] = "train"
val_df['type'] = "val"
test_df['type'] = "test"
full_df = pd.concat([train_df, val_df, test_df]).sort_
values(["LCLid", "timestamp"])
del train_df, test_df, val_df
```

Now, we have a `full_df` that combines the train, validation, and test datasets. Some of you may already have alarm bells ringing in your head at combining the train and test sets. What about **data leakage**? Let's check it out.

Avoiding data leakage

Data leakage occurs when the model is trained with some information that would not be available at the time of prediction. Typically, this leads to high performance in the training set, but very poor performance in unseen data. There are two types of data leakage:

- **Target leakage** is when the information about the target (that we are trying to predict) leaks into some of the features in the model, leading to an overreliance of the model on those features, ultimately leading to poor generalization. This includes features that use the target in any way.

- **Train-test contamination** is when there is some information leaking between the train and test datasets. This can happen because of careless handling and splitting of data. But it can also happen in more subtle ways, such as scaling the dataset before splitting the train and test sets.

When we are working with time series forecasting problems, the biggest and most common mistake that we can make is target leakage. We will have to think hard about each of the features to ensure we are not using any data that will not be available during prediction. The following diagram will help us remember and internalize this concept:

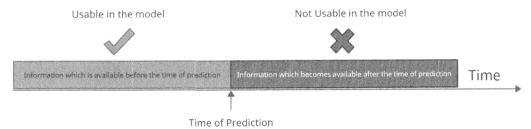

Figure 6.1 – Usable and not-usable information to avoid data leakage

To make this concept clearer and more relevant to the time series forecasting context, let's look at an example. Let's say we are forecasting sales for shampoo, and we are using sales for conditioner as a feature. We developed the model, trained it on the training data, and tested it on the validation data. The model is doing very well. The moment we start predicting for the future, we will see the problem. We don't know what the sales for conditioner are in the future either. While this example is pretty straightforward, there will be times when this becomes not so obvious. And that is why we need to exercise a fair amount of caution while creating features and always evaluate the features through the lens of, *will this feature be available at the time of prediction?*

Best practices

There are many ways of identifying target leakage, apart from thinking hard about the features:

• If the model you've built is too good to be true, you most likely have a leakage problem

• If any single feature has too much weightage in the feature importance of the model, that feature may have a problem with leakage

• Double-check the features that are highly correlated with the target

---

Now, let's learn about forecast horizons.

Setting a forecast horizon

Although we generated forecasts earlier in this book, we never explicitly discussed **forecast horizons**. A forecast horizon is the number of time steps into the future we want to forecast at any point in time. For instance, if we want to forecast the next 24 hours for the electricity consumption dataset that we have been working with, the forecast horizon becomes 48 (because the data is half-hourly). In *Chapter 5, Time Series Forecasting as Regression,* where we generated baselines, we just predicted the entire test data at once. In such cases, the forecast horizon becomes equal to the length of the test data.

We never had to worry about this until now because, in the classical statistical methods of forecasting, this decision is decoupled from modeling. If we train a model, we can use that model to predict any future point without retraining. But with *time series forecasting as regression,* we have a constraint on the forecast horizon and it has its roots in data leakage. For now, let's only look at single-step-ahead forecasting. In the context of the dataset we are working with, this means that we will be answering the question, *what is the energy consumption in the next half an hour?* We will talk about multi-step forecasting and other mechanics of forecasting in *Section 4 – The Mechanics of Forecasting.*

Now that we have set some ground rules, let's start looking at the different feature engineering techniques. To follow along with the Jupyter notebook, head over to the `chapter06` folder and use the `01-Feature Engineering.ipynb` file.

Time delay embedding

The basic idea behind time delay embedding is to embed time in terms of recent observations. If you want to head back to *Chapter 5*, *Time Series Forecasting as Regression*, and review this concept (*Figure 5.1*), please go ahead and do so now.

In *Figure 5.1*, we talked about including previous observations of a time series as **lags**. However, there are a few more ways to capture recent and seasonal information using this concept. Let's take a look.

Lags or backshift

Let's assume we have a time series with time steps, Y_L. Consider that we are at time t and that we have a time series where the length of history is L. So, our time series will have y_t as the latest observation in the time series, and then y_{t-1}, y_{t-2}, and so on as we move back in time. So, lags, as explained in *Chapter 5*, *Time Series Forecasting as Regression*, are features that include the previous observations in the time series, as shown in the following diagram:

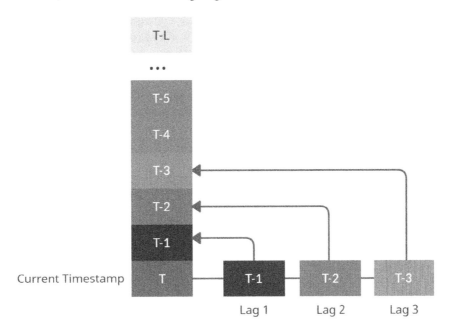

Figure 6.2 – Lag features

We can create multiple lags by including observations that are a timesteps before (y_{t-a}); we will call this *Lag a*. In the preceding diagram, we have shown **Lag 1**, **Lag 2**, and **Lag 3**. However, we can add any number of lags we like. Now, let's learn how to do that in code:

```
df["lag_1"]=df["column"].shift(1)
```

Remember when we combined the train and test datasets and I asked you to take it in good faith? It's time to put a reason to that faith. If we consider the lag operation (or any autoregressive feature), it relies on a continuous representation along the time axis. If we consider the test dataset, for the first few rows (or earliest dates), the lags would be missing because it is part of the training dataset. So, by combining the two, we create a continuous representation along the time axis where standard functions in pandas such as `shift` can be utilized to create these features easily and efficiently.

It is as simple as that, but we need to perform the lag operation for each `LCLid` separately. We have included a helpful method in `src.feature_engineering.autoregressive_features` called `add_lags` that adds all the lags you want for each `LCLid` in a fast and efficient manner. Let's see how we can use that.

We are going to import the method and use a few of its parameters to configure the lag operation the way we want:

```
from src.feature_engineering.autoregressive_features import
add_lags
# Creating first 5 lags and then same 5 lags but from previous
day and previous week to capture seasonality
lags = (
    (np.arange(5) + 1).tolist()
    + (np.arange(5) + 46).tolist()
    + (np.arange(5) + (48 * 7) - 2).tolist()
)
full_df, added_features = add_lags(
    full_df, lags=lags, column="energy_consumption", ts_
id="LCLid", use_32_bit=True
)
```

Now, let's look at the parameters that we used in the previous code snippet:

- `lags`: This parameter takes in a list of integers denoting all the lags we need to create as features.
- `column`: The name of the column to be lagged. In our case, this is `energy_consumption`.
- `ts_id`: The name of the column that contains the unique ID of a time series. If `None`, it assumes the DataFrame only contains a single time series. In our case, `LCLid` is the name of that column.
- `use_32_bit`: This parameter doesn't do anything functionally but makes the DataFrames much smaller in memory, sacrificing the precision of the floating-point numbers.

This method returns the DataFrame with the lags added and a list with column names of the newly added features.

Rolling window aggregations

With lags, we were connecting the present points to single points in the past, but with rolling window features, we are connecting the present with an aggregate statistic of a window from the past. Instead of looking at the observation from previous time steps, we would be looking at an average of the observations from the last three timesteps. Take a look at the following diagram to understand this better:

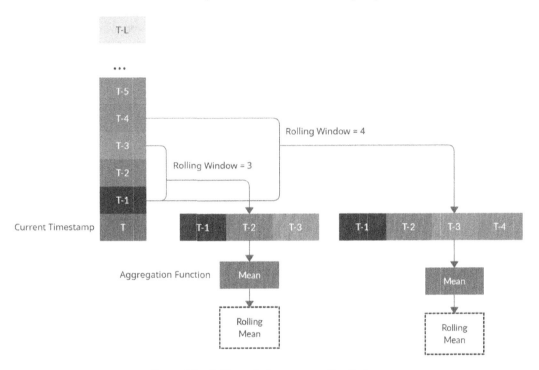

Figure 6.3 – Rolling window aggregation features

We can calculate rolling statistics with different widows, and each of them would capture slightly different aspects of the history. In the preceding diagram, we can see an example of a window of three and a window of four. When we are at timestep t, a rolling window of three would have $y_{t-3}, y_{t-2}, y_{t-1}$ as the vector of past observations. Once we have these, we can apply any aggregation functions, such as the mean, standard deviation, min, max, and so on. Once we have a scalar value after the aggregation function, we can include that as a feature for timestep t.

> **Important note**
> We are *not including* y_t in the vector of past observations because that leads to data leakage.

Let's see how we can do this with pandas:

```
# We shift by one to make sure there is no data leakage
df["rolling_3_mean"] = df["column"].shift(1).rolling(3).mean()
```

Similar to the lags, we need to do this operation for each LCLid column separately. We have included a helpful method in src.feature_engineering.autoregressive_features called add_rolling_features that adds all the rolling features you want for each LCLid in a fast and efficient manner. Let's see how we can use that.

We are going to import this method and use a few of its parameters to configure the rolling operation the way we want:

```
from src.feature_engineering.autoregressive_features import
add_rolling_features
full_df, added_features = add_rolling_features(
    full_df,
    rolls=[3, 6, 12, 48],
    column="energy_consumption",
    agg_funcs=["mean", "std"],
    ts_id="LCLid",
    use_32_bit=True,
)
```

Now, let's look at the parameters that we used in the previous code snippet:

- rolls: This parameter takes in a list of integers denoting all the windows over which we need to calculate the aggregate statistics.

- column: The name of the column to be lagged. In our case, this is energy_consumption.

- agg_funcs: This is a list of aggregations that we want to do for each window we declared in rolls. Allowable aggregation functions include {mean, std, max, min}.

- n_shift: This is the number of timesteps we need to shift before doing the rolling operation. This parameter avoids data leakage. Although we are shifting by one now, there are cases where we need to shift by more than one as well. This is typically used in multi-step forecasting, which we will cover in *Section 3 – Mechanics of Forecasting*.

- ts_id: The name of the column name that contains the unique ID of a time series. If None, it assumes that the DataFrame only has a single time series. In our case, LCLid is the name of that column.

- use_32_bit: This parameter doesn't do anything functionally but makes the DataFrames much smaller in memory, sacrificing the precision of the floating-point numbers.

This method returns the DataFrame with the rolling features added and a list with column names of the newly added features.

Seasonal rolling window aggregations

Seasonal rolling window aggregations are very similar to rolling window aggregations, but instead of taking past *n* consecutive observations in the window, this takes a seasonal window, skipping a constant number of timesteps between each item in a window. The following diagram will make this clearer:

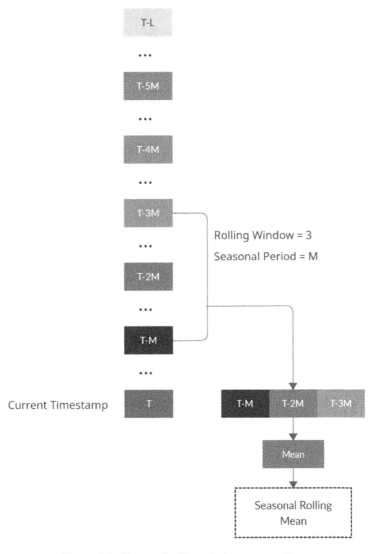

Figure 6.4 – Seasonal rolling window aggregations

The key parameter here is the seasonality period, which is commonly referred to as m. This is the number of timesteps after which we expect the seasonality pattern to repeat. When we are at timestep t, a rolling window of three would have $y_{t-3}, y_{t-2}, y_{t-1}$ as the vector of past observations. But the seasonal rolling window would skip m timesteps between each item in the window. This means that the observations that are there in the seasonal rolling window would be $y_{t-m}, y_{t-2m}, y_{t-3m}$. And as usual, once we have the window vector, we just need to apply the aggregation function to get a scalar value and include that as a feature.

> **Important note**
> We are *not including* y_t as an element in the seasonal rolling window vector to avoid data leakage.

This is not an operation that you can do easily and efficiently with pandas. Some fancy NumPy indexing and Python loops should do the trick. We are using an implementation from github.com/jmoralez/window_ops/ that uses NumPy and Numba to make the operation fast and efficient.

Just like the features we saw earlier, we need to do this operation for each LCLid separately. We have included a helpful method in src.feature_engineering.autoregressive_features called add_seasonal_rolling_features that adds all the seasonal rolling features you want for each LCLid in a fast and efficient manner. Let's see how we can use that.

We are going to import the method and use a few parameters of the method to configure the seasonal rolling operation the way we want:

```
from src.feature_engineering.autoregressive_features import
add_seasonal_rolling_features
full_df, added_features = add_seasonal_rolling_features(
    full_df,
    rolls=[3],
    seasonal_periods=[48, 48 * 7],
    column="energy_consumption",
    agg_funcs=["mean", "std"],
    ts_id="LCLid",
    use_32_bit=True,
)
```

Now, let's look at the parameters that we used in the previous code snippet:

- `seasonal_periods`: This is a list of seasonal periods that should be used in the seasonal rolling windows. In the case of multiple seasonalities, we can include the seasonal rolling features of all the seasonalities.

- `rolls`: This parameter takes in a list of integers denoting all the windows over which we need to calculate aggregate statistics.

- `column`: The name of the column to be lagged. In our case, this is `energy_consumption`.

- `agg_funcs`: This is a list of aggregations that we want to do for each window we declared in `rolls`. The allowable aggregation functions are {`mean`, `std`, `max`, `min`}.

- `n_shift`: This is the number of seasonal timesteps we need to shift before doing the rolling operation. This parameter avoids data leakage.

- `ts_id`: The name of the column name that contains the unique ID of a time series. If `None`, it assumes the DataFrame only contains a single time series. In our case, `LCLid` is the name of that column.

- `Use_32_bit`: This parameter doesn't do anything functionally but makes the DataFrames much smaller in memory, sacrificing the precision of the floating-point numbers.

As always, the method returns the DataFrame with seasonal rolling features and a list containing the column names of the newly added features.

Exponentially weighted moving averages (EWMA)

With the rolling window mean operation, we were calculating the average of the window, and it works synonymously with the **moving average**. EWMA is the slightly smarter cousin of the moving average. While the moving average considers a rolling window and considers each item in the window equally on the computed average, EWMA tries to do a weighted average on the window, and the weights decay at an exponential rate. There is a parameter, α, that determines how fast the weights decay. And because of this, we can consider all the history available as a window and let the α parameter decide how much recency is included in EWMA. This can be written simply and recursively, as follows:

$$EWMA_t = \alpha \times y_t + (1 - \alpha) \times EWMA_{t-1}$$

Here, we can see that the larger the value of α, the more the average is skewed toward recent values (see *Figure 6.6* to get a visual intuition of how the weights would be). If we expand the recursion, the weights of each term work out to be:

$$w\_\{t - k\} = \alpha \times (1 - \alpha)^\wedge k$$

where k is the number of timesteps behind t. If we plot the weights, we can see them in an exponential decay; α determines how fast the decay happens. Another way to think about α is in terms of **span**. Span is the number of periods at which the decayed weights approach zero (not in a strictly mathematical way, but intuitively). α and span are related through this equation:

$$\alpha = \frac{2}{1 + span}$$

This will become clearer in the following diagram, where we have plotted how the weights decay for different values of α:

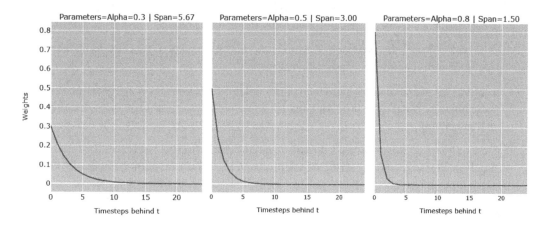

Figure 6.5 – Exponential weight decay for different values of α

Here, we can see that the weight becomes small by the time we reach the span.

Intuitively, we can think of EWMA as an average of the entire history of the time series, but with parameters such as α and **span**, we can make different periods of history more representative of the average. If we define a 60-period span, we can think that the last 60 time periods are what majorly drive the average. So, making EWMAs with different spans or αs gives us representative features that capture different periods of history.

The overall process is depicted in the following diagram:

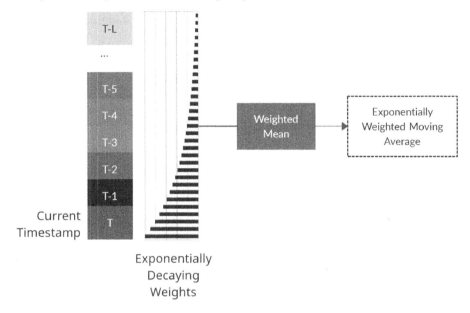

Figure 6.6 – EWMA features

Now, let's see how we can do this in pandas:

```
df["ewma"]=df['column'].shift(1).ewm(alpha=0.5).mean()
```

Like the other features we discussed earlier, EWMA also needs to be done for each LCLid separately. We have included a helpful method in src.feature_engineering.autoregressive_ features called add_ewma that adds all the EWMA features you want for each LCLid in a fast and efficient manner. Let's see how we can use that.

We are going to import the method and use a few parameters of the method to configure EWMA the way we want to:

```
from src.feature_engineering.autoregressive_features import
add_ewma
full_df, added_features = add_ewma(
    full_df,
    spans=[48 * 60, 48 * 7, 48],
    column="energy_consumption",
    ts_id="LCLid",
    use_32_bit=True,
)
```

Now, let's look at the parameters that we used in the previous code snippet:

- `alphas`: This is a list of all αs we need to calculate the EWMA features for.
- `spans`: Alternatively, we can use this to list all the spans we need to calculate the EWMA features for. If you use this feature, `alphas` will be ignored.
- `column`: The name of the column to be lagged. In our case, this is `energy_consumption`.
- `n_shift`: This is the number of seasonal timesteps we need to shift before doing the rolling operation. This parameter avoids data leakage.
- `ts_id`: The name of the column name that has a unique ID for a time series. If `None`, it assumes the DataFrame only contains a single time series. In our case, `LCLid` is the name of that column.
- `use_32_bit`: This parameter doesn't do anything functionally but makes the DataFrames much smaller in memory, sacrificing the precision of the floating-point numbers.

As always, the method returns the DataFrame containing EWMA features and a list with the column names of the newly added features.

These are a few standard ways of including time delay embedding in your ML model, but you are not restricted to just these. As always, feature engineering is a space that is not bound by rules and we can get as creative as we want and inject domain knowledge into the model. Apart from the features we have seen, we can include the difference in lag as custom lags that inject domain knowledge, and so on.

Now, let's look at the other class of features we can add via **temporal embedding**.

Temporal embedding

In *Chapter 5, Time Series Forecasting as Regression*, we briefly talked about temporal embedding as a process where we try to embed *time* into features that the ML model can leverage. If we think about *time* for a second, we will realize that there are two aspects of time that are important to us in the context of time series forecasting – *passage of time* and *periodicity of time*.

Let's look at a few features that can help us capture these aspects in an ML model.

Calendar features

The first set of features that we can extract are features based on calendars. Although the strict definition of time series is a set of observations taken sequentially in time, more often than not, we will have the timestamps of these collected observations alongside the time series. We can utilize these timestamps and extract calendar features such as the month, quarter, day of the year, hour, minutes, and so on. These features capture the periodicity of time and help the ML model capture seasonality well. Only the calendar features that are temporally higher than the frequency of the time series make sense. For instance, an hour feature in a time series with a weekly frequency doesn't make sense, but a month feature and week feature make sense. We can utilize inbuilt datetime functionalities in pandas to create these features and treat these as categorical features in the model.

Time elapsed

This is another feature that captures the passage of time in an ML model. This feature increases monotonically as time increases, giving the ML model a sense of the passage of time. There are many ways to create this feature, but one of the easiest and most efficient ways is to use the integer representation of dates in NumPy:

```
df['time_elapsed'] = df['timestamp'].values.astype(np.int64)/
(10**9)
```

We have included a helpful method in `src.feature_engineering.temporal_features` called `add_temporal_features` that adds all relevant temporal features in an automated way. Let's see how we can use it.

We are going to import the method and use a few parameters of this method to configure and create the temporal features:

```
full_df, added_features = add_temporal_features(
    full_df,
    field_name="timestamp",
    frequency="30min",
    add_elapsed=True,
    drop=False,
    use_32_bit=True,
)
```

Now, let's look at the parameters that we used in the previous code snippet:

- `field_name`: This is the column name that contains the datetime that should be used to create features.
- `frequency`: We should provide the frequency of the time series as input so that the method automatically extracts the relevant features. These are standard pandas frequency strings.
- `add_elapsed`: This flag turns the creation of the time elapsed feature on or off.
- `use_32_bit`: This parameter doesn't do anything functionally but makes the DataFrames much smaller in memory, sacrificing the precision of the floating-point numbers.

Just like the previous methods we discussed, this also returns the new DataFrame with the temporal features added and a list containing the column names of the newly added features.

Fourier terms

Previously, we extracted a few calendar features such as the month, year, and so on and talked about using them as categorical variables in the ML model. Another way we can represent the same information, but on a continuous scale, is by using **Fourier terms**. We discussed Fourier series in *Chapter 3, Analyzing and Visualizing Time Series Data*. Just to recall, the sine-cosine form of the Fourier series is as follows:

$$s_{N(x)} = \frac{a_0}{2} + \Sigma_{n=1}^{N}\left(a_n \cdot cos\left(\frac{2\pi}{P} \cdot n \cdot x\right) + b_n \cdot sin\left(\frac{2\pi}{P} \cdot n \cdot x\right)\right)$$

Here, s_N is the N-term approximation of the signal, S. Theoretically when N is infinite, the resulting approximation is equal to the original signal. P is the maximum length of the cycle. We can create these cosine and sine functions as features to represent the seasonal cycle. If we are encoding the month, we know that the month goes from 1 to 12 and then repeats itself. So, P, in this case, will be 12 and x will be 1, 2, …12. Therefore, for each x, we can calculate the cosine and sine terms and add them as features to the ML model. The following diagram shows the difference in representations between the month on an ordinal scale and as a Fourier series:

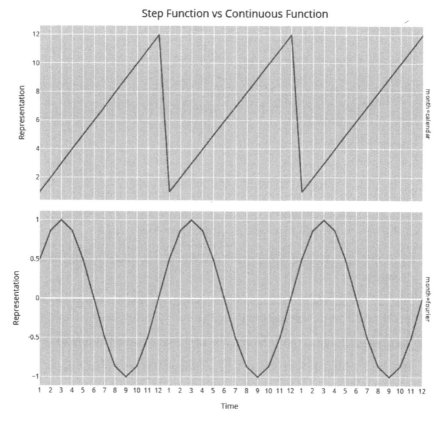

Figure 6.7 – Month as an ordinal step function (top) versus Fourier terms (bottom)

The preceding diagram shows just a single Fourier term; we can add multiple Fourier terms to help capture complex seasonality.

We cannot say that continuous representation of seasonality is better than categorical because it depends on the type of model you are using and the dataset. This is something we will have to find out empirically.

To make the process of adding Fourier features easy, we have made some easy-to-use methods available in `src.feature_engineering.temporal_features` in a file called `bulk_add_fourier_features` that adds Fourier features for all the calendar features we want in an automated way. Let's see how we can use that.

We are going to import the method and use a few parameters of the method to configure and create the Fourier series-based features:

```
full_df, added_features = bulk_add_fourier_features(
    full_df,
    ["timestamp_Month", "timestamp_Hour", "timestamp_Minute"],
    max_values=[12, 24, 60],
    n_fourier_terms=5,
    use_32_bit=True,
)
```

Now, let's look at the parameters that we used in the previous code snippet:

- `columns_to_encode`: This is the list of calendar features we need to encode using Fourier terms.

- `max_values`: This is a list of max values for the seasonal cycle for the calendar features in the same order as they are given in `columns_to_encode`. For instance, for `month` as a column to encode, we give `12` as the corresponding `max_value`. If not given, `max_value` will be inferred. This is only recommended if the data you have contains at least a single complete seasonal cycle.

- `n_fourier_terms`: The number of Fourier terms to be added. This is synonymous to n in the equation for the Fourier series mentioned previously.

- `use_32_bit`: This parameter doesn't do anything functionally but makes the DataFrames much smaller in memory, sacrificing the precision of the floating-point numbers.

Just like the previous methods we've discussed, this also returns a new DataFrame with the Fourier features added and a list with column names of the newly added features.

After executing the `01-Feature Engineering.ipynb` notebook in `chapter06`, we will have the following feature engineered files written to disk:

- `selected_blocks_train_missing_imputed_feature_engg.parquet`
- `selected_blocks_val_missing_imputed_feature_engg.parquet`
- `selected_blocks_test_missing_imputed_feature_engg.parquet`

In this section, we looked at a few popular and effective ways of generating features for time series. But there are many more and depending on your problem and the domain, many of them will be relevant.

> **Additional information**
>
> The world of feature engineering is vast and there are a few open source libraries that make exploring that space easier. A few of them include `https://github.com/Nixtla/tsfeatures`, `https://tsfresh.readthedocs.io/en/latest/`, and `https://github.com/DynamicsAndNeuralSystems/catch22`. A preprint by *Ben D. Fulcher* titled *Feature-based time-series analysis* at `https://arxiv.org/abs/1709.08055` also gives a nice summary of the space.

Summary

After a brief overview of the ML for time series forecasting paradigm in the previous chapter, in this chapter, we looked at this practically and saw how we can prepare the dataset with the required features to start using these models. We reviewed a few time series-specific feature engineering techniques such as lags, rolling, and seasonal features. All the techniques we learned in this chapter are tools with which we can quickly iterate through experiments to find out what works for our dataset. However, we only talked about feature engineering, which affects one side of the standard regression equation ($y = mX + c$). The other side, which is the target (y) we are predicting, is also equally important. In the next chapter, we'll look at a few concepts such as stationarity and some transformations that affect the target.

7

Target Transformations for Time Series Forecasting

In the previous chapter, we delved into how we can do temporal embedding and time delay embedding by making use of feature engineering techniques. But that was just one side of the regression equation – the features. Often, we see that the other side of the equation – the target – does not behave the way we want. In other words, the target doesn't have some desirable properties that make forecasting easier. One of the major culprits in this area is **stationarity** – or more specifically, the lack of it. And it creates problems with the assumptions we make while developing a **machine learning** (**ML**)/statistical model. In this chapter, we will look at some techniques for handling such problems with the target.

In this chapter, we will cover the following topics:

- Handling non-stationarity in time series
- Detecting and correcting for unit roots
- Detecting and correcting for trends
- Detecting and correcting for seasonality
- Detecting and correcting for heteroscedasticity
- AutoML approach to target transformation

Technical requirements

The following are the technical requirements for this chapter:

- You will need to set up the Anaconda environment following the instructions in the *Preface* of the book to get a working environment with all the packages and datasets required for the code in this book.

- You will need to run the following notebooks in this chapter:

  - `02-Preprocessing London Smart Meter Dataset.ipynb` in the `Chapter02` folder

  - `01-Setting up Experiment Harness.ipynb` in `Chapter04` folder

  - `01-Feature Engineering.ipynb` in `Chapter06` folder

- The associated code for this chapter can be found at `https://github.com/PacktPublishing/Modern-Time-Series-Forecasting-with-Python-/tree/main/notebooks/Chapter07`.

Handling non-stationarity in time series

Stationarity is a prevalent assumption in econometrics and is a rigorous and mathematical concept. But without getting into a lot of math, we can intuitively think about stationarity as the state where the statistical properties of the distribution from which the time series is sampled remain constant over time. This is relevant in time series as regression as well because we are estimating a single forecasting function across time. And if the *behavior* of the time series changes with time, the single function that we estimate may not be relevant all the time. For instance, if we think about the number of visitors to the nearby park in a day as a time series, we know that those patterns are going to be very different for pre- and post-pandemic periods. In the ML world, this phenomenon is called **concept drift**.

Intuitively, we can understand that it is easier to forecast a stationary series than a non-stationary series. But here comes the punchline: in the real world, almost all time series do not satisfy the stationarity assumption – more specifically, the **strict stationarity** assumption. Strict stationarity is when all the statistical properties such as the mean, variance, skewness, and so on do not change with time. Many times, this strict stationarity assumption is relaxed in favor of **weak stationarity**, where we only stipulate that the mean and the variance of the time series do not change with time.

There are four main questions we can ask ourselves to check whether our time series is stationary or not:

- Does the mean change over time? Or in other words, is there a trend in the time series?

- Does the variance change over time? Or in other words, is the time series heteroscedastic?

- Does the time series exhibit periodic changes in mean? Or in other words, is there seasonality in the time series?

- Does the time series have a unit root?

Out of these questions, the first three can be ascertained using a simple visual inspection. **Unit roots** are more difficult to understand. Let's take a look at a few time series and check whether we can tell whether they are stationary or not via visual inspection (you can note your answers):

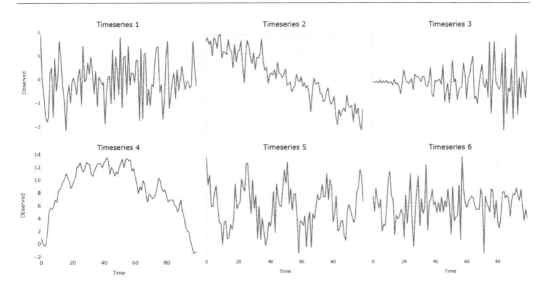

Figure 7.1 – Testing your understanding of stationarity

Now, check your responses and see how many of them you guessed correctly. If you got at least four out of six, you are doing great with your intuition of stationarity:

- **Timeseries 1** is *stationary* as it is a white noise process that, by definition, has zero mean and a constant variance. It checks our checklist for the first three questions.

- **Timeseries 2** is *non-stationary* as it has an obvious downward linear trend. This means that the mean of the series at the beginning of the series is not the same toward the end. So, it fails our first question in the checklist.

- **Timeseries 3** may look stationary at first because it is essentially oscillating around 0, but the oscillations are wider as we progress through time. This means that it has an increasing variance – or in other words, it is heteroscedastic. So, although this checks our first question, it doesn't pass our second check of having constant variance. Hence, it is *non-stationary*.

- Now, we are coming to the problem child – **Timeseries 4**. At first glance, we may think it is stationary because even though it had a trend in the beginning, it also reversed it, making the mean almost constant. And it's not obvious that the variance is also widely varying. But this is a time series with a unit root (we will talk about this in detail later in the *Unit roots* section) and typically unit root time series are difficult to judge visually.

- **Timeseries 5** checks out on the first two questions – the constant mean and constant variance – but it has a very obvious seasonal pattern and hence is *non-stationary*.

- **Timeseries 6** is another white noise process, included just to trick you. This is also *stationary*.

When we have hundreds, or even millions, of time series, we can't practically do a visual inspection to ascertain whether they are stationary or not. So, now, let's look at a few ways of detecting these key properties using statistical tests and also how to try and correct them.

> **Important note**
>
> Although we are talking about correcting or making a time series stationary, it is not always essential to do that in the ML paradigm because some of these can be handled by using the right kind of features in the model. Whether to make a series stationary or not is a decision we will have to make after experimenting with the techniques. This is because, as you will see, while there are advantages to making a series stationary, there are also disadvantages to using some of these techniques, as we will see when we discuss each transformation in detail.

> **Notebook alert**
>
> To follow along with the complete code, use the `02-Dealing with Non-Stationarity.ipynb` notebook in the `chapter06` folder.

Detecting and correcting for unit roots

Let's talk about unit roots first since this is what is most commonly tested for stationarity. Time series analysis has its roots in econometrics and statistics and unit root is a concept derived directly from those fields.

Unit roots

Unit roots are quite complicated to understand fully but to develop some intuition, we can look at a simplification. Let's consider an autoregressive model of order 1(AR(1) model):

$$y_t = \phi y_{t-1} + \epsilon_t \text{ , where } \epsilon_t \text{ is white noise and } \phi \text{ is the AR coefficient}$$

If we think about the different values of ϕ in the equation, we can come up with three scenarios (*Figure 7.2*):

- $|\phi| > 1$: When $|\phi|$ is greater than 1, every successive value in the time series is multiplied by a number greater than 1, which means it will have a strong and rapidly increasing/decreasing trend and thereby be non-stationary.

- $|\phi| < 1$: When $|\phi|$ is less than 1, every successive value in the time series is multiplied by a number less than 1, which means over the long term, the mean of the series trends to zero and will oscillate around it. Therefore, it is stationary.

- $|\phi| = 1$: When $|\phi|$ is equal to 1, things become trickier. When $|\phi| = 1$ for an AR(1) model, this is known as it having a unit root and the equation becomes $y_t = y_{t-1} + \epsilon_t$. This is called random walk in econometrics and is a very popular kind of time series in financial and economic domains. Mathematically, we can prove that such a series will have a constant mean but a non-constant variance:

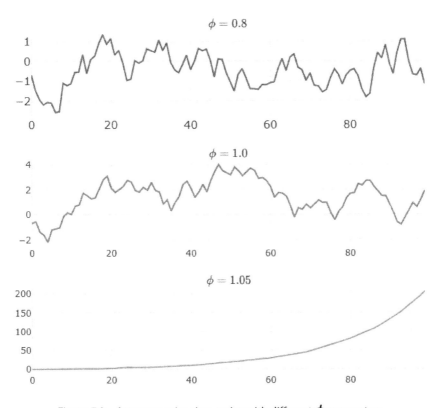

Figure 7.2 – Autoregressive time series with different ϕ parameters

While we discussed unit roots in an AR(1) process, we can extend the same intuition to multiple lags or an AR(p) model. Calculating and testing unit roots is more complicated there, but still possible.

So, now that we know what a unit root is, how can we statistically test this? This is where the Dickey-Fuller test comes in.

The Augmented Dickey-Fuller (ADF) test

The null hypothesis in this test is that the ϕ in an AR(1) model of the time series is equal to 1, and by extension non-stationary. The alternate hypothesis is that the ϕ in the AR(1) model is less than 1. The **ADF** test takes the Dickey-Fuller test and extends it to an AR(p) model because most time series are not defined by just one lag of the time series. This is the standard and most popular statistical test to check for unit roots.

Let's see how we can do this in Python using `statsmodels`:

```
from statsmodels.tsa.stattools import adfuller
result = adfuller(y)
```

`result` from `adfuller` is a tuple that contains the test statistic, p-value, and critical values at different confidence levels. Here, we are most interested in the p-value, which is an easy and practical way to check whether the null hypothesis is rejected or not. If $p<0.05$, there is a 95% probability that the series does not have a unit root; the series is stationary from a unit root perspective.

To make this process even easier, we have included a method called `check_unit_root` in `src.transforms.stationary_utils` that does the inference for you and returns a `namedtuple` with a Boolean attribute called `stationary`:

```
from src.transforms.stationary_utils import check_unit_root
# We pass the time series along with the confidence with which
we need the results
check_unit_root(y, confidence=0.05)
```

Now that we've learned how to check whether a series has a unit root or not, how do we make it stationary? Let's look at a few transforms that help us do that.

Differencing transform

The differencing transform is a very popular transform to make a time series stationary, or at least get rid of unit roots. The concept is simple: we transform the time series from the domain of observation to the domain of change in observations. The differencing transform subtracts subsequent observations from one another:

$$z_t = y_t - y_{t-1}$$

Differencing helps us stabilize the mean of the time series and, with that, reduce or eliminate trend and seasonality. Let's see how differencing can make a series stationary.

Let the time series in question be $y_t = \beta_0 + \beta_1 t + \epsilon_t$, where β_0 and β_1 are the coefficients and ϵ is white noise. From this equation, we can see that time, t, is part of the equation, making y_t a time series with a trend. So, the differenced time series z would be as follows:

$$z_t = y_t - y_{t-1} = (\beta_0 + \beta_1 t + \epsilon_t) - (\beta_0 + \beta_1(t-1) + \epsilon_{t-1}) = \beta_1 + (\epsilon_t - \epsilon_{t-1})$$

What we need to look for in this new equation is that there is no mention of t. This means that the dependence on t, which created the trend, has been removed, and now the time series has constant mean and variance at any point in time.

Differencing does not remove all kinds of non-stationarity but works for the majority of time series. But there are a few drawbacks to this approach as well. One of them is that we lose the scale of the time series while modeling. Many times, the scale of the time series holds some information that is useful for forecasting. For instance, in a supply chain, SKUs with higher sales exhibit a different kind of pattern from the SKUs with lower sales and when we do differencing, this information about the distinction is lost.

Another drawback is more from an operational point of view. When we use differencing for forecasting, we also need to inverse the transform after we get the differenced output from the model. This is an additional layer of complexity that we have to manage. One way is to keep the most recent observation in memory and keep adding the differences to it to inverse the transform. Another way is to have y_{t-1} ready for every t that we need to inverse transform and keep adding the difference to y_{t-1}.

We have implemented the latter using the datetime index as a key to align and fetch the y_{t-1} observation in `src.transforms.target_transformations.py` in this book's GitHub repository. Let's see how we can use it:

```
from src.transforms.target_transformations import
AdditiveDifferencingTransformer
diff_transformer = AdditiveDifferencingTransformer()
# [1:] because differencing reduces the length of the time
series by one
y_diff = diff_transformer.fit_transform(y, freq="1D")[1:]
```

`y_diff` will have the transformed series. To get back to the original time series, we can call `inverse_transform` using `diff_transformer`.

Here, we saw differencing as the process of subtracting subsequent values in the time series. But we can also do differencing with other operators such as division (y_t/y_{t-1}), which is implemented in the `src.transforms.target_transformations.py` file as `MultiplicativeDifferencingTransformer`. We can also experiment with these transforms to check whether these work best for your dataset.

Although differencing solves the majority of stationarity issues, it's not guaranteed to take care of all kinds of trends (non-linear or piecewise trends), seasonality, and so on. Sometimes, we may not want to difference the series but still handle trends and seasonality. So, let's see how we can detect and remove trends in a time series.

Detecting and correcting for trends

In *Chapter 5, Time Series Forecasting as Regression*, we talked about forecasting being a difficult problem because it is intrinsically an extrapolation problem. Trends are one of the major contributors to forecasting being an extrapolation problem. If we have a time series that is trending upward, any model that attempts to forecast it needs to extrapolate beyond the range of values it has seen during training. ARIMA handles this using autoregression, whereas exponential smoothing handles it by modeling the trend explicitly. But standard regression may not be naturally suited to extrapolation. However, with suitable features, such as lags, it can start to do that. But if we can confidently estimate and extract a trend in the time series, we can simplify the problem we have to apply regression to by detrending the time series.

But before we move ahead, it is worth learning about two major types of trends.

Deterministic and stochastic trends

Let's take the simple *AR(1)* model we saw earlier to develop intuitions about this one too. Earlier, we saw that having $\phi > 1$ in an *AR(1)* model leads to a trend in the time series. But another way we can think about a trending time series is if we include time as an ordinal variable in the equation defining the time series. For instance, let's consider two time series:

Time series 1: $y_t = \phi y_{t-1} + \epsilon_t; \epsilon_t \sim \mathcal{N}(0, \sigma^2)$

Time series 2: $y_t = \beta_0 + \beta_1 t + \epsilon_t; \epsilon_t \sim \mathcal{N}(0, \sigma^2)$

These can be seen in the following graphs:

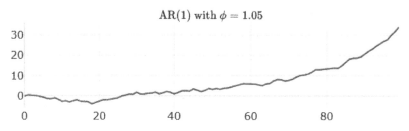

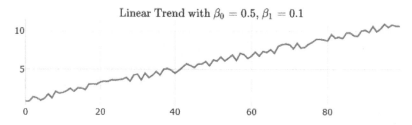

Figure 7.3 – Time series 1 (stochastic trend) and Time series 2 (deterministic trend)

We saw both of these equations earlier; *Time series 1* is the *AR(1)* model while *Time series 2* is the time series equation we chose to illustrate differencing. We already know that for $\phi > 1$, both *Time series 1* and *Time series 2* have trends. But there is a difference between the two trends. In *Time series 2*, the trend is constant and can be perfectly modeled. In this case, just a linear fit would explain the trend perfectly. But in *Time series 1*, the trend is not something that can be explained by a simple linear fit. It is inherently dependent on the previous value of the time series that has ϵ_{t-1} and hence is stochastic. Therefore, *Time series 2* has a deterministic trend and *Time series 1* has a stochastic trend.

We can use the same ADF test we saw earlier in this chapter to check whether a time series has deterministic or stochastic trends. Without going into the math of the statistical test, we know that it tests for a unit root by fitting an *AR(p)* model to the time series. There are a few variants of this test that we can specify using the `regression` parameter in the `statsmodels` implementation. This parameter takes in the following values:

- `c`: This means we are including a constant intercept in the *AR(p)* model. Practically, this means that we will be considering a time series as stationary even if the series is not around zero. This is the default setting in `statsmodels`.

- `n`: This means we do not even include a constant intercept in the *AR(p)* model.

- `ct`: If we supply this option, the *AR(p)* model will also have a constant intercept and a linear, deterministic trend component. What this means is that even if there is a deterministic trend in the time series, it will be ignored and the series will be tested as stationary.

- `ctt`: This is when we include a constant intercept – that is, a linear and quadratic trend.

So, if we run an ADF test with `regression="c"`, it will be non-stationary. Now, if we run the ADF test with `regression="ct"`, it will come out as stationary. This means that when we removed a deterministic trend from the time series, it became stationary. This test is what we can use to determine whether a trend that we observe in the time series is deterministic or stochastic. In the *Further reading* section, we have provided a link to a blog post by *Fabian Kostadinov*, where he experiments with a few time series to make the distinction between the different variants of ADF tests clear.

We have implemented this test in `src.transforms.stationary_utils` as `check_deterministic_trend`, which does the inference for you and returns a `namedtuple` with a Boolean attribute of `deterministic_trend`. Let's see how we can use this test:

```
check_deterministic_trend(y, confidence=0.05)
```

This will tell us whether the trend is stationary or deterministic. Now, let's look at a couple of ways to identify and statistically test trends (irrespective of whether it is deterministic or not) in a time series.

Kendall's Tau

Kendall's Tau is a measure of correlation but carried out on the ranks of the data. Similar to Spearman's correlation, which also calculates correlation on ranked data, Kendall's Tau is a non-parametric test and therefore does not make assumptions about the data. The correlation coefficient, Tau, returns a value between -1 and 1, where 0 shows no relationship and 1 or -1 is a perfect relationship. We will not dive into the details of how Kendall's Tau is calculated and how the significance test is done as this is outside the scope of this book. The *Further reading* section contains a link that explains this well.

In this section, we will see how we can use Kendall's Tau to measure the trend in our time series. As mentioned earlier, Kendall's Tau calculates a rank correlation between two variables. If we chose one of those variables as the time series and set the other as the ordinal representation of time, the resulting Kendall's Tau would represent the trend in the time series. An additional benefit is that the higher the value of Kendall's Tau, the stronger we expect the trend to be.

`scipy` has an implementation of Kendall's Tau that we can use as follows:

```
import scipy.stats as stats
tau, p_value = stats.kendalltau(y, np.arange(len(y)))
```

We can compare the returned p-value to our required confidence (typically, this is 0.05) and say that if `p_value < confidence`, we conclude that the trend is statistically significant. The sign of `tau` tells us whether this is an increasing trend or a decreasing one.

We have made an implementation of Kendall's Tau in `src.transforms.stationary_utils` as `check_trend`, which checks the presence of a trend for you. The only parameters we need to provide are as follows:

- `y`: The time series to check
- `confidence`: The confidence level against which the resulting p-value will be checked

A few more parameters are there, but those are for the **Mann-Kendall (M-K)** test, which will be explained next.

Let's see how we can use this test:

```
check_trend(y, confidence=0.05)
```

This method also checks whether the trend that has been identified is deterministic or stochastic and calculates the direction of the trend. The result is returned as a `namedtuple` with the following parameters:

- `trend`: A Boolean flag signifying the presence of a trend.
- `direction`: This will be either `increasing` or `decreasing`.
- `slope`: The slope of the estimated trend line. For Kendall's Tau, it will be the Tau.
- `p`: The p-value of the statistical test.
- `deterministic`: A Boolean flag signifying the deterministic trend.

Now, let's look at the Mann-Kendall test.

Mann-Kendall test (M-K test)

The Mann-Kendall test is used to check for the presence of a monotonic upward or downward trend. And since the M-K test is a non-parametric test, like Kendall's Tau, there is no assumption of normality or linearity. The test is done by analyzing the signs between consecutive points in the time series. The crux of the test is the idea that in the presence of a trend, the sign values, if summed up, increase or decrease constantly.

Although non-parametric, there were a few assumptions in the original test:

- There is no auto-correlation in the time series
- There is no seasonality in the time series

Numerous alterations have been made to the original tests to tackle these problems over the years and a lot of such alterations, along with the original test, have been implemented at `https://github.com/mmhs013/pyMannKendall`. They are available in `pypi` as `pymannkendall`.

Pre-whitening is a common technique used to remove the autocorrelation in a time series. In a nutshell, the idea is as follows:

1. Identify ϕ with an AR(1) model
2. $y_t^{prewhiten} = y_t - \phi * y_{t-1}$

M. Bayazit and B. Önöz (2007) suggested to not use pre-whitening before doing the M-K test if the sample size is larger than 50 and if the trend is strong enough (slope>0.01). For seasonal data, a seasonal variant of the M-K test has also been implemented in `pymannkendall`.

> **Reference Check**
>
> The research paper by M. Bayazit and B. Önöz is cited in the *References* section under reference number *1*.

The same method we discussed earlier, `check_trend`, also implements M-K tests that can be enabled by setting `mann_kendall=True`. However, one thing we need to keep in mind is that the M-K test is considerably slower than Kendall's Tau, especially for long time series. There are a few more parameters specific to the M-K test:

- `seasonal_period`: The default value is None. But if there is seasonality, we can provide `seasonal_period` here and the seasonal variant of the M-K test will be retrieved.
- `prewhiten`: This is a Boolean flag that's used to pre-whiten the time series before applying the M-K test. The default value is None. In that case, using the condition we discussed earlier (N>50), we decide whether to pre-whiten or not. If we explicitly pass True or False here, it will be respected.

Let's see how we can use this test:

```
check_trend(y, confidence=0.05, mann_kendall=True)
```

The result is returned as a `namedtuple` with the following parameters:

- `trend`: A Boolean flag signifying the presence of a trend.
- `direction`: This will be either `increasing` or `decreasing`.
- `slope`: The slope of the estimated trend line. For the M-K test, it will be the slope estimated using the Theil-Sen estimator.
- p: The p-value of the statistical test.
- `deterministic`: A Boolean flag signifying the deterministic trend.

Now that we know how to detect a trend, let's look at detrending.

Detrending transform

If the trend is deterministic, removing the trend would add some value to the modeling procedure. In *Chapter 3, Analyzing and Visualizing Time Series Data*, we discussed detrending as it was an integral part of the decomposition we were doing. But techniques such as moving average or LOESS regression have one drawback – they can't extrapolate. But if we are considering a deterministic linear (or even polynomial) trend, it can be easily estimated by using linear regression. The added advantage here is that the trend that is identified can easily be extrapolated.

The procedure is simple: we regress the time series on the ordinal representation of time and extract the parameters. Once we have these parameters, using the dates, we can extrapolate the trend to any point in the future.

We have made and implemented a detrender as a transformer in `src.transforms.target_transformations.py` as `DetrendingTransformer`. Let's see how we can use it:

```
from src.transforms.target_transformations import
DetrendingTransformer
detrending_transformer = DetrendingTransformer(degree=1)
y_detrended = detrending_transformer.fit_transform(y,
freq="1D")
```

`y_detrended` will contain the detrended series. To get the original time series back, we can call `inverse_transform` using `detrending_transformer`.

> **Best practice**
>
> We have to be careful with the trend assumptions, especially if we are forecasting for the long term. Even a linear trend assumption can lead to an unrealistic forecast because trends don't continue the same forever in the real world. It is always advisable to dampen the trend by some factor, ϕ, to be conservative in our extrapolation of the trend. This dampening can be as simple as $f_{t+h}^{damped} = f_{t+h} \times \phi^h, where\ \phi < 1.$

Another key aspect that makes a time series non-stationary is seasonality. Let's look at how to identify seasonality and remove it.

Detecting and correcting for seasonality

A vast majority of real-world time series have seasonality such as retail sales, energy consumption, and so on. And generally, the presence or absence of seasonality comes as part of the domain knowledge. But when we are working with a time series dataset, the domain knowledge becomes slightly diluted. The majority of time series may exhibit seasonality, but that doesn't mean every time series in the dataset is seasonal. For instance, within a retail dataset, there might be items that are seasonal and some items that are not. Therefore, when working with a time series dataset, being able to determine whether a particular time series is seasonal or not has some value.

Detecting seasonality

There are two popular ways to check for seasonality, apart from just eyeballing it: autocorrelation and fast Fourier transform. Either is equally capable of identifying the seasonality period automatically. For our discussion, we'll cover the autocorrelation method and examine how we can use that to determine seasonality.

Autocorrelation, as explained in *Chapter 3, Analyzing and Visualizing Time Series Data*, is the correlation of a time series to its lagged values. Typically, we expect the correlation to be higher in the immediate lags (lag 1, lag 2, and so on) and gradually die down as we move farther into the past. But for time series with seasonality, we will also see a spike in the seasonal periods.

Let's understand this by looking at an example. Consider a synthetic time series that is just white noise combined with a sinusoidal signal with a seasonality cycle of 25 (identical to the seasonal time series we saw earlier in *Figure 7.1*):

```
#WhiteNoise + Seasonal
y_random = pd.Series(np.random.randn(length), index=index)
t = np.arange(len(y_random))
y_seasonal = (y_random+1.9*np.cos((2*np.pi*t)/(length/4)))
```

If we plot the **autocorrelation function (ACF)** for this time series, it will look as follows (the code to calculate and plot this can be found in the `02-Dealing with Non-Stationarity. ipynb` notebook):

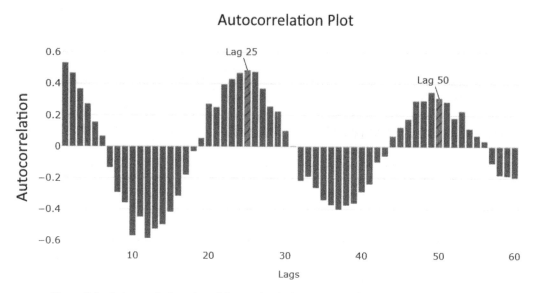

Figure 7.4 – Autocorrelation plot of the synthetic time series with a seasonality cycle of 25

We can see that apart from the first few lags, the autocorrelation increases as we approach the seasonal cycle and peaks at the exact seasonality. We can use this property of the ACF to detect seasonality. `darts`, the library we used to generate our baseline forecasts, has an implementation of this technique that identifies seasonality. But since it was designed to work for the time series data structure of `darts`, we have adapted the same logic to work on regular `pandas` series in `src. transforms.stationary_utils.py` under the name `check_seasonality`. The implementation can do two kinds of seasonality checks. It can take a `seasonality_period` as input and verify whether a seasonality corresponding to that `seasonality_period` exists in the data or not. If we do not give a `seasonality_period` ahead of time, it will return to you the shortest `seasonality_period` that is statistically significant.

The procedure, at a high level, does the following:

1. Calculates the ACF.
2. Finds all the relative maxima in the ACF. A relative maximum is a point where the function changes direction from increasing to decreasing.
3. Checks whether the provided `seasonal_period` is a relative maximum. If not, we conclude there is no seasonality associated with `seasonality_period`.

4. Now, we take the assumption that the ACF is normally distributed and compute the upper limit at the specified confidence level. The upper bound is given by:

$$UB = z_{1-\frac{\alpha}{2}} \times SE(r_h)$$

where r_h is the estimated autocorrelation at lag h, SE is the standard error, and $z_{1-\frac{\alpha}{2}}$ is the quantile of the normal distribution based on the required confidence, α. The SE is approximated using Bartlett's formula (for the math behind this, head over to the *Further reading* section).

5. Each of our candidates for `seasonality_period` is checked against this upper limit and the ones that are above this limit are deemed statistically significant.

There are only three parameters for this function, apart from the time series itself:

- `max_lag`: This specifies the maximum lag that should be included in the ACF and subsequent search for seasonality. This should be at least one more than the expected seasonality period.

- `seasonal_period`: This is where we give our intuition of the seasonality period from domain knowledge and the function verifies that assumption for us.

- `confidence`: This is the standard statistical confidence level. The default value is `0.05`.

Let's see how we can use this function with an example:

```
check_seasonality(y_seasonal, max_lag=30, seasonal_period=25,
confidence=0.05)
```

This will give you a `namedtuple` with `seasonal`, a Boolean flag to indicate seasonality, and `seasonal_periods`, the seasonal periods with significant seasonality, as parameters.

Now that we know how to identify and test for seasonality, let's talk about deseasonalizing.

Deseasonalizing transform

In *Chapter 3, Analyzing and Visualizing Time Series Data*, we reviewed techniques for seasonal decomposition. We can use the same techniques here as well, but with just one tweak. Earlier, we were not concerned with projecting the seasonality into the future. But when we are using deseasonalizing in forecasting, it is essential to be able to project it into the future as well. We are in luck since projecting the seasonal cycle forward is trivial. This is because we are looking at a fixed seasonality profile that will always keep repeating in the seasonal cycle. For instance, if we identified a seasonality profile for the 12 months of a year (yearly seasonality at monthly frequency data), the seasonality that's extracted for these 12 months will just be repeating itself in chunks of 12 months.

Using this property, we have implemented a transformer in `src.transforms.target_transformations.py` as `DeseasonalizingTransformer`. There are a few parameters and properties that we need to be aware of:

- `seasonality_extraction`: This transformer supports two ways of extracting seasonality – `"period_averages"`, where the seasonality profile is estimated using seasonal averaging, and `"fourier_terms"`, where we regress on Fourier terms to extract the seasonality.

- `seasonality_period`: Depending on the technique we use for seasonality extraction, this can either be an integer or a string. If `"period_averages"`, this parameter denotes the number of periods after which the seasonal cycle repeats. If `"fourier_terms"`, this denotes the seasonality to be extracted from the datetime index. pandas datetime properties such as `week_of_day`, `month`, and so on can be used to specify the most prominent seasonality. Similar to `FourierDecomposition`, which we saw earlier, we can also omit this parameter and provide custom seasonality in the `fit`/`transform` methods in the implementation.

- `n_fourier_terms`: This parameter specifies the number of Fourier terms to be included in the regression. Increasing this parameter makes the fitted seasonality more complex.

- There is no detrending in this implementation because we already saw a `DetrendingTransformer`. This implementation expects any trend to be removed before using the `fit` function.

Let's see how we can use it:

```
from src.transforms.target_transformations import
DeseasonalizingTransformer
deseasonalizing_transformer =
DeseasonalizingTransformer(seasonality_extraction="period_
averages",seasonal_period=25)
y_deseasonalized = deseasonalizing_transformer.fit_transform(y,
freq="1D")
```

`y_deseasonalized` will have the deseasonalized time series. To get back to the original time series, we can use the `inverse_transform` function. Typically, this can be used to add the seasonality back after making predictions.

Best practice

Modeling seasonality can be done either separately, as discussed here, or by using the seasonal features that we discussed earlier in this chapter. Although the final evaluation on which one works better has to be found out empirically for each dataset, we can have a few rules of thumb/ guidelines to decide on priority.

When we have enough data, letting the model learn seasonality as part of the main forecasting problem seems to work better. But in cases where data is not that rich, extracting seasonality separately before feeding it to an ML model works well.

When the dataset has varied seasonality (different seasonal cycles for different time series), then it should be treated accordingly. Either deseasonalize each time series separately or split the global ML model into different local models each with its own seasonality pattern.

The last aspect that we talked about earlier is heteroscedasticity. Let's quickly take a look at that as well.

Detecting and correcting for heteroscedasticity

Despite having a scary name, heteroscedasticity is a simple enough concept. It is derived from ancient Greek, where *hetero* means *different* and *skedasis* means *dispersion*. True to its name, heteroscedasticity is defined when the variability of a variable is different across another variable. In the context of a time series, we say a time series is heteroscedastic when the variability or dispersion of the time series varies with time. For instance, let's think about the spending of a household through the years. In these years, this particular household went from being poor to middle class and finally upper middle class. When the household was poor, the spending was less and only on essentials, and because of that, the variability in spending was less. But as they approached upper middle class, the household could afford luxuries, which created spikes in the time series and therefore higher variability. If we refer back to *Figure 7.1*, we can see what a heteroscedastic time series looks like.

But in addition to visual inspection, it would be neat if we could carry out an automated statistical test to ascertain heteroscedasticity.

Detecting heteroscedasticity

There are many ways to detect heteroscedasticity, but we will be using one of the most popular techniques, known as the **White test**, proposed by Halbert White in 1980. The White test uses an auxiliary regression task to check for constant variance. We run an initial regression using some covariates and calculate the residuals of this regression. Then, we fit another regression model with these residuals as the target and the covariates used in the first regression, and their squares and cross products. The final statistic is estimated by using the R^2 value of this auxiliary regression. For a detailed account of the test, head over to the *Further reading* section; for the rigorous mathematical procedure, the research paper is cited in the *References* section.

> **Reference check**
>
> To learn more about the rigorous mathematical procedure of the White test, take a look at the research paper cited in the *References* section under reference number *2*.

In the context of a time series, we adapt this formulation by using a deterministic trend model. The initial regression is done by using time as an ordinal variable and the residuals are used to carry out the White test. The White test has an implementation in statsmodels of het_white, which we will be using to carry out this test. We have wrapped all of this in a helpful function in src. transforms.stationary_utils as check_heteroscedasticity, which has only one additional parameter – confidence. Let's see how we can use that:

```
from src.transforms.stationary_utils import check_
heteroscedastisticity
check_heteroscedastisticity(y, confidence=0.05)
```

This returns a namedtuple with the following parameters:

- Heteroscedastic: A Boolean flag indicating the presence of heteroscedasticity
- lm_statistic: The **Lagrangian Multiplier** (**LM**) statistic
- lm_p_value: The p-value associated with the LM statistic

> **Best practice**
>
> The heteroscedasticity test we are doing only considers a trend in the regression and therefore, in the presence of seasonality, may not work very well. It is advised to deseasonalize the data before applying the function.

Detecting heteroscedasticity was the easier part. There are a few transforms that attempt to remove heteroscedasticity but with advantages and disadvantages. Let's take a look at a few such transforms.

Log transform

Log transform, as the name suggests, is about applying a logarithm to the time series. There are two main properties of a log transform – variance stabilization and reducing skewness – thereby making the data distribution more *normal*. And out of these, we are more interested in the first property because that is what combats heteroscedasticity.

Log transforms are typically known to reduce the variance of the data and thereby remove heteroscedasticity in the data. Intuitively, we can think of a log transform as something that *pulls in* the extreme values on the right of the histogram, at the same time stretching back the very low values on the left of the histogram.

But it has been shown that the log transform does not always stabilize the variance. In addition to that, the log transform poses another challenge in ML. The optimization of loss now happens on the log scale. This means that while optimizing the loss, the ML model might think that the loss is small enough, but when we inverse the transformation, a very small loss will blow up into a large number. Another key disadvantage is that the log transform can only be applied to strictly positive data. And if any of your data is zero or less than zero, then you will need to offset the whole distribution by adding some constant, *M*, and then applying the transform. This will also create some disturbance in the data, which can have adverse effects.

The bottom line is that we should be careful when applying a log transform. We have implemented a transformer in `src.transforms.target_transformations.py` as `LogTransformer` with just one parameter, `add_one`, which adds one before the transform and subtracts one after the inverse. Let's see how we can use it:

```
from src.transforms.target_transformations import
LogTransformer
log_transformer = LogTransformer(add_one=True)
y_log = log_transformer.fit_transform(y)
```

`y_log` is the log-transformed time series. We can call `inverse_transform` to get the original time series back.

Box-Cox transform

The log transform, although effective and common, is very *strong*. But the log is not the only monotonic transform that we can use. There are many other transforms, such as:

$$y^2, \frac{1}{y}, \frac{1}{\sqrt{y}}$$

and so on, which are collectively part of the family of power transforms. One set of transforms that is very famous and widely used in this family is the Box-Cox transforms:

$$y(\lambda) = \frac{y^\lambda - 1}{\lambda}, \text{if } \lambda \neq 0$$

$$\textit{And, } log(y), if \ \lambda = 0$$

> **Reference check**
>
> The original research paper by Box and Cox is cited in the *References* section under reference number 3.

Intuitively, we can see that the Box-Cox transform is a generalized logarithm transform. The log transform is just a special case of the Box-Cox transform (when $\lambda = 0$). At different values of λ, it approximates other transforms such as y^2 when $\lambda = 2$, $\frac{1}{\sqrt{y}}$ when $\lambda = -0.5$, $\sqrt{y}$ when $\lambda = 0.5$, and so on. When $\lambda = 1$, there is no major transformation.

A lot of the disadvantages that we mentioned for log transforms apply here as well, but the degree to which those effects are there varies, and we have a parameter, λ, to help us decide on the right level of those effects. Like log transforms, Box-Cox transforms also only use strictly positive data. The same addition of a constant to offset the data distribution has to be done here as well. The flip side of the parameter that there is one more hyperparameter to tune.

There are a few automated methods to find the optimum λ for any data distribution. One of them is by minimizing the log-likelihood of the data distribution, assuming normality. So, essentially, what we will be doing is finding the optimal λ that makes the data distribution most *normal*. This optimization is already implemented in popular implementations such as the boxcox function in the scipy. special module in scipy.

Another way to find the optimal λ is to use Guerrero's method, which is typically suited for a time series. In this method, instead of trying to conform the data distribution to a normal distribution, we try to minimize the variability of the time series across different sub-series in the time series that are homogenous. The definition of this sub-series is slightly subjective but usually, we can safely assume the sub-series as the seasonal length. Therefore, what we will be trying to minimize is the variability of the time series across different seasonality cycles.

> **Reference check**
>
> The research paper proposing Guerrero's method is cited in the *References* section under reference number *4*.

There are stark differences in the way both these optimization methods work and we need to be careful when using them. If our main concern is to remove the heteroscedastic behavior of the time series, Guerrero's method is what we can use.

We have made a transformer available in src.transforms.target_transformations. py called BoxCoxTransformer. There are a few parameters and properties that we need to be aware of:

- box_cox_lambda: This is the λ parameter to be used for the Box-Cox transform. If left set to None, the implementation will find an optimal λ.

- optimization: This can either be guerrero, which is the default setting, or loglikelihood. This determines how the λ parameter is estimated.

- seasonal_period: This is an input for finding the optimal λ parameter using Guerrero's method. Technically, this is the length of the sub-series, usually taken as the seasonality period.

- bounds: This is another parameter that controls the optimization using Guerrero's method. This is a tuple with lower and upper bounds in the search for the optimal λ parameter.

- add_one: This is a flag that adds one to the series before applying a log transform to avoid log 0.

Let's see how we can use it:

```
from src.transforms.target_transformations import
BoxCoxTransformer
boxcox_transformer = BoxCoxTransformer()
y_boxcox = boxcox _transformer.fit_transform(y)
```

y_boxcox will contain the Box-Cox transformed time series. To get back to the original time series, we can use the inverse_transform function.

When we approach the forecasting problem at scale, we will have hundreds, thousands, or millions of time series that we will need to analyze before forecasting. In such scenarios, an AutoML approach is needed to be practical.

AutoML approach to target transformation

So far, we have discussed many ways to make a series *more* stationary (we are using the word stationary here in the non-mathematical sense), such as detrending, deseasonalizing, differencing, and monotonic transformations. We've also looked at statistical tests to check whether trends, seasonality, and so on are present in a time series. So, the natural next step is to put it all together to carry out these transforms in an automated way while choosing good defaults wherever possible. This is exactly what we did and implemented an AutoStationaryTransformer in src.transforms.target_ transformations. The following flow chart explains the logic of this in an automated way:

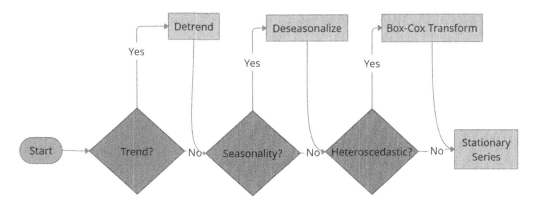

Figure 7.5 – Flow chart for AutoStationaryTransformer

We have excluded differencing from this implementation for two reasons:

- Differencing, in the context of predictions, comes with considerable baggage of technical debt. If you do differencing, you are inherently making it difficult to carry out multi-step forecasting. It is possible, but just more difficult and less flexible.

- Differencing can be looked at as a different way of doing what we have done here. This is because differencing removes linear trends and seasonal differencing removes seasonality as well. So, for autoregressive time series, differencing can do a lot and deserves to be a standalone transformation.

Now, let's see what parameters we can use to tweak `AutoStationaryTransformer`:

- `confidence`: The confidence level for the statistical tests. It defaults to `0.05`.

- `seasonal_period`: The number of periods after which the seasonality cycle repeats itself. If set to None, `seasonal_period` will be inferred from the data. It defaults to None.

- `seasonality_max_lags`: This is only used if `seasonality_period` is not given. This sets the maximum lags within which we search for seasonality. It defaults to None.

- `trend_check_params`: These are the parameters that are used in the statistical tests for trend. `check_trend` defaults to `{"mann_kendall": False}`.

- `detrender_params`: The parameters passed to `DetrendingTransformer`. This defaults to `{"degree":1}`.

- `deseasonalizer_params`: The parameters passed to `DeseasonalizingTransformer`. `seasonality_extraction` is fixed as `period_averages`.

- `box_cox_params`: The parameters that are passed to `BoxCoxTransformer`. Defaults to `{"optimization": "guerrero"}`.

Now, let's apply this automatic transformation to the dataset we have been working with:

```
train_df = pd.read_parquet(preprocessed/"selected_blocks_train_
missing_imputed_feature_engg.parquet")
transformer_pipelines = {}
for _id in tqdm(train_df["LCLid"].unique()):
    #Initialize the AutoStationaryTransformer with a
seasonality period of 48*7
    auto_stationary = AutoStationaryTransformer(seasonal_
period=48*7)

    #Creating the timeseries with datetime index
```

```
    y = train_df.loc[train_df["LCLid"]==_id, ["energy_
consumption","timestamp"]].set_index("timestamp")
    #Fitting and transforming the train
    y_stat = auto_stationary.fit_transform(y, freq="30min")
    # Setting the transformed series back to the dataframe
    train_df.loc[train_df["LCLid"]==_id, "energy_consumption"]
= y_stat.values
    #Saving the pipeline
    transformer_pipelines[_id] = auto_stationary
```

The code to execute this is split into two notebooks called `02-Dealing with Non-Stationarity.ipynb` and `02a-Dealing with Non-Stationarity-Train+Val.ipynb` in the `chapter06` folder. The former does the auto-stationary transformation on the train data, while the latter does it on train and validation data combined. This is to simulate how we would predict for validation data (by just using train data for training) and for test data (where we use the train and validation data for training).

This process is slightly time-consuming. I suggest that you run the notebook, grab lunch or a snack, and come back. Once it's done, the `02-Dealing with Non-Stationarity.ipynb` notebook will save a few files:

- `selected_blocks_train_auto_stat_target.parquet`: A DataFrame that has `LCLid` and `timestamp` as indices and the transformed target

- `auto_transformer_pipelines_train.pkl`: A Python dictionary of `Auto-StationaryTransformer` for each `LCLid` so that we can reverse the transformations in the future

The `02a-Dealing with Non-Stationarity-Train+Val.ipynb` notebook also saves the corresponding files for the train and validation datasets.

The dataset we are working on has almost negligible trends and is pretty stationary throughout. The impact of these transformations will be more evident in time series with strong trends and heteroscedasticity.

Best Practice

This kind of explicit detrending and deseasonalizing before modeling can also be seen as a form of **boosting**. This should be considered as just another alternative to modeling all of this together. There can be situations where letting the model learn from end to end in a data-driven manner performs better than injecting these strong inductive biases using explicit detrending and deseasonalization and vice versa. Cross-validated test scores should always have the last word.

Congratulations on making it through a heavy chapter full of new concepts, some statistics, and mathematics. From the point of view of applying ML models for time series, the concepts in this chapter will be really helpful in taking your models to the next level.

Summary

After getting down to a practical level in the previous chapter, we stayed there and plowed on to review concepts such as stationarity and how to deal with such non-stationary time series. We learned about techniques we can use to explicitly handle non-stationary time series such as differencing, detrending, deseasonalizing, and so on. To put this all together, we saw an automatic way of transforming the target, learned how to use the implementation provided, and applied it to our dataset. Now that we have the necessary skills to effectively transform a time series into an ML dataset, in the next chapter, we will start applying a few ML models to the dataset using the features we've created.

References

The following are the references for this chapter:

1. Bayazit M. and Önöz B. (2007), *To prewhiten or not to prewhiten in trend analysis?*, Hydrological Sciences Journal, 52:4, 611-624. https://doi.org/10.1623/hysj.52.4.611.

2. White, H. (1980), *A Heteroskedasticity-Consistent Covariance Matrix Estimator and a Direct Test for Heteroskedasticity*. Econometrica Vol. 48, No. 4 (May 1980), pp. 817-838 (22 pages). https://doi.org/10.2307/1912934.

3. Box, G. E. P. and Cox, D. R. (1964), *An analysis of transformations*. Journal of the Royal Statistical Society, Series B, 26, 211-252. http://www.ime.usp.br/~abe/lista/pdfQWaCMboK68.pdf.

4. Guerrero, Victor M. (1993), *Time-series analysis supported by power transformations*. Journal of Forecasting, Volume 12, Issue 1, 37-48. https://onlinelibrary.wiley.com/doi/10.1002/for.3980120104.

Further reading

To learn more about the topics that were covered in this chapter, take a look at the following resources:

- *Stationarity in time series analysis*, by Shay Palachy: https://towardsdatascience.com/stationarity-in-time-series-analysis-90c94f27322

- *Comparing ADF Test Functions in R*, by Fabian Kostadinov (the same concepts can be implemented in Python as well): https://fabian-kostadinov.github.io/2015/01/27/comparing-adf-test-functions-in-r/

- *Kendall's Tau*: https://www.statisticshowto.com/kendalls-tau/

- Mann-Kendall trend test: `https://www.statisticshowto.com/wp-content/uploads/2016/08/Mann-Kendall-Analysis-1.pdf`

- *Theil-Sen estimator*: `https://en.wikipedia.org/wiki/Theil%E2%80%93Sen_estimator`

- *Statistical inference with correlograms* – Wikipedia: `https://en.wikipedia.org/wiki/Correlogram#Statistical_inference_with_correlograms`

- *White test for Heteroscedasticity Detection*: `https://itfeature.com/heteroscedasticity/white-test-for-heteroskedasticity`

8

Forecasting Time Series with Machine Learning Models

In the previous chapter, we started looking at machine learning as a tool to solve the problem of time series forecasting. We talked about a few techniques such as time delay embedding and temporal embedding, both of which cast a time series forecasting problem as a classical regression problem from the machine learning paradigm. In this chapter, we'll look at these techniques in detail and go through them in a practical sense using the London Smart Meters dataset we have been working with throughout this book.

In this chapter, we will cover the following topics:

- Training and predicting with machine learning models
- Generating single-step forecast baselines
- Standardized code to train and evaluate machine learning models
- Training and predicting for multiple households

Technical requirements

You will need to set up the Anaconda environment following the instructions in the *Preface* of the book to get a working environment with all the packages and datasets required for the code in this book.

You must run the following notebooks for this chapter:

- `02 - Preprocessing London Smart Meter Dataset.ipynb` in `Chapter02`
- `01-Setting up Experiment Harness.ipynb` in `Chapter04`

- `01-Feature Engineering.ipynb` in Chapter06

- `02-Dealing with Non-Stationarity.ipynb` in Chapter07

- `02a-Dealing with Non-Stationarity-Train+Val.ipynb` in Chapter07

The code for this chapter can be found at `https://github.com/PacktPublishing/Modern-Time-Series-Forecasting-with-Python-/tree/main/notebooks/Chapter08`.

Training and predicting with machine learning models

In *Chapter 5*, *Time Series Forecasting as Regression*, we talked about a schematic for supervised machine learning (*Figure 5.2*). In the schematic, we mentioned that the purpose of a supervised learning problem is to come up with a function, $\hat{y} = h(X, \phi)$, where X is the set of features as the input, ϕ is the model parameters, and h is the approximation of the ideal function. In this section, we are going to talk about h in more detail and see how we can use different machine learning models to estimate it.

h is any function that approximates the ideal function, but it can be thought of as an element of all possible functions from a family of functions. More formally, we can say the following:

$$\hat{y} = h(X, \phi), \text{where } h \in \mathcal{H}$$

Here, $\mathcal{H}$ is a family of functions that we also call a model. For instance, linear regression is a type of model or a family of functions. For each value of the coefficients, the linear regression model gives you a different function and $\mathcal{H}$ becomes the set of all possible functions a linear regression model can produce.

There are many families of functions, or models, available. For a more complete understanding of the space, we will need to refer to machine learning books or resources. The *Further reading* section contains a few resources that may help you start the journey. As for the scope of this book, we narrowly define it as the application of machine learning models for forecasting, rather than machine learning in general. And although we can use any regression model, we will only review a few popular and useful ones for time series forecasting and see them in action. We leave it to you to strike out on your own and explore the other algorithms to become familiar with them as well. But before we look at the different models, we need to generate a few baselines again.

Generating single-step forecast baselines

We reviewed and generated a few baseline models back in *Chapter 4, Setting a Strong Baseline Forecast*. But there is a small issue – the prediction horizon. In *Chapter 6, Feature Engineering for Time Series Forecasting*, we talked about how the machine learning model can only predict one target at a time and that we are sticking with a single-step forecast. The baselines we generated earlier were not single-step, but multi-step. Generating a single-step forecast for baseline algorithms such as ARIMA or ETS requires us to fit on history, predict one step ahead, and then fit again using one more day. Predicting in such an iterative fashion for our test or validation period requires us to do this iteration ~1,440 times (48 data points a day for 30 days) and repeat this for all the households in our selected dataset (150, in our case). This would take quite a long time to compute.

We have chosen the naïve method and seasonal naïve (*Chapter 4, Setting a Strong Baseline Forecast*), which can be implemented as native `pandas` methods, as two baseline methods to generate single-step forecasts. Naïve forecasts perform unreasonably well for single-step ahead forecasts and can be considered a strong baseline. In the `chapter08` folder, there is a notebook named `00-Single Step Backtesting Baselines.ipynb` that generates these baselines and saves them to disk. Let's run the notebook now. The notebook generates the baselines for both the validation and test datasets and saves the predictions, metrics, and aggregate metrics to disk. The aggregate metrics for the test period are as follows:

	MAE	MSE	meanMASE	Forecast Bias
Naive	0.086	0.045	1.050	0.02%
Seasonal Naive	0.122	0.072	1.487	4.07%

Figure 8.1 – Aggregate metrics for a single-step baseline

To make training and evaluating these models easier, we have used a standard structure throughout. Let's quickly review that structure as well so that you can follow along with the notebooks closely.

Standardized code to train and evaluate machine learning models

There are two main ingredients while training a machine learning model – *data* and the *model* itself. Therefore, to standardize the pipeline, we defined three configuration classes (`FeatureConfig`, `MissingValueConfig`, and `ModelConfig`) and another wrapper class (`MLForecast`) over scikit-learn-style estimators (`.fit` - `.predict`) to make the process smooth. Let's look at each of them.

> **Notebook alert**
>
> To follow along with the code, use the `01-Forecasting with ML.ipynb` notebook in the `chapter08` folder and the code in the `src` folder.

FeatureConfig

`FeatureConfig` is a Python `dataclass` that defines a few key attributes and functions that are necessary while processing the data. For instance, continuous, categorical, and Boolean columns need separate kinds of preprocessing before being fed into the machine learning model. Let's see what `FeatureConfig` holds:

- `date`: A mandatory column that sets the name of the column with `date` in the DataFrame.

- `target`: A mandatory column that sets the name of the column with `target` in the DataFrame.

- `original_target`: If `target` contains a transformed target (log, differenced, and so on), `original_target` specifies the name of the column with the target without transformation. This is essential in calculating metrics such as MASE, which relies on training history. If not given, it is assumed that `target` and `original_target` are the same.

- `continuous_features`: A list of continuous features.

- `categorical_features`: A list of categorical features.

- `boolean_features`: A list of Boolean features. Boolean features are categorical but only have two unique values.

- `index_cols`: A list of columns that are set as a DataFrame index while preprocessing. Typically, we would give the datetime and, in some cases, the unique ID of a time series as indices.

- `exogenous_features`: A list of exogenous features. The features in the DataFrame may be from the feature engineering process, such as the lags or rolling features, but also external sources such as the temperature data in our dataset. This is an optional field that lets us bifurcate the exogenous features from the rest of the features. The items in this list should be a subset of `continuous_features`, `categorical_features`, or `boolean_features`.

In addition to a bit of validation on the inputs, there is also a helpful method called `get_X_y` in the class, with the following parameters:

- `df`: A DataFrame that contains all the necessary columns, including the target, if available

- `categorical`: A Boolean flag for including categorical features or not

- `exogenous`: A Boolean flag for including exogenous features or not

The function returns a tuple of (`features`, `target`, `original_target`).

All we need to do is initialize the class, like any other class, with the feature names separated into the parameters of the class. The entire code that contains all the features is available in the accompanying notebook.

After setting the `FeatureConfig` data class, we can pass any DataFrame with the features defined to the `get_X_y` function to get the features, target, and original target:

```
train_features, train_target, train_original_target = feat_
config.get_X_y(
    sample_train_df, categorical=False, exogenous=False
)
```

As you can see, we are not using categorical features or exogenous features here. We will talk about how to handle categorical features in *Chapter 15, Strategies for Global Deep Learning Forecasting Models*.

MissingValueConfig

Another key setting is how to deal with missing values. We saw a few ways to fill in missing values from a time series context in *Chapter 3, Analyzing and Visualizing Time Series Data*, and we have already filled in missing values and prepared our datasets. But a few missing values will be created in the feature engineering required to convert a time series into a regression problem. For instance, when creating lag features, the earliest date in the dataset will not have enough data to create a lag and will be left empty.

> **Best practice**
> Although filling with zero or mean is the default or go-to method for the majority of the data scientist community, we should always make an effort to fill the missing values as intelligently as possible. In terms of lag features, filling with zero can distort the feature. Instead of filling with zero, a backward fill (using the earliest value in the column to fill backward) might be a much better fit.

Some machine learning models handle empty or `NaN` features naturally, while for other machine learning models, we will need to deal with such missing values before training. It's helpful if we can define `config` in which we set for a few columns where we expect `NaN` information on how to fill those. `MissingValueConfig` is a Python `dataclass` that does just that. Let's see what it holds:

- `bfill_columns`: A list of column names that need to use a backward fill strategy to fill missing values.

- `ffill_columns`: A list of column names that need to use a forward fill strategy to fill missing values. If a column name is repeated across both `bfill_columns` and `ffill_columns`, that column is filled using backward fill first and the rest of the missing values are filled with the forward fill strategy.

- `zero_fill_columns`: A list of column names that need to be filled with zeros.

The order in which the missing values are filled is `bfill_columns` then `ffill_columns` and then `zero_fill_columns`. As the default strategy, the data class uses the column mean to fill in missing values so that even if you have not defined any strategy for a column, the missing value will be filled in by using a column mean. There is a method called `impute_missing_values` that takes in the DataFrame and fills the empty cells with a value according to the specified strategy.

ModelConfig

`ModelConfig` is a Python `dataclass` that holds a few details regarding the modeling process, such as whether to normalize the data, whether to fill missing values, and so on. Let's take a detailed look at what it holds:

- `model`: This is a mandatory parameter that can be any scikit-learn-style estimator.

- `name`: A string name or identifier for the model. If it's not used, it will revert to the name of the class that was passed in as `model`.

- `normalize`: A Boolean flag to set whether to apply `StandardScaler` to the input or not.

- `fill_missing`: A Boolean flag to set whether to fill empty values before training or not. Some models can handle NaN naturally, while others can't.

- `encode_categorical`: A Boolean flag to set whether to encode categorical columns as part of the fitting procedure. If `False`, categorical encoding is expected to be done separately and included as part of continuous features.

- `categorical_encoder`: If `encode_categorical` is True, `categorical_encoder` is the scikit-learn-style encoder we can use.

Let's see how we can define the `ModelConfig` data class:

```
model_config = ModelConfig(
    model=LinearRegression(),
    name="Linear Regression",
    normalize=True,
    fill_missing=True,
)
```

This has just one method, `clone`, that clones the estimator, along with the config, into a new instance.

MLForecast

Last but not least, we have the wrapper class around a scikit-learn-style model. It uses the different configurations we have discussed to encapsulate the training and prediction functions. Let's see what parameters are available when initializing the model:

- `model_config`: The instance of the `ModelConfig` class we discussed in the *ModelConfig* section.

- `feature_config`: The instance of the `FeatureConfig` class we discussed earlier.

- `missing_config`: The instance of the `MissingValueConfig` class we discussed earlier.

- `target_transformer`: The instance of target transformers from `src.transforms`. It should support `fit`, `transform`, and `inverse_transform`. It should also return `pd.Series` with a datetime index to work without errors. If we have done the target transform separately, then this is also used to perform `inverse_transform` during prediction.

`MLForecast` has a few functions that can help us manage the life cycle of a model, once initialized. Let's take a look.

The fit function

The `fit` function is similar in purpose to the scikit-learn `fit` function but does a little extra by handling the standardization, categorical encoding, and target transformations using the information in the three configs. The parameters of the function are as follows:

- X: The `pandas` DataFrame with features to be used in the model as columns.

- y: This is the target and can be a `pandas` DataFrame, `pandas` Series, or a `numpy` array.

- `is_transformed`: This is a Boolean parameter that lets us know whether the target is already transformed or not. If `True`, the `fit` method won't be transforming the target, even if we have initialized the object with `target_transformer`.

- `fit_kwargs`: This is a Python dictionary of keyword arguments that need to be passed to the `fit` function of the estimator.

The predict function

The `predict` function handles inferencing. It wraps around the `predict` function of the scikit-learn estimator, but like `fit`, it does a few other things, such as standardization, categorical encoding, and reversing the target transformation. There is only one parameter for this function:

- X: The `pandas` DataFrame with features to be used in the model as columns. The index of the DataFrame is passed on to the prediction.

The feature_importance function

The `feature_importance` function retrieves the feature importance from the model, if available. For linear models, it extracts the coefficients, while for tree-based models, it extracts the built-in importance and returns it in a sorted DataFrame.

Helper functions for evaluating models

In addition to these standard configurations and wrapper classes, we have also defined a couple of helper functions for evaluating different models in the notebook:

```
def evaluate_model(
    model_config,
    feature_config,
    missing_config,
    train_features,
    train_target,
    test_features,
    test_target,
):
    ml_model = MLForecast(
        model_config=model_config,
        feature_config=feat_config,
        missing_config=missing_value_config,
    )
    ml_model.fit(train_features, train_target)
    y_pred = ml_model.predict(test_features)
    feat_df = ml_model.feature_importance()
    metrics = calculate_metrics(test_target, y_pred, model_
config.name, train_target)
    return y_pred, metrics, feat_df
```

This provides us with a standard way of evaluating all the different models, as well as automating the process at scale.

Important note

The standard implementation that we have provided with this book is in no way a one-size-fits-all approach, but rather something that works best with the flow and dataset of this book. However, it does form a good starting point and guide for designing systems with your data.

Now that we have the baselines and a standard way to apply different models, let's get back to what the different models are. For the discussion ahead, let's keep *time* out of our mind because we have converted a time series forecasting problem into a regression problem and factored in *time* as a feature of the problem (the lags and rolling features).

Linear regression

Linear regression is a family of functions that takes the following form:

$$\hat{y} = \beta_0 + \sum_{i=1}^{k} X_i \beta_i,$$

Here, k is the number of features in the model and β are the parameters of the model. There is a β for each feature and a β_0, which we call the intercept, which is estimated from data. Essentially, the output is a linear combination of the feature vectors, X. As the name suggests, this is a linear function.

The model parameters can be estimated from data, $D(X_i, y_i)$, using an optimization method and loss, but the most popular method of estimation is using **ordinary least squares** (**OLS**). Here, we find the model parameters, β, which minimizes the residual sum of squares (**mean squared error** (**MSE**)):

$$RSS = \sum_{i=1}^{N} (y_i - \hat{y}_i)^2$$

The loss function here is very intuitive. We are essentially minimizing the distance between the training samples and our predicted points. The square term acts as a technique that does not cancel out positive and negative errors. Apart from the intuitiveness of the loss, another reason why this is widely chosen is that an analytical solution exists for least squares and because of that, we don't need to resort to more compute-intensive optimization techniques such as gradient descent.

Linear regression has one foot firmly planted in statistics and with the right assumptions, it can be a powerful tool. Commonly, five assumptions are associated with linear regression, as follows:

- The relationship between the independent and dependent variables is linear.
- The errors are normally distributed.
- The variance of the errors is constant across all the values of the independent variable.
- There is no autocorrelation in the errors.
- There is little to no correlation between independent variables (multi-collinearity).

But unless you are concerned about using linear regression to come up with prediction intervals (a band in which the prediction would lie with some probability), we can disregard all but the first assumption to some extent.

The linearity assumption (the first assumption) is relevant because if the variables are not linearly related, it will result in an underfit and thus poor performance. We can get around this problem to some extent by projecting the inputs into a higher dimensional space. Theoretically, we can project a non-linear problem into a higher-dimensional space, where the problem is linear. For instance, let's consider a non-linear function, $y = 3x_1^2 + 2x_2^2 + 6x_1x_2$. If we run linear regression in the input space of x_1 and x_2, we know the resulting model will be highly underfitting. But if we project the input space from x_1 and x_2 to x_1^2, x_2^2, and xy by using a polynomial transform, the function for y becomes a perfect linear fit.

The multi-collinearity assumption (the final assumption) is partly relevant to the fit of the linear function because when we have highly correlated independent variables, the estimated coefficients are highly unstable and difficult to interpret. The fitted function would still be working well, but because we have multi-collinearity, even small changes in the inputs would make the coefficients change magnitude and sign. It is best practice to check for multi-collinearity if you are using a pure linear regression. This is typically a problem in time series because the features we have extracted, such as the lag and rolling features, may be correlated with each other. Therefore, we will have to be careful while using and interpreting linear regression on time series data.

Now, let's see how we can use linear regression and evaluate the fit on a sample household from our validation dataset:

```
from sklearn.linear_model import LinearRegression
model_config = ModelConfig(
    model=LinearRegression(),
    name="Linear Regression",
    # LinearRegression is sensitive to normalized data
    normalize=True,
    # LinearRegression cannot handle missing values
    fill_missing=True,
)

y_pred, metrics, feat_df = evaluate_model(
    model_config,
    feat_config,
    missing_value_config,
    train_features,
    train_target,
    test_features,
    test_target,
)
```

The single-step forecast looks good and is already better than the naïve forecast (MAE = 0.173):

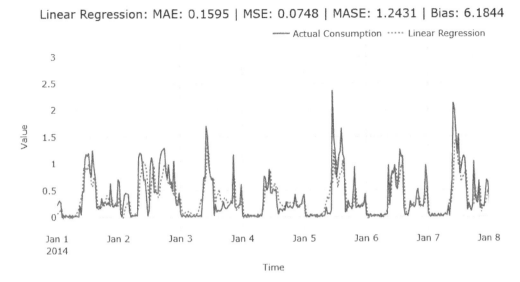

Figure 8.2 – Linear regression forecast

The coefficients of the model, β (which can be accessed using the `coef_` attribute of a trained scikit-learn model), show how much influence each feature has on the output. So, extracting and plotting them gives us our first level of visibility into the model. Let's take a look at the coefficients of the model:

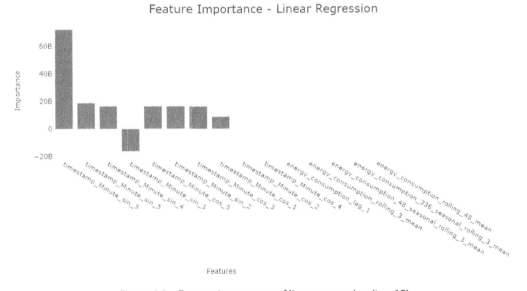

Figure 8.3 – Feature importance of linear regression (top 15)

If we look at the Y-axis in the feature importance chart, we can see it is in billions as the coefficient for a couple of features is in orders of magnitude in billions. We can also see that those features are Fourier series-based features, which are correlated with each other. Even though we have a lot of coefficients that are in billions, we can find them on both sides of zero, so they will essentially cancel out each other in the function. This is the problem with multi-collinearity that we talked about earlier. We can go about removing multi-collinear features and then perform some sort of feature selection (forward selection or backward elimination) to make the linear model even better.

But instead of that, let's look at a few modifications we can make to the linear model that are a bit more robust to multi-collinearity and feature selection.

Regularized linear regression

We briefly talked about regularization in *Chapter 5, Time Series Forecasting as Regression*, and mentioned that regularization, in the general sense, is any kind of constraint we place on the learning process to reduce the complexity of the learned function. One of the ways linear models can become more complex is by having a high magnitude of coefficients. For instance, in the linear fit, we have a coefficient of 20 billion. Any small change in that feature is going to cause a huge fluctuation in the resulting prediction. Intuitively, if we have a large coefficient, the function becomes more flexible and complex. One way we can fix this is to apply regularization in the form of weight decay. Weight decay is when we add a term that penalizes the magnitude of the coefficients to the loss function. The loss function, residual sum of squares, now becomes as follows:

$$RSS = \sum_{i=1}^{N} (y_i - \hat{y}_i)^2 + \lambda \mathcal{W}$$

Here, $\mathcal{W}$ is the weight decay and $\lambda > 0$ is the strength of regularization.

$\mathcal{W}$ is typically the norm of the weight matrix. In linear algebra, the norm of a matrix is a measure of how large its elements are. There are many norms for a matrix, but the two most common norms that are used for regularization are the **L1** and **L2** norms. When we use the L1 norm to regularize linear regression, we call it **lasso regression**, while when we use the L2 norm, we call it **ridge regression**. When we apply weight decay regularization, we are forcing the coefficients to be lower, which means that it also acts as an internal feature selection because the features that don't add a lot of value will get very low or zero (depending on the type of regularization) coefficients, which means they contribute little to nothing in the resulting function.

The L1 norm is defined as the sum of the absolute values of the matrix. For weight decay regularization, the L1 norm would be as follows:

$$\mathcal{W} = \sum_{i=1}^{k} |\beta_i|$$

L2 norm is defined as the sum of squared values of a matrix. For weight decay regularization, the L2 norm would be as follows:

$$\mathcal{W} = \sum_{i=1}^{k} \beta_i^2$$

By adding this term to the loss function of linear regression, we are forcing the coefficients to be small because while the optimizer is reducing the RSS, it is also incentivized to reduce $\mathcal{W}$.

Another way we can think about regularization is in terms of linear algebra and geometry.

> **Important note**
>
> The following section discusses the geometric intuition of regularization. Although it would make your understanding of regularization more solid, it is not essential to be able to follow the rest of this book. So, feel free to skip the next section and just read the *Key Point* callout if you are pressed for time or if you want to come back to it later when you have time.

Regularization – a geometric perspective

If we look at the L1 and L2 norms from a slightly different perspective, we will see that they are measures of distance.

Let **B** be the vector of all the coefficients, β, in linear regression. A vector is an array of numbers, but geometrically, it is also an arrow from the origin to a point in the n-dimensional coordinate space. Now, the L2 norm is nothing but the Euclidean distance from the origin on that point in space defined by the vector, **B**. The L1 norm is the Manhattan distance or taxicab distance from the origin on that point in space defined by the vector, **B**. Let's see this visually:

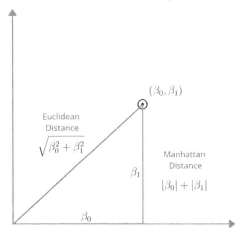

Figure 8.4 – Euclidean versus Manhattan distance

Euclidean distance is the length of the direct path from the origin to the point. But if we can only move parallel to the two axes, we will have to travel the distance of β_0 along the one axis first, and then a distance of β_1 along the other. This is the Manhattan distance.

Let's say we are in a city (for example, Manhattan) where the buildings are laid out in square blocks where the straight streets intersect at right angles, and we want to travel from point A to point B. Euclidean distance is the direct distance from point A to point B, which in the real sense is only possible if we parkour through the top of the buildings. On the other hand, the Manhattan distance is the actual distance a taxicab would take while traveling the right-angled roads from point A to point B.

To develop further geometrical intuition about the L1 and L2 norms, let's do one thought experiment. If we move the point, (β_0, β_1), in the 2D space while keeping the Euclidean distance or the L2 norm the same, we will end up with a circle with its center at the origin. This becomes a sphere in 3D and a hypersphere in n-D. If we trace out the same but keep the L1 norm the same, we will end up with a diamond with its center at the origin. This would become a cube in 3D and a hypercube in n-D.

Now, when we are optimizing for the weights, in addition to the main objective of reducing the loss function, we are also encouraging the coefficients to stay within a defined distance (norm) from the origin. Geometrically, this means that we are asking the optimization to find a vector, β, that minimizes the loss function and stays within the geometric shape (circle or square) defined by the norm. We can see this in the following diagram:

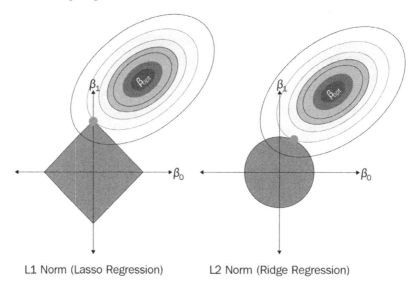

L1 Norm (Lasso Regression)   L2 Norm (Ridge Regression)

Figure 8.5 – Regularization with the L1 Norm (lasso regression) versus the L2 Norm (ridge regression)

The concentric circles in the diagram are the contours of the loss function, with the innermost being the lowest. As we move outward, the loss increases. So, instead of selecting a β_{opt}, regularized regression will select a β that intersects with the norm geometry.

This geometric interpretation also makes understanding another key difference between ridge and lasso regression. Lasso regression, because of the L1 norm, produces a sparse solution. Earlier, we mentioned that weight decay regularization does implicit feature selection. But depending on whether you are applying the L1 or L2 norm, the kind of implicit feature selection differs.

> **Key point**
>
> For an L2 norm, the coefficients of less relevant features are pushed to zero, but not exactly zero. The feature will still play a role in the final function, but its influence will be minuscule. The L1 norm, on the other hand, pushes the coefficients of such features completely to zero, resulting in a sparse solution.

This can be understood better using the geometrical interpretation of regularization. In optimization, the interesting points are usually found in the extrema or *corners* of a shape. There are no corners in a circle, so an L2 norm is created; the minima can lie anywhere on the edge of the circle. But for the diamond, we have four corners, and the minima would lie in those corners. So, with the L2 norm, the solution can move very close to zero, but not necessarily zero. However, with the L1 norm, the solution would be on the corners, where the coefficient can be pushed to an absolute zero.

Now, let's see how we can use ridge regression and evaluate the fit on a sample household from our validation dataset:

```
from sklearn.linear_model import RidgeCV
model_config = ModelConfig(
    model=RidgeCV(),
    name="Ridge Regression",
    # RidgeCV is sensitive to normalized data
    normalize=True,
    # RidgeCV does not handle missing values
    fill_missing=True
)
y_pred, metrics, feat_df = evaluate_model(
    model_config,
    feat_config,
    missing_value_config,
    train_features,
    train_target,
    test_features,
    test_target,
)
```

Let's look at the single-step ahead forecast from `RidgeCV`. It looks very similar to linear regression. Even the MAE is the same for this household:

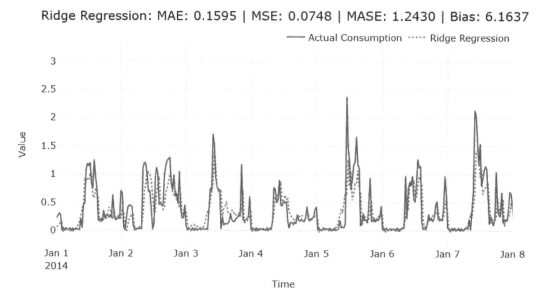

Figure 8.6 – Ridge regression forecast

But it is interesting to look at the coefficients with the L2 regularized model. Let's take a look at the coefficients of the model:

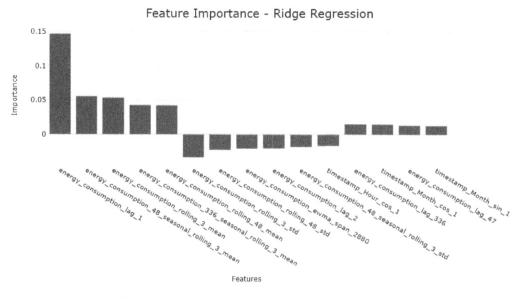

Figure 8.7 – Feature importance of ridge regression (top 15)

Now, the *Y*-axis looks reasonable and small. The coefficients for the multi-collinear features have shrunk to a more reasonable level. Features such as the lag features, which should ideally be highly influential, have gained the top spots. As you may recall, in the linear regression (*Figure 8.3*), these features were dwarfed by the huge coefficients on the Fourier features. We have just plotted the top 15 features here, but if you look at the entire list, you will see that there will be a lot of features for which the coefficients are close to zero.

Now, let's try lasso regression on the sample household:

```
from sklearn.linear_model import LassoCV
model_config = ModelConfig(
    model=LassoCV(),
    name="Lasso Regression",
    # LassoCV is sensitive to normalized data
    normalize=True,
    # LassoCV does not handle missing values
    fill_missing=True
)
y_pred, metrics, feat_df = evaluate_model(
    model_config,
    feat_config,
    missing_value_config,
    train_features,
    train_target,
    test_features,
    test_target,
)
```

Let's look at the single-step ahead forecast from `LassoCV`. Like ridge regression, there is hardly any visual difference from linear regression:

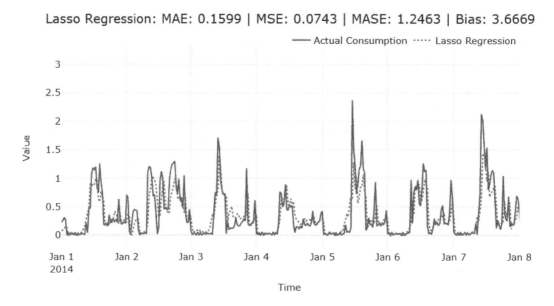

Figure 8.8 – Lasso regression forecast

Let's look at the coefficients of the model:

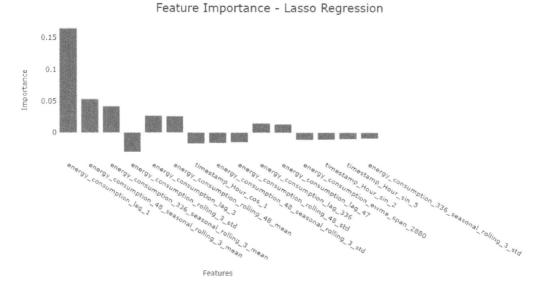

Figure 8.9 – Feature importance of lasso regression (top 15)

The coefficients are very similar to ridge regression, but if you look at the full list of coefficients (in the notebook), you will see that there are a lot of features where the coefficients will be zero.

Even with the same MAE, MSE, and so on, ridge or lasso regression is preferred to linear regression because of the additional stability and robustness that comes with regularized regression, especially for forecasting, where multi-collinearity is almost always there. But we need to keep in mind that all the linear regression models are still only capturing linear relationships. If the dataset has a non-linear relationship, the resulting fit from linear regression won't be as good and, sometimes, will be terrible.

Now, let's switch tracks and look at another class of models – **decision trees**.

Decision trees

Decision trees are another family of functions that is much more expressive than a linear function. Decision trees split the feature space into different sub-spaces and fit a very simple model (such as an average) to each. Let's understand how this partitioning works with an example. Let's consider a regression problem for predicting Y with just one feature, X, as shown in the following diagram:

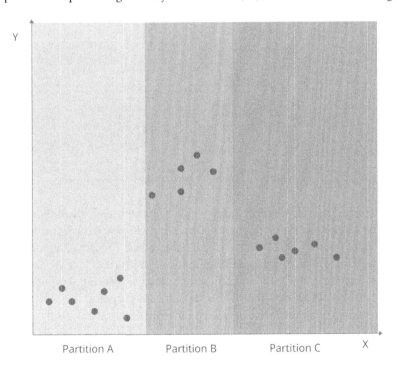

Figure 8.10 – The feature space partitioned by a decision tree

Right away, we can see that fitting a linear function would result in an underfit. But what decision trees do is split the feature space (here, it is just X) into different regions where the target, Y, is similar and then fit a simple function such as an average (because it is a regression problem). In this case, the decision tree has split the feature space into partitions – A, B, and C. Now, for any X that falls into partition A, the prediction function will return the average of all the points in partition A.

These partitions are formed by creating a decision tree using data. Intuitively, a decision tree creates a set of if-else conditions and tries to arrive at the best way to partition the feature space to maximize the homogeneity of the target variable within the partition. One helpful way to understand what a decision tree does is to think of data points as beads flowing down a tree, taking a path that is based on its features, and ending up in a final resting place. Before we talk about how to create a decision tree from data, let's take a look at its components and understand the terminology surrounding it:

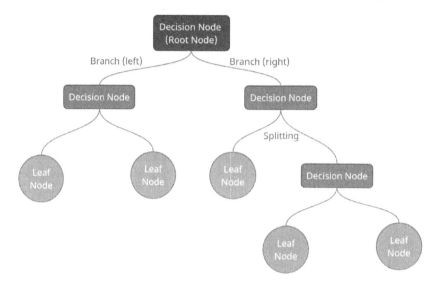

Figure 8.11 – Anatomy of a decision tree

There are two types of nodes in a decision tree – a **decision node** and a **leaf node**. A decision node is the *if-else* statement we mentioned previously. This node will have a condition based on which the data points that flow down the tree take the left or right **branch**. The decision node that sits right at the top has a special name – the **root node**. Finally, the process of dividing the data points based on a condition and directing it to the right or left branch is called **splitting**. Leaf nodes are nodes that don't have any other branches below them. These are final resting points in the *beads flowing down a tree* analogy. These are the partitions we discussed earlier in this section.

Formally, we can define the function that's been generated by a decision tree that has M partitions, $P_1, P_2, ..., P_M$, as follows:

$$\hat{y} = \sum_{m=1}^{M} c_m I(x \in P_m)$$

Here, x is the input, c_m is the constant response for the region, P_m, and I is a function that is 1 if $x \in P_m$; otherwise, it's 0.

For regression trees, we usually adopt the squared loss as the loss function. In that case, c_m is usually set as the average of all y, where the corresponding x falls in the P_m partition.

Now that we know how a decision tree functions, the only thing left to understand is how to decide which feature to split on and where to split the feature.

> **Additional note**
>
> Many algorithms have been proposed over the years on how to create a decision tree from data such as ID3, C4.5, CART, and so on. **Classification and Regression Trees (CART)** is one of the most popular methods out of the lot and it supports regression as well. Therefore, we will just stick to CART in this book.

The most optimal set of binary partitions that minimizes the sum of squares globally is generally intractable. So, we adopt a greedy algorithm to create the decision tree. Greedy optimization is a heuristic that builds up a solution stage by stage, selecting a local optimum at each stage. Therefore, instead of finding the best feature splits globally, we will create the decision tree, decision node by decision node, where we choose the most optimal feature split at each stage. For a regression tree, we choose a split feature, f, and split point, s, so that it creates two partitions, P_1 and P_2, that minimize, as follows:

$$\sum_{x_i \in P_1} (y_i - c_1)^2 + \sum_{x_i \in P_2} (y_i - c_2)^2$$

Here, c_1 and c_2 is the average of all y, where the corresponding x falls in-between P_1 and P_2, respectively.

Therefore, by using this criterion, we can keep splitting the regions further and further. With each level we split, we increase the **depth** of the tree by one. But at some point, we will start overfitting the dataset. But if we don't do enough splits, we might be underfitting the data as well. One strategy is to stop creating further splits when we reach a predetermined depth. In the scikit-learn implementation of `DecisionTreeRegressor`, this corresponds to the `max_depth` parameter. This is a hyperparameter that needs to be estimated using a validation dataset. There are other strategies to stop the splits, such as setting a minimum number of samples required to split (`min_samples_split`), or a minimum decrease in cost to carry out a split (`min_impurity_decrease`). For a complete list of parameters in `DecisionTreeRegressor`, please refer to the documentation at `https://scikit-learn.org/stable/modules/generated/sklearn.tree.DecisionTreeRegressor.html`.

Now, let's see how we can use a decision tree and evaluate the fit on a sample household from our validation dataset:

```
from sklearn.tree import DecisionTreeRegressor
model_config = ModelConfig(
    model=DecisionTreeRegressor(max_depth=4, random_state=42),
    name="Decision Tree",
```

```
    # Decision Tree is not affected by normalization
    normalize=False,
    # Decision Tree in scikit-learn does not handle missing
values
    fill_missing=True,
)
y_pred, metrics, feat_df = evaluate_model(
    model_config,
    feat_config,
    missing_value_config,
    train_features,
    train_target,
    test_features,
    test_target,
)
```

Let's take a look at the single-step forecast from `DecisionTreeRegressor`. It's not doing as well as the linear or regularized linear regression models we have run so far:

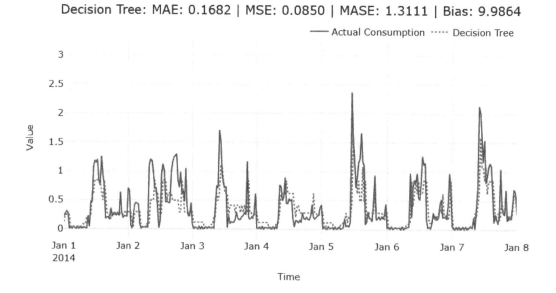

Figure 8.12 – Decision tree forecast

For the linear models, some coefficients helped us understand how much each feature was important to the prediction function. In decision trees, we don't have any coefficients, but the feature importance is still estimated using the mean decrease in the loss function, which is attributed to each feature in the tree construction process. This can be accessed in scikit-learn models by using the `feature_importance_` attribute of the trained model. Let's take a look at this feature importance:

Figure 8.13 – Feature importance of a decision tree (top 15)

Best practice

Although the default feature importance is a quick and easy way to check how the different features are used, due diligence should be applied before using them for any other purposes, such as feature selection or making business decisions. This way of assessing feature importance gives misleadingly high values for some continuous features and high cardinality categorical features. It is recommended to use permutation importance (`sklearn.inspection.permutation_importance`) for an easy but better assessment of feature importance. The *Further reading* contains some resources regarding the interpretability of models, which can be a good start to understanding what influences the models.

Here, we can see that the important features such as the lag and seasonal rolling features are coming up at the top.

We talked about overfitting and underfitting in *Chapter 5, Time Series Forecasting as Regression*. These are also referred to high bias (underfitting) and high variance (overfitting) in machine learning parlance (the *Further reading* section contains links if you wish to read up more about bias and variance and the trade-off between them). A decision tree is an algorithm that is highly prone to overfitting or high variance because, unlike the linear function, if given enough expressiveness, it can memorize the training dataset by partitioning the feature space. Another key disadvantage is a decision tree's inability to extrapolate. Let's consider a feature, f, that linearly increases our target variable, y. The training data we have has f_{max} as the maximum value for f and y_{max} as the maximum value for y. Since the decision tree partitions the feature space and assigns a constant value for that partition, even if we provide $f > f_{max}$, we will still only get a prediction of $\hat{y} \le y_{max}$.

Now, let's look at a model that uses decision trees, but in an ensemble and doesn't overfit as much.

Random forest

Ensemble learning is a process in which we use multiple models, or experts, and combine them in a way to solve the problem at hand. It taps into the *wisdom of the crowd* approach, which suggests that the decision-making of a group of people is typically better than any individual in that group. In the machine learning context, these individual models are called **base learners**. A single model may not perform well because it's overfitting the dataset, but when we combine multiple such models, they can form a strong learner.

Bagging is a form of ensemble learning where we use bootstrap sampling (sampling repeatedly with replacement from a population) to draw different subsets of the dataset, train weak learners on each of these subsets, and combine them by averaging or voting (for regression and classification, respectively). Bagging works best for high-variance, low-bias weak learners and the decision tree is a prime successful candidate with bagging. Theoretically, bagging maintains the same level of bias on the weak learners but reduces the variance, resulting in a better model. But if the weak learners are correlated with each other, the benefits of bagging will be limited.

In 2001, Leo Brieman proposed **Random forest**, which substantially modifies standard bagging by building a large collection of decorrelated trees. He proposed to alter the tree building procedure slightly to make sure all the trees that are grown on bootstrapped datasets are not correlated with each other.

> **Reference check**
>
> The original research paper for Random Forest is cited in the *References* section as reference *1*.

In the Random Forest algorithm, we decide how many trees to build. Let's call that *M* trees. Now, for each tree, the following steps are repeated:

1. Draw a bootstrap sample from the training dataset.

2. Select *f* features at random from all the features.

3. Pick the best split just using *f* features and split the node into two child nodes.

4. Repeat *steps 2* and *3* until we hit any of the defined stopping criteria.

This set of *M* trees is the Random Forest. The key difference here from regular trees is the random sampling of features at each split, which increases randomness and reduces the correlation in the outputs of different trees. While predicting, we use each of these *M* trees to get a prediction. For regression problems, we average them, while for classification problems, we take the majority vote. The final prediction function that we learn from the Random Forest for regression is as follows:

$$\hat{y} = \frac{1}{M} \sum_{t=1}^{M} \mathcal{T}_t(x)$$

Here, $\mathcal{T}_t(x)$ is the output of the *t*th tree in the Random Forest.

All the hyperparameters that we have to control the complexity of the decision tree are applicable here as well (RandomForestRegressor from scikit-learn) and in addition to those, we have two other important parameters – the number of trees to build in the ensemble (n_estimators) and the number of features randomly chosen for each split (max_features).

Now, let's see how we can use Random Forest and evaluate the fit on a sample household from our validation dataset:

```
from sklearn.ensemble import RandomForestRegressor
model_config = ModelConfig(
    model=RandomForestRegressor(random_state=42, max_depth=4),
    name="Random Forest",
    # RandomForest is not affected by normalization
    normalize=False,
    # RandomForest in scikit-learn does not handle missing
values
    fill_missing=True,
)
y_pred, metrics, feat_df = evaluate_model(
    model_config,
    feat_config,
    missing_value_config,
```

```
    train_features,
    train_target,
    test_features,
    test_target,
)
```

Let's take a look at this single-step forecast from `RandomForestRegressor`. It's better than the decision tree, but it's not as good as the linear models. However, we should keep in mind that we have not tuned the model and may be able to get better results by setting the right hyperparameters.

Now, let's take a look at the forecast that was generated using Random Forest:

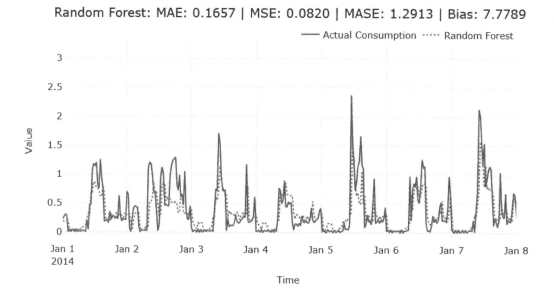

Figure 8.14 – Random Forest forecast

Just like the feature importance in decision trees, Random Forests also have a very similar mechanism for estimating the feature importance. Since we have a lot of trees in the Random Forest, we accumulate the decrease in split criterion across all the trees in the forest and arrive at a single feature of importance for the Random Forest. This can be accessed in scikit-learn models by using the `feature_importance_` attribute of the trained model. Let's take a look at this feature importance:

Figure 8.15 – Feature importance of a decision tree (top 15)

Here, we can see that the feature importance is very much similar to decision trees. The same caveat about this kind of feature importance applies here as well. This is just a quick and dirty way of looking at what the model is using internally.

Typically, Random Forest achieves good performance on many datasets with very little tuning, so Random Forests are a very popular option in machine learning. The fact that it is difficult to overfit with a Random Forest also increases their appeal. But since Random Forest uses decision trees as the weak learners, the inability of decision trees to extrapolate is passed down to Random Forest as well.

> **Additional note**
>
> The scikit-learn implementation of Random Forest can get a bit slow for a large number of trees and data sizes. Instead, we can use the Random Forest implementation from XGBoost, called XGBRFRegressor, and very similar hyperparameters. In most cases, this is a drop-in replacement and gives almost the same results. The minor difference is due to small implementation details. We have used this variant as well in the notebooks. This variant is preferred going forward because of obvious runtime considerations. It also handles missing values natively and saves us from an additional preprocessing step. More details about the implementation and how to use it can be found here: https://xgboost.readthedocs.io/en/latest/tutorials/rf.html.

Now, let's look at one last family of functions that is one of the most powerful learning methods and has proven exceedingly well in a wide variety of datasets – gradient boosting.

Gradient boosting decision trees

Boosting, like bagging, is another ensemble method that uses a few weak learners to produce a powerful committee of models. The key difference between bagging and boosting is in the way the weak learners are combined. Instead of building different models in parallel on bootstrapped datasets, as bagging does, boosting uses the weak learners in a sequential manner, with each weak learner applied to repeatedly modified versions of the data.

To understand the additive function formulation, let's consider this function:

$$F(x) = 25 + x^2 + cos(x)$$

We can break this function into $f_1(x) = 25, f_2(x) = x^2, f_3(x) = cos(x)$ and rewrite $F(x)$ as follows:

$$F(x) = f_1(x) + f_2(x) + f_3(x)$$

This is the kind of additive ensemble function we are learning in boosting. Although, in theory, we can use any weak learner, decision trees are the de facto and most popular choice. So, let's use decision trees to explore how gradient boosting works.

Earlier, when we were discussing decision trees, we saw that a decision tree that has M partitions, $P_1, P_2, ..., P_M$, is as follows:

$$\mathcal{T}(x) = \sum_{m=1}^{M} c_m I(x \in P_m)$$

Here, x is the input, c_m is the constant response for the region, P_m, and I is a function that is 1 if $x \in P_m$; otherwise, it is 0. A boosted decision tree model is a sum of such trees:

$$\hat{y} = \sum_{k=1}^{M} \mathcal{T}_k(x)$$

Since finding the optimal partitions, P, and the constant value, c, for all the trees in the ensemble is a very difficult optimization problem, we usually adopt a suboptimal, stagewise solution where we optimize each step as we build the ensemble. In gradient boosting, we use the gradient of the loss to direct our optimization, hence the name.

Let the loss function we are using in the training be $\mathcal{L}(y, y)$. Since we are looking at a stagewise additive functional form, we can replace $\hat{Y}_k$ with $\hat{y}_{k-1} + \mathcal{T}_k(x)$, where $\hat{y}_{k-1}$ is the prediction of the sum of all trees until k-1 and $\mathcal{T}_k(x)$ is the prediction of the tree at stage k. Let's look at what the gradient boosting learning procedure for a training data $\mathcal{D}$ with N samples is:

1. Initialize the model with a constant value by minimizing the loss function:

$$F_{0(x)} = \arg \min_{b_0} \sum_{i=1}^{N} \mathcal{L}(y_i, b_0)$$

- b_0 is the prediction of the model that minimizes the loss function at the 0th iteration. At this iteration, we do not have any weak learners yet and this optimization is independent of any feature.

- For squared error loss, this works out to be the average of all training samples, while for the absolute error loss, it's the median.

2. Now that we have the initial solution, we can start the tree-building process. For $k=1$ to M, we must do the following:

   I.   Compute $r_k = -[\frac{\delta \mathcal{L}(y, F_{k-1(x)})}{\delta F_{k-1(x)}}]$ for all the training samples:

   - r_k is the derivative of the loss function with respect to $F(x)$ from the last iteration. It's also called pseudo-residuals.

   - For squared error loss, this is just the residual, $(\hat{y} - y)$.

   II. Build a regular regression tree to the r_k values with M_k partitions or leaf nodes, P_{mk}.

   III. Compute $\rho_t = \arg \min_{\rho} \sum_{i=1}^{N} \mathcal{L}(y_i, F_{k-1(x_i)} + \rho \mathcal{T}_k(x_i))$:

   - ρ_k is the scaling factor of the leaf or partition values for the current stage.

   - $\mathcal{T}_k(x_i)$ is the function that was learned by the decision tree from the current stage.

   IV. Update $F_k(x) = F_{k-1}(x) + \eta \times \rho_k \times \mathcal{T}_k(x_i)$:

   - η is the shrinkage parameter or learning rate.

Boosting, typically, is a high variance algorithm. This means that the chance of overfitting the training dataset is quite high and that enough measures need to be taken to make sure it doesn't happen. There are many ways regularization and capacity constraining have been implemented in gradient-boosted trees. As always, all the key parameters that decision trees have to reduce capacity to fit the data are valid here because the weak learner is a decision tree. In addition to that, there are two other key parameters – the number of trees, M (n_estimators in scikit-learn), and the learning rate, η (learning_rate in scikit-learn).

When we apply a learning rate in the additive formulation, we are essentially shrinking each weak learner, thus reducing the effect of any one weak learner on the overall function. This was originally referred to as shrinkage, but now, in all the popular implementations of gradient-boosted trees, it is referred to as the learning rate. The number of trees and the learning rate are highly interdependent. For the same problem, we will need a greater number of trees if we reduce the learning rate. It has been empirically shown that a lower learning rate improves the generalization error. Therefore, a very effective and convenient way is to set the learning rate to a very low value (<0.1) and a very high value for the number of trees (>5,000) and train the gradient boosted tree with early stopping. Early stopping is when we use a validation dataset to monitor the out-of-sample performance while training the model. We stop adding more trees to the ensemble when the out-of-sample error stops reducing.

Another key technique a lot of the implementations adopt is subsampling. Subsampling can be done on rows and columns. Row subsampling is similar to bootstrapping, where each candidate in the ensemble is trained on a subsample of the dataset. Column subsampling is similar to random feature selection in Random Forest. Both these techniques introduce a regularization effect to the ensemble and help reduce generalization error. Some implementations of gradient boosted trees, such as `XGBoost` and `LightGBM`, implement L1 and L2 regularization directly in the objective function as well.

There are many implementations of regression gradient-boosted trees. A few popular implementations are as follows:

- `GradientBoostingRegressor` and `HistGradientBoostingRegressor` in scikit-learn

- XGBoost by T Chen

- LightGBM from Microsoft

- CatBoost from Yandex

Each of these implementations offer changes that range from subtle to very fundamental regarding the standard gradient boosting algorithm. We have included a few resources in the *Further reading* section so that you can read up on these differences and get acquainted with the different parameters they support.

For our exercise, we are going to use LightGBM from Microsoft Research because it is one of the fastest and best-performing implementations. LightGBM and CatBoost also support categorical features out of the box and handle missing values natively.

Reference check

The original research papers for XGBoost, LightGBM, and CatBoost are cited in the *References* section as *2*, *3*, and *4*, respectively.

Now, let's see how we can use LightGBM and evaluate the fit on a sample household from our validation dataset:

```python
from lightgbm import LGBMRegressor
model_config = ModelConfig(
    model=LGBMRegressor(random_state=42),
    name="LightGBM",
    # LightGBM is not affected by normalization
    normalize=False,
    # LightGBM handles missing values
    fill_missing=False,
)
y_pred, metrics, feat_df = evaluate_model(
    model_config,
    feat_config,
    missing_value_config,
    train_features,
    train_target,
    test_features,
    test_target,
)
```

Let's take a look at the single-step forecast from `LGBMRegressor`. It's already significantly better than all the other models we have tried so far:

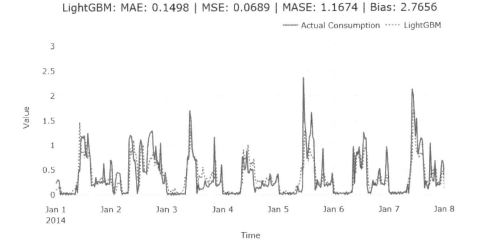

Figure 8.16 – LightGBM forecast

Just like the feature importance in decision trees, gradient boosting implementations also have a very similar mechanism for estimating the feature importance. The feature importance for the ensemble is given by the average of split criteria reduction attributed to each feature in all the trees. This can be accessed in the scikit-learn API as the `feature_importance_` attribute of the trained model. Let's take a look at this feature importance:

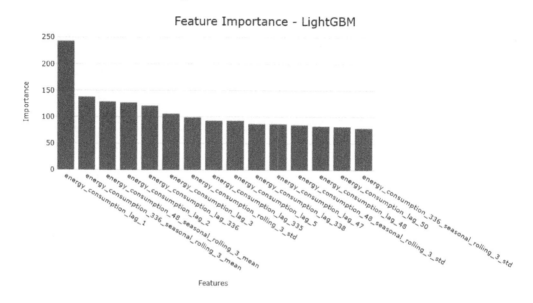

Figure 8.17 – Feature importance of LightGBM (top 15)

There are multiple ways of getting feature importance from the model, and each implementation has slightly different ways of calculating it. This is controlled by parameters. The most common ways of extracting it (sticking to LightGBM terminology) are `split` and `gain`. If we choose `split`, the feature importance is the number of times a feature is used to split nodes in the trees. On the other hand, `gain` is the total reduction in the split criterion. This can be attributed to any feature. *Figure 8.17* shows `split`, which is the default value in LightGBM. We can see that the order of the feature importance is very much similar to decision trees, or Random Forests with almost the same features taking the top three spots.

Gradient boosted decision trees (GBDTs) typically give us very good performance on tabular data and time series as regression is no exception. This very strong model has usually been part of almost all winning entries in Kaggle competitions on time series forecasting in the recent past. While it is one of the best machine learning model families, it still has a few disadvantages:

- GBDTs are high variance algorithms and hence prone to overfitting. This is why all kinds of regularization are applied in different ways in most of the successful implementations of GBDTs.

- GBDTs usually take longer to train (although many modern implementations have made this faster) and are not easily parallelizable as a Random Forest. In Random Forest, we can train all the trees in parallel because they are independent of each other. But in GBDTs, the sequential nature of the algorithm restricts parallelization. All the successful implementations have clever ways of enabling parallelization when creating a decision tree. LightGBM has many parallelization strategies, such as feature parallel, data parallel, and voting parallel. Details regarding these can be found at `https://lightgbm.readthedocs.io/en/latest/Features.html#optimization-in-distributed-learning` and are worth understanding. The documentation of the library also contains a helpful guide in choosing between these parallelization strategies in a table:

	Data is Small	Data is Large
# of Features is Small	Feature Parallel	Data Parallel
# of Features is Large	Feature Parallel	Voting Parallel

Table 8.1 – Parallelization strategies in LightGBM

- Extrapolation is a problem for GBDTs just like it is a problem for all tree-based models. There is some very weak potential for extrapolation in GBDTs, but nothing that solves the problem. Therefore, if your time series has some strong trends, tree-based methods will, most likely, fail to capture the trend. Either training the model on detrended data or switching to another model class would be the way forward. An easy way to do detrending would be to use `AutoStationaryTransformer`, which we discussed in *Chapter 6, Feature Engineering for Time Series Forecasting*.

To summarize, let's look at the metrics and runtime that were taken by these machine learning models. If you have run the notebook along with this chapter, then you will find the following summary table in there as well:

Algorithm	MAE	MSE	MASE	Forecast Bias	Time Elapsed
Naive	0.1753	0.1050	1.3664	0.03%	nan
Seasonal Naive	0.2377	0.1709	1.8521	4.80%	nan
Linear Regression	0.1595	0.0748	1.2431	6.18%	0.490227
Ridge Regression	0.1595	0.0748	1.2430	6.16%	0.425553
Lasso Regression	0.1599	0.0743	1.2463	3.67%	0.949244
Decision Tree	0.1682	0.0850	1.3111	9.99%	0.474296
Random Forest	0.1657	0.0820	1.2913	7.78%	26.353781
XGB Random Forest	0.1644	0.0818	1.2808	9.35%	1.786139
LightGBM	0.1498	0.0689	1.1674	2.77%	0.435123

Figure 8.18 – Summary of the metrics and runtimes for a sample household

Right off the bat, we can see that all of the machine learning models we tried have performed better than the baselines in all metrics except the forecast bias. The three linear regression models perform well with almost equal performance on MAE, MASE, and MSE, with a slight increase in runtimes for regularized models. The decision tree has underperformed, but this is usually expected. Decision trees need to be tuned a little better to reduce overfitting. Random Forest (both the scikit-learn and XGBoost implementations) have improved the decision tree's performance, which is what we would expect. One key thing to note here is that the XGBoost implementation of Random Forest is almost six times faster than the scikit-learn one. Finally, LightGWM has the best performance across all metrics and a faster runtime.

Now, this was just one household out of all the selected ones. To see how well these models are doing, we need to evaluate them on all selected households.

Training and predicting for multiple households

We have picked a few models (LassoCV, XGBRFRegressor, and LGBMRegressor) that are doing better in terms of metrics, as well as runtime, to run on all the selected households in our validation dataset. The process is straightforward: loop over all the unique combinations, inner loop over the different models to run, and then train, predict, and evaluate. The code is available in the 01-Forecasting with ML.ipynb notebook in chapter08, under the *Running an ML Forecast For All Consumers* heading. You can run the code and take a break because this is going to take a little less than an hour. The notebook also calculates the metrics and contains a summary table that will be ready for you when you're back. Let's look at the summary now:

Algorithm	MAE	MSE	meanMASE	Forecast Bias
Naive	0.0882	0.0450	1.1014	-0.00%
Seasonal Naive	0.1292	0.0777	1.6004	-1.00%
Lasso Regression	0.0802	0.0271	1.0052	-0.29%
XGB Random Forest	0.0808	0.0306	1.0177	-2.43%
LightGBM	0.0772	0.0275	0.9781	0.05%

Figure 8.19 – Aggregate metrics on all the households in the validation dataset

Here, we can see that even at the aggregated level, the different models we used perform as expected. The notebook also saves the predictions for the validation set on disk.

> **Notebook alert**
>
> We also need to run another notebook, called 01a-Forecasting with ML for Test Dataset.ipynb, in chapter08. This notebook follows the same process, generates the forecast, and calculates the metrics on the test dataset.

The aggregate metrics for the test dataset are as follows (from the notebook):

Algorithm	MAE	MSE	meanMASE	Forecast Bias
Naive	0.086	0.045	1.050	0.02%
Seasonal Naive	0.122	0.072	1.487	4.07%
Lasso Regression	0.077	0.026	0.946	0.99%
XGB Random Forest	0.078	0.030	0.966	-0.18%
LightGBM	0.075	0.027	0.914	2.57%

Figure 8.20 – Aggregate metrics on all the households in the test dataset

In *Chapter 6, Feature Engineering for Time Series Forecasting*, we used `AutoStationaryTransformer` on all the households and saved the transformed dataset.

Using AutoStationaryTransformer

The process is really similar to what we did earlier in this chapter, but with small changes. We read in the transformed targets and joined them to our regular dataset in such a way that the original target is named `energy_consumption` and the transformed target is named `energy_consumption_auto_stat`:

```
#Reading the missing value imputed and train test split data
train_df = pd.read_parquet(preprocessed/"block_0-7_train_
missing_imputed_feature_engg.parquet")
auto_stat_target = pd.read_parquet(preprocessed/"block_0-7_
train_auto_stat_target.parquet")
transformer_pipelines = joblib.load(preprocessed/"auto_
transformer_pipelines_train.pkl")
#Reading in validation as test
test_df = pd.read_parquet(preprocessed/"block_0-7_val_missing_
imputed_feature_engg.parquet")
# Joining the transformed target
train_df = train_df.set_index(['LCLid','timestamp']).join(auto_
stat_target).reset_index()
```

And while defining `FeatureConfig`, we used `energy_consumption_auto_stat` as `target` and `energy_consumption` as `original_target`.

> **Notebook check**
>
> The `02-Forecasting with ML and Target Transformation.ipynb` and `02a-Forecasting with ML and Target Transformation for Test Dataset.ipynb` notebooks use these transformed targets to generate the forecasts for the validation and test datasets, respectively.

Let's look at the summary metrics that were generated by these notebooks on the transformed data:

Algorithm	MAE	MSE	meanMASE	Forecast Bias
Naive	0.088	0.045	1.101	-0.00%
Seasonal Naive	0.129	0.078	1.600	-1.00%
Lasso Regression	0.080	0.027	1.005	-0.29%
XGB Random Forest	0.081	0.031	1.018	-2.43%
LightGBM	0.077	0.028	0.978	0.05%
Lasso Regression_auto_stat	0.083	0.030	1.055	-3.50%
XGB Random Forest_auto_stat	0.086	0.033	1.098	-8.33%
LightGBM_auto_stat	0.079	0.029	1.002	-4.41%

Figure 8.21 – Aggregate metrics on all the households with transformed targets in the validation dataset

The target transformed models are not performing as well as the original ones. This might be because the dataset doesn't have any strong trends.

Congratulations on making it through a very heavy and packed chapter full of theory as well as practice. We hope this has enhanced your understanding of machine learning and skills in applying these modern techniques to time series data.

Summary

This was a very practical and hands-on chapter where we developed some standard code to train and evaluate multiple models. Then, we reviewed a few key machine learning models and how they work behind the hood. To complete and reinforce what we learned, we applied the machine learning models we learned about to the dataset and saw how well they did.

In the next chapter, we will start combining different forecasts into a single forecast and explore concepts such as combinatorial optimization and stacking to achieve state-of-the-art results.

References

The following references were provided in this chapter:

1. Breiman, L. *Random Forests*, Machine Learning 45, 5–32 (2001): `https://doi.org/10.1023/A:1010933404324`.

2. Chen, Tianqi and Guestrin, Carlos. (2016). *XGBoost: A Scalable Tree Boosting System*. Proceedings of the 22nd ACM SIGKDD International Conference on Knowledge Discovery and Data Mining (KDD '16). Association for Computing Machinery, New York, NY, USA, 785–794: `https://doi.org/10.1145/2939672.2939785`.

3. Ke, Guolin et.al. (2017), *LightGBM: A Highly Efficient Gradient Boosting Decision Tree*. Advances in Neural Information Processing Systems, pages 3149-3157: `https://dl.acm.org/doi/pdf/10.5555/3294996.3295074`.

4. Prokhorenkova, Liudmila, Gusev, Gleb et al. (2018), *CatBoost: unbiased boosting with categorical features*. Proceedings of the 32nd International Conference on Neural Information Processing Systems (NIPS'18): `https://dl.acm.org/doi/abs/10.5555/3327757.3327770`.

Further reading

To learn more about the topics that were covered in this chapter, take a look at the following resources:

- *The difference between L1 and L2 regularization*, by Terrence Parr: `https://explained.ai/regularization/L1vsL2.html`

- *L1 Norms versus L2 Norms*, by Aleksey Bilogur: `https://www.kaggle.com/residentmario/l1-norms-versus-l2-norms`

- *Interpretability – Cracking Open the Black Box*, by Manu Joseph: `https://deep-and-shallow.com/2019/11/13/interpretability-cracking-open-the-black-box-part-ii/`

- *The Gradient Boosters – Part III: XGBoost*, by Manu Joseph: `https://deep-and-shallow.com/2020/02/12/the-gradient-boosters-iii-xgboost/`

- *The Gradient Boosters – Part IV: LightGBM*, by Manu Joseph: `https://deep-and-shallow.com/2020/02/21/the-gradient-boosters-iii-lightgbm/`

- *The Gradient Boosters – Part V: CatBoost*, by Manu Joseph: `https://deep-and-shallow.com/2020/02/29/the-gradient-boosters-v-catboost/`

- *The Gradient Boosters – Part II: Regularized Greedy Forest*, by Manu Joseph: `https://deep-and-shallow.com/2020/02/09/the-gradient-boosters-ii-regularized-greedy-forest/`

- LightGBM Distributed Learning Guide: `https://lightgbm.readthedocs.io/en/latest/Parallel-Learning-Guide.html`

9

Ensembling and Stacking

In the previous chapter, we looked at a few machine learning algorithms and used them to generate forecasts on the London Smart Meters dataset. Now that we have multiple forecasts for all the households in the dataset, how do we come up with a single forecast by choosing or combining these different forecasts? That is what we will be doing in this chapter – we will learn how to leverage combinatorial and mathematical optimization to come up with a single forecast.

In this chapter, we will cover the following topics:

- Strategies for combining forecasts
- Stacking or blending

Technical requirements

You will need to set up the Anaconda environment following the instructions in the *Preface* of the book to get a working environment with all the packages and datasets required for the code in this book.

You need to run the following notebooks for this chapter:

- `02 - Preprocessing London Smart Meter Dataset.ipynb` in Chapter02
- `01-Setting up Experiment Harness.ipynb` in Chapter04
- `02-Baseline Forecasts using darts.ipynb` in Chapter04
- `01-Feature Engineering.ipynb` in Chapter06
- `02-Dealing with Non-Stationarity.ipynb` in Chapter07
- `02a-Dealing with Non-Stationarity-Train+Val.ipynb` in Chapter07
- `00-Single Step Backtesting Baselines.ipynb` in Chapter08

- `01-Forecasting with ML.ipynb` in Chapter08
- `01a-Forecasting with ML for Test Dataset.ipynb` in Chapter08
- `02-Forecasting with Target Transformation.ipynb` in Chapter08
- `02a-Forecasting with Target Transformation(Test).ipynb` in Chapter08

The code for this chapter can be found at `https://github.com/PacktPublishing/Modern-Time-Series-Forecasting-with-Python-/tree/main/notebooks/Chapter09`.

Combining forecasts

We have generated forecasts by using many techniques – some univariate, some machine learning, and so on. But at the end of the day, we would need a single forecast, and that means choosing a forecast or combining a variety. The most straightforward option is to choose the algorithm that does the best in the validation dataset, which in our case is LightGBM. We can think of this *selection* as another function that takes the forecasts that we generated as inputs and combines them into a final forecast. Mathematically, this can be represented as follows:

$$Y = \mathcal{F}(Y_1, Y_2, \dots, Y_N)$$

Here, $\mathcal{F}$ is the function that combines N forecasts. We can use the $\mathcal{F}$ function to choose the best-performing model in the validation dataset. However, this function can be as complex as it wants to be, and choosing the right $\mathcal{F}$ function while balancing bias and variance is a must.

> **Notebook alert**
>
> To follow along with the code, use the `01-Forecast Combinations.ipynb` notebook in the `chapter09` folder.

We will start by loading all the forecasts (both the validation and test forecasts) and the corresponding metrics for all the forecasts we have generated so far and combining them into `pred_val_df` and `pred_test_df`. Now, we must reshape the DataFrame using `pd.pivot` to get it into the shape we want. Up to this point, we have been tracking multiple metrics. But to meet this objective, we will need to choose one. For this exercise, we are going to choose MAE as the metric. The validation metrics can be combined and reshaped into `metrics_combined_df`:

LCLid	timestamp	FFT	Lasso Regression	Lasso Regression_auto_stat	LightGBM	LightGBM_auto_stat	Theta	XGB Random Forest	XGB Random Forest_auto_stat	energy_consumption
MAC000002	2014-01-01 00:00:00	0.255057	0.455158	0.418127	0.419273	0.414226	0.398836	0.39043	0.347244	0.496
	2014-01-01 00:30:00	0.234834	0.471182	0.422963	0.425602	0.403881	0.380464	0.39043	0.328894	0.427
	2014-01-01 01:00:00	0.207254	0.443879	0.418469	0.373510	0.378720	0.369484	0.39043	0.317926	0.469
	2014-01-01 01:30:00	0.175136	0.438553	0.382969	0.345316	0.333053	0.328537	0.39043	0.276990	0.362
	2014-01-01 02:00:00	0.144155	0.309471	0.295905	0.304884	0.277279	0.306195	0.36219	0.242762	0.452

Figure 9.1 – Reshaped predictions DataFrame

Now, let's look at some different strategies for combining the forecasts.

Best fit

This strategy of choosing the best forecast is by far the most popular and is as simple as choosing the best forecast for each time series based on the validation metrics. This strategy has been made popular by many automated forecasting software, which calls this the "best fit" forecast. The algorithm is very simple:

1. Find the best-performing forecast for each time series using a validation dataset.

2. For each time series, select the forecast from the same model for the test dataset.

We can do this easily:

```
# Finding the lowest metric for each LCLid
best_alg = metrics_combined_df.idxmin(axis=1)
#Initialize two columns in the dataframe
pred_wide_test["best_fit"] = np.nan
pred_wide_test["best_fit_alg"] = ""
#For each LCL id
for lcl_id in tqdm(pred_wide_test.index.get_level_values(0).
unique()):
    # pick the best algorithm
    alg = best_alg[lcl_id]
    # and store the forecast in the best_fit column
    pred_wide_test.loc[lcl_id, "best_fit"] = pred_wide_test.
loc[lcl_id, alg].values
    # also store which model was chosen for traceability
    pred_wide_test.loc[lcl_id, "best_fit_alg"] = alg
```

This will create a new column called `best_fit` with the forecasts that have been chosen according to the strategy we discussed. Now, we can evaluate this new forecast and get the metrics for the test dataset. The following table shows the best individual model (`LightGBM`) and the new strategy – `best_fit`:

Algorithm	MAE	MSE	meanMASE	Forecast Bias
LightGBM	0.0751	0.0271	0.9142	2.57%
best_fit	0.0740	0.0269	0.8971	0.14%

Figure 9.2 – Aggregate metrics for the best fit strategy

Here, we can see that the best fit strategy is not performing as well as the best individual model overall, which is not what we expect when combining forecasts. One drawback is the fundamental assumption of this strategy – whatever model does best in the validation period also performs the best in the test period. Given the dynamic nature of time series, this is not always the best strategy. Another drawback of this approach is the instability of the final forecast. When we are using such a rule in a live environment, where we retrain and rerun the best fit every week, the forecast for any time series can jump back and forth between different forecast models, which can generate wildly different forecasts. Therefore, the final forecast shows a lot of week-over-week instability, which hampers the downstream actions we use these forecasts for.

Measures of central tendency

Another prominent strategy is to use either an average or median to combine the forecasts. This is a function, $\mathcal{F}$, that is independent of validation metrics. This is both the appeal and angst of this method. It is impossible to overfit the validation metrics because we are not using them at all. But on the other hand, without any information from the validation metric, we may be including some very bad models, which pulls down the ensemble. However, empirically, this simple averaging of taking the median has proven to be a very strong combination method for forecast and is hard to outperform. Let's see how this can be done:

```
# ensemble_forecasts is a list of column names(forecast) we
want to combine
pred_wide_test["average_ensemble"] = pred_wide_test[ensemble_
forecasts].mean(axis=1)
pred_wide_test["median_ensemble"] = pred_wide_test[ensemble_
forecasts].median(axis=1)
```

The preceding code will create two new columns called `average_ensemble` and `median_ensemble` with the combined forecasts. Now, we can evaluate this new forecast and get the metrics for the test dataset. The following table shows the best individual model (`LightGBM`) and the new strategies:

Algorithm	MAE	MSE	meanMASE	Forecast Bias
LightGBM	0.0751	0.0271	0.9142	2.57%
best_fit	0.0740	0.0269	0.8971	0.14%
median_ensemble	0.0767	0.0279	0.9304	-0.86%
average_ensemble	0.0828	0.0285	1.0159	1.58%

Figure 9.3 – Aggregate metrics for the mean and median strategies

Here, we can see that neither the mean nor median strategy is working better than the best individual model overall. This can be because we are including methods such as Theta and FFT, which are performing considerably worse than the other machine learning methods. But since we are not taking any information from the validation dataset, we do not know this information. We can make an exception and say that we are going to use the validation metrics to choose which models we include in the average or median. But we have to be careful because now, we are moving closer to the assumption that what works in the validation period is going to work in the test period.

There are a few manual techniques we can use here, such as **trimming** (discarding the worst-performing models in the ensemble) and **skimming** (selecting only the best few models in the ensemble). While effective, these are a bit subjective, and often, they become hard to use, especially when we have scores of models to choose from.

If we think about this problem, it is essentially a combinatorial optimization problem where we have to select the best combination of models that optimizes our metric. If we consider the average for combining the different forecasts, mathematically, it can be thought of as follows:

$$\hat{Y} = \underset{w}{\arg\min}\, \mathcal{L}\left(\frac{1}{\sum_{i=1}^{N} w_i} \sum_{i=1}^{N} w_i \times \hat{Y}_i, Y\right)$$

Here, $\mathcal{L}$ is the loss or metric that we are trying to minimize. In our case, we chose that to be the MAE. $w_N \in [0,1]$ is the binary weights of each of the base forecasts. Finally, $\widehat{Y_N}$ is the set of N base forecasts and Y is the real observed values of the time series.

But unlike pure optimization, where there is no concept of bias and variance, we need an optimal solution that can be generalized. Therefore, selecting the global minima in the training data is not advisable because in that case, we might be further overfitting the training dataset, increasing the variance of the resulting model. For this minimization, we typically use out-of-sample predictions, which in this case can be the forecast during the validation period.

The most straightforward solution is to find w, which minimizes this function on validation data. But there are two problems with this approach:

- The possible candidates (different combinations of the base forecasts) increase exponentially as we increase the number of base forecasts, N. This becomes computationally intractable very soon.

- Selecting the global minima in the validation period may not be the best strategy because of overfitting the validation period.

Now, let's take a look at a few heuristics-based solutions to this combinatorial optimization problem.

Simple hill climbing

We briefly talked about greedy algorithms while discussing decision trees, as well as gradient-boosted trees. Greedy optimization is a heuristic that builds up a solution stage by stage, selecting a local optimum at each stage. In both these machine learning models, we adopt a greedy, stagewise approach to finding the solution to a computationally infeasible optimization problem. To select the best subset that gives us the best combination of forecasts, we can employ a simple greedy algorithm called hill climbing. If we consider the objective function surface as a hill, to find the maxima, we would need to climb the hill. As its name suggests, hill climbing ascends the hill, one step at a time, and in each of those steps, it takes the best possible path, which increases the objective function. Let's see how the algorithm works.

Here, C is a set of candidates (base forecasts) and O is the objective we want to minimize. The algorithm for the simple hill-climb is as follows:

1. Initialize a starting solution, C_{best}, as the candidate that gives the minimum value in O, O_{best}, and remove C_{best} from C.

2. While the length of $C > 0$, do the following:

   I. Evaluate all members of C by averaging the base forecasts in C_{best} with each element in C and select the best member ($C_{stage\ best}$) that was added to C_{best} to minimize the objective function, O ($O_{stage\ best}$).

   II. If $O_{stage\ best} > O_{best}$, then do the following:

      i. $C_{best} = C_{best} \cup C_{stage\ best}$.

      ii. $O_{best} = O_{stage\ best}$.

      iii. Remove $C_{stage\ best}$ from C.

   III. Otherwise, exit.

At the end of the run, we have c_{best}, which is the best combination of forecasts we got through greedy optimization. We have made an implementation of this available in `src.forecasting.ensembling.py` under the `greedy_optimization` function. The parameters for this function are as follows:

- `objective`: This is a callable that takes in a list of strings as the candidates and returns a `float` objective value.

- `candidates`: This is a list of candidates to be included in the optimization.

- `verbose`: A flag that specifies whether progress is printed or not.

The function returns a tuple of the best solution as a list of strings and the best score that was obtained through optimization.

Let's see how we can use this in our example:

1. Import all the required libraries/functions:

    ```
    # Used to partially construct a function call
    from functools import partial
    # calculate_performance is a custom method we defined
    to calculate the MAE provided a list of candidates and
    prediction dataframe
    from src.forecasting.ensembling import calculate_
    performance, greedy_optimization
    ```

2. Define the objective function and run greedy optimization:

    ```
    # We partially construct the function call by passing the
    necessary parameters
    objective = partial(
        calculate_performance, pred_wide=pred_wide_val,
    target="energy_consumption"
    )
    # ensemble forecasts is the list of candidates
    solution, best_score = greedy_optimization(objective,
    ensemble_forecasts)
    ```

3. Once we have the best solution, we can create the combination forecast in the test DataFrame:

    ```
    pred_wide_test["greedy_ensemble"] = pred_wide_
    test[solution].mean(axis=1)
    ```

Once we run this code, we will have the combination forecast under the name `greedy_ensemble` in our prediction DataFrame. The candidates that are part of the optimal solution are `LightGBM`, `Lasso Regression`, and `LightGBM_auto_stat`. Now, let's evaluate the results and look at the aggregated metrics:

Algorithm	MAE	MSE	meanMASE	Forecast Bias
LightGBM	0.0751	0.0271	0.9142	2.57%
best_fit	0.0740	0.0269	0.8971	0.14%
median_ensemble	0.0767	0.0279	0.9304	-0.86%
average_ensemble	0.0828	0.0285	1.0159	1.58%
greedy_ensemble	0.0733	0.0251	0.8951	0.81%

Figure 9.4 – Aggregate metrics for a simple hill climbing-based ensemble

As we can see, the simple hill-climb is performing better than any individual models or any other ensemble techniques we have seen so far. This greedy approach seems to be working well in this case. Now, let's understand a few limitations of hill climbing, as follows:

- **Runtime considerations**: Since a simple hill-climb requires us to evaluate all the candidates at any step, this can cause a bottleneck in terms of runtime. If the number of candidates is large, this approach can take longer to finish.

- **Short-sightedness**: Hill climbing optimization is short-sighted. During optimization, it always picks the best in each step. Sometimes, by choosing a slightly worse solution in a step, we may get to a better overall solution.

- **Forward-only**: Hill climbing is a forward-only algorithm. Once a candidate has been admitted into the solution, we can't go back and remove it.

The greedy approach may not always get us the best solution, especially when there are scores of models to combine. So, let's look at a small variation of hill climbing that tries to get over some of the limitations of the greedy approach.

Stochastic hill climbing

The key difference between simple hill climbing and stochastic hill climbing is in the evaluation of candidates. In a simple hill-climb, we *evaluate all possible options* and pick the best among them. However, in a stochastic hill-climb, we *randomly pick a candidate* and add it to the solution if it is better than the current solution. This addition of stochasticity helps the optimization not get the local maxima/minima. Let's take a look at the algorithm.

Here, C is a set of candidates (base forecasts), O is the objective we want to minimize, and N is the maximum number of iterations we want to run the optimization for. The algorithm for stochastic hill climbing is as follows:

1. Initialize a starting solution, C_{best}, as the candidate. This can be done by picking a candidate at random or choosing the best-performing model.

2. Set the value of the objective function for C_{best}, O, as O_{best}, and remove C_{best} from C.

3. Repeat this for N iterations:

    I.   Draw a random sample from C, add it to C_{best}, and store it as C_{stage}.

    II.   Evaluate C_{stage} on the objective function, O, and store it as O_{stage}.

    III. If $O_{stage} > O_{best}$, then do the following:

        i. $C_{best} = C_{best} \cup C_{stage}$.

        ii. $O_{best} = O_{stage}$.

        iii. Remove C_{best} from C.

At the end of the run, we have C_{best}, which is the best combination of forecasts we got through stochastic hill climbing. We have made an implementation of this available in `src.forecasting.ensembling.py` under the `stochastic_hillclimbing` function. The parameters for this function are as follows:

- `objective`: This is a callable that takes in a list of strings as the candidates and returns a `float` objective value.
- `candidates`: This is a list of candidates to be included in the optimization.
- `n_iterations`: The number of iterations to run the hill-climb for. If this is not given, a heuristic (twice the number of candidates) is used to set this.
- `init`: This determines the strategy to be used for the initial solution. This can be `random` or `best`.
- `verbose`: A flag that specifies whether progress is printed or not.
- `random_state`: A seed that gets repeatable results.

The function returns a tuple of the best solution as a list of strings and the best score obtained through optimization.

This can be used in a very similar fashion to `greedy_optimization`. We will only show the different parts here. The full code is available in the notebook:

```
from src.forecasting.ensembling import stochastic_hillclimbing
# ensemble forecasts is the list of candidates
```

```
solution, best_score = stochastic_hillclimbing(
    objective, ensemble_forecasts, n_iterations=10,
init="best", random_state=9
)
```

Once we run this code, we will have the combination forecast called `stochastic_hillclimb__ensemble` in our prediction DataFrame. The candidates that are part of the optimal solution are `LightGBM`, `Lasso Regression_auto_stat`, `LightGBM_auto_stat`, and `Lasso Regression`. Now, let's evaluate the results and look at the aggregated metrics:

Algorithm	MAE	MSE	meanMASE	Forecast Bias
LightGBM	0.0751	0.0271	0.9142	2.57%
best_fit	0.0740	0.0269	0.8971	0.14%
median_ensemble	0.0767	0.0279	0.9304	-0.86%
average_ensemble	0.0828	0.0285	1.0159	1.58%
greedy_ensemble	0.0733	0.0251	0.8951	0.81%
stochastic_hillclimb__ensemble	0.0751	0.0257	0.9206	1.18%

Figure 9.5 – Aggregate metrics for a stochastic hill climbing-based ensemble

The stochastic hill-climb is not doing better than the greedy approach but is better than the mean, median, and best fit ensembles. We discussed three disadvantages of simple hill climbing earlier – runtime considerations, short-sightedness, and forward-only. Stochastic hill climbing solves the runtime consideration because we are not evaluating all the combinations and selecting the best. Instead, we are randomly evaluating the combinations and adding them to the ensemble as soon as we see a solution that performs better. It partly solves the short-sightedness purely because the randomness in the algorithm may end up choosing a sub-optimal solution for each stage. But it still only chooses solutions that are better than the current solution.

Now, let's look at another modification of hill climbing that handles this issue as well.

Simulated annealing

Simulated annealing is a modification of hill climbing that is inspired by a physical phenomenon – annealing solids. Annealing is the process of heating a solid to a predetermined temperature (usually above its melting point), holding it for a while, and then slowly cooling it. This is done to ensure that the atoms assume a new globally minimum energy state, which induces desirable properties to some metals, such as iron.

In 1952, Metropolis proposed simulated annealing as an optimization technique. The annealing analogy applies to the optimization context as well. When we say we heat the system, we encourage random perturbations. So, when we start an optimization with a high temperature, the algorithm explores the space and comes up with an initial structure of the problem. And as we reduce the temperature, the structure is refined to arrive at a final solution. This technique helps us avoid getting stuck in any local optima. Local optima are extrema in the objective function surface that are better than other values nearby but may not be the absolute best solution possible. The *Further reading* section contains a resource that explains what local and global optima are in a concise language.

Now, let's look at the algorithm.

Here, $\mathcal{C}$ is a set of candidates (base forecasts), $\mathcal{O}$ is the objective we want to minimize, $\mathcal{N}$ is the maximum number of iterations we want to run the optimization for, T_{max} is the maximum temperature, and α is the temperature decay. The algorithm for simulated annealing is as follows:

1. Initialize a starting solution, C_{best}, as the candidate. This can be done by picking a candidate at random or choosing the best-performing model.

2. Set the value of the objective function for C_{best}, $\mathcal{O}$, as O_{best}, and remove C_{best} from $\mathcal{C}$.

3. Set the current temperature, t, as T_{max}.

4. Repeat this for $\mathcal{N}$ iterations:

    I. Draw a random sample from $\mathcal{C}$, add it to C_{best}, and store it as C_{stage}.

    II. Evaluate C_{stage} on the objective function, $\mathcal{O}$, and store it as O_{stage}.

    III. If $O_{stage} > O_{best}$, then do the following:

        i. $C_{best} = C_{best} \cup C_{stage}$.

        ii. $O_{best} = O_{stage}$.

        iii. Remove C_{best} from $\mathcal{C}$.

    IV. Otherwise, do the following:

        i. Calculate the acceptance probability, $s = e^{-\frac{O_{best}-O_{stage}}{t}}$.

        ii. Draw a random sample between 0 and 1, as p.

        iii. If $p < s$, then do the following:

            i. $C_{best} = C_{best} \cup C_{stage}$.

            ii. $O_{best} = O_{stage}$.

            iii. Remove C_{best} from $\mathcal{C}$.

    V. $t = t - \alpha$ (for linear decay) and $t=t/\alpha$ (for geometric decay).

    VI. Exit when $\mathcal{C}$ is empty.

At the end of the run, we have c_{best}, which is the best combination of forecasts we got through simulated annealing. We have provided an implementation of this in `src.forecasting.ensembling. py` under the `simulated_annealing` function. Setting the temperature to the right value is key for the algorithm to work well and is typically the hardest hyperparameter to set. More intuitively, we can think of temperature in terms of the probability of accepting a worse solution in the beginning. In the implementation, we have also made it possible to input the starting and ending probability of accepting a worse solution.

In 1989, D.S. Johnson et al. proposed a procedure for estimating the temperature range from the given probability range. This has been implemented in `initialize_temperature_range`.

Reference check

The research paper by D.S. Johnson, titled *Optimization by Simulated Annealing: An Experimental Evaluation; Part I, Graph Partitioning*, is cited in the *References* section as reference 1.

The parameters for the `simulated_annealing` function are as follows:

- `objective`: This is a callable that takes in a list of strings as the candidates and returns a `float` objective value.

- `candidates`: This is a list of candidates to be included in the optimization.

- `n_iterations`: The number of iterations to run simulated annealing for. This is a mandatory parameter.

- `p_range`: The starting and ending probabilities as a tuple. This is the probability with which a worse solution is accepted in simulated annealing. The temperature range (`t_range`) is inferred from `p_range` during optimization.

- `t_range`: We can use this if we want to directly set the temperature range as a tuple (start, end). If this is set, `p_range` is ignored.

- `init`: This determines the strategy that's used for the initial solution. This can be `random` or `best`.

- `temperature_decay`: This specifies how to decay the temperature. It can be `linear` or `geometric`.

- `verbose`: A flag that specifies whether progress is printed or not.

- `random_state`: The seed for getting repeatable results.

The function returns a tuple of the best solution as a list of strings and the best score that was obtained through optimization.

This can be used in a very similar fashion to the other ways of combining forecasts. We will show just the part that is different here. The full code is available in the notebook:

```
from src.forecasting.ensembling import simulated_annealing
# ensemble forecasts is the list of candidates
solution, best_score = simulated_annealing(
    objective,
    ensemble_forecasts,
    p_range=(0.5, 0.0001),
    n_iterations=50,
    init="best",
    temperature_decay="geometric",
    random_state=42,
)
```

Once we run this code, we will have a combination forecast called `simulated_annealing_ensemble` in our prediction DataFrame. The candidates that are part of the optimal solution are `LightGBM`, `Lasso Regression_auto_stat`, `LightGBM_auto_stat`, and `XGB Random Forest`. Let's evaluate the results and look at the aggregated metrics:

Algorithm	MAE	MSE	meanMASE	Forecast Bias
LightGBM	0.0751	0.0271	0.9142	2.57%
best_fit	0.0740	0.0269	0.8971	0.14%
median_ensemble	0.0767	0.0279	0.9304	-0.86%
average_ensemble	0.0828	0.0285	1.0159	1.58%
greedy_ensemble	0.0733	0.0251	0.8951	0.81%
stochastic_hillclimb_ensemble	0.0751	0.0257	0.9206	1.18%
simulated_annealing_ensemble	0.0735	0.0248	0.9041	0.26%

Figure 9.6 – Aggregate metrics for a simulated annealing-based ensemble

Simulated annealing seems to be doing better than stochastic hill climbing. We discussed three disadvantages of simple hill climbing earlier – runtime considerations, short-sightedness, and forward-only. Simulated annealing solves the runtime consideration because we are not evaluating all the combinations and selecting the best. Instead, we are randomly evaluating the combinations and adding them to the ensemble as soon as we see a solution that performs better. It also solves the short-sightedness problem because, by using temperature, we are also accepting solutions that are slightly worse toward the beginning of the optimization. However, it is still a forward-only procedure.

So far, we have looked at combinatorial optimization because we said $w_N \in [0,1]$. But if we can relax this constraint and make $w_N \in \mathbb{R}$ (real numbers), the combinatorial optimization problem can be relaxed to a general mathematical optimization problem. Let's see how we can do that.

Optimal weighted ensemble

Previously, we defined the optimization problem we are trying to solve as follows:

$$\hat{Y} = \underset{w}{\arg\min} \, \mathcal{L} \left(\frac{1}{\sum_{i=1}^{N} w_i} \sum_{i=1}^{N} w_i \times \hat{Y}_i, Y \right)$$

Here, $\mathcal{L}$ is the loss or metric that we are trying to minimize. In our case, we chose that to be the MAE. $\hat{Y}_N$ is the set of N base forecasts while Y is the real observed values of the time series. Instead of defining $w_N \in [0,1]$, let's make $w_N \in \mathbb{R}$, the continuous weights of each of the base forecasts. With this new relaxation, the combination becomes a weighted average between the different base forecasts. Now, we are looking at a soft mixing of the different forecasts as opposed to the hard-choice-based combinatorial optimization (which was what we had been using up until this point).

This is an optimization problem that can be solved using off-the-shelf algorithms from `scipy`. Let's see how we can use `scipy.optimize` to solve this problem.

First, we need to define a loss function that takes in a set of weights as a list and returns the metric we need to optimize:

```
def loss_function(weights):
        # Calculating the weighted average
        fc = np.sum(pred_wide[candidates].values *
np.array(weights), axis=1)
        # Using any metric function to calculate the metric
        return metric_fn(pred_wide[target].values, fc)
```

Now, all we need to do is call `scipy.optimize` with the necessary parameters. Let's learn how to do this:

```
from scipy import optimize
opt_weights = optimize.minimize(
        loss_function,
        # set x0 as initial values, which is a uniform
distribution over all the candidates
        x0=[1 / len(candidates)] * len(candidates),
        # Set the constraint so that the weights sum to one
        constraints=({"type": "eq", "fun": lambda w: 1 -
```

```
sum(w) }),
        # Choose the optimization technique. Should be
gradient-free and bounded.
        method="SLSQP",
        # Set the lower and upper bound as a tuple for each
element in the candidate list.
        # We set the maximum values between 1 and 0
        bounds=[(0.0, 1.0)] * len(candidates),
        # Set the tolerance for termination
        options={"ftol": 1e-10},
    )["x"]
```

The optimization is usually fast and we will get the weights as a list of floating-point numbers. We have wrapped this in a function in src.forecasting.ensembling.py called under the find_optimal_combination function. The parameters for this function are as follows:

- candidates: This is a list of candidates to be included in the optimization. They are returning in the same order in which the returned weights would.

- pred_wide: This is the prediction DataFrame on which we need to learn the weights.

- target: This is the column name of the target.

- metric_fn: This is any callable with a metric(actuals, pred) signature.

The function returns the optimal weights as a list of floating-point numbers. Let's see what the optimal weights are when we learned them through our validation forecast:

Forecast	Weights
LightGBM	0.4221
LightGBM_auto_stat	0.2991
Lasso Regression_auto_stat	0.1266
Lasso Regression	0.1012
XGB Random Forest	0.0510
FFT	0.0000
Theta	0.0000
XGB Random Forest_auto_stat	0.0000

Figure 9.7 – The optimal weights that were learned through optimization

Here, we can see that the optimization automatically learned to ignore FFT, Theta, XGB Random Forest, and XGB Random Forest_auto_stat because they didn't add much value to the ensemble. It has also learned some non-zero weights for each of the forecasts. The weights already resemble the selection we made using the techniques we discussed previously. Now, we can use these weights to come up with a weighted average and call it optimal_combination_ensemble. The aggregated results should be as follows:

Algorithm	MAE	MSE	meanMASE	Forecast Bias
LightGBM	0.0751	0.0271	0.9142	2.57%
best_fit	0.0740	0.0269	0.8971	0.14%
median_ensemble	0.0767	0.0279	0.9304	-0.86%
average_ensemble	0.0828	0.0285	1.0159	1.58%
greedy_ensemble	0.0733	0.0251	0.8951	0.81%
stochastic_hillclimb__ensemble	0.0751	0.0257	0.9206	1.18%
simulated_annealing_ensemble	0.0735	0.0248	0.9041	0.26%
optimal_combination_ensemble	0.0732	0.0248	0.8956	0.81%

Figure 9.8 – Aggregate metrics for the optimal combination-based ensemble

Here, we can see that this soft mixing of the forecasts is doing much better than all of the hard-choice-based ensembles on all three metrics.

> **Additional note**
>
> In all the techniques we discussed, we were using MAE as the objective function. But we can use any metric, a combination of metrics, or even metrics with regularization as the objective function. When we discussed Random Forest, we talked about how decorrelated trees were essential to getting better performance. A very similar principle applies while choosing ensembles as well. Having decorrelated base forecasts adds value to the ensemble. So, we can use any measure of variety to regularize our metric as well. For instance, we can use correlation as a measure and create a regularized metric to be used in these techniques. The 01-Forecast Combinations.ipynb notebook in the chapter09 folder contains a bonus section that shows how to do that.

We started by discussing combining forecasts with a mathematical formulation:

$$Y = \mathcal{F}(Y_1, Y_2, \dots, Y_N)$$

Here, $\mathcal{F}$ is the function that combines the N forecasts.

We did all this while looking at ways to come up with this function as an optimization problem, using something such as a mean or median to combine the metrics. But we have also seen another way to learn this function, $\mathcal{F}$, from data, haven't we? Let's see how that can be done.

Stacking or blending

We started this chapter by talking about machine learning algorithms, which learn a function from a set of inputs and outputs. While using those machine learning algorithms, we learned about the functions that forecast our time series, which we'll call base forecasts now. Why not use the same machine learning paradigm to learn this new function, $\mathcal{F}$, that we are trying to learn as well?

This is exactly what we do in stacking (often called stacked generalization), where we train another learning algorithm on the predictions of some base learners to combine these predictions. This second-level model is often called a **stacked model** or a **meta model**. And typically, this meta model performs equal to or better than the base learners.

Although the idea originated with Wolpert in 1992, Leo Breiman formalized this idea in the way it is used now in his 1996 paper titled *Stacked Regressions*. And in 2007, Mark J. Van der Laan et al. established the theoretical underpinnings of the technique and provided proof that this meta model will perform at least as well or even better than the base learners.

> Reference check
>
> The research papers by Leo Breiman (1996) and Mark J. Van der Laan (2007) are cited in the *References* section as *2* and *3*, respectively.

This is a very popular technique in machine learning competitions such as Kaggle and is considered a black art among machine learning practitioners. We also discussed some other techniques, such as bagging and boosting, which combine base learners into something more. But those techniques require the base learner to be a weak learner. This is where stacking differs because stacking tries to combine a *diverse* set of *strong* learners.

The intuition behind stacking is that different models or families of functions learn the output function slightly differently, capturing different properties of the problem. For instance, one model may have captured the seasonality very well, whereas the other may have captured any particular interaction with an exogenous variable better. The stacking model will be able to combine these base models into a model that learns to look toward one model for seasonality and the other for interaction. This is done by making the meta model learn the predictions of the base models. But to avoid data leakage and thereby avoid overfitting, the meta model should be trained on out-of-sample predictions. There are two small variations of this technique that are used today – stacking and blending.

Stacking is when the meta model is trained on the entire training dataset, but with out-of-sample predictions. The following steps are involved in stacking:

1. Split the training dataset into *k* parts.

2. Iteratively, train the base models on *k-1* parts, predict on the *kth* part, and save the predictions. Once this step is done, we have the out-of-sample predictions for the training dataset from all base models.

3. Train a meta model on these predictions.

Blending is similar to this but slightly different in the way we generate out-of-sample predictions. The following steps are involved in blending:

1. Split the training dataset into two parts – train and holdout.

2. Train the base models on the training dataset and predict on the holdout dataset.

3. Train a meta model on the validation dataset with the predictions of the base model as the features.

Intuitively, we can see that stacking can work better because it is using a much larger dataset (usually all the training data) as the out-of-sample prediction, so the meta model may be more generalized. But there is a caveat: we assume that the entire training data is **independent and identically distributed** (**iid**). This is typically an assumption that is hard to meet in time series since the data generating process can change at any time (either gradually or drastically). If we know that the data distribution has changed significantly over time, blending the holdout period (which is usually the most recent part of the dataset) is better because the meta model is only learning on the latest data, thus paying respect to the temporal changes in the distribution of data.

There is no limit to the number of models we can include as base models, but usually, there is a plateau that we reach where additional models do not add much to the stacked ensemble. We can also add multiple levels of stacking. For instance, let's assume there are four base learners: B_1, B_2, B_3, and B_4. We have also trained two meta models M_1 and M_2, on the base models. Now, we can train a second-level meta model, $\mathcal{M}$, on the outputs of M_1 and M_2 and use that as the final prediction. We can use the pystacknet Python library (https://github.com/h2oai/pystacknet), which is the Python implementation of an older library, called stacknet, to make the process of creating multi-level (or single-level) stacked ensembles easy.

Another key point to keep in mind is the type of models we usually use as meta models. It is assumed that the bulk of the learning has been taken care of by the base models, which are the multi-dimensional data for patterns for prediction. Therefore, the meta models are usually simple models such as linear regression, a decision tree, or even a random forest with much lower depth than the base models. Another way to think about this is in terms of bias and variance. Stacking can overfit the training or holdout set and by including model families with larger flexibility or expressive power, we are enabling this overfitting. The *Further reading* section contains a few links that explain different techniques of stacking from a general machine learning perspective.

Now, let's quickly see how we can use this in our dataset:

```
from sklearn.linear_model import LinearRegression
stacking_model = LinearRegression()
# ensemble_forecasts is the list of candidates
stacking_model.fit(
    pred_wide_val[ensemble_forecasts], pred_wide_val["energy_
consumption"]
)
pred_wide_test["linear_reg_blending"] = stacking_model.predict(
    pred_wide_test[ensemble_forecasts]
)
```

This would save the blended prediction for linear regression as `linear_reg_blending`. We can use the same code but swap the models to try out other models as well.

Best practice

When there are many base models and we want to do implicit base model selection as well, we can opt for one of the regularized linear models, such as ridge or lasso regression. Breiman, in his original paper, *Stacked Regressions*, proposed to use linear regression with positive coefficients and no intercept as the meta model. He argued that this gives a theoretical guarantee that the stacked model will give at least as good as any best individual model. But in practice, we can relax those assumptions while experimenting. Non-negative regression without intercepts is very close to the optimal weighted ensemble we discussed earlier. Finally, if we are evaluating multiple stacked models to select which one works well, we should resort to either having a separate validation dataset (instead of a *train-validation-test* split, we can use a *train-validation-validation_meta-test* split) or use cross-validated estimates. If we just pick the stacked model that performs best on the test dataset, we are overfitting the test dataset.

Now, let's see how the blended models are doing on our test data:

Algorithm	MAE	MSE	meanMASE	Forecast Bias
LightGBM	0.0751	0.0271	0.9142	2.57%
best_fit	0.0740	0.0269	0.8971	0.14%
median_ensemble	0.0767	0.0279	0.9304	-0.86%
average_ensemble	0.0828	0.0285	1.0159	1.58%
greedy_ensemble	0.0733	0.0251	0.8951	0.81%
stochastic_hillclimb__ensemble	0.0751	0.0257	0.9206	1.18%
simulated_annealing_ensemble	0.0735	0.0248	0.9041	0.26%
optimal_combination_ensemble	0.0732	0.0248	0.8956	0.81%
linear_reg_blending	0.0755	0.0245	0.9260	4.35%
ridge_reg_blending	0.0737	0.0243	0.9082	1.84%
lasso_reg_blending	0.0736	0.0243	0.9068	1.94%
huber_reg_blending	0.0704	0.0246	0.8989	-6.42%

Figure 9.9 – Aggregate metrics for blending models

Here, we can see that a simple linear regression has learned a meta model that performs much better than any of our average ensemble methods. And the Huber regression (which is a way to optimize the MAE directly) performs much better on the MAE benchmark. However, keep in mind that this is not universal and has to be evaluated for each problem you come across. Choosing the metric to optimize for and the model to use to combine makes a lot of difference. And often, the simple average ensemble is a very formidable benchmark for combining models.

> **Additional reading**
>
> There are other more innovative ways to combine base forecasts. This is an active area of research. The *Further reading* section contains links to two such ideas that are very similar. **Feature-Based Forecast Model Averaging (FFORMA)** extracts a set of statistical features from the time series and uses it to train a machine learning model that predicts the weights in which the base forecast should be combined. Another technique, from Facebook (Meta) Research, trains a classifier to predict which of the base learners does best, given a set of statistical features extracted from the time series.

Summary

Continuing with the streak of practical lessons in the previous chapter, we completed yet another hands-on lesson. In this chapter, we generated forecasts from different machine learning models from the previous chapter. We learned how to combine these different forecasts into a single forecast that performs better than any single model. Then, we explored concepts such as combinatorial optimization and stacking to achieve state-of-the-art results.

In the next chapter, we will start talking about global models of forecasting and explore strategies, feature engineering, and so on to enable such modeling.

References

The following references were provided in this chapter:

1. David S. Johnson, Cecilia R. Aragon, Lyle A. McGeoch, and Catherine Schevon (1989), *Optimization by Simulated Annealing: An Experimental Evaluation; Part I, Graph Partitioning*. Operations Research, 1989, vol. 37, issue 6, 865-892 – `http://dx.doi.org/10.1287/opre.37.6.865`

2. *L. Breiman* (1996), *Stacked regressions*. Mach Learn 24, 49–64 – `https://doi.org/10.1007/BF00117832`

3. Mark J. van der Laan; Eric C.Polley; and Alan E.Hubbard (2007), *Super Learner*. U.C. Berkeley Division of Biostatistics Working Paper Series. Working Paper 222: `https://biostats.bepress.com/ucbbiostat/paper222`

Further reading

To learn more about the topics that were covered in this chapter, take a look at the following resources:

- *A Kaggler's Guide to Model Stacking in Practice*, by Ha Nguyen: `https://datasciblog.github.io/2016/12/27/a-kagglers-guide-to-model-stacking-in-practice/`

- Kai Ming Ting and Ian H. Witten (1997), *Stacked Generalization: when does it work?*: `https://www.ijcai.org/Proceedings/97-2/Papers/011.pdf`

- Pablo Montero-Manso, George Athanasopoulos, Rob J. Hyndman, Thiyanga S. Talagala (2020), *FFORMA: Feature-based forecast model averaging*. International Journal of Forecasting, Volume 36, Issue 1: `https://robjhyndman.com/papers/fforma.pdf`

- Peiyi Zhang, et al. (2021), *Self-supervised learning for fast and scalable time-series hyper-parameter tuning*: `https://www.ijcai.org/Proceedings/97-2/Papers/011.pdf`

- Local versus Global Optima: `https://www.mathworks.com/help/optim/ug/local-vs-global-optima.html`

10

Global Forecasting Models

In previous chapters, we saw how we can use modern machine learning models on time series forecasting problems, essentially replacing traditional models such as ARIMA or exponential smoothing. However, before now, we were looking at the different time series in any dataset (such as households in the *London Smart Meters* dataset) in isolation, just as the traditional models did.

However, we will now explore a different paradigm of modeling where we use a single machine learning model to forecast a bunch of time series together. As we will learn in the chapter, this paradigm brings many benefits with it, from the perspective of both computation and accuracy.

In this chapter, we will be covering these main topics:

- Why Global Forecasting Models (GFMs)?
- Creating GFMs
- Strategies to improve GFMs
- Bonus – interpretability

Technical requirements

You will need to set up an Anaconda environment, following the instructions in the *Preface* of the book, to get a working environment with all the packages and datasets required for the code in this book.

The associated code for the chapter can be found at `https://github.com/PacktPublishing/Modern-Time-Series-Forecasting-with-Python-/tree/main/notebooks/Chapter10`.

You need to run the following notebooks for this chapter:

- `02-Preprocessing London Smart Meter Dataset.ipynb` in `Chapter02`
- `01-Setting up Experiment Harness.ipynb` in `Chapter04`
- From the `Chapter06` and `Chapter07` folders:
  - `01-Feature Engineering.ipynb`
  - `02-Dealing with Non-Stationarity.ipynb`
  - `02a-Dealing with Non-Stationarity-Train+Val.ipynb`
- From the `Chapter08` folder:
  - `00-Single Step Backtesting Baselines.ipynb`
  - `01-Forecasting with ML.ipynb`
  - `01a-Forecasting with ML for Test Dataset.ipynb`
  - `02-Forecasting with Target Transformation.ipynb`
  - `02a-Forecasting with Target Transformation(Test).ipynb`

Why Global Forecasting Models (GFMs)?

We talked about global models briefly in *Chapter 5, Time Series Forecasting as Regression*, where we mentioned related datasets. We can think of many scenarios where we would encounter related time series. We may need to forecast the sales for all the products of a retailer, the number of rides requested for a cab service across different areas of a city, or the energy consumption of all the households in a particular area (which is what the London Smart Meters dataset does). We call these related time series because all the different time series in the dataset can have a lot of factors in common with each other. For instance, the yearly seasonality that might occur in retail products might be present for a large section of products, or the way an external factor such as temperature affects energy consumption may be similar for a large number of households. Therefore, one way or the other, the different time series in a related time series dataset share attributes between them.

Traditionally, we used to consider each time series an independent time series; in other words, each time series was assumed to be generated using a different data generating process. Classical models such as ARIMA and exponential smoothing are trained for each time series. However, we can also consider all the time series in the dataset as being generated from a single data generating process, and the subsequent modeling approach would be to train a single model to forecast all the time series in the dataset. The latter is what we refer to as GFMs and, in contrast, the traditional approach is referred to as **Local Forecasting Models (LFMs)**.

Although we briefly talked about the drawbacks of LFMs in *Chapter 5, Time Series Forecasting as Regression*, let's summarize them in a more concrete fashion and see why GFMs help us tide over a lot of those drawbacks.

Sample size

In most real-world applications (especially in business forecasting), the time series we have to forecast is not very long. Adopting a completely data-driven approach to modeling such a small time series is problematic. Training a highly flexible model with a handful of data points will lead to the model memorizing the training data, resulting in an overfit.

Traditionally, this has been overcome by placing strong priors or inductive bias into the models we use for forecasting. Inductive bias loosely refers to a set of assumptions or restrictions that are built into a model that should help the model predict feature combinations it has not encountered while training. For instance, double exponential smoothing has strong assumptions about seasonality and trend. The model does not allow any other more complicated patterns to be learned from the data. Therefore, using these strong assumptions, we are restricting the model search to a small section of the hypothesis space. While this helps in low-data regimes, the flip side is that these assumptions may limit accuracy.

Recent developments in the field of machine learning have shown us without a doubt that using a data-driven approach (with much fewer assumptions or priors) on large training sets will lead to us training better models. However, conventional statistical wisdom tells us that the number of data points needs to be at least 10 to 100 times the number of parameters that we are trying to learn from those data points.

So, if we stick to LFMs, scenarios in which we can adopt a completely data-driven approach will be very rare. This is where GFMs shine. A GFM is able to use the history of *all* the time series in a dataset to train the model and learn a single set of parameters that work for all the time series in the dataset. Borrowing the terminology introduced in *Chapter 5, Time Series Forecasting as Regression*, we increase the *width* of the dataset, keeping the *length* the same (refer back to *Figure 5.2*). This explosion of historical information available to a single model lets us use completely data-driven techniques on time series datasets.

Cross-learning

GFMs, by design, promote cross-learning across different time series in a dataset. Imagine we have a time series that is quite new and does not have a history rich enough for teaching the model – for instance, the sales of a newly introduced retail product or the electricity consumption of a new household in a region. If we consider these time series in isolation, it will be a while before we start to get reasonable forecasts from the models we train on them, but GFMs make that process easier by enabling cross-learning. GFMs have an implicit sense of similarity between different time series and they will be able to use patterns they have seen in similar time series with a rich history to come up with a forecast on the new time series.

Another way cross-learning helps is by acting like a regularizer while estimating common parameters such as seasonality. For instance, the seasonality exhibited by similar products in a retail scenario is best estimated at an aggregate level, because each individual time series will have some sort of noise that can creep into the seasonality extraction. By enforcing common seasonality across multiple products, we are essentially regularizing the seasonality estimation and, in the process, making the seasonality estimate more robust. The good thing about GFMs is that they take a data-driven approach to define the seasonality of which products should be estimated together and which ones have different patterns. If you have different seasonality patterns in different products, a GFM may struggle to model them together. However, when provided with enough information on how to distinguish between different products, the GFM will be able to learn that difference too.

Multi-task learning

GFMs can be considered multi-task learning paradigms where a single model is trained to learn multiple tasks (as forecasting each time series is a separate task). Multi-task learning is an active area of research, and there are many benefits to using multi-task models:

- When the model is learning from noisy, high-dimensional data, it becomes harder for the model to distinguish between useful and non-useful features. When we train the model on a multi-task paradigm, the model can understand useful features by looking at features that are useful for other tasks as well, thus providing the model with an additional perspective for discerning useful features.

- Sometimes, features such as seasonality might be hard to learn from a particularly noisy time series. However, under a multi-task framework, the model can learn the difficult feature using other time series in the dataset.

- Finally, multi-task learning introduces a kind of regularization that forces the model to find a model that works well on all tasks, thus reducing the risk of overfitting.

Engineering complexity

LFMs pose a challenge from the engineering side as well for large datasets. If we have thousands or millions of time series to forecast, it becomes increasingly difficult to both train and manage the life cycle of these LFMs. In *Chapter 8*, *Forecasting Time Series with Machine Learning Models*, we trained LFMs for just a subset of households in the dataset. It took almost 20 to 30 minutes to train a machine learning model for all 150 households and we ran them with the default hyperparameters. In a normal machine learning workflow, we train multiple machine learning models and do hyperparameter tuning to find the best configuration of the model. However, carrying out all these steps for thousands of time series in a dataset becomes increasingly complex and time-consuming.

Equally, then there is the issue of managing the life cycle of these models. All these individual models need to be deployed to production, the performance monitored to check for model and data drift, and retrained at a set frequency. This becomes increasingly complex, as we have more and more time series to forecast.

However, by shifting to a GFM paradigm, we drastically reduce the time and effort required to train and manage a machine learning model throughout its life cycle. As we will see in this chapter, training a GFM on these 150 households takes only a fraction of the time it takes to train LFMs.

Despite all the advantages of GFMs, they are not without some drawbacks. The main drawback is that we are assuming that all the time series in a dataset are generated by a single **Data Generating Process** (**DGP**). This might not be a valid assumption and this can lead to the GFM underfitting some specific types of time series patterns that are underrepresented in the dataset.

Another open issue is whether a GFM is good for use with unrelated tasks or time series. The jury is out on this one, but Montero-Manso et al. proved that there are also gains in modeling unrelated time series with a GFM. The same finding has been put forward, although from another perspective, by Oreshkin et al., who trained a global model on the M4 dataset (a set of unrelated datasets) and obtained state-of-the-art performance. They attributed it to the meta-learning capabilities of the model. That being said, relatedness does help the GFM, as the learning task becomes easier this way. We will see a practical application of this in upcoming sections of this chapter as well.

In the larger scheme of things, the benefits we derive from a GFM paradigm far outweigh the drawbacks. On most tasks, the GFMs either perform on par with or better than local models. It has been proven theoretically as well, by Montero-Manso et al., that a GFM, in a worst-case scenario, learns the same function as a local model. We will see this clearly in the models we are going to train in the upcoming sections. Finally, the training time and engineering complexity drop drastically as you move to a GFM paradigm.

Now that we have motivated you as far as why a GFM is a worthwhile paradigm to adopt, let's see how we can train one.

Creating GFMs

Training a GFM is very straightforward. While we were training LFMs in *Chapter 8*, *Forecasting Time Series with Machine Learning Models*, we were looping over different households in the London Smart Meters dataset and training a model for each household. However, if we just take all the households into a single dataframe (our dataset is already that way) and train a single model on it, we get a GFM. One thing we want to keep in mind is to make sure that all the time series in the dataset have the same frequency. In other words, if we mix daily time series with weekly ones while training these models, the performance drop will be noticeable – especially if we are using time-varying features and other time-based information. For a purely autoregressive model, mixing time series in this way is much less of a problem.

> **Notebook alert**
>
> To follow along with the complete code, use the notebook named `01-Global Forecasting Models-ML.ipynb` in the `chapter10` folder.

The standard framework we developed in *Chapter 8, Forecasting Time Series with Machine Learning Models*, is general enough to work for GFMs as well. So, as we did in that chapter, we define `FeatureConfig` and `MissingValueConfig` in the `01-Global Forecasting Models-ML.ipynb` notebook. We also slightly tweaked the Python function to train and evaluate the machine learning to make it work for all households. The details and exact functions can be found in the notebook.

Now, instead of looping over different households, we input the entire training dataset into the `get_X_y` function:

```
# Define the ModelConfig
from lightgbm import LGBMRegressor
model_config = ModelConfig(
    model=LGBMRegressor(random_state=42),
    name="Global LightGBM Baseline",
    # LGBM is not sensitive to normalized data
    normalize=False,
    # LGBM can handle missing values
    fill_missing=False,
)
# Get train and test data
train_features, train_target, train_original_target = feat_
config.get_X_y(
    train_df, categorical=True, exogenous=False
)
test_features, test_target, test_original_target = feat_config.
get_X_y(
    test_df, categorical=True, exogenous=False
)
```

Now that we have the data, we need to train the model. Training the model is also exactly the same as we saw in *Chapter 8, Forecasting Time Series with Machine Learning Models*. We will just choose LightGBM, which was the best-performing LFM model, and use functions we have defined earlier to train the model and evaluate the results:

```
y_pred, feat_df = train_model(
        model_config,
        _feat_config,
        missing_value_config,
        train_features,
        train_target,
```

```
        test_features,
    )
agg_metrics, eval_metrics_df = evaluate_forecast(
        y_pred, test_target, train_target, model_config
    )
```

Now in `y_pred`, we will have the forecast for all the households and `feat_df` will have the feature importance. `agg_metrics` will have the aggregated metric for all the selected households.

Let's look at how well our GFM model did:

Algorithm	MAE	MSE	meanMASE	Forecast Bias	Time Elapsed
LightGBM	0.077183	0.027510	0.978056	0.050231	NaN
GFM Baseline	0.079581	0.027326	1.013393	0.218127	28.718087

Figure 10.1 – Aggregate metrics with the baseline GFM

We are not doing better than the best LFM (in the first row) in terms of the metrics. However, one thing we should note is the time taken to train the model – ~30 seconds. The LFM for all the selected households was taking ~30 minutes. This huge reduction in time taken gives us a lot of flexibility to iterate faster with different features and techniques.

With that said, let's now look at a few techniques with which we can improve the accuracy of the GFMs.

Strategies to improve GFMs

GFMs have been in use in many forecasting competitions in Kaggle and outside of it. They have been battle-tested empirically, although very little work has gone into examining why they work so well from a theoretical point of view. Montero-Manso and Hyndman (2020) have a working paper titled *Principles and Algorithms for Forecasting Groups of Time Series: Locality and Globality*, which is an in-depth investigation, both theoretical and empirical, of GFMs and the many techniques that have been developed by the data science community collectively. In this section, we will try to include strategies to improve GFMs and, wherever possible, try to give theoretical justifications for why they would work.

> **Reference check**
>
> The Montero-Manso and Hyndman (2020) research paper is cited in *References* under reference number 1.

In the paper, Montero-Manso and Hyndman use a basic result in machine learning about generalization error to carry out the theoretical analysis and it is worth spending a bit of time to understand that, at last on a high level. **Generalization error**, as we know, is the difference between out-of-sample error and in-sample error. Yaser S Abu-Mostafa has a free, online **Massive Open Online Course (MOOC)** and an associated book (both of which are linked in the *Further reading* section). It is a short course on machine learning and is a course that I would recommend to anyone in the machine learning field for developing a stronger theoretical and conceptual basis for what we do. One of the important concepts the course and book put forward is the use of Hoeffding's inequality from probability theory to derive bounds on a learning problem. Let's quickly look at the result to develop our understanding:

$$E_{out} < E_{in} + \sqrt{\frac{log(|\mathcal{H}|) + log\left(\frac{2}{\delta}\right)}{2N}}$$

It has a probability of at least $1 - \delta$.

E_{in} is the in-sample average error and E_{out} is the expected out-of-sample error. N is the total number of samples in the dataset from which we are learning and $\mathcal{H}$ is the hypothesis class of models. It is a finite set of functions that can potentially fit the data. The size of $\mathcal{H}$, denoted by $|\mathcal{H}|$, is the complexity of $\mathcal{H}$. Although the formula of the bound looks intimidating, let's simplify the way we look at it to develop the necessary understanding.

We want E_{out} to be as close to E_{in} as possible and for that, we need the terms in the square root to be as small as possible. There are two terms under the square root that are in our *control*, so to speak – N and $|\mathcal{H}|$. Therefore, to make the generalization error ($E_{in} - E_{out}$) as small as possible, we either need to increase N (have more data) or decrease $|\mathcal{H}|$ (have a less complex model). This is a result that is applicable to all machine learning but Montero-Manso and Hyndman, with a few assumptions, made this applicable to time series models as well. It is this result that they used to give theoretical backing to the arguments put forward in their working paper.

Montero-Manso and Hyndman have taken Hoeffding's inequality and applied it to LFMs and GFMs to compare them. We can see the result here (for full mathematical and statistical understanding, refer to the original paper under *References*):

$$E_{out}^{Local} < E_{in}^{Local} + \sqrt{\frac{log\left(\prod_{i=1}^{K}|\mathcal{H}_i|\right) + log\left(\frac{2}{\delta}\right)}{2NK}}$$

$$E_{out}^{Global} < E_{in}^{Global} + \sqrt{\frac{log(|\mathcal{J}|) + log\left(\frac{2}{\delta}\right)}{2NK}}$$

E_{out}^{Local} and E_{out}^{Global} are the average in-sample errors across all the time series using the local and global approaches, respectively. E_{out}^{Global} and E_{in}^{Global} are the out-of-sample expectations under the local and global approaches, respectively. $\mathcal{H}_i$ is the hypothesis class for the i-th time series and $\mathcal{J}$ is the hypothesis class for the global approach (the global approach only fits a single function and hence, has just a single hypothesis class).

One of the most interesting results that comes out of this is that the complexity term for LFMs $\left(log\left(\prod_{i=1}^{K}|\mathcal{H}_i|\right)\right)$ grows the size of the dataset. The greater the number of time series we have in the dataset, the more the complexity and the worse the generalization error, whereas with GFMs, the complexity term $(log(|\mathcal{J}|))$ stays constant. Therefore, for a dataset of moderate size, the overall complexity of LFMs (such as exponential smoothing) can be much higher than a single GFM, no matter how complex the GFM is. As a corollary, we can also think that with the available dataset (NK), we can afford to train a model with much higher complexity than a model for LFMs. There are many ways to increase the complexity of the model, which we will see in the following section.

Now, let's return to the GFMs we were training. We saw that the performance of the GFM we trained was not up to the mark when we compared it with the best LFM (LightGBM), but it is better than the baseline and other models we tried, so right off the bat, we know the GFM we trained is not terrible. Now, let's look at a few ways to improve the performance of the model.

Increasing memory

As we discussed in *Chapter 5, Time Series Forecasting as Regression*, the machine learning models that we discuss in this book are finite memory models or Markov models. A model such as exponential smoothing takes into account the entire history of a time series while forecasting, but models such as any of the machine learning models we discussed only take in a finite memory to make their predictions. In a finite memory model, the amount of memory we allow the model to access is called the size of the memory (M) or order of autoregression (from econometrics).

Providing a greater amount of memory to the model increases the complexity of the model. Therefore, one of the ways to increase the performance of the GFM is to increase the amount of memory the model has access to. There are many ways to increase the amount of memory.

Adding more lag features

If you have prior exposure to ARIMA models, you will know that the number of **Autoregressive (AR)** terms are sparingly used. We usually see AR models with single-digit lags. However, when we are moving to GFMs, we can afford to have much larger lags. Montero-Manso and Hyndman empirically showed the benefits of adding more lags to GFMs. For highly seasonal time series, a peculiar phenomenon was observed. The accuracy improves with an increase in lags but it then saturates and suddenly worsens when the lag becomes equal to the seasonal cycle. On further increasing the lags beyond the seasonal cycle, the accuracy shows huge gains. This may be because of the overfitting that happens because of seasonality. It becomes very easy for the model to favor the seasonal lag because it works very well in a sample, so it's better to add a few more lags on the plus side of the seasonal cycle.

Adding rolling features

Another way to increase the memory of the model is to include rolling averages as features. Rolling averages take information from extended windows on memory and encode that information by way of descriptive statistics (such as the mean or max). This is an efficient way of including the memory because we can take very large windows for memory and include the information as a single feature in the model.

Adding EWMA features

An **Exponentially Weighted Moving Average** (**EWMA**) is a way to include infinite memory into a finite memory model. The EWMA essentially takes the average of the entire history but is weighted according to the α that we set. Therefore, with different values of α, we get different kinds of memory, again encoded as a single feature. Including different EWMA features has also empirically proved beneficial.

We have already included these kinds of features in our feature engineering and they are part of the baseline GFM we trained, so let's move on to the next strategy for improving the accuracy of GFMs.

Using time series meta-features

The baseline GFM we trained earlier in the *Creating Global Forecasting Models (GFMs)* section had lag features, rolling features, and EWMA features, but we have given no feature that helps the model distinguish between different time series in the dataset. The baseline GFM model learned a generalized function that generates a forecast provided the features. This might work well enough for homogenous datasets where all the time series are very similar in nature, but for heterogenous datasets, the information with which the model can distinguish each time series comes in handy.

So, information about the time series itself is what we call meta-features. In a retail context, it can be the product ID, the category of products, the store number, and so on. In our dataset, we have features such as `stdorToU`, `Acorn`, `Acorn_grouped`, and `LCLid`, which give some information about the time series itself. Including these meta-features in the GFM will improve the performance of the model.

However, there is just one problem – more often than not, these meta-features are categorical in nature. A feature is categorical when the values in the feature can only take discrete values. For instance, `Acorn_grouped` can only have one of three values – `Affluent`, `Comfortable`, or `Adversity`. Most machine learning models do not work well with categorical features. All the models in `scikit-learn`, the most popular machine learning library in the Python ecosystem, do not allow categorical features at all. To include categorical features in machine learning models, we need to encode them into numerical form, and there are many ways to encode categorical columns. Let's review a few popular options.

Ordinal encoding and one-hot encoding

The most popular ways of encoding categorical features are ordinal encoding and one-hot encoding, but they are not always the best choices. Let's quickly review what these techniques are and when they are suitable.

Ordinal encoding is the simplest of them all. We simply assign a numerical code to the unique values of a category and then replace the categorical value with the numerical code. To encode the Acorn_grouped feature from our dataset, all we need to do is assign codes, say 1 for Affluent, 2 for Comfortable, and 3 for Adversity, and replace all instances of the categorical values with the code we assigned. While this is really easy, this kind of encoding introduces meanings to the categorical values that we may or may not intend. When we assign numerical codes, we are implicitly saying that the categorical value that gets assigned 2 as a code is better than the categorical value with 1 as the code. This kind of encoding only works for ordinal features (features whose categorical values have an intrinsic sense of rank in their meaning) and should be sparingly used. Another way we can think about the problem is in terms of distance. When we do ordinal encoding, the distance between Comfortable and Affluent can be higher than the distance between Comfortable and Adversity, depending on the way we encode.

One-hot encoding is a better way of representing categorical features with no ordinal meaning. It essentially encodes the categorical features in a higher dimension, placing the categorical values equally distant in that space. The size of the dimension it requires to encode the categorical values is equal to the cardinality of the categorical variable. **Cardinality** is the number of unique values in the categorical feature. Let's see how sample data would be encoded in a one-hot encoding scheme:

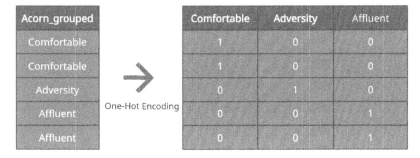

Figure 10.2 – One-hot encoding of categorical features

We can see that the resulting encoding will have a column for each unique value in the categorical feature and the value is indicated by 1 in the column. For instance, the first row is Comfortable, and therefore, every other column except the Comfortable column will have 0 and the Comfortable column will have 1. If we calculate the Euclidean distance between any two categorical values, we can see that they are the same.

However, there are three main issues with this encoding, all of which become a problem with high cardinality categorical variables:

- The embedding is inherently sparse and many machine learning models (for instance, tree-based models and neural networks) do not really work well with sparse data (sparse data is when a majority of values in the data are zeros). When the cardinality is just 5 or 10, the sparsity introduced may not be that much of a problem, but when we consider a cardinality of 100 or 500, the encoding becomes really sparse.

- Another issue is the explosion of dimensions of the problem. When we increase the total number of features of a problem due to the large number of new features that are created through one-hot encoding, we make the problem harder to solve. This can be explained by the **curse of dimensionality**. The *Further reading* section has a link with more information on the curse of dimensionality.

- The last problem is related to practical concerns. For a large dataset, if we one-hot encode a categorical value with hundreds or thousands of unique values, the resulting dataframe is not going to be easy to work with because it will not fit in the computer memory.

There is a slightly different way of one-hot encoding where we drop one of these dimensions, called **dummy variable encoding**. This has the added benefit of making the encoding linearly independent, which, in turn, has some advantages, especially for vanilla linear regression. The *Further reading* section has a link if you want to know more.

Since the categorical columns that we must encode have high cardinality (at least a few of them), we will not be doing this encoding. Instead, let's look at a few encoding techniques that can handle high cardinality categorical variables better.

Frequency encoding

Frequency encoding is an encoding schema that does not increase the dimensions of the problem. It takes a single categorical array and returns a single numeric array. The logic is very simple – it replaces the categorical values with the number of times the value occurs in the training dataset. Although it's not perfect, this works pretty well, as it lets the model distinguish between different categories based on how frequently they occur.

There is a popular library, `category_encoders`, that implements a lot of different encoding schemes in a standard `scikit-learn` style estimator, and we will be using that in our experiments as well. The standard framework we developed in *Chapter 8, Forecasting Time Series with Machine Learning Models*, also had a couple of functionalities that we didn't use – `encode_categorical` and `categorical_encoder`. So, let's use these and train our model now:

```
from category_encoders import CountEncoder
from lightgbm import LGBMRegressor
#Define which columns names are categorical features
cat_encoder = CountEncoder(cols=cat_features)

model_config = ModelConfig(
    model=LGBMRegressor(random_state=42),
    name="Global LightGBM with Meta Features (CountEncoder)",
```

```
    # LGBM is not sensitive to normalized data
    normalize=False,
    # LGBM can handle missing values
    fill_missing=False,
    # Turn on categorical encoding
    encode_categorical=True,
    # Pass the categorical encoder to be used
    categorical_encoder=cat_encoder
)
```

The rest of the process is the same as what we saw in the *Creating Global Forecasting Models (GFMs)* section and we get the forecast using the encoded meta-features:

Algorithm	MAE	MSE	meanMASE	Forecast Bias	Time Elapsed
LightGBM	0.077183	0.027510	0.978056	0.050231	NaN
GFM Baseline	0.079581	0.027326	1.013393	0.218127	28.718087
GFM+Meta (CountEncoder)	0.079411	0.027233	1.011801	0.037475	68.020298

Figure 10.3 – Aggregate metrics with the GFM with meta-features (frequency encoding)

Right away, we can see that there is a reduction in error, although it is minimal. We can also see that the training time has almost doubled. This may be because now we have an additional step of encoding the categorical features in addition to training the machine learning model.

The main issue with frequency encoding is that it doesn't work with features that are uniformly distributed in the dataset. For instance, the LCLid feature, which is just a unique code for each household, is uniformly distributed in the dataset and when we use frequency encoding, all the LCLid features will come to almost the same frequency, and hence the machine learning model considers them almost the same.

Let's now look at a slightly different approach.

Target mean encoding

Target mean encoding, in its most vanilla form, is a very simple concept. It is a *supervised* approach that uses the target in the training dataset to encode the categorical columns. Let's look at an example:

Acorn_grouped	energy_consumption
Comfortable	10
Comfortable	15
Adversity	5
Affluent	15
Affluent	20
Adversity	8
Adversity	7

Mean Encoding

Acorn_grouped	Encoded Value
Comfortable	(10 + 15)/2
Adversity	(5 + 8 + 7)/3
Affluent	(15 + 20)/2

Figure 10.4 – Target mean encoding

The vanilla target mean encoding has a few limitations. It increases the chance of overfitting the training data because we are using the mean targets directly and thereby leaking the target into the model in a way. Another problem with the approach is that when the categorical values are unevenly distributed, there may be a few categorical values with very small sample sizes, and therefore, the mean estimate becomes noisy. Extending this problem to the extreme, we get another case where an unseen categorical value comes up in test data. This is also not supported in the vanilla version. Therefore, in practice, this simple version is almost never used, but slightly more sophisticated versions of this concept are widely used and are an effective strategy while encoding categorical features.

In `category_encoders`, there are many variations of this concept, but let's look at two popular and effective ones here.

In 2001, Daniele Micci-Barreca proposed a variant of mean encoding. If we consider the target as a binary variable, say 1 and 0, the mean (which is the number of 1s or number of samples) is also the probability of having 1. Using this interpretation of the means, Daniele proposed to blend two probabilities – prior and posterior probabilities – as the final encoding for the categorical features.

> **Reference check**
>
> The research paper by Daniele Micci-Barreca is cited in *References* under reference number 2.

The prior probability is defined as follows:

$$P_{prior} = \frac{n_y}{n_{TR}}$$

Here, n_y is the number of cases such that $target = 1$, and n_{TR} is the number of samples in the training data.

The posterior probability is defined for category i as follows:

$$P_{posterior}^i = \frac{n_{iY}}{n_i}$$

Here, n_{iY} is the number of samples in the dataset where category $= i$ and $Y = 1$, and n_i is the number of samples in the dataset where $category = i$.

Now, the final encoding for category i is as follows:

$$S_i = \lambda(n_i) \times P_{posterior}^i + \left(1 - \lambda(n_i)\right) \times P_{prior}$$

Here, λ is the weighting factor, which is a monotonically increasing function on n_i that is bounded between 0 and 1. So, this function gives a larger weight to the posterior probability as the number of samples increases.

Adapting this to the regression setting, the probabilities change to expected values so that the formula becomes the following:

$$S_i = \lambda(n_i) \times \frac{\sum_{k \in TR_i} Y_k}{n_i} + \left(1 - \lambda(n_i)\right) \times \frac{\sum_{k \in LTR} Y_k}{n_{TR}}$$

Here, TR_i is all the rows where $category = 1$ and $\sum_{k \in TR_i} Y_k$ is the sum of Y for TR_i. $\sum_{k \in TR} Y_k$ is the sum of Y for all the rows in the training dataset. As with the binary variable, we are mixing the expected value of Y, given $category = i$ ($E[Y \mid category = i]$) and the expected value of Y ($E[Y]$) for the final categorical encoding.

There are many functions that we can use for λ. Daniele mentions a very common functional form (sigmoid):

$$\lambda(n_i) = \frac{1}{1 + e^{-\frac{n_i - k}{f}}}$$

Here, n_i is the number of samples in the dataset where, $category = i$ and k and f are tunable hyperparameters. k determines half of the minimal sample size for which we completely trust the estimate. If $k = 1$, what we are saying is that we trust the posterior estimate from a category that has only two samples. f determines how fast the sigmoid transitions between the two extremes. As f tends to infinity, the transition becomes a hard threshold between prior and posterior probabilities. `TargetEncoder` from `category_encoders` has implemented this λ. The k parameter is called `min_samples_leaf` with a default value of 1, and the f parameter is called `smoothing` with a default value of 1. Let's see how this encoding works on our problem. Using a different encoder in the framework we are working on is as simple as passing a different `cat_encoder` (the initialized categorical encoder) to `ModelConfig`:

```
from category_encoders import TargetEncoder
cat_encoder = TargetEncoder(cols=cat_features)
```

The rest of the code is exactly the same. We can find the full code in the corresponding notebook. Let's see how well the new encoding has done:

Algorithm	MAE	MSE	meanMASE	Forecast Bias	Time Elapsed
LightGBM	0.077183	0.027510	0.978056	0.050231	NaN
GFM Baseline	0.079581	0.027326	1.013393	0.218127	28.718087
GFM+Meta (CountEncoder)	0.079411	0.027233	1.011801	0.037475	68.020298
GFM+Meta (TargetEncoder)	0.079537	0.027218	1.012400	0.335610	43.607325

Figure 10.5 – Aggregate metrics with the GFM with meta-features (target encoding)

It's not doing that well, is it? As with machine learning models, the **No Free Lunch Theorem** (**NFLT**) applies to categorical encoding as well. There is no one encoding scheme that works well all the time. Although not directly related to the topic, if you want to know more about the NFLT, head to *the Further reading section*.

> **Important note**
>
> With all these *supervised* categorical encoding techniques, such as target mean encoding, we have to be really careful not to induce data leakage. The encoder should be fit using training data and not using the validation or test data. Another very popular technique is to generate categorical encoding using cross-validation and use the out-of-sample encodings to absolutely avoid data leakage or overfitting.

There are many more encoding schemes, such as `MEstimateEncoder` (which uses additive smoothing as the λ), `HashingEncoder`, and so on, in `category_encoders`. Another very effective way of encoding categorical features is using embedding from deep learning. The *Further reading* section has a link to a tutorial for doing this.

Before now, all this categorical encoding was a separate step before the modeling. Now, let's look at a technique that considers categorical features natively for model training.

LightGBM's native handling of categorical features

A few machine learning model implementations handle categorical features natively, especially gradient-boosting models. CatBoost and LightGBM, two of the most popular GBM implementations, handle categorical features out of the box. CatBoost has a unique way of encoding categorical features into numerical ones internally using something similar to additive smoothing. The *Further reading* section has links to further information on how this encoding is done. `category_encoders` has implemented this logic as `CatBoostEncoder` so that we can use this type of encoding for any machine learning model as well.

While CatBoost handles this internal conversion into numerical features, LightGBM takes a more native approach to dealing with categorical features. LightGBM considers the categorical features as is while growing and splitting the trees. For a categorical feature with k unique values (cardinality of k), there are $2^{k-1} - 1$ possible partitions. This soon becomes intractable, but for regression trees, Walter D. Fisher proposed a technique back in 1958 that makes the complexity of finding an optimal split much lesser. The essence of the method is to use average target statistics for each categorical value to order them and then find the optimal split in the ordered categorical values.

Reference check

The research paper by Fisher is cited in *References* under reference number 3.

LightGBM's `scikit-learn` API supports this feature by taking an argument, `categorical_feature`, which has a list of categorical feature names, during `fit`. We can use the `fit_kwargs` argument in the fit of our `MLModel` that we defined in *Chapter 8, Forecasting Time Series with Machine Learning Models*, to pass in this parameter. Let's see how we can do this:

```
from lightgbm import LGBMRegressor
model_config = ModelConfig(
    model=LGBMRegressor(random_state=42),
    name="Global LightGBM with Meta Features (NativeLGBM)",
    # LGBM is not sensitive to normalized data
    normalize=False,
    # LGBM can handle missing values
    fill_missing=False,
    # We are using inbuilt categorical feature handling
    encode_categorical=False,
)
# Training the model and passing in fit_kwargs
y_pred, feat_df = train_model(
    model_config,
    _feat_config,
    missing_value_config,
    train_features,
    train_target,
    test_features,
    fit_kwargs=dict(categorical_feature=cat_features),
)
```

`y_pred` has the forecasts, which we evaluate as usual. Let's also see the results:

Algorithm	MAE	MSE	meanMASE	Forecast Bias	Time Elapsed
LightGBM	0.077183	0.027510	0.978056	0.050231	NaN
GFM Baseline	0.079581	0.027326	1.013393	0.218127	28.718087
GFM+Meta (CountEncoder)	0.079411	0.027233	1.011801	0.037475	68.020298
GFM+Meta (TargetEncoder)	0.079537	0.027218	1.012400	0.335610	43.607325
GFM+Meta (NativeLGBM)	0.079209	0.027329	1.002630	-0.083755	30.316029

Figure 10.6 – Aggregate metrics with the GFM with meta-features (native LightGBM)

We can observe a good reduction in **MAE** as well as **meanMASE** with the native handling of categorical features. We can also see a reduction in the total training time because we don't have a separate step for encoding the categorical feature. Empirically, the native handling of categorical features works better most of the time.

Now that we have encoded the categorical features, let's look at another way to improve accuracy.

Tuning hyperparameters

Although hyperparameter tuning is common practice in machine learning, we haven't been able to do so because of the sheer number of models we had under the LFM paradigm. Now that we have a GFM that finishes training in 30 seconds, hyperparameter tuning becomes feasible. From a theoretical perspective, we also saw that GFMs can afford a larger complexity and can therefore evaluate a greater number of functions to pick the best without overfitting.

Wikipedia defines mathematical optimization as *"the selection of a best element, with regard to some criterion, from some set of available alternatives."* In most cases, this involves finding the maximum or minimum value of some function (an **objective function**) from a set of alternatives (the **search space**) subject to some conditions (**constraints**). The search space can be discrete variables, continuous variables, or a mixture of both, and the objective function can be differentiable or non-differentiable. There is a large body of research that tackles these variations.

You may be wondering why we are talking about mathematical optimization now, right? Hyperparameter tuning is a mathematical optimization problem. The objective function here is non-differentiable and returns the metric for which we are optimizing – for instance, the **Mean Absolute Error** (**MAE**). The search space comprises the different hyperparameters we are tuning – say, the number of trees or depth of the trees. It could be a mixture of continuous and discrete variables and the constraints would be any restriction on the search space we impose – for instance, a particular hyperparameter cannot be negative, or a particular combination of hyperparameters cannot occur. Therefore, being aware of the terms used in mathematical optimization will help us in our discussion.

Even though hyperparameter tuning is a standard machine learning concept, we will quickly review three main techniques (besides manual trial and error) for doing hyperparameter tuning.

Grid search

Grid search can be thought of as a brute-force method where we define a discrete grid over the search space, check the objective function at each point in the grid, and pick the best point in that grid. The grid is defined as a set of discrete points for each of the hyperparameters we choose to tune. Once the grid is defined, all the intersections of the grid are evaluated to search for the best objective value. If we are tuning 5 hyperparameters and the grid has 20 discrete values for each parameter, the total number of trials for a grid search would be 3,200,000 (20^5). This means training a model 3.2 million times and evaluating it. This becomes quite limiting because most modern machine learning models have many hyperparameters. For instance, LightGBM has more than 100 and out of that, at least 20 are highly impactful parameters when tuned. So, using a brute force approach such as grid search forces us to make the search space quite small so that it becomes feasible to carry out the tuning in a reasonable amount of time.

For our case, we have defined a very small grid of just 27 trials by limiting ourselves to a really small search space. Let's see how we do that:

```
from sklearn.model_selection import ParameterGrid

grid_params = {
    "num_leaves": [16, 31, 63],
    "objective": ["regression", "regression_l1", "huber"],
    "random_state": [42],
    "colsample_bytree": [0.5, 0.8, 1.0],
}
parameter_space = list(ParameterGrid(grid_params))
```

We just tune three hyperparameters (num_leaves, objective, and colsample_bytree), and with just three options for each parameter. Performing the grid search after this is just about looping over the parameter space and evaluating the model at each combination of hyperparameters:

```
scores = []
for p in tqdm(parameter_space, desc="Performing Grid Search"):
    _model_config = ModelConfig(
        model=LGBMRegressor(**p, verbose=-1),
        name="Global Meta LightGBM Tuning",
        # LGBM is not sensitive to normalized data
        normalize=False,
```

```
        # LGBM can handle missing values
        fill_missing=False,
    )
    y_pred, feat_df = train_model(
        _model_config,
        _feat_config,
        missing_value_config,
        train_features,
        train_target,
        test_features,
        fit_kwargs=dict(categorical_feature=cat_features),
    )
    scores.append(ts_utils.mae(
            test_target['energy_consumption'], y_pred
        ))
```

This takes about 15 minutes to complete and gives us the best MAE of 0.73454, which is already a great improvement from our untuned GFM.

However, this makes us wonder whether there is an even better solution that we haven't covered in the grid we defined. One option is to expand the grid and run the grid search again. This increases the number of trials exponentially and soon becomes infeasible.

Let's look at a different method where we can explore a larger search space with the same number of trials.

Random search

Random search takes a slightly different route. In random search, we also define the search space, but instead of discretely defining specific points in the space, we define probability distributions over the range we want to explore. These probability distributions can be anything from a uniform distribution (which says any point in the range is equally likely) to Gaussian distribution (which has the familiar peak in the middle) or any other esoteric distributions such as gamma or beta distributions. As long as we can sample from the distribution, we can use it for random search. Once we define the search space, we can sample points from the distribution and evaluate each of the points to find the best hyperparameter.

While the number of trials is a function of the defined search space for grid search, it is a user input for random search, so we get to decide how much time or computational budget we need to use for hyperparameter tuning and, because of that, we can also search over a larger search space.

With this new flexibility, let's define a larger search space for our problem and use random search:

```
import scipy
from sklearn.model_selection import ParameterSampler


random_search_params = {
    # A uniform distribution between 10 and 100, but only
integers
    "num_leaves": scipy.stats.randint(10,100),
    # A list of categorical string values
    "objective": ["regression", "regression_l1", "huber"],
    "random_state": [42],
    # List of floating point numbers between 0.3 and 1.0 with a
resolution of 0.05
    "colsample_bytree": np.arange(0.3,1.0,0.05),
    # List of floating point numbers between 0 and 10 with a
resolution of 0.1
    "lambda_l1":np.arange(0,10,0.1),
    # List of floating point numbers between 0 and 10 with a
resolution of 0.1
    "lambda_l2":np.arange(0,10,0.1)
}
# Sampling from the search space number of iterations times
parameter_space = list(ParameterSampler(random_search_params,
n_iter=27, random_state=42))
```

This also runs for about 15 minutes, but we have explored a larger search space. However, the best MAE reported was just 0.73752, which is lower than with grid search. Maybe if we run the search for a greater number of iterations, we will get a better score, but that is just a shot in the dark. Ironically, that is pretty much what random search also does. It closes its eyes and throws the dart at random places on the dartboard and hopes it hits the bull's eye.

There are two terms in mathematical optimization called exploration and exploitation. Exploration ensures the optimization algorithm reaches different regions of the search space, whereas exploitation makes sure we search more in regions that are giving us better results. Random search is purely explorative and is unaware of what is happening as it evaluates different trials.

Let's look at one last technique that tries to balance between exploration and exploitation.

Bayesian optimization

Bayesian optimization has a lot of similarities with random search. Both define their search space as probability distributions, and in both techniques, the user decides how many trials it needs to evaluate, but where they differ is the key advantage of Bayesian optimization. While random search is randomly sampling from the search space, Bayesian optimization is doing it intelligently. Bayesian optimization is aware of its past trials and the objective values that came out of those trials so that it can adapt future trials to exploit the regions where better objective values were seen. At a high level, it does this by building a probability model of the objective function and using it to focus trials on promising areas. The details of the algorithm are worth knowing and we have linked to a couple of resources in *Further reading* to help you along the way.

Now, let's use a popular library, `optuna`, to implement Bayesian optimization for hyperparameter tuning on the GFM we have been training.

The process is quite simple. We need to define a function that takes in a parameter called `trial`. Inside the function, we sample the different parameters we want to tune from the `trial` object, train the model, evaluate the forecast, and return the metric we want to optimize (the MAE). Let's quickly do that:

```python
def objective(trial):
    params = {
        # Sample an integer between 10 and 100
        "num_leaves": trial.suggest_int("num_leaves", 10, 100),
        # Sample a categorical value from the list provided
        "objective": trial.suggest_categorical(
            "objective", ["regression", "regression_l1",
"huber"]
        ),
        "random_state": [42],
        # Sample from a uniform distribution between 0.3 and
1.0
        "colsample_bytree": trial.suggest_uniform("colsample_
bytree", 0.3, 1.0),
        # Sample from a uniform distribution between 0 and 10
        "lambda_l1": trial.suggest_uniform("lambda_l1", 0, 10),
        # Sample from a uniform distribution between 0 and 10
        "lambda_l2": trial.suggest_uniform("lambda_l2", 0, 10),
    }
    _model_config = ModelConfig(
        # Use the sampled params to initialize the model
```

```
        model=LGBMRegressor(**params, verbose=-1),
        name="Global Meta LightGBM Tuning",
        # LGBM is not sensitive to normalized data
        normalize=False,
        # LGBM can handle missing values
        fill_missing=False,
    )
    y_pred, feat_df = train_model(
        _model_config,
        _feat_config,
        missing_value_config,
        train_features,
        train_target,
        test_features,
        fit_kwargs=dict(categorical_feature=cat_features),
    )
    # Return the MAE metric as the value
    return ts_utils.mae(test_target["energy_consumption"], y_
pred)
```

Once we have defined the objective function, we need to initialize a sampler. optuna has many samplers such as GridSampler, RandomSampler, and TPESampler. For all standard use cases, TPESampler is the one to use. GridSampler does grid search and RandomSampler does random search. When defining a **Tree Parzen Estimator** (**TPE**) sampler, there are two parameters that we should pay attention to:

- seed – This sets the seed for the random sampling. This makes the process reproducible.
- n_startup_trials – This is the number of trials that are purely exploratory. This is done to understand the search space before the exploitation kicks in. The default value is 10. We can reduce or increase this depending on how large our sample space is and how many trials we are planning to do.

The rest of the parameters are best left untouched for the most common use cases.

Now, we create a study, which is the object that runs the trials and stores all the details about the trials:

```
# Create a study
study = optuna.create_study(direction="minimize",
sampler=sampler)
# Start the optimization run
study.optimize(objective, n_trials=27, show_progress_bar=True)
```

Here, we define the direction of optimization, and we pass in the sampler we initialized earlier. Once the study is defined, we need to call the `optimize` method and pass the objective function we defined, the number of trials we need to run, and some other parameters. A full list of parameters for the `optimize` method is available here –`https://optuna.readthedocs.io/en/ stable/reference/generated/optuna.study.Study.html#optuna.study. Study.optimize`.

This runs slightly longer, maybe because of the additional computation required to generate new trials, but still only takes about 20 minutes for the 27 trials. As expected, this has come up with another combination of hyperparameters for which the objective value is `0.72838` (the lowest before now).

To fully illustrate the difference between the three, let's compare how the three techniques spent their computational budget:

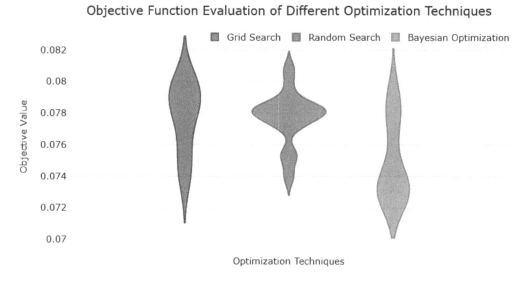

Figure 10.7 – Distribution of computational effort (grid versus random versus Bayesian optimization)

We can see that the Bayesian optimization has a fat tail on the lower side, indicating that it spent most of its computational budget evaluating and exploiting the optimal regions in the search space.

Let's look at how the different trials with these techniques fared as the optimization procedure progressed.

The notebook has a more detailed comparison and commentary on the three techniques.

The bottom line is that if we have unlimited computation, grid search with a well-defined and fine-grained grid is the best option, but if we value the efficiency of our computational effort, we should go for Bayesian optimization.

Let's see how the new parameters worked out for us:

Algorithm	MAE	MSE	meanMASE	Forecast Bias	Time Elapsed
LightGBM	0.077183	0.027510	0.978056	0.050231	NaN
GFM Baseline	0.079581	0.027326	1.013393	0.218127	28.718087
GFM+Meta (CountEncoder)	0.079411	0.027233	1.011801	0.037475	68.020298
GFM+Meta (TargetEncoder)	0.079537	0.027218	1.012400	0.335610	43.607325
GFM+Meta (NativeLGBM)	0.079209	0.027329	1.002630	-0.083755	30.316029
Tuned GFM+Meta	0.072918	0.030641	0.900749	-12.412786	57.936451

Figure 10.8 – Aggregate metrics with the tuned GFM with meta-features

We have had huge improvements in **MAE** and **meanMASE**, mostly because we were optimizing for the MAE when hyperparameter tuning. The MAE and MSE have slightly different priorities and we will spend more time on that in *Part 4, Mechanics of Forecasting*. The runtime also increased because the new parameters build more leaves for a tree than before and are more complex than the default parameters.

Now, let's look at another strategy for improving the performance of a GFM.

Partitioning

Out of all the strategies we have discussed so far, this is the most counter-intuitive, especially if you are coming from a standard machine learning or statistics background. Normally, we would expect the model to do well with more data, but partitioning or splitting the dataset into multiple, almost equal parts has been shown (empirically) to improve the accuracy of the model. While this has been seen empirically, why this happens is something that is still not quite clear. One explanation is that the GFMs have a slightly simpler job of learning when trained on a subset of similar entities and hence, can learn specific functions to subsets of similar entities. Another explanation for the phenomenon has been put forward by Montero-Manso and Hyndman (number 1 in *References*). They put forward that partitioning the data is another form of increasing the complexity because instead of having $log(|\mathcal{J}|)$ as the complexity term, we have $log\left(\prod_{i=1}^{P}|\mathcal{H}_i|\right)$, where P is the number of partitions. With this rationale, the LFMs are special cases where P is equal to the number of time series in the dataset.

There are many ways we can partition the data, each with varying degrees of complexity.

Random partition

The simplest method is to randomly split the dataset into P-equal partitions and train separate models for each partition. This method faithfully follows the explanation that Montero-Manso and Hyndman provide because we are splitting the dataset randomly, with no concern for the similarity of the different households. Let's see how we can do that:

```
# Define a function which splits a list into n partitions
def partition (list_in, n):
```

```
    random.shuffle(list_in)
    return [list_in[i::n] for i in range(n)]
# split the unique LCLids into partitions
partitions = partition(train_df.LCLid.cat.categories.tolist(),
3)
```

Then, we just loop over these partitions and train separate models for each partition. The exact code can be found in the notebook. Let's see how well the random partition does:

Algorithm	MAE	MSE	meanMASE	Forecast Bias	Time Elapsed
LightGBM	0.077183	0.027510	0.978056	0.050231	NaN
GFM Baseline	0.079581	0.027326	1.013393	0.218127	28.718087
GFM+Meta (CountEncoder)	0.079411	0.027233	1.011801	0.037475	68.020298
GFM+Meta (TargetEncoder)	0.079537	0.027218	1.012400	0.335610	43.607325
GFM+Meta (NativeLGBM)	0.079209	0.027329	1.002630	-0.083755	30.316029
Tuned GFM+Meta	0.072918	0.030641	0.900749	-12.412786	57.936451
Tuned GFM+Meta+Random Part	0.072598	0.030681	0.898618	-12.361642	49.178089

Figure 10.9 – Aggregate metrics with the tuned GFM with meta-features and random partitioning

We can see a decrease in **MAE** and **meanMASE** even with a random partition. There is even a decrease in runtime because the individual models are working on less data and hence, train faster.

Now, let's see another way of partitioning, keeping the similarity of different time series in mind.

Judgmental partitioning

Judgmental partitioning is when we use some attribute of the time series to split the dataset, and this is called judgmental because usually, this depends on the judgment of the person who is working on the model. There are many ways of doing this. We can use some meta-feature, or we can use some characteristics of the time series (such as volume, variability, intermittency, or a combination of these) to partition the dataset.

Let's use a meta-feature called Acorn_grouped to partition the dataset. Again, we will just loop over the unique values in Acorn_grouped and train a model for each value. We will also not use Acorn_grouped as a feature. The exact code is in the notebook. Let's see how well this partitioning is doing:

Algorithm	MAE	MSE	meanMASE	Forecast Bias	Time Elapsed
LightGBM	0.077183	0.027510	0.978056	0.050231	NaN
GFM Baseline	0.079581	0.027326	1.013393	0.218127	28.718087
GFM+Meta (CountEncoder)	0.079411	0.027233	1.011801	0.037475	68.020298
GFM+Meta (TargetEncoder)	0.079537	0.027218	1.012400	0.335610	43.607325
GFM+Meta (NativeLGBM)	0.079209	0.027329	1.002630	-0.083755	30.316029
Tuned GFM+Meta	0.072918	0.030641	0.900749	-12.412786	57.936451
Tuned GFM+Meta+Random Part	0.072598	0.030681	0.898618	-12.361642	49.178089
Tuned GFM+Meta+ACORN Part	0.072567	0.030786	0.898071	-12.316822	52.118687

Figure 10.10 – Aggregate metrics with the tuned GFM with meta-features and Acorn_grouped partitioning

This is doing even better than random partitioning. We can assume each of the partitions (Affluent, Comfortable, and Adversity) have some kind of similarity, which makes the learning easier, and hence, we get better accuracy.

Now, let's look at another way to partition the dataset, again, using similarity.

Algorithmic partitioning

In judgmental partitioning, we were picking some meta-features or time series characteristics for partitioning the dataset. We are picking a handful of dimensions to partition the dataset because we are doing it in our minds and our mental faculties cannot handle more than two or three dimensions well, but we can see this partitioning as an unsupervised clustering approach and this approach is called algorithmic partitioning.

There are two ways we can cluster time series:

- Extracting features for each time series and using those features to form clusters
- Using time series clustering techniques using the **Dynamic Time Warping** (**DTW**) distance

tslearn is an open source Python library that has implemented a few time series clustering approaches based on the distances between time series. There is a link in *Further reading* for more information on the library and how it can be used for time series clustering.

In our example, we are going to use the first method, where we derive a few time series characteristics and use them for clustering. There are many features from statistical and temporal literature, such as autocorrelation, mean, variance, entropy, and the peak-to-peak distance, that we can extract from the time series. We can use another open source Python library called the **Time Series Feature Extraction Library** (tsfel) to make the process easier.

The library has many classes of features – statistical, temporal, and spectral domains – that we can choose, and the rest is handled by the library. Let's see how we can generate these features and create a dataframe to perform clustering:

```
import tsfel
cfg = tsfel.get_features_by_domain("statistical")
cfg = {**cfg, **tsfel.get_features_by_domain("temporal")}

uniq_ids = train_df.LCLid.cat.categories

stat_df = []
for id_ in tqdm(uniq_ids, desc="Calculating features for all
households"):
    ts = train_df.loc[train_df.LCLid==id_, "energy_
consumption"]
    res = tsfel.time_series_features_extractor(cfg, ts,
verbose=False)
    res['LCLid'] = id_
    stat_df.append(res)

stat_df = pd.concat(stat_df).set_index("LCLid")
```

The dataframe looks something like this:

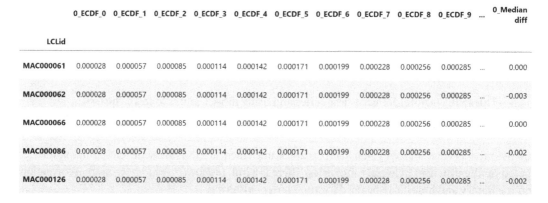

LCLid	0_ECDF_0	0_ECDF_1	0_ECDF_2	0_ECDF_3	0_ECDF_4	0_ECDF_5	0_ECDF_6	0_ECDF_7	0_ECDF_8	0_ECDF_9	...	0_Median diff
MAC000061	0.000028	0.000057	0.000085	0.000114	0.000142	0.000171	0.000199	0.000228	0.000256	0.000285	...	0.000
MAC000062	0.000028	0.000057	0.000085	0.000114	0.000142	0.000171	0.000199	0.000228	0.000256	0.000285	...	-0.003
MAC000066	0.000028	0.000057	0.000085	0.000114	0.000142	0.000171	0.000199	0.000228	0.000256	0.000285	...	0.000
MAC000086	0.000028	0.000057	0.000085	0.000114	0.000142	0.000171	0.000199	0.000228	0.000256	0.000285	...	-0.002
MAC000126	0.000028	0.000057	0.000085	0.000114	0.000142	0.000171	0.000199	0.000228	0.000256	0.000285	...	-0.002

Figure 10.11 – Features extracted from different time series

Now that we have the dataframe with each row representing a time series with different features, we can ideally apply any clustering method, such as k-means, k-medoids, or HDBSCAN, and find clusters. However, in high dimensions, a lot of the distance metrics (including Euclidean) do not work as well as they are supposed to. There is a seminal paper on the topic by Charu C. Agarwal et al. from 2001 that explores the topic. When we increase the dimensionality of the space, our common sense (which conceptualizes three dimensions) does not work as well and, as a consequence, common distance metrics such as Euclidean distance do not work very well with high dimensions. We have linked to a blog summarizing the paper (in *Further reading*) and the paper itself (in *References* under number 5), which make the concept clearer. So, a common way of handling high dimensional clustering is by performing dimensionality reduction first and then using normal clustering.

Principal Component Analysis (**PCA**) had been the go-to tool in the field, but since PCA only captures and retails linear relationships while reducing the dimensions, nowadays, another class of techniques is starting to become more popular – manifold learning.

t-distributed Stochastic Neighbor Embeddings (**t-SNE**) is a popular technique from this category, which is really popular for high-dimensional visualization. It is a really clever technique where we project the points from a high-dimensional space to a lower dimension, keeping the distribution of distance in the original space as close as possible to the one in lower dimensions. There is a lot to learn here, which is beyond the scope of this book. There are links in the *Further reading* section that can help you get started.

To cut a long story short, we will be using t-SNE to reduce the dimensions of the dataset we have and then cluster the dataset with the reduced dimensions. Let's see how we do that:

```python
from sklearn.preprocessing import StandardScaler
from sklearn.cluster import KMeans
from src.utils.data_utils import replace_array_in_dataframe
from sklearn.manifold import TSNE #T-Distributed Stochastic
Neighbor Embedding
# Standardizing to make distance calculation fair
X_std = replace_array_in_dataframe(stat_df, StandardScaler().
fit_transform(stat_df))
#Non-Linear Dimensionality Reduction
tsne = TSNE(n_components=2, perplexity=50, learning_
rate="auto", init="pca", random_state=42, metric="cosine",
square_distances=True)
X_tsne = tsne.fit_transform(X_std.values)
# Clustering reduced dimensions into 3 clusters
kmeans = KMeans(n_clusters=3, random_state=42).fit(X_tsne)
cluster_df = pd.Series(kmeans.labels_, index=X_std.index)
```

Since we reduced the dimensions to two, we can also visualize the clusters formed:

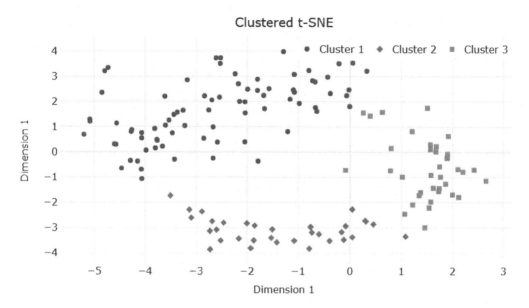

Figure 10.12 – Clustered time series after t-SNE dimensionality reduction

We have three well-defined clusters formed and now we are just going to use these clusters to train a model for each cluster. As usual, we loop over the three clusters and train the models. Let's see how we did so:

	Algorithm	MAE	MSE	meanMASE	Forecast Bias	Time Elapsed
0	LightGBM	0.077183	0.027510	0.978056	0.050231	NaN
1	GFM Baseline	0.079581	0.027326	1.013393	0.218127	28.718087
2	GFM+Meta (CountEncoder)	0.079411	0.027233	1.011801	0.037475	68.020298
3	GFM+Meta (TargetEncoder)	0.079537	0.027218	1.012400	0.335610	43.607325
4	GFM+Meta (NativeLGBM)	0.079209	0.027329	1.002630	-0.083755	30.316029
5	Tuned GFM+Meta	0.072918	0.030641	0.900749	-12.412786	57.936451
6	Tuned GFM+Meta+Random Part	0.072598	0.030681	0.898618	-12.361642	49.178089
7	Tuned GFM+Meta+ACORN Part	0.072567	0.030786	0.898071	-12.316822	52.118687
8	Tuned GFM+Meta+Clustered Part	0.072347	0.029976	0.905182	-12.521149	66.373510

Figure 10.13 – Aggregate metrics with the tuned GFM with meta-features and clustered partitioning

It looks as though this is the best MAE we have seen in all our experiments, but the three partition techniques have very similar MAEs. We can't see whether any one is better than the other just by looking at a single hold-out set. For good measure, we can run these forecasts with a test dataset using the `01a-Global Forecasting Models-ML-test.ipynb` notebook in the `chapter08` folder. Let's see how the aggregate metrics are on the test dataset:

Algorithm	MAE	MSE	meanMASE	Forecast Bias	Time Elapsed
LightGBM	0.0751	0.0271	0.9142	2.57%	nan
GFM Baseline	0.0773	0.0280	0.9586	0.71%	38.147337
GFM+Meta (CountEncoder)	0.0772	0.0276	0.9600	0.69%	71.797225
GFM+Meta (TargetEncoder)	0.0773	0.0276	0.9612	0.99%	48.736455
GFM+Meta (NativeLGBM)	0.0770	0.0279	0.9483	0.84%	32.467879
Tuned GFM+Meta	0.0700	0.0310	0.8384	-12.38%	62.091281
Tuned GFM+Meta+Random Part	0.0706	0.0339	0.8405	-12.96%	55.361825
Tuned GFM+Meta+ACORN Part	0.0696	0.0305	0.8342	-12.43%	52.066995
Tuned GFM+Meta+Clustered Part	0.0685	0.0285	0.8282	-11.94%	57.231065

Figure 10.14 – Aggregate metrics on test data

As expected, the clustered partition is still the methodology that performs the best in this case.

In *Chapter 8, Forecasting Time Series with Machine Learning Models*, it took us 8 minutes and 20 seconds to train an LFM for all the households in our dataset. Now, with the GFM paradigm, we finished training a model in 57 seconds (in the worst-case scenario). That's 777% less training time and this comes with an 8.78% decrease in the MAE.

We chose to do these experiments with LightGBM. This does not mean that LightGBM or any other gradient-boosting model is the only choice for GFMs, but they are a pretty good default. A well-tuned gradient-boosted trees model is a very difficult baseline to beat, but as always in machine learning, we should check what works best using well-defined experiments.

Although there are no hard and fast rules or cutoffs for when a GFM makes more sense than an LFM, as the number of time series in a dataset increases, the GFM becomes more favorable, both from the perspective of accuracy and computation.

Bonus – interpretability

Interpretability can be defined as the degree to which a human can understand the cause of a decision. In machine learning and artificial intelligence, that translates to the degree to which someone can understand the how and why of an algorithm and its predictions. There are two ways to look at interpretability – **transparency** and **post hoc interpretation**.

Transparency is when the model is inherently simple and can be simulated or thought about using human cognition. A human should be able to fully understand the inputs and the process a model takes to convert these inputs to outputs. This is a very stringent condition that almost none of the model machine learning or deep learning models satisfy.

This is where *post hoc interpretation* techniques shine. There are a wide variety of techniques that use the inputs and outputs of a model to understand why a model has made the predictions it has.

There are many popular techniques such as permutation feature importance, Shapley values, and LIME. All of these are general-purpose interpretation techniques that can be used on any machine learning model and that includes the GFMs we were discussing.

For more extensive coverage of such techniques, I have included a few links in *Further reading*.

Congratulations on finishing the second part of the book! It has been quite an intensive part where we went over quite a bit of theory and practical lessons, and we hope you are now comfortable with using machine learning for time series forecasting.

Summary

To round up the second part of the book nicely, we explored GFMs in detail and saw why they are important and why they are an exciting new direction in time series forecasting. We saw how we can use a GFM using machine learning models and also reviewed many techniques to make GFMs perform better, most of which are quite frequently used in competitions and industry use cases alike. Now that we have wrapped up the machine learning section of the book, we will move on to a specific type of machine learning that has become well-known over the past few years – **deep learning** – in the next chapter.

References

The following are sources that we have referenced throughout the chapter:

1. Montero-Manso, P., Hyndman, R.J. (2020), *Principles and algorithms for forecasting groups of time series: Locality and globality.* arXiv:2008.00444[cs.LG]: https://arxiv.org/abs/2008.00444.

2. Micci-Barreca, D. (2001), *A preprocessing scheme for high-cardinality categorical attributes in classification and prediction problems. SIGKDD Explor. Newsl.* 3, 1 (July 2001), 27–32: https://doi.org/10.1145/507533.507538.

3. Fisher, W. D. (1958). *On Grouping for Maximum Homogeneity. Journal of the American Statistical Association*, 53(284), 789–798: `https://doi.org/10.2307/2281952`.

4. Fisher, W.D. (1958), *A preprocessing scheme for high-cardinality categorical attributes in classification and prediction problems. SIGKDD Explor. Newsl.* 3, 1 (July 2001), 27–32.

5. Aggarwal, C. C., Hinneburg, A., and Keim, D. A. (2001). *On the Surprising Behavior of Distance Metrics in High Dimensional Spaces.* In *Proceedings of the 8th International Conference on Database Theory* (ICDT '01). Springer-Verlag, Berlin, Heidelberg, 420–434: `https://dl.acm.org/doi/10.5555/645504.656414`.

6. Oreshkin, B. N., Carpov D., Chapados N., and Bengio Y. (2020). *N-BEATS: Neural basis expansion analysis for interpretable time series forecasting. 8th International Conference on Learning Representations, ICLR 2020*: `https://openreview.net/forum?id=r1ecqn4YwB`.

Further reading

The following are a few resources that you can explore for a detailed study:

- *Learning From Data* by Yaser Abu-Mostafa: `https://work.caltech.edu/lectures.html`.

- *Curse of Dimensionality* – Georgia Tech: `https://www.youtube.com/watch?v=OyPcbeiwps8`.

- *Dummy Variable Trap*: `https://www.learndatasci.com/glossary/dummy-variable-trap/`.

- Using deep learning to learn categorical embeddings: `https://pytorch-tabular.readthedocs.io/en/latest/tutorials/03-Extracting%20and%20Using%20Learned%20Embeddings/`.

- Handling categorical features – CatBoost: `https://catboost.ai/en/docs/concepts/algorithm-main-stages_cat-to-numberic`.

- *Exploring Bayesian Optimization* – from Distil.pub: `https://distill.pub/2020/bayesian-optimization/`.

- Frazier, P.I. (2018). *A Tutorial on Bayesian Optimization.* arXiv:1807.02811 [stat.ML]: `https://arxiv.org/abs/1807.02811`.

- Time series clustering using `tslearn`: `https://tslearn.readthedocs.io/en/stable/user_guide/clustering.html`.

- *The Surprising Behaviour of Distance Metrics in High Dimensions*: `https://towardsdatascience.com/the-surprising-behaviour-of-distance-metrics-in-high-dimensions-c2cb72779ea6`.

- *An illustrated introduction to the t-SNE algorithm*: https://www.oreilly.com/content/an-illustrated-introduction-to-the-t-sne-algorithm/.

- *How to Use t-SNE Effectively* – from Distil.pub: https://distill.pub/2016/misread-tsne/.

- The NFLT: https://en.wikipedia.org/wiki/No_free_lunch_in_search_and_optimization.

- *Interpretability: Cracking open the black box* – parts I, II, and III by Manu Joseph: https://deep-and-shallow.com/2019/11/13/interpretability-cracking-open-the-black-box-part-i/.

- *Interpretable Machine Learning: A Guide for Making Black Box Models Explainable* by Christoph Molnar: https://christophm.github.io/interpretable-ml-book/.

Part 3 –
Deep Learning for Time Series

In this part, we focus on the exciting field of deep learning to tackle time series problems. This part starts with a good introduction of the necessary concepts and slowly builds up to different specialized architectures that are suited to handle time series data. It also talks about global models in deep learning and some strategies to make them work better.

This part comprises the following chapters:

- *Chapter 11, Introduction to Deep Learning*
- *Chapter 12, Building Blocks of Deep Learning for Time Series*
- *Chapter 13, Common Modeling Patterns for Time Series*
- *Chapter 14, Attention and Transformers for Time Series*
- *Chapter 15, Strategies for Global Deep Learning Forecasting Models*
- *Chapter 16, Specialized Deep Learning Architectures for Forecasting*

Introduction to Deep Learning

In the previous chapter, we understood how to use modern machine learning models to tackle time series forecasting. Now, let's focus our attention on a subfield of machine learning that has shown a lot of promise in the last few years – **deep learning**. We will be trying to demystify deep learning and go into why it is popular nowadays. We will also break down deep learning into major components and learn about the workhorse behind deep learning – gradient descent.

In this chapter, we will be covering these main topics:

- What is deep learning and why now?
- Components of a deep learning system
- Representation learning
- Linear layers and activation functions
- Gradient descent

Technical requirements

You will need to set up the Anaconda environment following the instructions in the *Preface* of the book to get a working environment with all the packages and datasets required for the code in this book.

The associated code for the chapter can be found at `https://github.com/PacktPublishing/ Modern-Time-Series-Forecasting-with-Python-/tree/main/notebooks/ Chapter11`.

What is deep learning and why now?

In *Chapter 5*, *Time Series Forecasting as Regression*, we talked about machine learning and borrowed a definition from Arthur Samuel: "*Machine Learning is a field of study that gives computers the ability to learn without being explicitly programmed.*" And we further saw how we can learn useful functions from data using machine learning. Deep learning is a subfield of this same field of study. The objective of deep learning is also to learn useful functions from data, but with a few specifications on how it does that.

Before we talk about what is special about deep learning, let's answer another question first. Why are we talking about this subfield of machine learning as a separate topic? The answer to that lies in the unreasonable effectiveness of deep learning methods in countless applications. Deep learning has taken the world of machine learning by storm, overthrowing state-of-the-art systems across types of data such as images, videos, text, and so on. If you remember the speech recognition systems on phones a decade ago, they were more meme-worthy than really useful. But today, you can say *Hey Google, play Pink Floyd* and *Comfortably Numb* will start playing on your phone or speakers. Multiple deep learning systems made this process possible in a smooth way. The voice assistant in your phone, self-driving cars, web search, language translation… the list of applications of deep learning in our day-to-day lives just keeps on going.

By now, you might be wondering what this new technology called deep learning is all about, right? Deep learning is not a new technology. The origins of deep learning can be traced way back to the late 1940s and early 1950s. It only appears to be new because of the recent surge in popularity of the field.

Let's quickly see why deep learning is suddenly popular.

Why now?

There are two main reasons why deep learning has gained a lot of ground in the last two decades:

- Increase in compute availability
- Increase in data availability

Let's discuss the preceding points in detail in the following sections.

Increase in compute availability

Back in 1960, Frank Rosenblatt wrote a paper about a three-layer neural network and stated that it went a long way in demonstrating the ability of neural networks as a pattern-recognizing device. But in the same paper, he noted the burden on a digital computer (of the 1960s) was too great as we increase the number of connections. However, in the decades that followed, computer hardware showed close to 50,000 times more improvement, which provided a good boost to neural networks and deep learning. Although it was still not enough as neural networks were still not considered to be good enough for *large-scale applications*.

This is when a particular type of hardware, which was initially developed for gaming, came to the rescue – GPUs. It's not entirely clear who started using GPUs for deep learning. Kyoung-Su Oh and Keechul Jung published a paper titled *GPU implementation of neural networks* back in 2004, which seems to be the first to show massive speed-ups in using GPUs for deep learning. One of the earliest and more popular research papers on the topic came from Rajat Raina, Anand Madhavan, and Andrew Ng, who published a paper titled *Large-scale deep unsupervised learning using graphics processors* back in 2009. It showed the effectiveness of GPUs for deep learning.

Although many groups led by LeCun, Schmidhuber, Bengio, and so on were playing around with using GPUs, the turning point really came when Alex Krizhevsky, Ilya Sutskever, and Geoffrey E. Hinton used a GPU-based deep learning system that outperformed all the other competing technologies in an image recognition contest called the *ImageNet Large Scale Visual Recognition Challenge 2012*. The introduction of GPUs provided the much-needed boost to the widespread use of deep learning and accelerated the progress in the field.

Reference check

The research papers *GPU implementation of neural networks*, *Large-scale deep unsupervised learning using graphics processors*, and *ImageNet Classification with Deep Convolutional Neural Networks* are cited in the *References* section under 1, 2, and 3, respectively.

Increase in data availability

In addition to the skyrocketing compute capability, the other main factor that helped deep learning is the sheer increase in data. As the world became more and more digitized, the amount of data that we generate increased drastically. Tables that had hundreds and thousands of rows now exploded into millions and billions of rows, and the ever-decreasing cost of storage helped this explosion of data collection.

And why would an increase in data availability help deep learning? This lies in the way deep learning works. Deep learning is quite data-hungry and needs large amounts of data to learn good models. Therefore, if we keep increasing the data that we provide to a deep learning model, the model will be able to learn better and better functions. But the same can't be said for the traditional machine learning models. Let's cement this learning with a chart that Andrew Ng, a world-renowned ML educator and an adjunct professor at Stanford, popularized in his famous machine learning course – *Machine Learning by Stanford University* in Coursera (*Figure 11.1*).

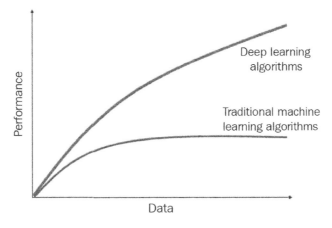

Figure 11.1 – Deep learning versus traditional machine learning as we increase the data size

In *Figure 11.1*, which was popularized by Andrew Ng, we can see that as we increase the data size, traditional machine learning hits a plateau and won't improve anymore.

It has been proven empirically that there are significant benefits to the overparameterization of a deep learning model. **Overparameterization** means that there are more parameters in the model than the number of data points available to train. In classical statistics, this is a big no-no because, under this scenario, the model invariably overfits. But deep learning seems to flaunt this rule with ease. One of the examples of overparameterization is the current state-of-the-art image recognition system, **NoisyStudent**. It has 480 million parameters, but it was trained on *ImageNet* with 1.2 million data points.

It has been argued that the way deep learning models are trained (stochastic gradient descent, which we will be explaining soon) is the key because it has a regularizing effect. In a research paper titled *The Computational Limits of Deep Learning*, Niel C. Thompson and others tried to illustrate this using a simple experiment. They set up a dataset with 1,000 features, but only 10 of them had any signal in them. Then they tried to learn four models based on the dataset using varying dataset sizes:

- **Oracle model** – A model that uses the exact 10 parameters that have any signal in them.

- **Expert model** – A model that uses 9 out of 10 significant parameters.

- **Flexible model** – A model that uses all 1,000 parameters.

- **Regularized model** – A model that uses all 1,000 parameters, but is now a regularized (**lasso**) model. (We covered regularization back in *Chapter 8, Forecasting Time Series with Machine Learning Models*.)

Let's see *Figure 11.2* from the research paper with the study:

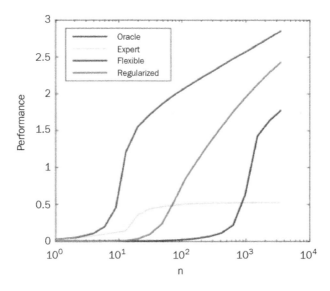

Figure 11.2 – The chart shows how different models perform under different sizes of data

The chart has a number of data points used on the x axis, and the performance (*-log(Mean Squared Error)*) on the y axis. The different colored lines show the different types of models. The regularized model (which is a proxy for deep learning models) keeps improving as we give the model more and more data, whereas the expert model (a proxy for machine learning model) plateaus. This strengthens the concept Andrew Ng popularized once more – with more data, deep learning starts to outperform traditional machine learning.

A lot more factors, apart from compute and data availability, have contributed to the success of deep learning. Sara Hooker, in her essay *The Hardware Lottery* (#9 in *References*), talks about how an idea wins not necessarily because it is superior to other ideas, but because it is suited to the software and hardware available at the time. And once a research direction gets the lottery, it snowballs because more funding and big research organizations get behind that idea and it eventually becomes the most prominent idea in the space of ideas.

We have talked about deep learning for some time but have still not understood what it is. Let's do that now.

What is deep learning?

There is no single definition of deep learning because it means slightly different things to different people. However, a large majority of people agree on one thing: a model is called deep learning when it involves automatic feature learning from raw data. As Yoshua Bengio (a Turing Award winner and one of the *godfathers* of AI) explains it in his 2021 paper titled *Deep Learning of Representations for Unsupervised and Transfer Learning*:

> *"Deep learning algorithms seek to exploit the unknown structure in the input distribution in order to discover good representations, often at multiple levels, with higher-level learned features defined in terms of lower-level features."*

Peter Norvig, the Director of Research at Google, has a similar but simpler definition:

> *"A kind of learning where the representation you form have (sic) several levels of abstraction, rather than a direct input to output."*

Another key feature of deep learning a lot of people agree upon is compositionality. Yann LeCun, a Turing Award winner and another one of the *godfathers* of AI, has a slightly more complex, but more exact definition of deep learning:

> *"DL is methodology: building a model by assembling parameterized modules into (possibly dynamic) graphs and optimizing it with gradient-based methods."*

The key points we would like to highlight here are as follows:

- *Assembling parametrized modules* – This refers to the compositionality of deep learning. Deep learning systems, as we will shortly see, are composed of a few submodules with a few parameters (some without) assembled into a graph-like structure.

- *Optimizing it with gradient-based methods* – Although having gradient-based learning as a sufficient criterion for deep learning is not widely accepted, we can still see empirically that, today, most successful deep learning systems are trained using gradient-based methods. (If you are not aware of what a gradient-based optimization method is, don't worry. We will be covering it soon in this chapter.)

If you have read anything about deep learning before, you may have seen neural networks and deep learning used together, or interchangeably. But we haven't talked about neural networks till now. Before we do that, let's look at a fundamental unit of any neural network.

Perceptron – the first neural network

A lot of what we call deep learning and neural networks are deeply influenced by the human brain and its inner workings. The human desire to create intelligent beings like themselves was manifested as early as back in Greek mythology (Galatea and Pandora). And owing to this desire, humans have studied and looked for inspiration from human anatomy for years. One of the organs of the human body that has been studied intensely is the brain because it is the center of intelligence, creativity, and everything else that makes a human.

Even though we still don't know a lot about the brain, we do know a bit about it, and we use that little information to design artificial systems. The fundamental unit of a human brain is something we call a **neuron**, shown here:

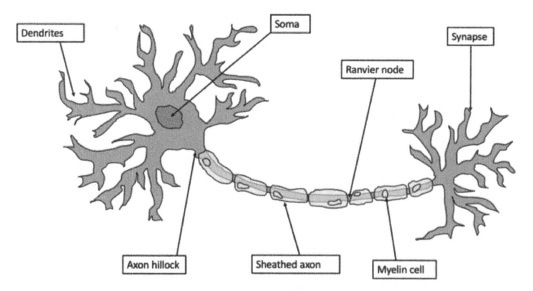

Figure 11.3 – A biological neuron

Many of you might have come across this in biology or in the context of machine learning as well. But let's refresh this anyway. The biological neuron has the following parts:

- **Dendrites** are branched extensions of the nerve cell that collect inputs from surrounding cells or other neurons.

- **Soma**, or the cell body, collects these inputs, joins them, and is passed on.

- **Axon hillock** connects the soma to the axon, and it controls the firing of the neuron. If the strength of a signal exceeds a threshold, the axon hillock fires an electrical signal through the axon.

- **Axon** is the fiber that connects the soma to the nerve endings. It is the axon's duty to pass on the electrical signal to the endpoints.

- **Synapses** are the end points of the nerve cell and transmit the signal to other nerve cells.

McCulloch and Pitts (1943) were the first to design a mathematical model for the biological neuron. But the McCulloch-Pitts model had a few limitations:

- It only accepted binary variables.

- It considered all input variables equally important.

- There was only one parameter, a threshold, which was not learnable.

In 1957, Frank Rosenblatt generalized the McCulloch-Pitts model and made it a full model whose parameters could be learned.

> **Reference check**
> The original research paper for Frank Rosenblatt's *Perceptron* is cited in *References* under reference number 5.

Let's understand the Perceptron in detail because it is the fundamental building block of all neural networks:

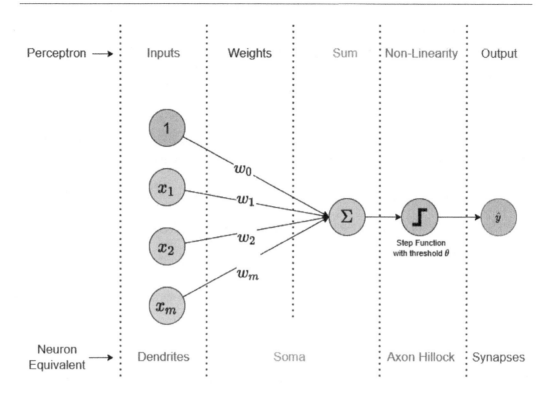

Figure 11.4 – Perceptron

As we see from *Figure 11.4*, the Perceptron has the following components:

- **Inputs** – These are the real-valued inputs that are fed to a Perceptron. This is like the dendrites in neurons that collect the input.

- **Weighted sum** – Each input is multiplied by a corresponding weight and summed up. The weights determine the importance of each input in determining the outcome.

- **Non-linearity** – The weighted sum goes through a non-linear function. For the original Perceptron, it was a step function with a threshold activation. The output would be positive or negative based on the weighted sum and the threshold of the unit. Modern-day Perceptrons and neural networks use different kinds of activation functions, but we will see that later on.

We can write the Perceptron in the mathematical form as follows:

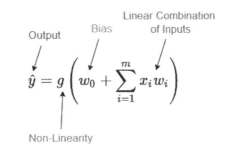

$$\hat{y} = g\left(\mathbb{X}_T \mathbb{W}\right)$$

Vector Form $\longrightarrow$ where

$$\mathbb{X} = \begin{bmatrix} 1 \\ x_1 \\ \dots \\ x_m \end{bmatrix} \text{ and } \mathbb{W} = \begin{bmatrix} w_0 \\ w_1 \\ \dots \\ w_m \end{bmatrix}$$

Figure 11.5 – Perceptron – a math perspective

As shown in *Figure 11.5*, the Perceptron output is defined by the weighted sum of inputs, which is passed in through a non-linear function. Now, we can think of this using linear algebra as well. This is an important perspective for two reasons:

- The linear algebra perspective will help you understand neural networks faster.

- It will also make the whole thing feasible because matrix multiplications are something that our modern-day computers and GPUs are really good at. Without linear algebra, multiplying these inputs with corresponding weights would require us to loop through the inputs, and it quickly becomes infeasible.

Linear algebra intuition recap

Let's take a look at a couple of concepts as a refresher.

Vectors and vector spaces

At the superficial level, a **vector** is an array of numbers. But in linear algebra, a vector is an entity that has both magnitude and direction. Let's take an example to elucidate:

$$A = \begin{bmatrix} 5 \\ 0 \end{bmatrix}$$

We can see that this is an array of numbers. But if we plot this point in the two-dimensional coordinate space, we get a point. And if we draw a line from the origin to this point, we will get an entity with direction and magnitude. This is a vector.

The two-dimensional coordinate space is called a **vector space**. A two-dimensional vector space, informally, is all the possible vectors with two entries. And extending it to n-dimensions, an n-dimensional vector space is all the possible vectors with n entries.

The final intuition I want to leave with you is this: *a vector is a point in the n-dimensional vector space.*

Matrices and transformations

Again, at the superficial level, a **matrix** is a rectangular arrangement of numbers that looks like this:

$$M = \begin{bmatrix} 1 & 0 \\ 0 & 0 \end{bmatrix}$$

Matrices have many uses but the one intuition that is most relevant for us is that a matrix specifies a linear transformation of the vector space it resides in. When we multiply a vector with a matrix, we are essentially transforming the vector, and the values and dimensions of the matrix define the kind of transformation that happens. Depending on the content of the matrix, it does *rotation, reflection, scaling, shearing*, and so on.

We have included a notebook in the `chapter11` folder titled `01-Linear Algebra Intuition.ipynb`, which explores matrix multiplication as a transformation. We also apply these transformation matrices to vector spaces to develop intuition on how matrix multiplication can rotate and warp the vector spaces.

I highly suggest heading over to the *Further reading* section where we have given a few resources to get started and solidify necessary intuition.

If we consider the inputs as vectors in the feature space (vector space with m-dimensions), the term $\sum_{i=1}^{m} x_i w_i$ is nothing but a linear combination of input vectors. We can convert this to vector dot products by $x_T w$. We can include the bias also in there by adding an additional dummy input with a fixed value of 1 and adding w_0 to the W vector. This is what is shown in *Figure 11.5* as the vector representation.

Now that we have had an introduction to deep learning, let us recall one of the aspects of deep learning we discussed earlier – compositionality – and explore it a bit more deeply in the next section.

Components of a deep learning system

Let us recall Yann LeCun's definition of deep learning:

> *"Deep learning is a methodology: building a model by assembling parameterized modules into (possibly dynamic) graphs and optimizing it with gradient-based methods."*

The core idea here is that deep learning is an extremely modular system. Deep learning is not just one model, but rather a language to express any model in terms of a few parametrized modules with these specific properties:

- It should be able to produce an output from a given input through a series of computations.

- If the desired output is given, they should be able to pass on information to its inputs on how to change, to arrive at the desired output. For instance, if the output is lower than what is desired, the module should be able to tell its inputs to change in some direction so that the output becomes closer to the desired one.

The more mathematically inclined may have figured out the connection to the second point of differentiation. And you would be correct. To optimize these kinds of systems, we predominantly use gradient-based optimization methods. Therefore, condensing the two properties into one, we can say that these parameterized modules should be *differentiable functions*.

Let's take the help of a visual to aid further discussion:

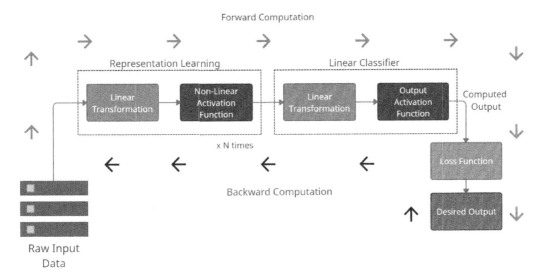

Figure 11.6 – A deep learning system

As shown in *Figure 11.6*, deep learning can be thought of as a system that takes in raw input data through a series of linear and non-linear transforms to provide us with an output. It also can adjust its internal parameters to make the output as close as possible to the desired output through learning. To make the diagram simpler, we have chosen a paradigm that fits most of the popular deep learning systems. It all starts with raw input data. The raw input data goes through *N* blocks of linear and non-linear functions that do representation learning. Let's explore this block in some detail.

Representation learning

Representation learning, informally, learns the best features by which we can make the problem linearly separable. Linearly separable means when we can separate the different classes (in a classification problem) with a straight line (*Figure 11.7*):

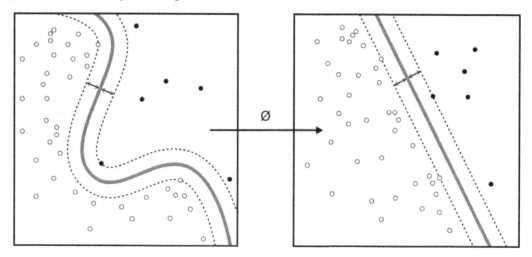

Figure 11.7 – Transforming non-linearly separable data into linearly separable using a function, Φ

The *representation learning* block in *Figure 11.6* may have multiple linear and non-linear functions stacked on top of each other and the overall function of the block is to learn a function, Φ, which transforms the raw input into good features that make the problem linearly separable.

Another way to look at this is through the lens of linear algebra. As we explored earlier in the chapter, matrix multiplication can be thought of as a linear transformation of vectors. And if we extend that intuition to the vector spaces, we can see that matrix multiplication warps the vector space in some way or another. And when we stack multiple linear and non-linear transformations on top of each other, we are essentially warping, twisting, and squeezing the input vector space (with the features) into another space. When we are asking a parameterized system to warp the input space (pixels of images) in such a way as to perform a particular task (such as the classification of dogs versus cats), the representation learning block learns the right transformations, which makes the task (separating cats from dogs) easier.

I have created a video illustrating this because nothing establishes an intuition better than a video of what is happening. I've taken a sample dataset that is not linearly separable, trained a neural network on the problem to classify, and then visualized how the input space was transformed by the model into a linearly separable representation. You can find the video here: `https://www.youtube.com/watch?v=5xYEa9PPDTE`.

Now, let's look inside the representation learning block. We can see there is a linear transformation and a non-linear activation.

Linear transformation

Linear transformations are just transformations that are applied to the vector space. When we say linear transformation in a neural network context, we actually mean affine transformations.

A linear transformation fixes the origin while applying the transformation, but an affine transformation doesn't. Rotation, reflection, scaling, and so on are purely linear transformations because the origin won't change while we do this. But something like a translation, which moves the vector space, is an affine transformation. Therefore $A \cdot X^T$ is a linear transformation, but $A \cdot X^T + b$ is an affine transformation.

So, linear transformations are simply matrix multiplications that transform the input vector space, and this is at the heart of any neural network or deep learning system today.

What happens if we stack linear transformations on top of each other? For instance, we first multiply the input, X, with a transformation matrix, A, and then multiply the results with another transformation matrix, B:

$$T = B \cdot (A \cdot X)$$

By the associative property (which is applicable for linear algebra as well), we can rewrite this equation as follows:

$$T = (B \cdot A) \cdot X$$

Generalizing this to a stack of N transformation matrices, we can see that it all works out to be a single linear transformation. This kind of defeats the purpose of stacking N layers, doesn't it?

This is where the non-linearity becomes essential and we introduce non-linearities by using a non-linear function, which we call activation functions.

Activation functions

Activation functions are non-linear differentiable functions. In a biological neuron, the axon hillock decides whether to fire a signal based on the inputs. The activation functions serve a similar function and are key to the neural network's ability to model non-linear data. Or in other words, activation functions are key in neural networks' ability to transform input vector space (which is linearly inseparable) to a linearly separable vector space, informally. To *unwarp* a space such that linearly inseparable points become linearly separable, we need to have non-linear transformations.

We repeated the same experiment we did in the last section, where we visualized the trained transformation of a neural network on the input vector space, but this time without any non-linearities. The resulting video can be found here: `https://www.youtube.com/watch?v=z-nV8oBpH2w`. The best transformation that the model learned is just not sufficient and the points are still linearly inseparable.

Theoretically, an activation function can be any non-linear differentiable (differentiable almost everywhere, to be exact) function. But over the course of time, there are a few non-linear functions that are popularly used as activation functions. Let's look at a few of them.

Sigmoid

Sigmoid is one of the most common activation functions around, and probably one of the oldest. It is also known as the logistic function. When we discussed Perceptron, we mentioned a step (also called *heavyside* in literature) function as the activation function. The step function is not a continuous function and hence *is not* differentiable everywhere. A very close substitute is the sigmoid function.

It is defined as follows:

$$g(x) = \frac{1}{1 + e^{-x}}$$

Sigmoid is a continuous function and therefore *is* differentiable everywhere. The derivative is also computationally simpler to calculate. Because of these properties of the sigmoid, it was adopted widely in the early days of deep learning as a standard activation function.

Let's see what a sigmoid function looks like and how it transforms a vector space:

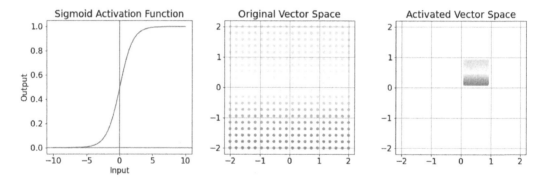

Figure 11.8 – Sigmoid activation function (left) and original, and activated vector space (middle and right)

The sigmoid function squashes the input between 0 and 1 as seen in *Figure 11.8 (left)*. We can observe the same phenomenon in the vector space. One of the drawbacks of the sigmoid function is that the gradients tend to zero on the flat portions of the sigmoid. When a neuron approaches this area in the function, the gradients that it receives and propagates become negligible and the unit stops learning. We call this *saturating of the activation*. Because of this, nowadays, *sigmoid* is not typically used in deep learning, except in the output layer (we will be talking about this usage soon).

Hyperbolic tangent (tanh)

Hyperbolic tangents are another popular activation. They can be easily defined as follows:

$$tanh(x) = \frac{sinh(x)}{cosh(x)}$$

It is very similar to sigmoid. In fact, we can express *tanh* as a function of sigmoid. Let's see what the activation function looks like:

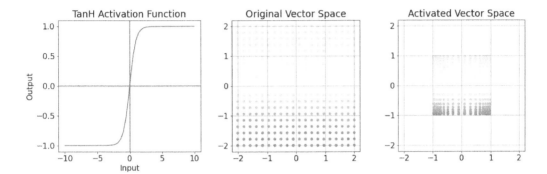

Figure 11.9 – TanH activation function (left) and original, and activated vector space (middle and right)

We can see that the shape is similar to sigmoid, although a bit sharper. But the key difference is that the *tanh* function outputs a value between -1 and 1. And because of the sharpness, we can also see the vector space getting pushed out to the edges as well. The fact that the function outputs a value that is symmetrical around the origin (0) works well with the optimization of the network and hence *tanh* was preferred over *sigmoid*. But since the *tanh* function is also a saturating function, the same problem of very small gradients hampering the flow of gradients and, in turn, learning plagues *tanh* activations as well.

Rectified linear unit and variants

As neuroscience gained more information about the human brain, researchers found out that only one to four percent of neurons in the brain are activated at any time. But with all the activation functions such as *sigmoid* or *tanh*, almost half of the neurons in a network are activated. In 2010, Vinod Nair and Geoffrey Hinton proposed **rectified linear units** (**ReLUs**) in the seminal paper *Rectified Linear Units Improve Restricted Boltzmann Machines*. And ever since, ReLUs have taken over as the de facto activation functions for deep neural networks.

ReLU

A ReLU is defined as follows:

$$g(x) \;=\; max(x, 0)$$

It is just a linear function, but with a kink at zero. Any value greater than zero is retained as is, but all values below zero are squashed to zero. The range of the output goes from 0 to ∞. Let's see how it looks visually:

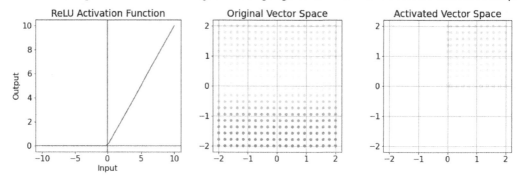

Figure 11.10 – ReLU activation function (left) and original, and activated vector space (middle and right)

We can see that the points in the left and bottom quadrants are all pushed into the axes' lines. This squashing is what gives the non-linearity to the activation function. And because of the way the activation sharply becomes zero and does not tend to zero like the sigmoid or tanh, ReLUs are non-saturating.

> **Reference check**
>
> The research paper that proposed ReLU is cited in *References* under reference number 7.

There are a lot of advantages to using ReLUs:

- The computations of the activation function as well as its gradients are really cheap.

- Training converges much faster than those with saturating activation functions.

- ReLU helps bring sparsity in the network (by having the activation as zero, a large majority of neurons in the network can be turned off) and resembles how biological neurons work.

But ReLUs are not without problems:

- When $x < 0$, the gradients become zero. This means a neuron that has an output < 0 will have zero gradients and therefore, the unit will not learn anymore. These are called dead ReLUs.

- Another disadvantage is that the average output of a ReLU unit is positive and when we stack multiple layers, this might lead to a positive bias in the output.

Let's see a few variants that tried to resolve the problems we discussed for ReLU.

Leaky ReLU and parametrized ReLU

Leaky ReLU is a variant of standard ReLU that resolves the *dead ReLU* problem. It was proposed by Maas and others in 2013. A Leaky ReLU can be defined as follows:

$$g(x) = x, \ if \ x \geq 0$$

$$\alpha \, x, \ if \ x < 0$$

Here, α is the slope parameter (typically set to a very small value such as 0.001) and is considered a hyperparameter. This makes sure the gradients are not zero when $x<0$ and thereby ensures there are no *dead* ReLUs. But the sparsity that ReLU provides is lost here because there is no zero output that turns off a unit completely. Let's visualize this activation function:

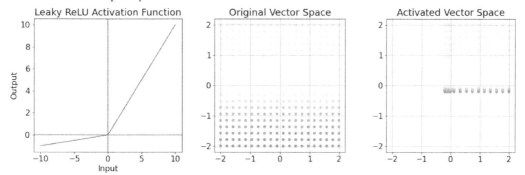

Figure 10.11 – Leaky ReLU activation function (left) and original,
and activated vector space (middle and right)

In 2015, He and others proposed another minor modification to Leaky ReLU called **parametrized ReLU**. In parametrized ReLU, instead of considering α as a hyperparameter, they considered it as a learnable parameter.

> **Reference check**
>
> The research paper that proposed leaky ReLU is cited in *References* under reference number 8, and parametrized ReLU is cited under reference number 9.

There are many other activation functions that are less popularly used but still have enough use cases to be included in *PyTorch*. You can find a list of them here: `https://pytorch.org/docs/stable/nn.html#non-linear-activations-weighted-sum-nonlinearity`. We encourage you to use the notebook titled `02-Activation Functions.ipynb` in the Chapter 11 folder to try out different activation functions and see how they warp the vector space.

And with that, we now have an idea of the components of the first block in *Figure 11.6*, representation learning. The next block in there is the linear classifier, which has a linear transformation and an output activation. We already know what a linear transformation is, but what is an output activation?

Output activation functions

Output activation functions are functions that enforce a few desirable properties to the output of the network.

Additional reading

These functions have a deeper connection with **maximum likelihood estimation** (MLE) and the chosen loss function, but we will not be getting into that because it is out of the scope of this book. We have linked to the book *Deep Learning* by Ian Goodfellow, Yoshua Bengio, and Aaron Courville in the *Further reading* section. If you are interested in a deeper understanding of deep learning, we suggest you use the book to that effect.

If we want the neural network to predict a continuous number in the case of regression, we just use a linear activation function (which is like saying there is no activation function). The raw output from the network is considered the prediction and fed into the loss function.

But in the case of classification, the desired output is a class out of all possible classes. If there are only two classes, we can use our old friend, the *sigmoid* function, which has an output between 0 and 1. We can also use *tanh* because its output is going to be between -1 and 1. The *sigmoid* function is preferred because of the intuitive probabilistic interpretation that comes along with it. The closer the value is to one, the more confident the network is about that prediction.

Now, *sigmoid* works for binary classification. What about multiclass classification where the possible classes are more than two?

Softmax

Softmax is a function that converts a vector of K real values into another K-positive real value, which sums up to one. *Softmax* is defined as follows:

$$Softmax(x_i) = \frac{e^{x_i}}{\sum_{j=1}^{K} e^{x_j}}$$

This function converts the raw output from a network into something that resembles a probability across K classes. This has a strong relation with *sigmoid* – *sigmoid* is a special case of *softmax* when $K=2$. In the following figure, let's see how a random vector of size 3 is converted into probabilities that add up to one:

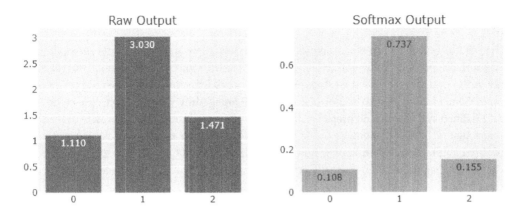

Figure 11.12 – Raw output versus softmax output

If we look closely, we can see that in addition to converting the real values into something that resembles probability, it also increases the relative gap between the maximum and the rest of the values. This activation is a standard output activation for multiclass classification problems.

Now, there is only one major component left in the diagram (*Figure 11.6*) – the loss function.

Loss function

The loss function we touched upon in *Chapter 5, Time Series Forecasting as Regression*, translates nicely to deep learning. In deep learning also, the loss function is a way to tell how good the predictions of the model are. If the predictions are way off the target, the loss function would be higher and as we get closer to the truth, it becomes smaller. In the deep learning paradigm, we just have one more additional requirement from the loss function – it should be differentiable.

Common loss functions from classical machine learning, such as **mean squared error** or **mean absolute error,** are valid in deep learning as well. In fact, in regression tasks, they are the default choices that practitioners adopt. For classification tasks, we adopt a concept borrowed from information theory called **cross-entropy loss**. But since deep learning is a very flexible framework, we can use any loss function as long as it is differentiable. There are a lot of loss functions people have already tried and found working in many situations. A lot of them are part of PyTorch's API as well. You can find them here: `https://pytorch.org/docs/stable/nn.html#loss-functions`.

Now that we have covered all the components of a deep learning system, let's also briefly look at how we train the whole system.

Forward and backward propagation

In *Figure 11.6*, we can see two sets of arrows, one going toward the desired output from input, marked as *Forward Computation*, and another going backward to the input from the desired output, marked *Backward Computation*. These two steps are at the core of learning a deep learning system. In the *Forward Computation*, popularly known as **Forward Propagation**, we use the series of computations that are defined in the layers and propagate the input all the way through the network to get the output. And now that we have the output, we would use the loss function to assess how close or far we are from the desired output. This information is now used in the *Backward Computation*, popularly known as **Backward Propagation**, to calculate the gradient with respect to all the parameters.

Now, what is a gradient and why do we need it? In high school math, we might have come across gradients or derivatives in another form called **slope**. It is the rate of change of a quantity when we change a variable by unit measure. Derivatives inform us of the local slope of a scalar function. While derivatives are always with respect to a single variable, gradients are a generalization of derivatives to multivariate functions. Intuitively, both gradient and derivatives inform us of the local slope of the function. And with the gradient of the loss function, we can use one of the techniques from mathematical optimization called **gradient descent**, to optimize our loss function.

Let's see this with an example.

Gradient descent

Any machine learning or deep learning model can be thought of as a function that converts an input, x, to an output, $\hat{y}$ using a few parameters, θ. Here, θ can be the collection of all the matrix transformations that we do to the input throughout the network. But to simplify the example, let's assume there are only two parameters, a and b. And if we think about the whole process of learning a bit, we will see that by keeping the input and expected output the same, the way to change your loss would be by changing the parameters of the model. Therefore, we can postulate the loss function to be parameterized by the parameters, in this case, a and b.

> Notebook alert
>
> To follow along with the complete code, use the notebook named `03-Gradient Descent.ipynb` in the `chapter11` folder and the code in the `src` folder.

Let's assume the loss function takes the following form:

$$\mathcal{L}(a,b) = (a - 8)^2 + (b - 2)^2$$

Let's see what the function looks like. We can use a three-dimensional plot to visualize a function with two parameters, as seen in *Figure 11.13*. Two dimensions will be used to denote the two parameters and at each point in that two-dimensional mesh, we can plot the loss value in the third dimension. This kind of plot of the loss function is also called a loss curve (in univariate settings), or loss surface (in multivariate settings).

Loss Surface for $\mathcal{L}(a, b) = (a - 8)^2 + (b - 2)^2$

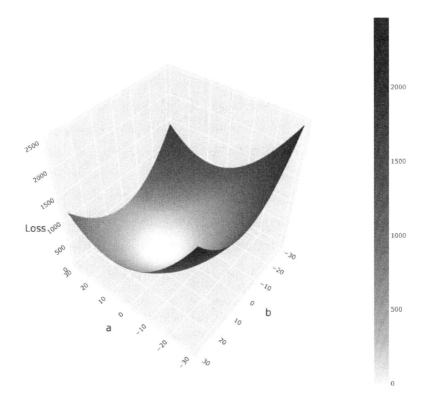

Figure 11.13 – Loss surface plot

The lighter portion of the 3D shape is where the loss function is less and as we move away from there, it increases.

In machine learning, our aim is to minimize the loss function, or in other words, find the parameters that make our predicted output as close as possible to the ground truth. This falls under the realm of mathematical optimization and a particular technique lends itself suitable for this approach – **gradient descent**.

Gradient descent is a mathematical optimization algorithm used to minimize a cost function by iteratively moving in the direction of the steepest descent. In a univariate function, the derivative (or the slope) gives us the direction (and magnitude) of the steepest ascent. For instance, if we know that the slope of a function is 1, we know if we move to the right, we are climbing up the slope, and moving to the left, we will be climbing down. Similarly, in the multivariate setting, the gradient of a function at any point will give us the direction (and magnitude) of the steepest ascent. And since we are concerned with minimizing a loss function, we will be using the negative gradient, which will point us in the direction of the steepest descent.

So, let's define the gradient for our loss function. We are using high school calculus, but even if you are not comfortable, you don't need to worry:

$$\nabla f(a,b) = \begin{bmatrix} \dfrac{df}{da} \\ \dfrac{df}{db} \end{bmatrix} = \begin{bmatrix} 2(a-8) \\ 2(b-2) \end{bmatrix}$$

Now, how does the algorithm work? Very simply, as follows:

1. Initialize the parameters to random values.
2. Compute the gradient at that point.
3. Make a step in the direction opposite to the gradient.
4. Repeat steps 2 and 3 until it converges, or we reach maximum iterations.

There is just one more aspect that needs more clarity: how much of a step do we take in each iteration?

Ideally, the magnitude of the gradient tells you how fast the function is changing in that direction, and we should just take the step equal to the gradient. But there is a property of the gradient that makes that a bad idea. The gradient only defines the direction and magnitude of the steepest ascent in the infinitesimally small locality of the current point and is blind to what happens beyond it. Therefore, we use a hyperparameter, commonly called the **learning rate**, to temper the steps we take in each iteration. Therefore, instead of taking a step equal to the gradient, we take a step equal to the learning rate multiplied by the gradient.

Mathematically, if θ is the vector of parameters, at each iteration, we update the parameters using the following formula:

$$\theta = \theta - \eta \times \Delta f(a,b)$$

Here, η is the learning rate and Δf is the gradient at the point.

Let's see a very simple implementation of gradient descent. First, let's define a function that returns us the gradient at any point:

```
def gradient(a, b):
    return 2*(a-8), 2*(b-2)
```

Now we define a few initial parameters such as the maximum iterations, learning rate, and initial value of *a* and *b*:

```
# maximum number of iterations that can be done
maximum_iterations = 500
# current iteration
current_iteration = 0
# Learning Rate
learning_rate = 0.01
#Initial value of a, b
current_a_value = 28
current_b_value = 27
```

Now all that is left is the actual process of gradient descent:

```
while current_iteration < maximum_iterations:
    previous_a_value = current_a_value
    previous_b_value = current_b_value
    # Calculating the gradients at current values
    gradient_a, gradient_b = gradient(previous_a_value,
previous_b_value)
    # Adjusting the parameters using the gradients
    current_a_value = current_a_value - learning_rate *
gradient_a * (previous_a_value)
    current_b_value = current_b_value - learning_rate *
gradient_b * (previous_b_value)
    current_iteration = current_iteration + 1
```

We know the minimum for this function will be at $a=8$ and $b=2$ because that would make the loss function zero. And gradient descent finds a solution that is pretty accurate – $a = 8.000000000000005$ and $b = 2.000000002230101$. We can also visualize the path it took to reach the minimum, as seen in *Figure 11.14*:

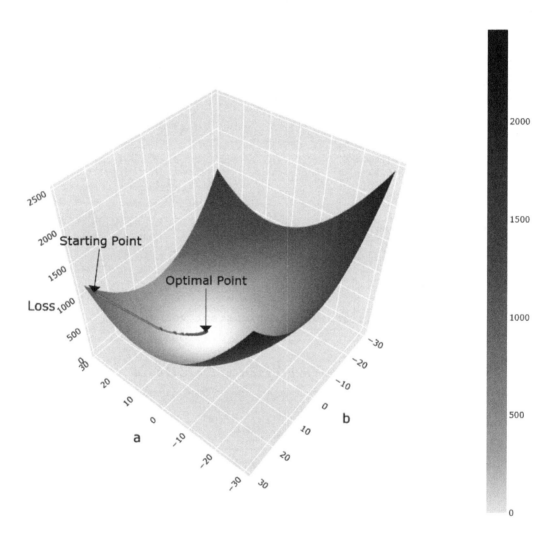

Figure 11.14 – Gradient descent optimization on the loss surface

We can see that even though we initialized the parameters far from the actual origin, the optimization algorithm makes a direct path to the optimal point. At each point, the algorithm looks at the gradient of the point and moves in the opposite direction, and eventually converges on the optimum.

When gradient descent is adopted in a learning task, there are a few kinks to be noted. Let's say we have a dataset of N samples. There are three popular variants of gradient descent that are used in learning and each of them has its pros and cons.

Batch gradient descent

We run *all N* samples through the network and average the losses across *all N* instances. Now, we use this loss to calculate the gradient and make a step in the right direction and repeat.

The pros are as follows:

- The optimization path is direct, and it has guaranteed convergence.

The cons are as follows:

- The entire dataset needs to be evaluated for a single step and that is computationally expensive. The computation per optimization step becomes prohibitively high for huge datasets.
- The time taken per optimization step is high and hence the convergence will also be slow.

Stochastic gradient descent (SGD)

In SGD, we randomly sample *one* instance from N samples, calculate the loss and gradients, and then make an update to the parameters.

The pros are as follows:

- Since we only use a single instance to make the optimization step, computation per optimization step is very low.
- Time taken per optimization step is also faster.
- Stochastic sampling also acts as regularization and helps to avoid overfitting.

The cons are as follows:

- The gradient estimates are noisy because we are making the step based on just one instance. Therefore, the path toward optimum will be choppy and noisy.
- Just because the time taken per optimization is low, it need not mean convergence is faster. We may not be taking the right step many times because of noisy gradient estimates.

Mini-batch gradient descent

Mini-batch gradient descent is a technique that falls somewhere between the spectrum of batch gradient descent and SGD. In this variant, we have another quality called mini-batch size (or simply batch size), b. And in each optimization step, we randomly pick b instances from N samples and calculate gradients on the average loss of all b instances. With $b = N$, we have *batch gradient descent*, and with $b = 1$, we have *stochastic gradient descent*. This is the most popular way neural networks are trained today. By varying the batch size, we can travel between the two variants and manage the pros and cons of each option.

Nothing develops intuition better than a visual playground where we can see the effects of the different components we discussed. *Tensorflow Playground* is an excellent resource (see the link in the *Further reading* section) to do just that. I strongly urge you to head over there and play with the tool, train a few neural networks right in the browser, and see in real time how the learning happens.

Summary

We kicked off a new section of the book with an introduction to deep learning. We started with a bit of history to understand why deep learning is so popular today and we also explored its humble beginnings in Perceptron. We understood the composability of deep learning and understood and dissected the different components of deep learning such as the representation learning block, linear layers, activation functions, and so on. Finally, we rounded off the discussion by looking at how a deep learning system uses gradient descent to learn from data. With that understanding, we are now ready to move on to the next chapter, where we will drive the narrative toward time series models.

References

Following is the list of the reference used throughout this chapter:

1. Kyoung-Su Oh and Keechul Jung. (2004), *GPU implementation of neural networks*. Pattern Recognition, Volume 37, Issue 6, 2004: `https://doi.org/10.1016/j.patcog.2004.01.013`.

2. Rajat Raina, Anand Madhavan, and Andrew Y. Ng. (2009), *Large-scale deep unsupervised learning using graphics processors*. In Proceedings of the 26th Annual International Conference on Machine Learning (ICML '09): `https://doi.org/10.1145/1553374.1553486`.

3. Alex Krizhevsky, Ilya Sutskever, and Geoffrey E. Hinton. (2012), *ImageNet Classification with Deep Convolutional Neural Networks*. Commun. ACM 60, 6 (June 2017), 84–90: `https://doi.org/10.1145/3065386`.

4. Neil C. Thompson, Kristjan Greenewald, Keeheon Lee, and Gabriel F. Manso. (2020). *The Computational Limits of Deep Learning*. arXiv:2007.05558v1 [cs.LG]: `https://arxiv.org/abs/2007.05558v1`.

5. Frank Rosenblatt. (1957), *The perceptron – A perceiving and recognizing automaton*, Technical Report 85-460-1, Cornell Aeronautical Laboratory.

6. Charu C. Aggarwal, Alexander Hinneburg, and Daniel A. Keim. (2001). *On the Surprising Behavior of Distance Metrics in High Dimensional Spaces.* In Proceedings of the 8th International Conference on Database Theory (ICDT '01). Springer-Verlag, Berlin, Heidelberg, 420–434: `https://dl.acm.org/doi/10.5555/645504.656414`.

7. Nair, V., and Hinton, G.E. (2010). *Rectified Linear Units Improve Restricted Boltzmann Machines.* ICML: `https://icml.cc/Conferences/2010/papers/432.pdf`.

8. Andrew L. Maas and Awni Y. Hannun and Andrew Y. Ng. (2013). *Rectifier nonlinearities improve neural network acoustic models.* ICML Workshop on Deep Learning for Audio, Speech, and Language Processing: `https://ai.stanford.edu/~amaas/papers/relu_hybrid_icml2013_final.pdf`.

9. He, K., Zhang, X., Ren, S., and Sun, J. (2015). *Delving Deep into Rectifiers: Surpassing Human-Level Performance on ImageNet Classification.* 2015 IEEE International Conference on Computer Vision (ICCV), 1026-1034: `https://ieeexplore.ieee.org/document/741048.0`

10. Sara Hooker. (2021). *The hardware lottery.* Commun. ACM, Volume 64: `https://doi.org/10.1145/3467017`.

Further reading

You can check out the following sources if you want to read more about a few topics covered in this chapter:

- *Linear Algebra* course from Gilbert Strang: `https://ocw.mit.edu/resources/res-18-010-a-2020-vision-of-linear-algebra-spring-2020/videos/`

- *Essence of Linear Algebra* from 3Blue1Brown: `https://www.youtube.com/playlist?list=PLZHQObOWTQDPD3MizzM2xVFitgF8hE_ab`

- *Neural Networks – A Linear Algebra Perspective* by Manu Joseph: `https://deep-and-shallow.com/2022/01/15/neural-networks-a-linear-algebra-perspective/`

- *Deep Learning* – Ian Goodfellow, Yoshua Bengio, Aaron Courville: `https://deep-and-shallow.com/2022/01/15/neural-networks-a-linear-algebra-perspective/`

- *Tensorflow Playground*: `https://playground.tensorflow.org/`

12

Building Blocks of Deep Learning for Time Series

While we laid the foundations of deep learning in the previous chapter, it was very general. Deep learning is a vast field with applications in all possible domains, but the focus of this book is time series forecasting.

So, in this chapter, let's strengthen the foundation by looking at a few building blocks of deep learning that are commonly used in time series forecasting. Even though the global machine learning models perform well in time series problems, some deep learning approaches have also shown good promise. They are a good addition to your toolset due to the flexibility they allow when modeling.

In this chapter, we will cover the following topics:

- Understanding the encoder-decoder paradigm
- Feed-forward networks
- Recurrent neural networks
- Long short-term memory (LSTM) networks
- Gated recurrent unit (GRU)
- Convolution networks

Technical requirements

You will need to set up the Anaconda environment following the instructions in the *Preface* of the book to get a working environment with all the packages and datasets required for the code in this book.

The associated code for this chapter can be found at `https://github.com/PacktPublishing/Modern-Time-Series-Forecasting-with-Python-/tree/main/notebooks/Chapter12`.

Understanding the encoder-decoder paradigm

In *Chapter 5, Time Series Forecasting as Regression*, we saw that machine learning is all about learning a function that maps our inputs to the desired output:

$$y = h(x), where\ x\ is\ the\ input\ and\ y\ is\ our\ desired\ output$$

Adapting this to time series forecasting (considering univariate time series forecasting to keep it simple), we can rewrite it as follows:

$$y_t = h(y_{t-1}, y_{t-2}, \cdots, y_{t-N})$$

Here, t is the current timestep and N is the total amount of history available at time t.

Deep learning, like any other machine learning approach, is tasked with learning this function, which maps history to the future. In *Chapter 11, Introduction to Deep Learning*, we saw how deep learning learns good features using representation learning and then uses the learned features to carry out the task at hand. This understanding can be further refined to the time series perspective by using the encoder-decoder paradigm.

Like everything in research, it is not entirely clear when and who proposed this idea of the encoder-decoder architecture. In 1997, Ramon Neco and Mikel Forcada proposed an architecture for machine translation that had ideas reminiscent of the encoder-decoder paradigm. In 2013, Nal Kalchbrenner and Phil Blunsom proposed an encoder-decoder model for machine translation, although they did not call it that. But it is when Ilya Sutskever et al. (2014) and Cho et al. (2014) proposed two new models for machine translation, which worked independently, that this idea took off. Cho et al. called it the encoder-decoder architecture, while Sutskever et al. called it the Seq2Seq architecture. The key innovation it drove was the ability to model variable-length inputs and outputs in an end-to-end fashion.

> **Reference check**
>
> The research papers by Ramon Neco et al., Nal Kalchbrenner et al., Cho et al., and Ilya Sutskever et al. are cited in the *References* section as *1*, *2*, *3*, and *4*, respectively.

The idea is very straightforward, but before we get into that, we need to have a high-level understanding of latent spaces and feature/input spaces.

The **feature space**, or the **input space**, is the vector space where your data resides. If the data has 10 dimensions, then the input space is the 10-dimensional vector space. Latent space is an abstract vector space that encodes a meaningful internal representation of the feature space. To understand this, we can think about how we, as humans, recognize a tiger. We do not remember every minute detail of a tiger; we just have a general idea of what a tiger looks like and its prominent features, such as its stripes. It is a compressed understanding of this concept that helps our brain process and recognize a tiger faster.

Now that we have an idea about latent spaces, let's see what an encoder-decoder architecture does.

An encoder-decoder architecture has two main parts – an encoder and a decoder:

- **Encoder**: The encoder takes in the input vector, x, and encodes it into a latent space. This encoded representation is called the latent vector, z.

- **Decoder**: The decoder takes in the latent vector, z, and decodes it into the kind of output we need ($\hat{y}$).

The following diagram shows the encoder-decoder setup visually:

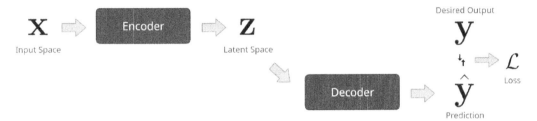

Figure 12.1 – The encoder-decoder architecture

In the context of time series forecasting, the encoder consumes the history and retains the information that is required for the decoder to generate the forecast. As we learned previously, time series forecasting can be written as follows:

$$y_t = h(y_{t-1}, y_{t-2}, \cdots, y_{t-N})$$

Now, using the encoder-decoder paradigm, we can rewrite it as follows:

$$z_t = h(y_{t-1}, y_{t-2}, \cdots, y_{t-N})$$

$$y_t = g(z_t)$$

Here, h is the encoder and g is the decoder.

Each encoder and decoder can be some special architecture suited for time series forecasting. Let's look at a few common components that are used in the encoder-decoder paradigm.

Feed-forward networks

Feed-forward networks (FFNs) or **fully connected networks** are the most basic architecture a neural network can take. We discussed perceptrons in *Chapter 11, Introduction to Deep Learning*. If we stack multiple perceptrons (both linear units and non-linear activations) and create a network of such units, we get what we call an FFN. The following diagram will help us understand this:

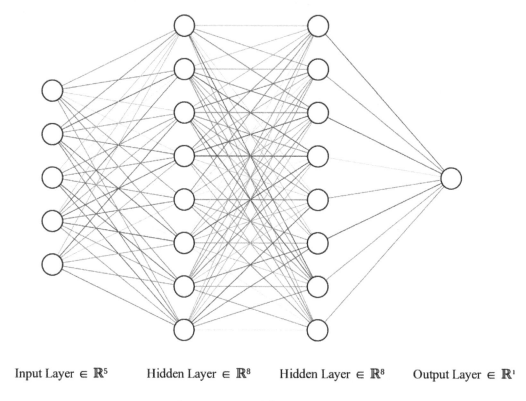

Input Layer $\in \mathbb{R}^5$　　　Hidden Layer $\in \mathbb{R}^8$　　　Hidden Layer $\in \mathbb{R}^8$　　　Output Layer $\in \mathbb{R}^1$

Figure 12.2 – Feed-forward network

An FFN takes a fixed-size input vector and passes it through a series of computational layers leading up to the desired output. This architecture is called feed-forward because the information is fed forward through the network. This is also called a **fully connected network** because every unit in a layer is connected to every unit in the previous layer and every unit in the next layer.

The first layer is called the input layer, and this is equal to the dimension of the input. The last layer is called the output layer, which is defined as per our desired output. If we need a single output, we will need one unit, while if we need 10 outputs, we will need 10 units. All the layers in between are called **hidden layers**. Two hyperparameters define the structure of the network – the number of hidden layers and the number of units in each layer. For instance, in *Figure 12.2*, we have a network with two hidden layers and eight units per layer.

In the time series forecasting context, an FFN can be used as an encoder as well as a decoder. As an encoder, we can use an FFN just like we used machine learning models in *Chapter 5, Time Series Forecasting as Regression*. We embed time and convert a time series problem into a regression problem before feeding it into the FFN. As a decoder, we use it on the latent vector (the output from the encoder) to get to the output (this is the most common usage of an FFN in time series forecasting).

> **Additional reading**
>
> We are going to be using PyTorch throughout this book to work with deep learning. If you are not comfortable with PyTorch, don't worry – I'll try and explain the concepts when necessary. To get a head start, you can go through the 01-PyTorch Basics.ipynb notebook in Chapter12, where we have explored the basic functionalities of tensors and trained a very small neural network from scratch using PyTorch. I also suggest heading over to the *Further reading* section at the end of this chapter, where you'll find a few resources to learn PyTorch.

Now, let's put on our practical hats and see some of these in action. PyTorch is an open source deep learning framework developed primarily by the **Facebook AI Research Lab** (**FAIR**). Although it is a library that can manipulate **tensors** (which are *n*-dimensional matrices) and accelerate such manipulations with a GPU, a large part of the use case for such a library is in building and training deep learning systems. Because of that, PyTorch provides a lot of ready-to-use components that we can use to build a deep learning system. Let's see how we can use PyTorch for an FFN.

> **Notebook alert**
>
> To follow along with the complete code, use the 02-Building Blocks.ipynb notebook in the Chapter12 folder and the code in the src folder.

As we learned earlier in the section, an FFN is a network of linear and non-linear units arranged in a network. A linear operation consists of multiplying the input vector, X, with a weight matrix, W, and adding a bias term, b. This operation, $WX + b$, is encapsulated in a Linear class in the nn module of the PyTorch library. We can import this from the library using torch.nn import Linear. But usually, we must import the nn module as a whole because we would be using a lot of components from that module. For non-linearity, let's use ReLU (as introduced in *Chapter 11, Introduction to Deep Learning*), which is also a class in the nn module.

Before moving on, let's create a random walk time series whose length is 20:

```
N = 20
df = pd.DataFrame({
    "date": pd.date_range(periods=N, start="2021-04-12",
freq="D"),
    "ts": np.random.randn(N)
})
```

We can use this tensor directly in the FFN, but usually, we use a sliding window technique to split the tensor and train the networks. We do this for multiple reasons:

- We can see this as a data augmentation technique that is creating a greater number of samples as opposed to using the entire sequence just once.

- It helps us reduce and restrict computation by limiting the calculation to a fixed window.

Let's do that now:

```
ts = torch.from_numpy(df.ts.values).float()
window = 15
# Creating windows of 15 over the dataset
ts_dataset = ts.unfold(0, size=window, step=1)
```

Now, we have a tensor, `ts_dataset`, whose size is *6x15* (this can create 6 samples of 15 input features each when we move the sliding window across the length of the series). For a standard FFN, the input shape is specified as *batch size x input features*. So, 6 becomes our batch size and 15 becomes the input feature size.

Now, let's define the layers in the FFN. For this exercise, let's assume the network's structure is as follows:

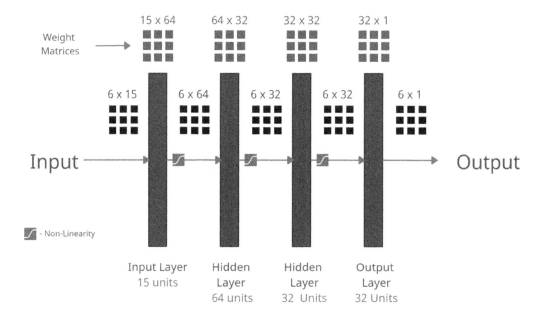

Figure 12.3 – FFNs – a matrix multiplication perspective

The input data (6x15) will be passed through these layers one by one. Here, we can see how the tensor dimensions are changing as it flows through the network. Each of the linear layers is essentially a matrix multiplication that converts the input into the output of a specified dimension. After each linear transformation, we stack a non-linear activation function in there. These alternative linear and non-linear modules are what give the neural network the expressive power it has. The linear layers are an affine transformation of the vector space (rotation, translation, and so on), and the non-linearity *squashes* the vector space. Together, they can morph the input space so that it's useful for the task at hand. Now, let's see how we can code this in PyTorch. We are going to use a handy module from PyTorch called `Sequential`, which allows us to stack different sub-components together and use them with ease:

```
# The FFN we define would have this architecture
# window(windowed input) >> 64 (hidden layer 1) >> 32 (hidden
layer 2) >> 32 (hidden layer 2) >> 1 (output)
ffn = nn.Sequential(
    nn.Linear(in_features=window,out_features=64), # (batch-
size x window) --> (batch-size x 64)
    nn.ReLU(),
    nn.Linear(in_features=64,out_features=32), # (batch-size x
64) --> (batch-size x 32)
    nn.ReLU(),
    nn.Linear(in_features=32,out_features=32), # (batch-size x
32) --> (batch-size x 32)
    nn.ReLU(),
    nn.Linear(in_features=32,out_features=1), # (batch-size x
32) --> (batch-size x 1)
)
```

Now that we have defined the FFN, let's see how we can use it:

```
ffn(ts_dataset)
# or more explicitly
ffn.forward(ts_dataset)
```

This will return a tensor whose shape is based on *batch size x output units*. We can have any number of output units, not just one. Therefore, when using an encoder, we can have an arbitrary dimension for the latent vector. Then, when we are using it as a decoder, we can have the output units equal the number of time steps we are forecasting.

> **Sneak peek**
>
> We have not seen multi-step forecasting until now because it will be covered in more detail in *Part 4, Mechanics of Forecasting*. But for now, just understand that there are cases where we will need to forecast multiple time steps into the future. The classical statistical models do this out of the box. But for machine learning and deep learning, we need to design systems that can do that. Fortunately, there are a few different techniques to do so which will be covered in *Part 4* of the book.

FFNs are designed for non-temporal data. We can use FFNs by embedding our data temporally and then passing that to the network. Also, the computational cost in an FFN is directly proportional to the memory we use in the embedding (the number of previous time steps we include as features). We will also not be able to handle variable-length sequences in this setting.

Now, let's look at another common architecture that is specifically designed for temporal data.

Recurrent neural networks

Recurrent neural networks (RNNs) are a family of neural networks specifically designed to handle sequential data. They were first proposed by *Rumelhart et al.* (1986) in their seminal work, *Learning Representations by Back-Propagating Errors*. The work borrows ideas such as parameter sharing and recurrence from previous work in statistics and machine learning to come up with a neural network architecture that helps overcome many of the disadvantages FFNs have when processing sequential data.

Parameter sharing is when we use the same set of parameters for different parts of the model. Apart from a regularization effect (restricting the model to using the same set of weights for multiple tasks, which regularizes the model by constraining the search space while optimizing the model), parameter sharing enables us to extend and apply the model to examples of different forms. RNNs can scale to much longer sequences because of this. In an FFN, each timestep (each feature) has a fixed weight and even if the motif we are looking for shifts by one timestep, the network may not capture it correctly. In an RNN enabled by parameter sharing, they are captured in a much better way.

In sentences (which are also sequences), we want the model to recognize that "*Tomorrow I will go to the bank*" and "*I will go to the bank tomorrow*" are the same thing. An FFN can't do this, but an RNN will be able to because it uses the same parameters at all positions and will be able to identify the motif "*I will go to the bank*" wherever it occurs. Intuitively, we can think of RNNs as applying the same FFN at each time window but enhanced with some kind of memory to store relevant information for the task at hand.

Let's visualize how an RNN processes inputs:

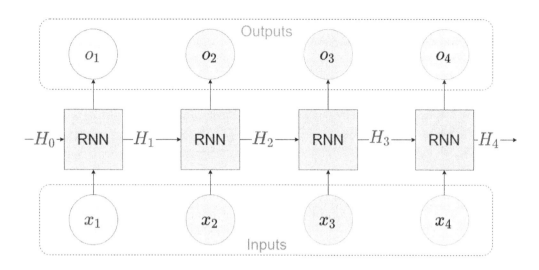

Figure 12.4 – How an RNN processes input sequences

Let's assume we are talking about a sequence with four elements in it, x_1 to x_4. Any RNN block (let's consider it as a black box for now) consumes input and a hidden state (memory) and produces an output. In the beginning, there is no memory, so we start with an initial memory (H_0), which is typically an array filled with zeroes. Now, the RNN block takes in the first input (x_1) along with the initial hidden state (H_0) and produces an output (o_1) and a hidden state (H_1).

To process the second element in the sequence, *the same RNN* block takes in the hidden state from the previous timestep (H_1) and the input at the current timestep (x_2) to produce the output at the second timestep (o_2) and a new hidden state (H_2). This process continues until we reach the end of the sequence. After processing the entire sequence, we will have all the outputs at each timestep (o_1 through o_4) and the final hidden state (H_4).

These outputs and the hidden state will have encoded the information contained in the sequence and can be used for further processing, such as to predict the next step using a decoder. The RNN block can also be used as a decoder that takes in the encoded representation and produces the outputs. Because of this flexibility, the RNN blocks can be arranged to suit a wide variety of input and output combinations, such as the following:

- Many-to-one, where we have many inputs and a single output – for instance, single-step forecasting or time series classification

- Many-to-many, where we have many inputs and many outputs – for instance, multi-step forecasting

Now let's look at what happens inside an RNN.

Let the input to the RNN at time t be x_t, and the hidden state from the previous timestep be H_{t-1}. The updated equations are as follows:

$$A_t = W \cdot H_{t-1} + U \cdot x_t + b_1$$

$$H_t = tanh(A_t)$$

$$o_t = V \cdot H_t + b_2$$

Here, U, V, and W are learnable weight matrices and b_1 and b_2 are two learnable bias vectors. U, V, and W can be easily remembered as *input-to-hidden*, *hidden-to-output*, and *hidden-to-hidden* matrices based on the kind of transformation they perform, respectively. Intuitively, we can think of the operation that the RNN is doing as a kind of learning and forgetting the information as it sees fit. The *tanh* activation, as we saw in *Chapter 11, Introduction to Deep Learning*, produces a value between -1 and 1, which acts analogous to forgetting and remembering. So, the RNN transforms the input into a latent dimension, uses the *tanh* activation to decide what information from the current timestep and previous memory to keep and forget, and uses this new memory to generate an output.

In standard backpropagation, we backpropagate the gradients from one unit to another. But in recurrent nets, we have a special situation where we have to backpropagate the gradients within a single unit, but through time or the different time steps. A special case of backpropagation, called **Back Propagation Through Time** (BPTT), has been developed for RNNs. Thankfully, all the major deep learning frameworks are capable of doing this without any problems. For a more detailed understanding and mathematical foundations of BPTT, please to the *Further reading* section.

PyTorch has made RNNs available as ready-to-use modules – all you need to do is import one of the modules from the library and start using it. But before we do that, we need to understand a few more concepts.

The first concept we will look at is the possibility of *stacking multiple layers* of RNNs on top of each other so that the outputs at each timestep become the input to the RNN in the next layer. Each layer will have a hidden state or memory. This enables hierarchical feature learning, which is one of the bedrocks of the successes of deep learning today.

Another concept is *bidirectional* RNNs, introduced by Schuster and Paliwal in 1997. Bidirectional RNNs are very similar to RNNs. In a vanilla RNN, we process the inputs sequentially from start to end (forward). However, a bidirectional RNN uses one set of input-to-hidden and hidden-to-hidden weights to process the inputs from start to end and another set to process the inputs in reverse (end to start) and concatenate the hidden states from both directions. It is on this concatenated hidden state that we apply the output equation.

> **Reference check**
>
> The research papers by Rumelhart et al and Schuster and Paliwal are cited in the *References* section as 5 and 6, respectively.

The RNN layer in PyTorch

Now, let's understand the PyTorch implementation for RNN. As with the `Linear` module, the RNN module is also available from `torch.nn`. Let's look at the different parameters the implementation provides while initializing:

- `input_size`: The number of expected features in the input. If we are using just the history of the time series, then this would be 1. However, when we use history along with some other features, then this will be >1.

- `hidden_size`: The dimension of the hidden state. This defines the size of the input-to-hidden and hidden-to-hidden matrices.

- `num_layers`: This is the number of RNNs that will be stacked on top of each other. The default is 1.

- `nonlinearity`: The non-linearity to use. Although tanh is the originally proposed non-linearity, PyTorch also allows us to use ReLU (`relu`). The default is `'tanh'`.

- `bias` This parameter decides whether or not to add bias to the update equations we discussed earlier. If the parameter is `False`, there will be no bias. The default is `True`.

- `batch_first`: There are two input data configurations that the RNN cell can use – we can have the input as *(batch size, sequence length, number of features)* or *(sequence length, batch size, number of features)*. `batch_first = True` selects the former as the expected input dimensions. The default is `False`.

- `dropout`: This parameter, if non-zero, uses a dropout layer on the outputs of each RNN layer except the last. Dropout is a popular regularization technique where randomly selected neurons are ignored during training (the *Further reading* section contains a link to the paper that proposed this). The dropout probability will be equal to `dropout`. The default is 0.

- `bidirectional`: This parameter enables a bidirectional RNN. If `True`, a bidirectional RNN is used. The default is `False`.

To continue applying the model to the same synthetic data we generated earlier in this chapter, let's initialize the RNN model, as follows:

```
rnn = nn.RNN(
    input_size=1,
    hidden_size=32,
```

```
    num_layers=1,
    batch_first=True,
    dropout=0,
    bidirectional=False,
)
```

Now, let's look at the inputs and outputs that are expected from an RNN cell.

As opposed to the `Linear` layer we saw earlier, the RNN cell takes in *two inputs* – the input sequence and the hidden state vector. The input sequence can be either (*batch size, sequence length, number of features*) or (*sequence length, batch size, number of features*), depending on whether we have set `batch_first=True`. The hidden state is a tensor whose size is (*D*number of layers, batch size, hidden size*), where *D = 1* for `bidirectional=False` and *D = 2* for `bidirectional=True`. The hidden state is an optional input and will default to zero tensors if left blank.

There are two outputs of the RNN cell: an output and a hidden state. The output can be either (*batch size, sequence length, D*hidden size*) or (*sequence length, batch size, D*hidden size*), depending on `batch_first`. The hidden state has the dimension of (*D*number of layers, batch size, hidden size*). Here, *D = 1* or *2* is based on the `bidirectional` parameter.

So, let's run our sequence through an RNN and look at the inputs and outputs (for more detailed steps, refer to the accompanying notebook):

```
#input dim: torch.Size([6, 15, 1])
# batch size = 6, sequence length = 15 and number of features =
1, batch_first = True
output, hidden_states = rnn(rnn_input)
# output.shape -> torch.Size([6, 15, 32])
# hidden_states.shape -> torch.Size([1, 6, 32]))
```

> **Important note**
> Although we saw that the RNN cell contains the output as well as the hidden state, we also know that the output is just an affine transformation of the hidden state. Therefore, to provide flexibility to the users, PyTorch only implements the update equations regarding the hidden states in the module. There are cases where we have no use for the outputs at each timestep (such as in a many-to-one scenario) and we can save computation if we do not do the output update at each step. Therefore, `output` from the PyTorch RNN is just the hidden states at each timestep and `hidden_states` is the latest hidden state.

We can verify this by checking whether the hidden state tensor is equal to the last output tensor:

```
torch.equal(hidden_states[0], output[:,-1]) # -> True
```

To make this clearer, let's look at it visually:

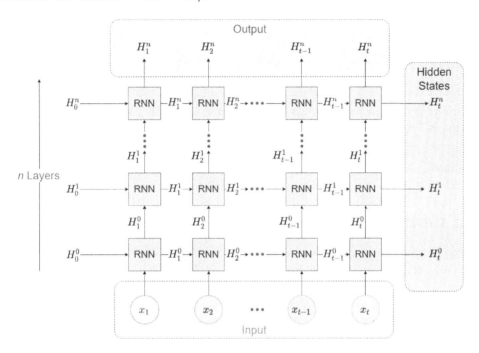

Figure 12.5 – PyTorch implementation of stacked RNNs

The hidden states at each timestep are used as input for the subsequent layer of RNNs and the hidden states of the last layer of RNNs are collected as the output. But each layer has a hidden state (that's not shared with the others) and the PyTorch RNN collects the last hidden state from each layer and gives us that as well. Now, it is up to us to decide how to use these outputs. For instance, in a one-step-ahead forecast, we can use the output hidden states and stack a few linear layers on top of it to get the next timestep prediction. Alternatively, we can use the hidden states to transfer memory into another RNN as a decoder and generate predictions for multiple time steps. There are many more ways we can use this output and PyTorch gives us that flexibility.

RNNs, while very effective in modeling sequences, have one big flaw. Because of BPTT, the number of units through which you need to backpropagate increases drastically with the length of the sequence to be used for training. When we have to backpropagate through such a long computational graph, we will encounter **vanishing** or **exploding gradients**. This is when the gradient, as it is backpropagated through the network, either shrinks to zero or explodes to a very high number. The former makes the network stop learning, while the latter makes the learning unstable.

We can think of what's happening as akin to what happens when we multiply a scalar number repeatedly by itself. If the number is less than one, with every subsequent multiplication, the number becomes smaller and smaller until it is practically zero. If the number is greater than one, then the number becomes larger and larger at an exponential scale. This was discovered, independently, by Hochreiter in his diploma thesis (1991) and Yoshua Bengio et al. in two papers published in 1993 and 1994. Over the years, many tweaks to the model and training process have been proposed to tackle this disadvantage. Nowadays, vanilla RNNs are hardly used in practice and have been replaced almost completely by their newer cousins.

> **Reference check**
>
> The references for Hochreiter (1991) and Bengio et al. (1993, 1994) are cited in the *References* section as *7, 8*, and *9*, respectively.

Now, let's look at two key improvements that have been made to the RNN architecture that have shown good performance and gained popularity in the machine learning community.

Long short-term memory (LSTM) networks

Hochreiter and Schmidhuber proposed a modification of the classical RNNs in 1997 – LSTM networks. It aimed to resolve the vanishing and exploding gradients in vanilla RNNs. The design of the LSTM was inspired by the logic gates of a computer. It introduces a new component, called a **memory cell**, which serves as long-term memory and is used in addition to the hidden state memory of classical RNNs. In an LSTM, multiple gates are tasked with reading, adding, and forgetting information from these memory cells. This memory cell acts as a *gradient highway*, allowing the gateways to pass relatively unhindered through the network. This is the key innovation that avoided vanishing gradients in RNNs.

Let the input to the LSTM at time t be x_t, and the hidden state from the previous timestep be H_{t-1}. Now, there are three gates that process information. Each gate is nothing but two learnable weight matrices (one for the input and one for the hidden state from the last step) and a bias term that is multiplied/added to the input and hidden state and finally passed through a sigmoid activation. The output of these gates will be a real number between 0 and 1. Let's look at each of these gates in detail:

- **Input gate**: The function of this gate is to decide how much information to read from the current input and previous hidden state. The update equation for this is:

$$I_t = \sigma(W_{xi} \cdot x_i + W_{hi} \cdot H_{t-1} + b_i)$$

- **Forget gate**: The forget gate decides how much information to forget from long-term memory. The updated equation for this is:

$$F_t = \sigma\left(W_{xf} \cdot x_i + W_{hf} \cdot H_{t-1} + b_f\right)$$

- **Output gate**: The output gate decides how much of the current cell state should be used to create the current hidden state, which is the output of the cell. The update equation for this is:

$$O_t = \sigma(W_{xo} \cdot x_i + W_{ho} \cdot H_{t-1} + b_o)$$

Here, W_{xi}, W_{xf}, W_{xo}, W_{hi}, W_{hf}, and W_{ho} are learnable weight parameters and b_i, b_f, and b_o are learnable bias parameters.

Now, we can introduce a new long-term memory (cell state), C_t. The three gates mentioned previously serve to update and forget from this memory. If the cell state from the previous timestep is C_{t-1}, then the LSTM cell calculates a candidate cell state, $\widetilde{C}_t$, using another gate, but this time with *tanh* activation:

$$\widetilde{C}_t = tanh(W_{xc} \cdot x_t + W_{hc} \cdot H_{t-1} + b_c)$$

Here, W_{xc}, and W_{xh} are learnable weight parameters and b_c is the learnable bias parameter.

Now, let's look at the key update equation, which updates the cell state or long-term memory of the cell:

$$C_t = F_t \odot C_{t-1} + I_t \odot \widetilde{C}_t$$

Here, $\odot$ is elementwise multiplication. Here, we use the forget gate to decide how much information from the previous timestep to carry forward, and the input gate to decide how much of the current candidate cell state will be written into long-term memory.

Last but not least, we use the newly created current cell state and the output gate to decide how much information to pass on to the predictor through the current hidden state:

$$H_t = O_t \odot tanh(C_t)$$

A visual representation of this process can be seen in *Figure 12.6*.

The LSTM layer in PyTorch

Now, let's understand the PyTorch implementation of LSTM. It is very similar to the RNN implementation we saw earlier, but it has one key difference: the parameters to initialize the class are pretty much the same. The API for this can be found at `https://pytorch.org/docs/stable/generated/torch.nn.LSTM.html#torch.nn.LSTM`. The key difference here is how the hidden states are used. While the RNN has a single tensor as a hidden state, the LSTM expects a `tuple` of tensors of the same dimensions: `(hidden state, cell state)`. LSTMs, just like RNNs, have stacked and bidirectional variants, and PyTorch handles them in the same way.

Now, let's initialize some LSTM modules and use the synthetic data we have been using to see them in action:

```
lstm = nn.LSTM(
    input_size=1,
    hidden_size=32,
    num_layers=5,
    batch_first=True,
    dropout=0,
    # bidirectional=True,
)

output, (hidden_states, cell_states) = lstm(rnn_input)
output.shape # -> [6, 15, 32]
hidden_states.shape # -> [5, 6, 32]
cell_states.shape # -> [5, 6, 32]
```

Now, let's look at another modification that's been made to vanilla RNNs that has resolved the vanishing and exploding gradient problems.

Gated recurrent unit (GRU)

In 2014, *Cho et al.* proposed another variant of the RNN that has a much simpler structure than an LSTM, called a **gated recurrent unit** (**GRU**). The intuition behind this is similar to when we use a bunch of gates to regulate the information that flows through the cell, but a GRU eliminates the long-term memory component and uses just the hidden state to propagate information. So, instead of the memory cell becoming the *gradient highway*, the hidden state itself becomes the "gradient highway." In keeping with the same notation convention we used in the previous section, let's look at the updated equations for a GRU.

While we had three gates in an LSTM, we only have two in a GRU:

- **Reset gate**: This gate decides how much of the previous hidden state will be considered as the candidate's hidden state of the current timestep. The equation for this is:

$$R_t = \sigma(W_{xr} \cdot x_t + W_{hr} \cdot H_{t-1} + b_r)$$

- **Update gate**: The update gate decides how much of the previous hidden state should be carried forward and how much of the current candidate's hidden state will be written into the hidden state. The equation for this is:

$$U_t = \sigma(W_{xu} \cdot x_t + W_{hu} \cdot H_{t-1} + b_u)$$

Here W_{xr}, W_{xu}, W_{hr}, and W_{hu} are learnable weight parameters and b_r and $\backslash b_u$ are learnable bias parameters.

Now, we can calculate the candidate's hidden state ($\widetilde{H_t}$) as follows:

$$\widetilde{H_t} = tanh(W_{xh} \cdot x_t + W_{hh} \cdot R_t \odot H_{t-1} + b_h)$$

Here, W_{xh} and W_{hh} are learnable weight parameters and b_h is the learnable bias parameter. Here, we use the reset gate to throttle the information flow from the previous hidden state to the current candidate's hidden state.

Finally, the current hidden state (the output that goes to a predictor) is computed using the following equation:

$$H_t = U_t \odot H_{t-1} + (1 - U_t) \odot \widetilde{H_t}$$

We use the update gate to decide how much from the previous hidden state and how much from the current candidate will be passed to the next timestep or predictor.

Reference check

The research papers for LSTM and GRUs are cited in the *References* section as *10* and *11*, respectively.

A visual representation of this process can be found in *Figure 12.6*:

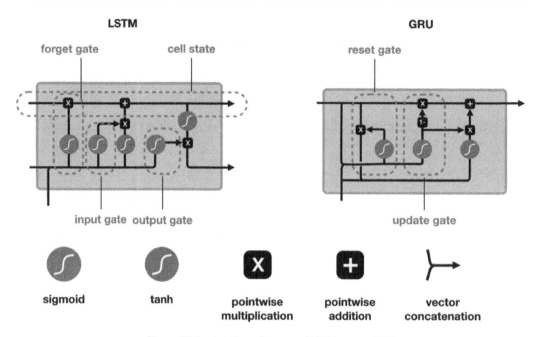

Figure 12.6 – A gating diagram of LSTM versus GRU

The GRU layer in PyTorch

Now, let's understand the PyTorch implementation of the GRU. The APIs, inputs, and outputs are the same as with an RNN. The API for this can be referenced here: https://pytorch.org/docs/stable/generated/torch.nn.GRU.html#torch.nn.GRU. The key difference is the internal workings of the modules, where the GRU update equations are used instead of the standard RNN ones.

Now, let's initialize a GRU module and use the synthetic data we have been using to see it in action:

```
Gru = nn.GRU(
    input_size=1,
    hidden_size=32,
    num_layers=5,
    batch_first=True,
    dropout=0,
    # bidirectional=True,
)
```

```
output, hidden_states = gru(rnn_input)
output.shape # -> [6, 15, 32]
hidden_states.shape # -> [5, 6, 32]
```

Now, let's look at another major component that can be used for sequential data.

Convolution networks

Convolution networks, also called **convolutional neural networks** (**CNNs**), are like neural networks for processing data in the form of a grid. This grid can be 2D, such as an image, 1D, such as a time series, 3D, such as data from LIDAR sensors, and so on. The basic idea behind CNNs is inspired by how human vision works. In 1979, Fukushima proposed Neocognitron. It was a one-of-a-kind architecture that was directly inspired by how human vision works. But CNNs came into existence as we know them today in 1989 when Yann LeCun used backpropagation to learn such a network and proved it by getting state-of-the-art results in handwritten digit recognition. In 2012, when AlexNet (a CNN architecture for image recognition) won the annual challenge of image recognition called ImageNet, that too by a large margin between it and competing non-deep learning approaches, the interest and research in CNNs peaked. People soon figured out that, apart from images, CNNs are effective with sequences, such as language and time series data.

Convolution

At the heart of CNNs is a mathematical operation called **convolution**. The mathematical interpretation of a convolution operation is beyond the scope of this book, but there are a couple of links in the *Further reading* section if you want to learn more. For our purposes, we'll develop an intuitive understanding of the convolution operation. Since CNNs rose to popularity on image data, let's start by discussing the image domain and then transition to the sequence domain.

Any image (for simplicity, let's assume it's grayscale) can be considered as a grid of pixel values, each value denoting how bright that point is, with 1 being pure white and 0 being pure black. Before we start talking about convolution, let's understand what a **kernel** is. For now, let's think of a kernel as a 2D matrix with some values in it. Typically, the kernel's size is smaller than the image's size we are using. Since the kernel is smaller than the image, we can "fit" the kernel inside the image. Let's start with the kernel aligned on the left top edge. With the kernel at the current position, there is a set of values in the image that this kernel is superpositioned over. We can perform element-wise multiplication between this subset of the image and the kernel, and then sum up all the elements into a single scalar. Now, we can repeat this process by "sliding" the kernel into all positions in the image. For instance, the following shows a sample image input whose size is 4x4 and how a convolution operation is carried out on that using a kernel whose size is 2x2:

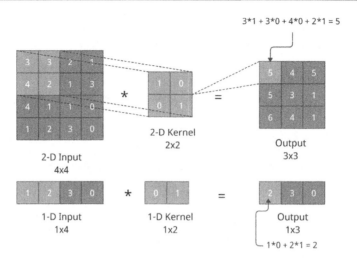

Figure 12.7 – A convolution operation on 2D and 1D inputs

So, if we place the 2x2 kernel at the top left position and perform the element-wise multiplication and the summation, we get the top left item in the 3x3 output. If we slide the kernel by one position to the right, we get the next element in the top row of the output, and so on. Similarly, if we slide the kernel by one position down, we get the second element in the first column in the output.

While this is interesting, we want to understand convolutions from a time series perspective. To do so, let's shift our paradigm to 1D convolutions – convolutions performed on 1-dimensional data such as a sequence. In the preceding diagram, we can also see an example of a 1D convolution where we take the 1D kernel and slide it across the sequence to get an output of 1x3.

Although we have set the kernel weights so that they're convenient to understand and compute, in practice, these weights are learned by the network from data. If we set the kernel size as n and all the kernel weights as $\frac{1}{n}$, what would such a convolution give us? This is something we covered in *Chapter 6, Feature Engineering for Time Series Forecasting*. Yes, they result in the rolling means with a window of n. Remember, we learned this as a feature engineering technique for machine learning models. So, 1D convolutions can be thought of as a more powerful feature generator, where the features are learned from data. With different weights on the kernels, we will be extracting different features. It is this intuition that we should hold on to while learning CNNs for time series data.

Padding, stride, and dilations

Now that we have understood what a convolution operation is, we need to understand a few more terms, such as **padding**, **stride**, and **dilations**.

Before we start talking about these terms, let's look at an equation that gives the output dimensions (O) of a convolutional layer, given the input dimensions (L), kernel size (k), padding size (p_l for left padding and p_r for right padding), stride (s), and dilation (d):

$$O = \frac{L + p_l + p_r - d \times (k - 1) - 1}{s} + 1$$

The default values (padding, strides, and dilations are special cases of a convolution process) of these terms are $p_r, p_l = 0, s = 1, d = 1$. Don't worry if you don't understand the formula or the terms in it – just keep the default values in mind so that when we understand each term, we can negate the others.

In *Figure 12.7*, we noticed that the convolution operation always reduces the size of the input. So, in the default case, the formula becomes $O = L - (k - 1)$. This is because the earliest position we can place the kernel in the sequence is from $t = 0$ to $t = k$. Then, by convolving through the sequence, we get $L - (k - 1)$ terms in the output. Padding is when we add some values to the beginning or the end of the sequence. The value we use for padding is dependent on the problem. Typically, we choose zero as a padding value. So, padding a sequence essentially increases the size of the input. So, in the preceding formula, we can think of $L + p_l + p_r$ as the effective length of the sequence after padding.

The next two terms (stride and dilation) are closely related to the **receptive field** of the convolutional layer. The receptive field of a convolutional layer is the region in the input space that influences the feature that's generated by the convolutional layer. Or, in other words, it is the size of the window of input over which we have performed the convolution operation. For a single convolutional layer (with default settings), this is pretty much the kernel size. For multi-layered CNNs, this calculation becomes a bit more complicated because of the hierarchical structure (the *Further reading* section contains a link to a paper by Arujo et al. who derived a formula to calculate the receptive field of a CNN). But generally, increasing the receptive field of a CNN is associated with an increase in the accuracy of the CNN. For computer vision, Araujo et al. noted the following:

> *"We observe a logarithmic relationship between classification accuracy and receptive field size, which suggests that large receptive fields are necessary for high-level recognition tasks, but with diminishing rewards."*

In time series, this is important because if the receptive field of a CNN is smaller than the long-term dependency, such as the seasonality, that we want to capture, then the network will fail to do so. Making the CNN deeper by stacking more convolutional layers on top of the others is one way to increase the receptive field of a network. But there are a few ways to increase the receptive field of a single convolutional layer. Strides and dilations are two such ways:

- **Stride**: Earlier, when we talked about *sliding* the kernel over the sequence, we mentioned that we move the kernel by one position at a time. This is called the stride of the convolutional layer and there is no necessity that the stride should be 1. If we set the stride to 2, the convolution operation would be performed by skipping a position in between, as shown in *Figure 12.8*. This can make each layer in the convolutional network look at a larger slice of history, thereby increasing the receptive field.

- **Dilation**: Another way we can tweak the basic convolutional layer is by dilating the input connections. In the standard convolutional layer with a kernel size of 3, we apply the kernel to three consecutive elements in the input with a dilation of 1. If we increase the dilation to 2, then the kernel will be dilated spatially and will be applied. Instead of being applied to three consecutive elements, an element in between will be skipped. *Figure 12.8* shows how this works. As we can see, this can also increase the receptive field of the network.

Both these techniques are similar but different and are compatible with each other. The following diagram shows what happens when we apply strides and dilations together (although this doesn't happen frequently):

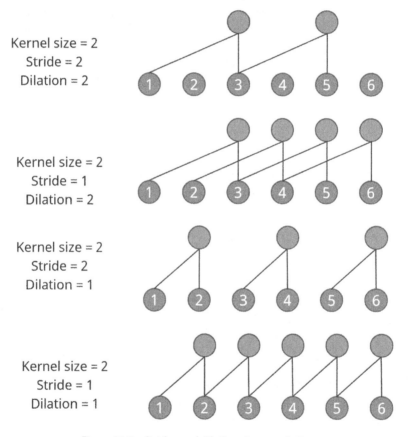

Figure 12.8 – Strides and dilations in convolutions

Now, what if we want to make the output dimensions the same as the input dimensions? By using some basic algebra and rearranging the previous formula, we get the following:

$$P_l + p_r = d(k - 1) + L(s - 1) - (s - 1)$$

And in time series, we typically pad on the left rather than the right because of the strong autocorrelation that is typically present. Padding the latest few entries with zeros or some other values will make the learning of the prediction function very hard because the latest hidden states are directly influenced by the padded values. The *Further reading* section contains a link to an article by Kilian Batzner about autoregressive convolutions. It is a must-read if you wish to really understand the concepts we have discussed here and also understand a few limitations. The *Further reading* section also contains a link to a GitHub repository that contains animations of convolutions for 2D inputs, which will give you a good intuition of what is happening.

There is just one more term that you may hear often in convolutions, especially in time series – **causal convolutions**. But all you have to keep in mind is that causal convolutions are not special types of convolutions. So long as we ensure that we won't be using future time steps to predict the current timestep while training, we are performing causal operations. This is typically done by offsetting the target and padding the inputs.

The convolution layer in PyTorch

Now, let's understand the PyTorch implementation of the CNN (a one-dimensional CNN, which is typically used for sequences such as time series). Let's look at the different parameters the implementation provides while initializing. We have just discussed the following terms, so they should be familiar to you by now:

- `in_channels`: The number of expected features in the input. If we are using just the history of the time series, then this would be 1. But when we use history along with some other features, then this will be >1. For subsequent layers, `out_channels` you have used in the previous layer become your `in_channels` in the current layer.

- `out_channels`: The number of kernels or filters applied to the input. Each kernel/filter produces a convolution operation with its own weights.

- `kernel_size`: This is the size of the kernel we use for convolving.

- `stride`: The stride of the convolution. The default is `1`.

- `padding`: This is the padding that is added to *both* sides. If we set the value as 2, the sequence that we pass to the layer will have a padded position on both the left and right. We can also give `valid` or `same` as input. These are easy ways of mentioning the kind of padding we need to add. `padding='valid'` is the same as no padding. `padding='same'` pads the input so that the output has the shape as the input. However, this mode doesn't support any stride values other than 1. The default is `0`.

- `padding_mode`: This defines how the padded positions should be filled with values. The most common and default option is *zeros*, where all the padded tokens are filled with zeros. Another useful mode that is relevant for time series is `replicate`, which behaves like forward and backward fill in pandas. The other two options – `reflect` and `circular` – are more esoteric and are only used for specific use cases. The default is `zeros`.

- dilation: The dilation of the convolution. The default is 1.

- groups: This parameter lets you control the way input channels are connected to output channels. The number specified in groups specifies how many groups will be formed so that the convolutions happen within a group and not across. For instance, group=2 means that half the input channels will be convolved by one set of kernels and that the other half will be convolved by a separate set of kernels. This is equivalent to running two convolution layers side by side. Check the documentation for more information on this parameter. Again, this is for an esoteric use case. The default is 1.

- bias: This parameter adds a learnable bias to the convolutions. The default is True.

Let's apply a CNN model to the same synthetic data we generated earlier in this chapter with a kernel size of 3:

```
conv = nn.Conv1d(in_channels=1, out_channels=1, kernel_size=k)
```

Now, let's look at the inputs and outputs that are expected from a CNN.

Conv1d expects the inputs to have three dimensions – *(batch size, number of channels, sequence length)*. For the initial input layer, the number of channels is the number of features you are feeding into the network; for intermediate layers, it is the number of kernels we have used in the previous layer. The output from Conv1d is in the form of *(batch size, number of channels (output), sequence length (output))*.

So, let's run our sequence through Conv1d and look at the inputs and outputs (for more detailed steps, refer to the 02-Building Blocks.ipynb notebook):

```
#input dim: torch.Size([6, 1, 15])
# batch size = 6, number of features = 1 and sequence length =
15
output = conv(cnn_input)
# Output should be in_dim - k + 1
assert output.size(-1)==cnn_input.size(-1)-k+1
output.shape #-> torch.Size([6, 1, 13])
```

The notebook provides a slightly more detailed analysis of Conv1d, with tables showing the impact that the hyperparameters have on the shape of the output, what kind of padding is used to make the input and output dimensions the same, and how a convolution with equal weights is just like a rolling mean. I highly suggest that you check it out and play around with the different options to get a feel of what the layer does for you.

> **Additional information**
>
> The inbuilt padding in `Conv1d` has its roots in image processing, so the padding technique defaults to adding adding to both sides. But for sequences, it is preferable to use padding on the left and because of that, it is also preferable to handle how the input sequences are padded separately and not use the inbuilt mechanism. `torch.nn.functional` has a handy method called `pad` that can be used to this effect.

Other building blocks are used in time series forecasting because the architecture of a deep neural network is only limited by creativity. But the point of this chapter was to introduce you to the common ones that appear in many different architectures. We also intentionally left out one of the most popular architectures used nowadays: the transformer. This is because we have devoted another chapter (*Chapter 14, Attention and Transformers for Time Series*) to understanding attention before we look at transformers. Another major block that is slowly gaining popularity is graph neural networks, which can be thought of as specialized CNNS that operate on graph-based data rather than grids. However, this is outside the scope of this book since it is an area of active research.

Summary

After introducing deep learning in the previous chapter, in this chapter, we gained a deeper understanding of the common architectural blocks that are used for time series forecasting. The encoder-decoder paradigm was explained as a fundamental way we can structure a deep neural network for forecasting. Then, we learned about FFNs, RNNS, and CNNs and explored how they are used to process time series. We also saw how we can use all these major blocks in PyTorch by using the associated notebook and got our hands dirty with some PyTorch code.

In the next chapter, we'll learn about a few major patterns we can use to arrange these blocks to perform time series forecasting.

References

The following references were used in this chapter:

1. Neco, R. P., and Forcada, M. L. (1997), *Asynchronous translations with recurrent neural nets.* Neural Networks, 1997., International Conference on (Vol. 4, pp. 2535–2540). IEEE: https://ieeexplore.ieee.org/document/614693.

2. Kalchbrenner, N., and Blunsom, P. (2013), *Recurrent Continuous Translation Models.* EMNLP (Vol. 3, No. 39, p. 413): https://aclanthology.org/D13-1176/.

3. Kyunghyun Cho, Bart van Merriënboer, Caglar Gulcehre, Dzmitry Bahdanau, Fethi Bougares, Holger Schwenk, and Yoshua Bengio. (2014), *Learning Phrase Representations using RNN Encoder-Decoder for Statistical Machine Translation.* Proceedings of the 2014 Conference on Empirical Methods in Natural Language Processing (EMNLP), pages 1724–1734, Doha, Qatar. Association for Computational Linguistics: https://aclanthology.org/D14-1179/.

4.   Ilya Sutskever, Oriol Vinyals, and Quoc V. Le. (2014), *Sequence to sequence learning with neural networks*. Proceedings of the 27th International Conference on Neural Information Processing Systems – Volume 2: `https://dl.acm.org/doi/10.5555/2969033.2969173`.

5.   Rumelhart, D., Hinton, G., and Williams, R (1986). *Learning representations by back-propagating errors*. Nature 323, 533–536: `https://doi.org/10.1038/323533a0`.

6.   Schuster, M., and Paliwal, K. K. (1997). *Bidirectional recurrent neural networks*. IEEE Transactions on Signal Processing, 45(11), 2673–2681: `https://doi.org/10.1109/78.650093`.

7.   Sepp Hochreiter (1991) *Untersuchungen zu dynamischen neuronalen Netzen*. Diploma thesis, TU Munich: `https://people.idsia.ch/~juergen/SeppHochreiter1991ThesisAdvisorSchmidhuber.pdf`.

8.   Y. Bengio, P. Frasconi, and P. Simard (1993), *The problem of learning long-term dependencies in recurrent networks*. IEEE International Conference on Neural Networks, pp. 1183-1188 vol.3: `10.1109/ICNN.1993.298725`.

9.   Y. Bengio, P. Simard, and P. Frasconi (1994) *Learning long-term dependencies with gradient descent is difficult* in IEEE Transactions on Neural Networks, vol. 5, no. 2, pp. 157–166, March 1994: `10.1109/72.279181`.

10. Hochreiter, S., and Schmidhuber, J. (1997). *Long short-term memory*. Neural computation, 9(8), 1735–1780: `https://doi.org/10.1162/neco.1997.9.8.1735`.

11. Cho, K., Merrienboer, B.V., Gülçehre, Ç., Bahdanau, D., Bougares, F., Schwenk, H., and Bengio, Y. (2014). *Learning Phrase Representations using RNN Encoder-Decoder for Statistical Machine Translation*. EMNLP: `https://www.aclweb.org/anthology/D14-1179.pdf`.

12. Fukushima, K. *Neocognitron: A self-organizing neural network model for a mechanism of pattern recognition unaffected by shift in position*. Biol. Cybernetics 36, 193–202 (1980): `https://doi.org/10.1007/BF00344251`.

13. Y. Le Cun, B. Boser, J. S. Denker, R. E. Howard, W. Habbard, L. D. Jackel, and D. Henderson. 1990. *Handwritten digit recognition with a back-propagation network*. Advances in neural information processing systems 2. Morgan Kaufmann Publishers Inc., San Francisco, CA, USA, 396–404: `https://proceedings.neurips.cc/paper/1989/file/53c3bce66e43be4f209556518c2fcb54-Paper.pdf`.

Further reading

Take a look at the following resources to learn more about the topics that were covered in this chapter:

- Official PyTorch Tutorials: `https://pytorch.org/tutorials/beginner/basics/intro.html`

- *Essence of linear algebra*, by 3Blue1Brown: `https://www.youtube.com/playlist?list=PLZHQObOWTQDPD3MizzM2xVFitgF8hE_ab`

- *Neural Networks – A Linear Algebra Perspective*, by Manu Joseph: `https://deep-and-shallow.com/2022/01/15/neural-networks-a-linear-algebra-perspective/`

- *Deep Learning*, by Ian Goodfellow, Yoshua Bengio,and Aaron Courville: `https://deep-and-shallow.com/2022/01/15/neural-networks-a-linear-algebra-perspective/`

- *Understanding LSTMs*, by Christopher Olah: `http://colah.github.io/posts/2015-08-Understanding-LSTMs/`

- *Intuitive Guide to Convolution*: `https://betterexplained.com/articles/intuitive-convolution/`

- *Computing Receptive Fields of Convolutional Neural Networks*, by Andre Araujo, Wade Norris, and Jack Sim: `https://distill.pub/2019/computing-receptive-fields/`

- *Convolutions in Autoregressive Neural Networks*, by Kilian Batzner: `https://theblog.github.io/post/convolution-in-autoregressive-neural-networks/`

- *Convolution Arithmetic*, by Vincent Dumoulin and Francesco Visin: `https://github.com/vdumoulin/conv_arithmetic`

- *Dropout: A Simple Way to Prevent Neural Networks from Overfitting*, by Nitish Srivastava et al: `https://jmlr.org/papers/v15/srivastava14a.html`

13
Common Modeling Patterns for Time Series

We reviewed a few major and common building blocks of a **deep learning** (DL) system, specifically suited for time series, in the last chapter. Now that we know what those blocks are, it's time for a more practical lesson. Let's see how we can put these common blocks together in various common ways in which time series forecasting is modeled using the dataset we have been working with all through this book.

In this chapter, we will be covering these main topics:

- Tabular regression
- Single-step-ahead recurrent neural networks
- Sequence-to-sequence models

Technical requirements

You will need to set up the Anaconda environment following the instructions in the *Preface* of the book to get a working environment with all packages and datasets required for the code in this book.

The associated code for the chapter can be found at `https://github.com/PacktPublishing/Modern-Time-Series-Forecasting-with-Python-/tree/main/notebooks/Chapter13`.

You need to run the following notebooks for this chapter:

- `02-Preprocessing London Smart Meter Dataset.ipynb` in `Chapter02`
- `01-Setting up Experiment Harness.ipynb` in `Chapter04`
- `01-Feature Engineering.ipynb` in `Chapter06`

- `00-Single Step Backtesting Baselines.ipynb`, `01-Forecasting with ML.ipynb`, and `02-Forecasting with Target Transformation.ipynb` in Chapter08
- `01-Global Forecasting Models-ML.ipynb` in Chapter10

Tabular regression

In *Chapter 5, Time Series Forecasting as Regression*, we saw how we can convert a time series problem into a standard regression problem by temporal embedding and time delay embedding. In *Chapter 6, Feature Engineering for Time Series Forecasting*, we have already created the necessary features for the household energy consumption dataset we have been working on, and in *Chapter 8, Forecasting Time Series with Machine Learning Models, Chapter 9, Ensembling and Stacking*, and *Chapter 10, Global Forecasting Models*, we used traditional **machine learning** (**ML**) models to create a forecast.

Just as we used standard ML models for forecasting, we can also use DL models built for tabular data using the feature-engineered dataset we have created. One of the advantages of using a DL model in this setting, over the ML models, is the flexibility DL offers us. All through *Chapters 8, 9*, and *10*, we only saw how we can create single-step-ahead forecasting using ML models. We have a separate section on multi-step forecasting in *Part 3, Deep Learning for Time Series*, where we go into detail on different strategies with which we can generate multi-step forecasts, and we address one of the limitations of standard ML models in multi-step forecasting. But right now, let's just understand that standard ML models are designed to have a single output and, because of that fact, getting multi-step forecasts is not straightforward. But with tabular DL models, we have the flexibility to train the model to predict multiple targets, and this enables us to generate multi-step forecasts easily.

PyTorch Tabular is an open source library (`https://github.com/manujosephv/pytorch_tabular`) that makes it easy to work with DL models in the tabular data domain, and it also has ready-to-use implementations of many state-of-the-art DL models. We are going to use PyTorch Tabular to generate forecasts using the feature-engineered datasets we created in *Chapter 6, Feature Engineering for Time Series Forecasting*.

PyTorch Tabular has very detailed documentation and tutorials to get you started here: `https://pytorch-tabular.readthedocs.io/en/latest/`. Although we won't be going into detail on all the intricacies of the library, we will look at how we can use a bare-bones version to generate a forecast on the dataset we are working on using a `FTTransformer` model. `FTTransformer` is one of the state-of-the-art DL models for tabular data. DL for tabular data is a whole different kind of model, and I've linked a blog post in the *Further reading* section as a primer to the field of study. For our purposes, we can treat them as any standard ML model in scikit-learn.

> **Notebook alert**
>
> To follow along with the complete code, use the notebook named `01-Tabular Regression.ipynb` in the `Chapter13` folder and the code in the `src` folder.

We start off, pretty much like before, by loading the libraries and necessary datasets. Just one additional thing we are doing here is that instead of taking the same selection of blocks we worked with in *Part 2, Machine Learning for Time Series*, we take smaller-sized data by selecting half the number of blocks as before. This is done to make the **neural network** (**NN**) training smoother and faster and for it to fit into GPU memory (if any). I'd like to stress here that this is done purely for hardware reasons, and provided we have sufficiently powerful hardware, we need not have smaller datasets for DP. On the contrary—DL loves larger datasets. But since we want to keep the focus on the modeling side, the engineering constraints and techniques in working with larger datasets have been kept outside the scope of this book.

```
uniq_blocks = train_df.file.unique().tolist()
sel_blocks = sorted(uniq_blocks, key=lambda x: int(x.
replace("block_","")))[:len(uniq_blocks)//2]
train_df = train_df.loc[train_df.file.isin(sel_blocks)]
test_df = test_df.loc[test_df.file.isin(sel_blocks)]
sel_lclids = train_df.LCLid.unique().tolist()
```

After handling the missing values, we are ready to start using PyTorch Tabular. We first import the necessary classes from the library, like so:

```
from pytorch_tabular.config import DataConfig, OptimizerConfig,
TrainerConfig
from pytorch_tabular.models import FTTransformerConfig
from pytorch_tabular import TabularModel
```

PyTorch Tabular uses a set of config files to define the parameters required for running the model, and these configs include everything from how the dataframe is configured to what kind of preprocessing needs to be applied, what kind of training we need to do, what model we need to use, what the hyperparameters of the model are, and so on. Let's see how we can define a bare-bones configuration (because PyTorch Tabular makes use of intelligent defaults wherever possible to make the usage easier for the practitioner):

```
data_config = DataConfig(
    target=[target], #target should always be a list
    continuous_cols=[
        "visibility",
        "windBearing",
        ...
        "timestamp_Is_month_start",
    ],
    categorical_cols=[
```

```
        "holidays",
        ...
        "LCLid"
    ],
    normalize_continuous_features=True
)
trainer_config = TrainerConfig(
    auto_lr_find=True, # Runs the LRFinder to automatically
derive a learning rate
    batch_size=1024,
    max_epochs=1000,
    auto_select_gpus=True,
    gpus=-1
)
optimizer_config = OptimizerConfig()
```

We use a very high max_epochs parameter in TrainerConfig because by default, PyTorch Tabular employs a technique called **early stopping,** where we continuously keep track of the performance on a validation set and stop the training when the validation loss starts to increase.

Selecting which model to use from the implemented models in PyTorch Tabular is as simple as choosing the right configuration. Each model is associated with a configuration that defines the hyperparameters of the model. So, just by using that specific configuration, PyTorch Tabular understands which model the user wants to use. Let's choose the FTTransformerConfig model and define a few hyperparameters:

```
model_config = FTTransformerConfig(
    task="regression",
    num_attn_blocks=3,
    num_heads=4,
    transformer_head_dim=64,
    attn_dropout=0.2,
    ff_dropout=0.1,
    out_ff_layers="32",
    metrics=["mean_squared_error"]
)
```

The main and only mandatory parameter here is task, which tells PyTorch Tabular whether it is a *regression* or *classification* task.

> **Additional note**
>
> Although PyTorch Tabular provides the best defaults, we only set these parameters to make the training faster and fit into the memory of the GPU we are running on. If you are not running the notebook on a machine with a GPU, choosing a smaller and faster model such as `CategoryEmbeddingConfig` would be better.

Now, all that is left to do is put all these configs together in a class called `TabularModel`, which is the workhorse of the library, and as with any scikit-learn model, call `fit` on the object. But, unlike a scikit-learn model, you don't need to split X and y; we just need to provide the dataframe, as follows:

```
tabular_model.fit(train=train_df)
```

Once the training completes, you can save the model by just running the following code:

```
tabular_model.save_model("notebooks/Chapter13/ft_transformer_
global")
```

If for any reason you have to close your notebook instance after training, you can always load the model back by using the following code:

```
tabular_model = TabularModel.load_from_checkpoint("notebooks/
Chapter13/ft_transformer_global")
```

This way, you don't need to spend a lot of time training the model again, but instead, use it for prediction.

Now, all that is left is to predict on the unseen data and evaluate the performance. Here's how we can do this:

```
forecast_df = tabular_model.predict(test_df)
agg_metrics, eval_metrics_df = evaluate_forecast(
    y_pred=forecast_df[f"{target}_prediction"],
    test_target=forecast_df["energy_consumption"],
    train_target=train_df["energy_consumption"],
    model_name=model_config._model_name,
)
```

We have used the untuned global forecasting model with metadata that we trained in *Chapter 10, Global Forecasting Models*, as the baseline against which we can do a cursory check on how well the DL model is doing, as illustrated in the following screenshot:

Algorithm	MAE	MSE	meanMASE	Forecast Bias
GFM+Meta (NativeLGBM)	0.0873	0.0340	1.0627	-0.68%
FTTransformerModel	0.0913	0.0332	1.1598	5.90%

Figure 13.1 – Evaluation of the DL-based tabular regression

We can see that the `FTTransformer` model is competitive with the `LightGBM` model we trained in *Chapter 10*. Maybe, with the right amount of tuning and partitioning, the `FTTransformer` model can do as well or better than the `LightGBM` one. Training a competitive DL model in the same way as `LightGBM` is useful in many ways. First, this brings us flexibility and trains the model to predict multiple timesteps at once. Second, this can also be combined with the `LightGBM` model in an ensemble, and because of the variety the DL model brings to the mix, this can make the ensemble performance better.

> **Things to try**
>
> Use PyTorch Tabular's documentation and play around with other models or change the parameters to see how the performances changes.
>
> Select a few households and plot them to see how well the forecast matches up to the targets.

Now, let's look at how we can use RNN for single-step-ahead forecasting.

Single-step-ahead recurrent neural networks

Although we took a little detour to check out how DL regression models can be used to train the same global models we learned about in *Chapter 10, Global Forecasting Models*, now we are back to looking at DL models and architectures specifically built for time series. And as always, we will look at simple one-step-ahead and local models first before moving on to more complex modeling paradigms. In fact, we have another chapter (*Chapter 15, Strategies for Global Deep Learning Forecasting Models*) entirely devoted to techniques we can use to train global DL models.

Now, let's bring our attention back to one-step-ahead local models. We saw **recurrent neural networks (RNNs)** (vanilla RNN, **long short-term memory (LSTM)**, and **gated recurrent unit (GRU)**) as a few blocks we can use for sequences such as time series. Now, let's see how we can use them in an **end-to-end (E2E)** model on the dataset we have been working on (the *London smart meters* dataset).

Although we will be looking at a few libraries (such as `darts`) that make the process of training DL models for time series forecasting easier, in this chapter, we will be looking at how to develop such models from scratch. Understanding how a DL model for time series forecasting is put together from the ground up will give you a good grasp of the concepts that are needed to use and tweak the libraries that we will be looking at later.

We will be using PyTorch, and if you are not comfortable, I suggest you head to *Chapter 12, Building Blocks of Deep Learning for Time Series*, and the associated notebooks for a quick refresher. On top of that, we are also going to use PyTorch Lightning, which is another library built on top of PyTorch to make training models using PyTorch easy, among other benefits.

We talked about **time delay embedding** in *Chapter 5, Time Series Forecasting as Regression*, where we talked about using a window in time to embed the time series into a format more suitable for regression. When training NNs for time series forecasting also, we need such windows. Suppose we are training on a single time series. We can give this super long time series to an RNN as is, but then it only becomes one sample in the dataset. And with just one sample in the dataset, it's close to impossible to train any ML or DL models. So, it's advisable to sample multiple windows from the time series to convert the time series into a number of data samples in a process that is very much similar to time delay embedding. This window also sets the memory of the DL model.

The first step we need to take is to create a PyTorch dataset that takes the raw time series and prepares these samples' windows. A dataset is like an iterator over the data that gives us samples corresponding to a provided index. Defining a custom dataset for PyTorch is as simple as defining a class that takes in a few arguments (data being one of them) and defining two mandatory methods in the class, as follows:

- `__len__(self)` —This sets the maximum number of samples in the dataset.
- `__get_item__(self, idx)` —This picks the `idx`th sample from the dataset.

We have defined a dataset in `src/dl/dataloaders.py` with the name `TimeSeriesDataset`, which takes in the following parameters:

- `data`—This argument can either be a pandas dataframe or a NumPy array with the time series. This is the entire time series, including train, validation, and test, and the splits occur inside the class.
- `window`—This sets the length of each sample.
- `horizon`—This sets the number of future timesteps we want to get as the target.
- `n_val`—This parameter can either be a `float` or an `int` data type. If `int`, it represents the number of timesteps to be reserved as validation data. And if `float`, this represents the percent of total data to be reserved as validation data.
- `n_test`—This parameter is similar to `n_val`, but does the same for test data.

- `normalize`—This parameter defines how we want to normalize the data. This takes in three options: `none` means no normalizing; `global` means we calculate the mean and standard deviation of the train data and use it to standardize the entire series using this equation:

$$\frac{series - mean}{std}$$

`local` means we use the window mean and standard deviation to standardize the series.

- `normalize_params`—This parameter takes in a tuple of mean and standard deviations. If provided, this is be used to standardize in *global* standardization. This is typically used to use the train mean and standard deviation on validation and test data as well.

- `mode`—This parameter sets which dataset we want to make. It takes in one of three values: `train`, `val`, or `test`.

Each sample from this dataset returns to you two tensors—the window (X) and the corresponding target (Y) (see *Figure 13.2*):

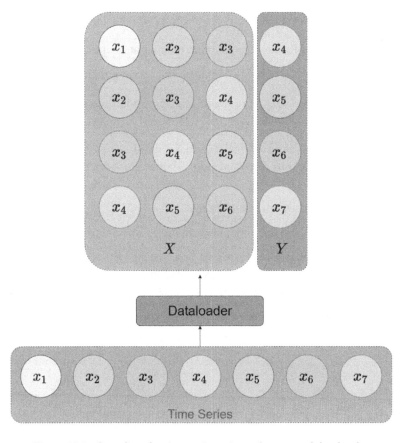

Figure 13.2 – Sampling the time series using a dataset and dataloader

Now that we have the dataset defined, we need another PyTorch artifact called a dataloader. A dataloader uses the dataset to pick samples into a batch of samples, among other things. In the PyTorch Lightning ecosystem, we have another concept called a datamodule, which is a standard way of generating dataloaders. We need train dataloaders, validation dataloaders, and test dataloaders. Datamodules provide a good abstraction to encapsulate the whole data part of the pipeline. We have defined a datamodule in `src/dl/dataloaders.py` called `TimeSeriesDataModule` that takes in the data along with the batch size and prepares the datasets and dataloaders necessary for training. The parameters are exactly the same as `TimeSeriesDataset`, with `batch_size` as the only additional parameter.

> **Notebook alert**
>
> To follow along with the complete code, use the notebook named `02-One-Step RNN.ipynb` in the `Chapter13` folder and the code in the `src` folder.

We will not be going into each and every step in the notebook but will be just stressing the key points. The code in the notebook is well commented, and we urge you to follow the code along with the book.

We have already sampled a household from the data, and now, let's see how we can define a datamodule:

```
datamodule = TimeSeriesDataModule(data = sample_df[[target]],
        n_val = sample_val_df.shape[0],
        n_test = sample_test_df.shape[0],
        window = 48, # giving enough memory to capture daily
seasonality
        horizon = 1, # single step
        normalize = "global", # normalizing the data
        batch_size = 32,
        num_workers = 0)
datamodule.setup()
```

`datamodule.setup()` is the method that calculates and sets up the dataloaders. Now, we can access the train dataloader by simply calling `datamodule.train_dataloader()`, and similarly, validation and test by `val_dataloader` and `test_dataloader` methods, respectively. And we can access the samples, as follows:

```
# Getting a batch from the train_dataloader
for batch in datamodule.train_dataloader():
    x, y = batch
    break
```

```
print("Shape of x: ",x.shape) #-> torch.Size([32, 48, 1])
print("Shape of y: ",y.shape) #-> torch.Size([32, 1, 1])
```

We can see that each sample has two tensors—x and y. There are three dimensions for the tensors, and they correspond to *batch size, sequence length, features*.

Now that we have the data pipeline ready, we need to build out the modeling and training pipelines. PyTorch Lightning has a standard way of defining these so that they can be plugged into the training engine they provide (which makes our life so much easier). The PyTorch Lightning documentation (https://pytorch-lightning.readthedocs.io/en/latest/starter/introduction.html) has good resources to get started with and go into depth on as well. We have also linked to a video in the *Further reading* section that makes the transition from pure PyTorch to PyTorch Lightning easy. I strongly urge you to take some time to familiarize yourself with it.

If you are familiar with standard PyTorch, you'll know that a standard method called `forward` is the only mandatory method you have to define, apart from `__init__`. This is because the training loop is something that we will have to write on our own. In the `01-PyTorch Basics.ipynb` notebook for *Chapter 12, Building Blocks of Deep Learning for Time Series*, we saw how we can write a PyTorch model and a training loop to train a simple classifier. But now that we are delegating the training loop to PyTorch Lightning, we have to include a few additional methods as well:

- `training_step`—This method takes in a batch and uses the model to get the outputs, calculate the loss/metrics, and return the loss.

- `validation_step` and `test_step`—These methods take in the batch and use the model to get the outputs and calculate the loss/metrics.

- `predict_step`—This method is used to define the step to be taken while inferencing. If there is anything special we have to do for inferencing, we can define this method. If this is not defined, it uses `test_step` for the prediction use case as well.

- `configure_optimizers`—This method defines the optimizer to be used; for instance, `Adam`, `RMSProp`, and so on.

We have defined a `BaseModel` class in `src/dl/models.py` that implements all the common functions, such as loss and metric calculation, logging of results, and so on, as a framework to implement new models. And using this `BaseModel` class, we have defined a `SingleStepRNNModel` class that takes in a standard config (`SingleStepRNNConfig`) and initializes an RNN, LSTM, or GRU model.

Before we look at how the model is defined, let's see what the different config (`SingleStepRNNConfig`) parameters are:

- `rnn_type`—This parameter takes in one of three strings as an input: RNN, GRU, or LSTM. This defines what kind of model we will initialize.

- `input_size`—This parameter defines the number of features the RNN is expecting.

- `hidden_size`, `num_layers`, `bidirectional`—These parameters are the same as the ones we saw in the RNN cell in *Chapter 12, Building Blocks of Deep Learning for Time Series*.

- `learning_rate`—This defines the learning rate of the optimization procedure.

- `optimizer_params`, `lr_scheduler`, `lr_scheduler_params`—These are parameters that let us tweak the optimization procedure. Let's not worry about these for now because all of them have been set to intelligent defaults.

With this setup, defining a new model is as simple as this:

```
rnn_config = SingleStepRNNConfig(
    rnn_type="RNN",
    input_size=1,
    hidden_size=128,
    num_layers=3,
    bidirectional=True,
    learning_rate=1e-3,
    seed=42,
)


model = SingleStepRNNModel(rnn_config)
```

Now, let's take a peek at the `forward` method, which is the heart of the model. We want our model to do one-step-ahead prediction, and from *Chapter 12, Building Blocks of Deep Learning for Time Series*, we know what a typical RNN output is and how PyTorch RNNs just output the hidden state at each timestep. Let's see what we want to do visually and then see how we can code it up:

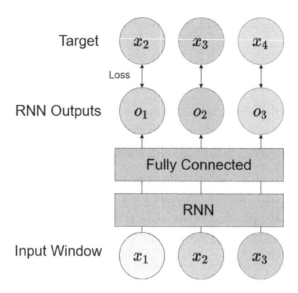

Figure 13.3 – A single-step RNN

Suppose we are using the same example we saw in the dataloader—a time series with the following entries :, $x_1, x_2, x_3, \dots x_7$ and a window of three. So, one of the samples the dataloader gives will have x_1, x_2, x_3 as the input (x) and x_4 as the target. One way we can use this is by passing the sequence through the RNN, ignoring all the outputs except the last one, and using that to predict the target, x_4. But that is not an efficient use of the samples we have, right? We also know that the output from the first timestep (using x_1) should output x_2, the second timestep should output x_3, and so on. Therefore, we can formulate the RNN in such a way that we maximize the usage of the data and, while training, use these additional points in time to also give a better signal to our model. Now, let's break down the `forward` method.

`forward` takes in a single argument called `batch`, which is a tuple of input and output. So, we unpack `batch` into two variables, x and y, like so:

```
x, y = batch
```

x will have the shape → *(batch size, window length, features)* and y will have the shape → *(batch size, target length, features)*.

Now we need to pass the input sequence (x) through the RNN (RNN, LSTM, or GRU), like so:

```
x, _ = self.rnn(x)
```

As we saw in *Chapter 12, Building Blocks of Deep Learning for Time Series*, the PyTorch RNNs process the input and return two outputs—hidden states for each timestep and output (which is the hidden state of the last timestep). Here, we need the hidden states from all the timesteps, and therefore we capture that in the x variable. x will now have the dimension → *(batch size, window length, hidden size of RNN)*.

We have the hidden states, but to get the output, we need to apply a fully connected layer over the hidden states, and this fully connected layer should be shared across timesteps. An easy way to do this is to just define a fully connected layer with an input size equal to the hidden size of the RNN and then do the following:

```
x = self.fc(x)
```

x is a three-dimensional tensor, and when we use a fully connected layer on a three-dimensional tensor, PyTorch automatically applies the fully connected layer to each of the timesteps. Now, this final output is captured in x, and its dimensions would be a *(batch size, window length, 1)*.

Now, we have got the output of the network, but we also must do a bit of rearrangement to prepare the targets. Currently, y has just the one timestep beyond the window, but if we skip the first timestep from x and concatenate it with y, we would get the target, as we have in *Figure 13.3*:

```
y = torch.cat([x[:, 1:, :], y], dim=1)
```

By using array indexing, we select everything except the first timestep from x and concatenate it with y on the first dimension (which is the *window length*).

And with that, we have the x and y variables, which we can return, and the BaseModel class will calculate loss and handle the rest of the training. For the entire class, along with the forward method, you can refer to src/dl/models.py.

Let's test the model we have initialized by passing the batch from the dataloader:

```
y_hat, y = model(batch)
print("Shape of y_hat: ",y_hat.shape) #-> ([32, 48, 1])
print("Shape of y: ",y.shape) #-> ([32, 48, 1])
```

Now that the model is working as expected, without errors, let's start training the model. For that, we can leverage Trainer from PyTorch Lightning. There are so many options in the Trainer class, and a full list of all parameters to tweak the training can be found here: https://pytorch-lightning.readthedocs.io/en/stable/api/pytorch_lightning.trainer.trainer.Trainer.html#pytorch_lightning.trainer.trainer.Trainer.

But here, we are just going to use the bare minimum. Let's go over the parameters we will be using here one by one:

- auto_select_gpus and gpus—Together, these parameters let us select GPUs for training if present. If we set auto_select_gpus to True and gpus to -1, the Trainer class will choose all GPUs present in the machine, and if there are no GPUs, it falls back to CPU-based training.

- `callbacks`—PyTorch Lightning has a lot of useful callbacks that can be used during training such as `EarlyStopping`, `ModelCheckpoint`, and so on. Most useful callbacks are automatically added even if we don't explicitly set them, but `EarlyStopping` is one useful callback that needs to be set explicitly. `EarlyStopping` is a callback that lets us monitor the validation loss or metrics while training and stop the training when this starts to become worse. This is a form of regularization and helps us keep our model from overfitting to the train data. `EarlyStopping` has the following major parameters (a full list of parameters can be found here: `https://pytorch-lightning.readthedocs.io/en/stable/api/pytorch_lightning.callbacks.EarlyStopping.html`):

  - `monitor`—This parameter takes a string input that specifies the exact name of the metric that we want to monitor for early stopping.

  - `patience`—This specifies the number of epochs with no improvement in the monitored metric before the callback stops the training. For instance, if we set patience as `10`, the callback will wait for 10 epochs of the degrading metric before stopping the training. There are finer points on these, which are explained in the documentation.

  - `mode`—This is a string input and takes one of `min` or `max`. This sets the direction of improvement. In `min` mode, training will stop when the quantity monitored has stopped decreasing, and in `max` mode, it will stop when the quantity monitored has stopped increasing.

- `min_epochs` and `max_epochs`—These parameters help us set `min` and `max` limits to the number of epochs the training should run. If we are using `EarlyStopping`, `min_epochs` decides the minimum number of epochs that will be run regardless of the validation loss/metrics, and `max_epochs` sets the upper limit on the number of epochs. So, even if the validation loss is still decreasing when we reach `max_epochs`, training will stop.

Glossary

Here are a few terms you should know to fully digest NN training:

Training step—This denotes a single gradient update to the parameter. In batched **stochastic gradient descent** (**SGD**), the gradient update after each batch is considered a step.

Batch—A batch is the number of data samples we run through the model and average the gradients over for the update in a training step.

Epoch—An epoch is when the model has seen all the samples in a dataset, or all the batches in the dataset have been used for a gradient update.

So, let's initialize a bare-bones `Trainer` class:

```
trainer = pl.Trainer(
    auto_select_gpus=True,
    gpus=-1,
```

```
    min_epochs=5,
    max_epochs=100,
    callbacks=[pl.callbacks.EarlyStopping(monitor="valid_loss",
patience=3)],
)
```

Now, all that is left is to trigger the training by passing in the `model` and `datamodule` to a method called `fit`:

```
trainer.fit(model, datamodule)
```

It will run for a while and, depending on when the validation loss starts to increase, it will stop the training. Once the model is trained, we can still use the `Trainer` class to predict on new data. The prediction uses the `predict_step` method that we defined in the `BaseModel` class, which in turn uses the `predict` method that we defined in the `SingleStepRNN` model. It's a very simple method that calls the `forward` method, takes in the model outputs, and just picks the last timestep from the output (which is the true output that we are projecting into the future). You can see an illustration of this here:

```
def predict(self, batch):
        y_hat, _ = self.forward(batch)
        return y_hat[:, -1, :]
```

So, let's see how we can use the `Trainer` class to predict on new data (or new dataloaders, to be exact):

```
pred = trainer.predict(model, datamodule.test_dataloader())
```

We just need to provide the trained model and the dataloader (here, we use the test dataloader that we have already set up and defined).

Now the output, `pred`, is a list of tensors, one for each batch in the dataloader. We just need to concatenate them, squeeze out any redundant dimensions, detach them from the computational graph, and convert them to a NumPy array. Here's how we can do this:

```
pred = torch.cat(pred).squeeze().detach().numpy()
```

Now, `pred` is a NumPy array of predictions for all the items in the test dataframe (which was used to define `test_dataloader`, but remember we had applied a transformation to the raw time series to standardize it. Now, we need to reverse the transformation. The mean and standard deviation we used for the initial transformation are still stored in the train dataset. We merely retrieve them and inverse the transformation we did earlier, like so:

```
pred = pred * datamodule.train.std + datamodule.train.mean
```

Now, we can do all kinds of actions on them, such as evaluate against actuals, visualize the predictions, and so on. Let's see how well the model has done. To get context, we have included the single-step ML models we did back in *Chapter 8, Forecasting Time Series with Machine Learning Models*, as well:

Algorithm	MAE	MSE	MASE	Forecast Bias
Lasso Regression	0.1598	0.0743	1.2452	3.78%
XGB Random Forest	0.1641	0.0819	1.2792	9.30%
LightGBM	0.1470	0.0666	1.1457	3.36%
RNN	0.2685	0.1721	2.0927	29.35%

Figure 13.4 – Metrics of the vanilla single-step-ahead RNN on MAC000193 household

It looks like the RNN model did pretty badly. Let's also look at the predictions visually:

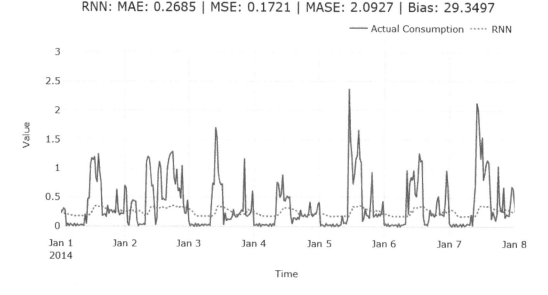

Figure 13.5 – Single-step-ahead RNN predictions for MAC000193 household

We can see that the model has failed to learn the scale of the peaks and the nuances of the patterns. Maybe this is because of the problem that we discussed in terms of RNNs because the seasonality pattern here is spread over 48 timesteps; remember that the pattern requires the RNN to have long-term memory. Let's quickly swap out the model with LSTM and GRU and see how they are doing. The only thing we need to change is the rnn_type parameter in SingleStepRNNConfig. The notebook has the code to train LSTM and GRU as well. But let's look at the metrics with LSTM and GRU:

Algorithm	MAE	MSE	MASE	Forecast Bias
Lasso Regression	0.1598	0.0743	1.2452	3.78%
XGB Random Forest	0.1641	0.0819	1.2792	9.30%
LightGBM	0.1470	0.0666	1.1457	3.36%
RNN	0.2685	0.1721	2.0927	29.35%
LSTM	0.1982	0.1125	1.5442	17.94%
GRU	0.1714	0.0899	1.3358	14.48%

Figure 13.6 – Metrics for single-step-ahead LSTM and GRU on MAC000193 household

Now, it looks competitive. LightGBM is still the best model, but now the LSTM and GRU models are competitive and not entirely lacking, like the vanilla RNN model. If we look at the predictions, we can see that the LSTM and GRU models have managed to capture the pattern much better as well:

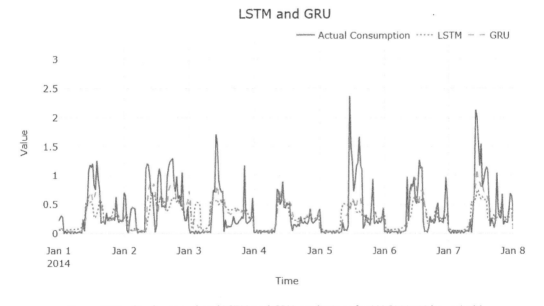

Figure 13.7 – Single-step-ahead LSTM and GRU predictions for MAC000193 household

> **Things to try**
> Try changing the parameters of the models and see how it works. How does a bidirectional LSTM perform? Can increasing the window increase performance?

Now that we have seen how a standard RNN can be used for single-step-ahead predictions, let's look at another modeling pattern that is more flexible than the one we just saw.

Sequence-to-sequence (Seq2Seq) models

We talked in detail about the sequence-to-sequence (Seq2Seq) architecture and the encoder-decoder paradigm in *Chapter 12, Building Blocks of Deep Learning for Time Series*. Just to refresh your memory, the Seq2Seq model is a kind of an encoder-decoder model by which an encoder encodes the sequence into a latent representation, and then the decoder steps in to carry out the task at hand using this latent representation. This setup is inherently more flexible because of the separation between the encoder (which does the representation learning) and the decoder, which uses the representation for predictions. One of the biggest advantages of this approach, from a time series forecasting perspective, is that the restriction of single step ahead is taken out. Under this modeling pattern, we can extend the forecast to any forecast horizon we want.

In this section, let's put together a few encoder-decoder models and test out our single-step-ahead forecasts, just like we have been doing with the *single-step-ahead RNNs*.

> **Notebook alert**
>
> To follow along with the complete code, use the notebook named `03-Seq2Seq RNN.ipynb` in the `Chapter13` folder and the code in the `src` folder.

We can use the same mechanism we developed in the last section such as `TimeSeriesDataModule`, the `BaseModel` class, and the corresponding code for our Seq2Seq modeling pattern as well. Let's define a new PyTorch model called `Seq2SeqModel`, inheriting the `BaseModel` class. While we are at it, let's also define a new config file, called `Seq2SeqConfig`, to set the hyperparameters of the model. The final version of both can be found in `src/dl/models.py`.

Before we explain the different parameters in the model and the config, let's talk about the different ways we can set this Seq2Seq model.

RNN-to-fully connected network

For our convenience, let's restrict the encoder to be from the RNN family—it can be a vanilla RNN, LSTM, or GRU. Now, we saw in *Chapter 12, Building Blocks of Deep Learning for Time Series,* that in PyTorch, all the models in the RNN family have two outputs—*output* and *hidden states*, and we also saw that output is nothing but all the hidden states (final hidden states in stacked RNNs) at all timesteps. The hidden state that we get has the latest hidden states (and cell states, in the case of LSTM) of all layers in the stacked RNN setup. The encoder can be initialized just like we initialized the RNN family of models in the previous section, like so:

```
self.encoder = nn.LSTM(
            **encoder_params,
            batch_first=True,
        )
```

And in the `forward` method, we can just do the following to encode the time series:

```
o, h = self.encoder(x)
```

Now, there are a few different ways we can decode the information. The first one we will discuss is using a fully connected layer. Either the fully connected layer can take the latest hidden state from the encoder and predict the desired output or we can flatten all the hidden states into a long vector and use that to predict the output. The latter provides more information to the decoder, but there can be more noise as well. Both are shown in *Figure 13.8*, using the same example we have been using in the last section as well:

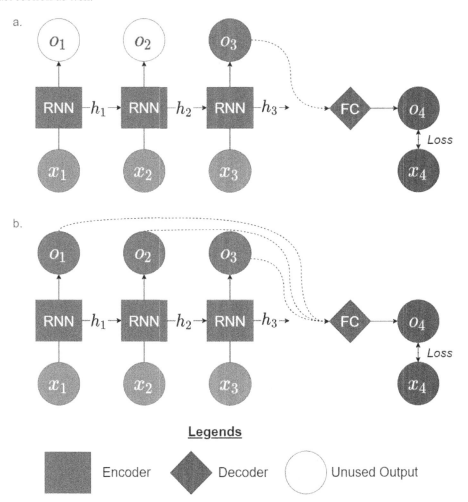

Figure 13.8 – RNN as the encoder and a fully connected layer as the decoder

Let's also see how we can put together this in code. The decoder in the first case, where we are using just the last hidden state of the encoder, will look like this:

```
self.decoder = nn.Linear(
                hidden_size*bi_directional_multiplier,
    horizon
                )
```

Here, `bi_directional_multiplier` is 2 if the encoder was bidirectional and 1 otherwise. This is done because if the encoder is bidirectional, there will be two hidden states concatenated together for each timestep. `horizon` is the number of timesteps ahead we want to forecast.

In the second case, where we are using the hidden states from all the timesteps, we need to make the decoder, as follows:

```
self.decoder = nn.Linear(
                hidden_size * bi_directional_multiplier *
    window_size, horizon
                )
```

Here, the input vector will be the flattened vector of all the hidden states from all the timesteps, and hence the input dimension would be `hidden_size * window_size`.

And in the `forward` method, we can do the following for case 1:

```
y_hat = self.decoder(o[:,-1,:]).unsqueeze(-1)
```

Here, we are just taking the hidden state from the latest timestep and unsqueezing to maintain three dimensions as the target, `y`.

For case 2, we can do the following:

```
y_hat = self.decoder(o.reshape(o.size(0), -1)).unsqueeze(-1)
```

Here, we first reshape the entire hidden state to flatten it and then pass it through the decoder to get the predictions. We unsqueeze to insert the dimension we collapsed so that the output and target, `y`, have the same dimensions.

Even though, in theory, we can use the fully connected decoder to predict as much into the future as possible, practically, there are limitations. When we have a large number of steps to forecast, the model will have to learn that big of a matrix to generate those outputs, and that becomes harder as the matrix becomes bigger. Another point worth noting is that each of these predictions happens independently with the information encoded in the latent representation. For instance, the prediction of five timesteps ahead is only dependent on the latent representation from the encoder and not predictions of timesteps 1 to 4. Let's look at another type of Seq2Seq, which makes the decoding more flexible and aware of the temporal aspect of the problem.

RNN-to-RNN

Instead of using a fully connected layer as the decoder, we can use another RNN for decoding as well—so, one model from the RNN family takes care of the encoding and another model from the RNN family takes care of the decoding. Initializing the decoder in the model is also similar to initializing the encoder. If we want an LSTM model as the decoder, we can do the following:

```
self.decoder = nn.LSTM(
                **decoder_params,
                batch_first=True,
            )
```

Let's develop our understanding of how this is done through a visual representation:

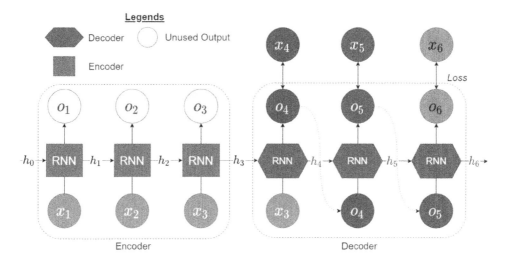

Figure 13.9 – RNN as the encoder and decoder

The encoder part remains the same: it takes in the input window x_1 to x_3 and produces outputs, o_1 to o_3, and the last hidden state, h_3. Now, we have another decoder (a model from the RNN family) that takes in h_3, as the initial hidden state, and the latest input from the window to produce the next output. And now, this output is fed back into the RNN as the input and we produce the next output, and this cycle continues until we have got the required number of timesteps in our prediction.

Some of you may be wondering why we don't use the target window (x_4 to x_6) during decoding as well. In fact, this is a valid way of training the model and is called **teacher forcing** in the literature. This has strong connections to maximum likelihood and is explained well in the *Deep Learning* book by Goodfellow et al. (see the *Further reading* section). So, instead of feeding in the output of the model from the previous timestep as the input to the RNN at the current timestep, we feed in the real observation, thereby eliminating the error that might have crept in in the previous timestep.

While this sounds like the most straightforward thing to do, it does come with a few disadvantages as well. The main one is that the kinds of inputs that the decoder sees during training may not the same as the ones it will see during actual prediction. During prediction, we will still be feeding the output of the model in the previous step to the decoder. This is because in the inference mode, we do not have access to real observations in the future. This can cause problems in some cases. One way to mitigate this problem is to randomly choose between the model's output at the previous timestep and real observation while training (Bengio et al., 2015).

> **Reference check**
>
> The research paper by Bengio et al., which proposed teacher forcing, is cited in the *References* section.

Now, let's see how we can code the `forward` method for both these cases using a parameter called `teacher_forcing_ratio`, which is a decimal from 0 to 1. This decides how frequently teacher forcing is implemented. For instance, if `teacher_forcing_ratio` = 0, then teacher forcing is never done, and if `teacher_forcing_ratio` = 1, then teacher forcing is always done.

The following code block has all the code necessary for decoding, and it comes with line numbers so that we can go line by line and explain what we are doing:

```
01   y_hat = torch.zeros_like(y, device=y.device)
02   dec_input = x[:, -1:, :]
03   for i in range(y.size(1)):
04       out, h = self.decoder(dec_input, h)
05       out = self.fc(out)
06       y_hat[:, i, :] = out.squeeze(1)
07       #decide if we are going to use teacher forcing or not
08       teacher_force = random.random() < teacher_forcing_ratio
09       if teacher_force:
10           dec_input = y[:, i, :].unsqueeze(1)
11       else:
12           dec_input = out
```

The first thing we need to do is declare a placeholder to store the desired output during decoding. In *line number 1*, we do that by using `zeros_like`, which generates a tensor with all zeros with the same dimension as y, and in *line number 2*, we set the initial input to the decoder as the last timestep in the input window. Now, we are all set to start the decoding process, and for that, in *line number 3*, we start a loop to run `y.size(1)` times. If you remember the dimensions of y, the second dimension was the sequence length, so we need to run the decoding process that many times.

In *line number 4*, we pass in the last input from the input window and the hidden state from the encoder to the decoder, and it returns the current output and the hidden state. We capture the current hidden state in the same variable, overwriting the old one. If you remember, the output from the RNN is the hidden state, and we will need to pass it through a fully connected layer for the prediction. So, in *line number 5*, we do just that. In *line number 6*, we store the output from the fully connected layer to the *i*-th timestep in y_hat.

Now, we just have one more thing to do—decide whether to use teacher forcing or not and move on to decoding the next timestep. This we can do by generating a random number between *0* and *1* and checking whether that number is less than the teacher_forcing_ratio parameter or not. random.random() samples a number from a uniform distribution between *0* and *1*. If the teacher_forcing_ratio parameter is *0.5*, checking whether random.random()<teacher_forcing_ratio automatically ensures we only do teacher forcing 50% of the time. So, in *line number 8*, we do this check and get a Boolean output, teacher_force, which tells us whether we need to do teacher forcing in the next timestep or not. For teacher forcing, we store the current timestep from y as dec_input (*line number 10*). Otherwise, we store the current output as dec_input (*line number 12*), and this dec_input parameter is used as the input to the RNN in the next timestep.

Now, all of this (both the fully connected decoder and the RNN decoder) has been put together into a single class called Seq2SeqModel in src/dl/models.py, and a config class (Seq2SeqConfig) has also been defined that has all the options and hyperparameters of the models. Let's take a look at the different parameters in the config:

- encoder_type—A string parameter that takes in one of three values: RNN, LSTM, or GRU. This decides the sequence model we need to use as the encoder.

- decoder_type—A string parameter that takes in one of four values: RNN, LSTM, GRU, or FC (for *fully connected*). This decides the sequence model we need to use as the decoder.

- encoder_params and decoder_params—These parameters take a dictionary of key-value pairs as the input. These are the hyperparameters of the encoder and the decoder, respectively. For the RNN family of models, there is another config class, RNNConfig, which sets standard hyperparameters such as hidden_size, num_layers, and so on. And for the FC decoder, we need to give two parameters: window_size as the number of timesteps included in the input window, and horizon as the number of timesteps ahead we want to be forecasting.

- decoder_use_all_hidden—We discussed two ways we can use the fully connected decoder. This parameter is a flag that switches between the two. If True, the fully connected decoder will flatten the hidden states of all timesteps and use them for the prediction, and if False, it will just use the last hidden state.

- `teacher_forcing_ratio`—We discussed teacher forcing earlier, and this parameter decided the strength of teacher forcing while training. If *0*, there will be no teacher forcing, and if *1*, every timestep will be teacher-forced.

- `optimizer_params`, `lr_scheduler`, `lr_scheduler_params`—These are parameters that let us tweak the optimization procedure. Let's not worry about these for now because all of them have been set to intelligent defaults.

Now, with this config and the model, let's run a few experiments. These work exactly the same as the set of experiments we ran in the previous section. The exact code for the experiments is available in the accompanying notebook. So, we ran the following experiments:

- `LSTM_FC_last_hidden`—Encoder = LSTM/Decoder = Fully Connected, using just the last hidden state

- `LSTM_FC_all_hidden`—Encoder = LSTM/Decoder = Fully Connected, using all the hidden states

- `LSTM_LSTM`—Encoder = LSTM/Decoder = LSTM

Let's see how they performed on the metrics we have been tracking:

Algorithm	MAE	MSE	MASE	Forecast Bias
Lasso Regression	0.1598	0.0743	1.2452	3.78%
XGB Random Forest	0.1641	0.0819	1.2792	9.30%
LightGBM	0.1470	0.0666	1.1457	3.36%
RNN	0.2685	0.1721	2.0927	29.35%
LSTM	0.1982	0.1125	1.5442	17.94%
GRU	0.1714	0.0899	1.3358	14.48%
LSTM_FC_last_hidden	0.1642	0.0815	1.2797	5.87%
LSTM_FC_all_hidden	0.1667	0.0799	1.2993	10.00%
LSTM_LSTM	0.1600	0.0795	1.2472	13.31%

Figure 13.10 – Metrics for Seq2Seq models on MAC000193 household

The `Seq2Seq` models seem to be performing better on the metrics and the *LSTM_LSTM* model is even better than the Random Forest model.

There are visualizations of each of these forecasts in the notebook. I urge you to look at those visualizations, zoom in, look at different places in the horizon, and so on. The astute observers among you must have figured out something weird with the forecast. Let's look at a zoomed-in version (on 1 day) of the forecasts we generated to make that point clear:

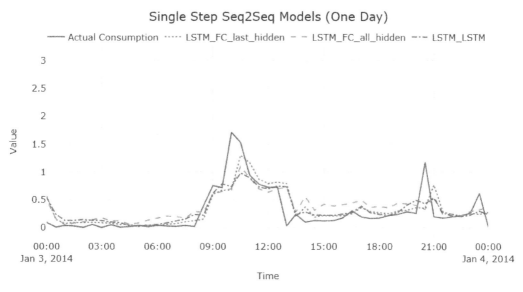

Figure 13.11 – Single-step-ahead Seq2Seq predictions for MAC000193 household (1 day)

What do you see now? Focus on the peaks in the time series. Are they aligned or do they seem at an offset? This phenomenon that you are seeing now is when a model learns to mimic the last seen timestep (like the naïve forecast) rather than learn the true pattern in the data. We will be getting good metrics and we might be happy with the forecast, but upon investigation, we can see that this is not the forecast we want. This is especially true in the case of single-step-ahead models where we are just optimizing to predict the next timestep. Therefore, the model has no real incentive to learn long-term patterns, such as seasonality and so on, and ends up learning a model like the naïve forecast.

Models that are trained to predict longer horizons overcome this problem because, in this scenario, the model is forced to learn the longer-term patterns in the model. Although multi-step forecasting is a topic that will be covered in detail in *Chapter 17, Multi-Step Forecasting*, let's do a little bit of a sneak peek now. In the notebook, we also train multi-step models using the Seq2Seq models.

The only changes we need to make are these:

- The horizon we define in the datamodule and the models should change.
- The way we evaluate the models should also have a small change.

Let's see how we can define a datamodule for multi-step forecasting. We have chosen to forecast a complete day, which is 48 timesteps. And as an input window, we are giving 2×48 timesteps:

```
HORIZON = 48
WINDOW = 48*2
datamodule = TimeSeriesDataModule(data = sample_df[[target]],
        n_val = sample_val_df.shape[0],
        n_test = sample_test_df.shape[0],
        window = WINDOW,
        horizon = HORIZON,
        normalize = "global", # normalizing the data
        batch_size = 32,
        num_workers = 0)
```

Now that we have the datamodule, we can initialize the models just like before and train them. The only change we have to make now is while predicting.

In the single-step setting, at each timestep, we were predicting the next one. But now, we are predicting the next 48 timesteps, at each step. There are multiple ways to look at this and measure the metrics, which we will cover in detail in *Part 3*. For now, let's choose a heuristic and say that we are considering that we are running this model only once a day, and each such prediction has 48 timesteps. But the test dataloader still increments by one—in other words, the test dataloader still gives us the next 48 timesteps, for each timestep. So, executing the following code, we will get a prediction array with dimensions—*(timesteps, horizon)*:

```
pred = trainer.predict(model, datamodule.test_dataloader())
# pred is a list of outputs, one for each batch
pred = torch.cat(pred).squeeze().detach().numpy()
```

The predictions start at 2014, Jan 1 00:00:00. So, if we select the 48 timesteps, every 48 timesteps apart, it'll be like considering only predictions that are made at the beginning of the day. Using a bit of fancy indexing numpy provides us, it is easy to do just that:

```
pred = pred[0::48].ravel()
```

We start at index 0, which is the first prediction of 48 timesteps, and pick every 48 indices (which are timesteps) and just flatten the array. We will get an array of predictions with the desired shape, and then the standard procedure of inverse transformation and metric calculation, and so on, proceeds.

The notebook has the code to do the following experiments:

- `MultiStep LSTM_FC_last_hidden`—Encoder = LSTM/Decoder = Fully Connected Layer, using only the last hidden state

- `MultiStep LSTM_FC_all_hidden`—Encoder = LSTM/Decoder = Fully Connected Layer, using all the hidden states

- `MultiStep LSTM_LSTM_teacher_forcing_0.0`—Encoder = LSTM/ Decoder = LSTM, using no teacher forcing

- `MultiStep LSTM_LSTM_teacher_forcing_0.5`—Encoder = LSTM/ Decoder = LSTM, using stochastic teacher forcing (randomly, 50% of the time teacher forcing is enabled)

- `MultiStep LSTM_LSTM_teacher_forcing_1.0`—Encoder = LSTM/ Decoder = LSTM, using complete teacher forcing

Let's look at the metrics of these experiments:

Algorithm	MAE	MSE	MASE	Forecast Bias
Lasso Regression	0.1598	0.0743	1.2452	3.78%
XGB Random Forest	0.1641	0.0819	1.2792	9.30%
LightGBM	0.1470	0.0666	1.1457	3.36%
RNN	0.2685	0.1721	2.0927	29.35%
LSTM	0.1982	0.1125	1.5442	17.94%
GRU	0.1714	0.0899	1.3358	14.48%
LSTM_FC_last_hidden	0.1642	0.0815	1.2797	5.87%
LSTM_FC_all_hidden	0.1667	0.0799	1.2993	10.00%
LSTM_LSTM	0.1600	0.0795	1.2472	13.31%
MultiStep LSTM_FC_last_hidden	0.2177	0.1305	1.6967	10.59%
MultiStep LSTM_FC_all_hidden	0.2344	0.1317	1.8265	9.33%
MultiStep LSTM_LSTM_teacher_forcing_0.0	0.2058	0.1241	1.6039	15.32%
MultiStep LSTM_LSTM_teacher_forcing_0.5	0.1866	0.0997	1.4544	11.90%
MultiStep LSTM_LSTM_teacher_forcing_1	0.1754	0.0912	1.3671	12.93%

Figure 13.12 – Metrics for multi-step Seq2Seq models on MAC000193 household

Although we cannot compare single-step-ahead accuracy to multi-step ones, for the time being, let's suspend that concern and use the single-step metrics as in the best-case scenario. So, we can see that our model that predicts 1 day ahead (48 timesteps) is not such a bad model after all, and if we visualize the predictions, the problem of imitating naïve forecasts is also not present because now the model is forced to learn long-term models and forecasts:

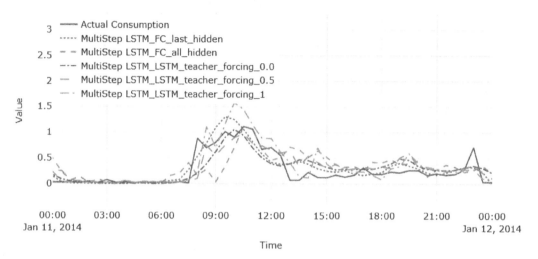

Figure 13.13 – Multi-step-ahead Seq2Seq predictions for MAC000193 household (1 day)

We can see that the model has tried to learn the daily patterns because it is forced to predict the next 48 timesteps. With some tuning and other training tricks, we might get a better model as well. But running a separate model for all `LCLid` (consumer ID) instances in the dataset may not be the best option, both from an engineering and a modeling perspective. We will tackle strategies for global modeling in *Chapter 15, Strategies for Global Deep Learning Forecasting Models*.

Things to try

Can you train a better model? Tweak the hyperparameters and try to get better performance. Use GRUs or combine a GRU with an LSTM—the possibilities are endless.

Congratulations on getting through yet another hands-on and practical chapter. If this is the first time you are training NNs, I hope this lesson has made you confident enough to try more: trying and experimenting with these techniques is the best way to learn.

Summary

Although we learned about the basic blocks of DL in the previous chapter, we put all of that into action while we used those blocks in common modeling patterns using PyTorch.

We saw how standard sequence models such as RNN, LSTM, and GRU can be used for time series prediction, and then we moved on to another paradigm of models, called Seq2Seq models. Here, we talked about how we can mix and match encoders and decoders to get the model we want. Encoders and decoders can be arbitrarily complex. Although we looked at simple encoders and decoders, it is very much possible to have something like a combination of a convolution block and an LSTM block working together for the encoder. Last but not least, we talked about teacher forcing and how it can help models train and converge faster and also with some performance boost.

In the next chapter, we will be tackling a subject that has captured a lot of attention (pun intended) in the past few years: attention and transformers.

Reference

Samy Bengio, Oriol Vinyals, Navdeep Jaitly, and Noam Shazeer (2015). *Scheduled Sampling for Sequence Prediction with Recurrent Neural Networks. Proceedings of the 28th International Conference on Neural Information Processing Systems - Volume 1 (NIPS'15)*: `https://proceedings.neurips.cc/paper/2015/file/e995f98d56967d946471af29d7bf99f1-Paper.pdf`.

Further reading

You can check out the following sources for further reading:

- *From PyTorch to PyTorch Lightning* by Alfredo Canziani and William Falcon: `https://www.youtube.com/watch?v=DbESHcCoWbM`

- *Deep Learning*—Ian Goodfellow, Yoshua Bengio, and Aaron Courville (pages 376-377): `https://www.deeplearningbook.org/contents/rnn.html`

- *A Short Chronology Of Deep Learning For Tabular Data* by Sebastian Raschka: `https://sebastianraschka.com/blog/2022/deep-learning-for-tabular-data.html`

14

Attention and Transformers for Time Series

In the previous chapter, we rolled up our sleeves and implemented a few **deep learning** (**DL**) systems for time series forecasting. We used the common building blocks we discussed in *Chapter 12, Building Blocks of Deep Learning for Time Series*, put them together in an encoder-decoder architecture, and trained them to produce the forecast we desired.

Now, let's talk about another key concept in DL that has taken the field by storm over the past few years—**attention**. Attention has a long-standing history, which has culminated in it being one of the most sought-after tools in the DL toolkit. This chapter takes you on a journey to understand attention and transformer models from the ground up from a theoretical perspective and solidify that understanding with practical examples.

In this chapter, we will be covering these main topics:

- What is attention?
- Generalized attention model
- Forecasting with sequence-to-sequence models and attention
- Transformers – Attention is all you need
- Forecasting with Transformers

Technical requirements

If you have not set up the Anaconda environment following the instructions in the *Preface*, please do that in order to get a working environment with all the packages and datasets required for the code in this book.

You need to run the following notebooks for this chapter:

- `02 - Preprocessing London Smart Meter Dataset.ipynb` in `Chapter02`
- `01-Setting up Experiment Harness.ipynb` in `Chapter04`
- `01-Feature Engineering.ipynb` in `Chapter06`
- `02-One-Step RNN.ipynb` and `03-Seq2Seq RNN.ipynb` in `Chapter13` (for benchmarking)
- `00-Single Step Backtesting Baselines.ipynb` and `01-Forecasting with ML.ipynb` in `Chapter08`

The associated code for the chapter can be found at `https://github.com/PacktPublishing/Modern-Time-Series-Forecasting-with-Python-/tree/main/notebooks/Chapter14`.

What is attention?

The idea of attention was inspired by human cognitive function. At any moment, the optic nerves in our eyes, the olfactory nerves in our noses, and the auditory nerves in our ears send a massive amount of sensory input to the brain. This is way too much information, definitely more than the brain can handle. But our brains have developed a mechanism that helps us to pay *attention* to only the stimuli that matter—such as a sound or a smell that doesn't belong. Years of evolution have *trained* our brains to pick out anomalous sounds or smells because that was key for us surviving in the wild where predators roamed free.

Apart from this kind of instinctive attention, we are also able to control our attention by what we call *focusing* on something. You are doing it right now by choosing to ignore all the other stimuli that you are getting and focusing your attention on the contents of this book. While you are reading, your mobile phone pings you, and the screen lights up. And your brain decides to focus its attention on the mobile screen, even though the book is still open in front of you. This feature of the human cognitive function has been the inspiration behind the attention mechanism in DL. Giving learning machines the ability to acquire this kind of attention has led to big breakthroughs in all fields of AI today.

The idea was first applied to DL in Seq2Seq models, which we learned about in *Chapter 13, Common Modeling Patterns for Time Series*. In the chapter, we saw how the handshake between the encoder and decoder was done. For the **recurrent neural network** (**RNN**) family of models, we use the hidden states from the encoder at the end of the sequence as the initial hidden states in the decoder. Let's call this handshake—the **context**. The assumption here is that all the information required for the decoding task is encoded in the context. This creates a kind of information bottleneck (*Figure 14.1*). There may be information in previous hidden states that can be useful for the decoding task. In 2015, Bahdanau et al. proposed the first known attention model in the context of DL. They proposed to learn attention weights, α, for each hidden state corresponding to the input sequence and combine them into a single context vector while decoding. And these attention weights are re-calculated for each decoding step using the similarity between the hidden states during decoding and all the hidden states in the input sequence (*Figure 14.2*):

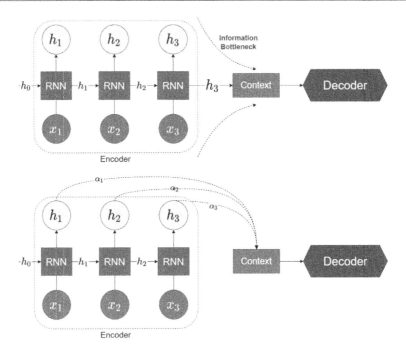

Figure 14.1 – Traditional (top) versus attention model (bottom) in Seq2Seq models

To make things clearer, let's adopt a formal way of describing the mechanism. Let $H = h_i$, $i \in \{1,2, \dots, T_s\}$ be the hidden states generated during the encoding process and $S = s_j$, $j \in \{1,2, \dots, T_t\}$ be the hidden states generated during decoding. The context vector will be c_j:

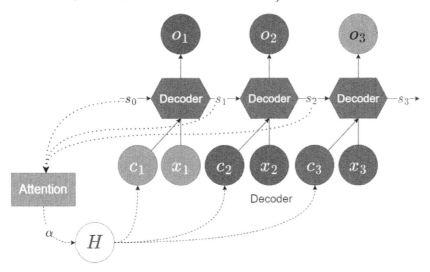

Figure 14.2 – Decoding using attention

So, now we have the hidden states from the encoding stage (H), and we need to have a way to use this information at each step of decoding. The key here is that at each step of the decoding process, information from different hidden states might be relevant. And this is exactly what attention weights do. So, for decoding step j, we use s_{j-1} and calculate attention weights (we'll look at how attention weights are learned in detail soon) $\alpha_{i,j}$, using the similarity between s_{j-1} and each hidden state in H. Now, we calculate the context vector, which combines the information in H in the right way:

$$c_j = \sum_{i=1}^{T_s} \alpha_{i,j} h_i$$

There are two main ways we can use this context vector, which we will go into in detail later in the chapter. This breaks the information bottleneck that was present in the traditional Seq2Seq model and allows the models to access a larger pool of information and decide which information is relevant at each step of the decoding process.

Now, let's see how these attention weights, α, are calculated.

The generalized attention model

Over the course of years, researchers have come up with different ways of calculating attention weights and using attention in DL models. Sneha Choudhari et al. published a survey paper on attention models that proposes a generalized attention model that tries to incorporate all the variations in a single framework. Let's structure our discussion around this generalized framework.

We can think of an attention model as learning an attention distribution (α) for a set of keys, K, using a set of queries, q. In the example we discussed in the last section, the query would be s_{j-1}—the hidden state from the last timestep during decoding—and the keys would be H—all the hidden states generated using the input sequence. In some cases, the generated attention distribution is applied to another set of inputs called values, V. In many cases, K and V are the same, but to maintain the general form of the framework, we consider these separately. Using these terminologies, we can define an attention model as a function of q, K, and V:

$$\mathcal{A}(q, K, V) = \sum_i p(a(k_i, q)) \times v_i$$

Here, a is an **alignment function** that calculates a similarity or a notion of similarity between the queries and keys. In the example we discussed in the previous section, this alignment function calculates how relevant an encoder hidden state is to a decoder hidden state, and p is a **distribution function** that converts this score into attention weights that sum up to 1.

Reference check

The research papers by Sneha Choudhari et al. are cited in the *References* section under *8*.

Since we have the generalized attention model now, let's also see how we can implement this in PyTorch. The full implementation can be found in the `Attention` class in `src/dl/attention.py`, but we will cover the key parts of it here.

The only information we require beforehand to initialize such a module is the hidden dimension of the queries and keys (encoder and decoder). So, the class definition and the `__init__` function of the class look like this:

```python
class Attention(nn.Module, metaclass=ABCMeta):
    def __init__(self, encoder_dim: int, decoder_dim: int):
        super().__init__()
        self.encoder_dim = encoder_dim
        self.decoder_dim = decoder_dim
```

Now, we need to define a `forward` function, which takes in two inputs:

- query: The query vector of size (*batch size, decoder dimension*), which we are going to use to find the attention weights with which to combine the keys. This is the q in $\mathcal{A}(q, K, V)$.

- key: The key vector of size (*batch size, sequence length, encoder dimension*), which is the sequence of hidden states across which we will be calculating the attention weights. This is the K in $\mathcal{A}(q, K, V)$.

We are assuming keys and values are the same because in most cases, they are. So, from the generalized attention model, we know that there are a few steps we need to perform:

1. Calculate an alignment score—$a(k_i, q)$—for each query and key combination.
2. Convert the scores to weights by applying a function—$p(a(k_i, q))$.
3. Use the learned weights to combine the values—$\sum_i p(a(k_i, q)) \times v_i$.

So, let's see those steps in code in the `forward` method:

```python
def forward(
        self,
        query: torch.Tensor,   # [batch_size, decoder_dim]
        values: torch.Tensor,  # [batch_size, seq_length, encoder_dim]
    ):
        scores = self._get_scores(query, values)  # [batch_size, seq_length]
        weights = torch.nn.functional.softmax(scores, dim=-1)
        return (values*weights.unsqueeze(-1)).sum(dim=1)  # [batch_size, encoder_dim]
```

The three lines of code in the `forward` method correspond to the three steps we discussed earlier. The first step, which is calculating the scores, is the key step that has led to many different types of attention, and therefore we have generalized that into a `_get_scores` abstract method that must be implemented by any class inheriting the `Attention` class. For the second line, we have used the `softmax` function for converting the scores to weights, and in the last line, we are doing an element-wise multiplication (`*`) between weights and values and summing across the sequence length to get the weighted value.

Now let's turn our attention toward alignment functions.

Alignment functions

There are many variations of the alignment function that have come up over the years. Let's review a few popular ones that are used today.

Dot product

This is probably the simplest alignment function of all. Luong et al. proposed this form of attention in 2015. From linear algebra intuition, we know that a dot product between two vectors tells us what amount of one vector goes in the direction of another. It measures some kind of similarity between the two vectors, and this similarity considers both the magnitude of the vectors and the angle between them in the vector space. Therefore, when we take a dot product between our query and key vectors, we get a notion of similarity between them. One thing to note here is that the hidden dimensions of the query and key should be the same for dot product attention to be applied. Formally, the similarity function can be defined as follows:

$$a(k_i, q) = q^T k_i$$

We need to calculate this score for each of the elements in the key, K, and instead of running a loop over each element in K, we can use a clever matrix multiplication trick to calculate the scores for all the keys in K in one shot. Let's see how we can define the `_get_scores` function for dot product attention.

We know from the previous section that the query and values (which are the same as keys in our case) are of (*batch size, decoder dimension*) and (*batch size, sequence length, encoder dimension*) dimensions respectively, and will be called q and v in the `_get_scores` function. And in this particular case, the decoder dimension and the encoder dimension are the same, so the scores can be calculated as follows:

```
scores = (q @ v.transpose(1,2))
```

Here, @ is shorthand for `torch.matmul`, which does matrix multiplication. The entire implementation is named `DotProductAttention` and can be found in `src/dl/attention.py`.

Scaled dot product attention

In 2017, Vaswani et al. proposed this type of attention in the seminal paper, *Attention is All you Need*. We will delve into that paper later in this chapter, but now, let's understand one key modification they suggested to the dot product attention. The modification is motivated by the concern that when the input is large, the *softmax function* we use to convert scores to weights may have very small gradients and hence makes efficient learning difficult.

This is because the *softmax* function is not scale-invariant. The exponential function in the *softmax* function is the reason for this behavior. So, the higher we scale the inputs to the function, the more the largest input dominates the output, and this throttles the gradient flow in the network. If we assume q and v are d_k dimensional vectors with 0 mean and a variance of 1, then their dot product would have a mean of zero and a variance of d_k. Therefore, if we scale the output of the dot product by $\sqrt{d_k}$, then we bring the variance of the dot product back to 1. So, by controlling for the scale of the inputs to the *softmax* function, we manage a healthy gradient flow through the network. The *Further reading* section has a link to a blog post that goes into this in more depth. Therefore, the scaled dot product alignment function can be defined as follows:

$$a(k_i, q) = \frac{1}{\sqrt{d_k}} \times q^T k_i$$

And consequently, the only change we will have to make in the `PyTorch` implementation is one additional line:

```
scores = scores/math.sqrt(encoder_dim)
```

This has been implemented as a parameter in `DotProductAttention` in `src/dl/attention.py`. If you pass `scaled=True` while initializing the class, it will perform scaled dot product attention. We need to keep in mind that similar to dot product attention, the scaled variant also requires the query and values to have the same dimensions.

General attention

In 2015, Luong et al. also proposed a slight variation of dot product attention by introducing a learnable W matrix into the calculation. They called it general attention. We can think of it as an attention mechanism that allows for the query to be projected into a learned plane of the same dimension as the values/keys using the W matrix before computing the similarity score using a dot product. The alignment function can be written as follows:

$$a(k_i, q) = q^T W k_i$$

The corresponding `PyTorch` implementation can be found under the name `GeneralAttention` in `src/dl/attention.py`. The key line calculating the attention scores can be written as follows:

```
scores = (q @ self.W) @ v.transpose(1,2)
```

Here, self.W is a tensor of size (*encoder hidden dimension x decoder hidden dimension*). General attention can be used in cases where the query and key/value dimensions are different.

Additive/concat attention

In 2015, Bahdanau et al. proposed additive attention, which was one of the first attempts at introducing attention to DL systems. Instead of using a defined similarity function such as the dot product, Bahdanau et al. proposed that the similarity function can be learned, giving the network more flexibility in deciding what it deems to be similar. They suggested that we can concatenate the query and the key into a single tensor and use a learnable matrix, W, to calculate the attention scores. This alignment function can be written as follows:

$$a(k_i, q) = w_{imp}^T \tanh\left(W_q q^T + W_k k_i + b\right)$$

Here, v_t, W_q and W_k are learnable matrices. In cases where the query and key have different hidden dimensions, we can use W_q and W_k to project them into a single dimension and then perform a similarity calculation on them. In the case that the query and key have the same hidden dimension, this is also equivalent to the variant of attention used in Luong et al., which they call *concat* attention, represented as follows:

$$a(k_i, q) = w_{imp}^T \tanh(W[q^T; k_i] + b)$$

It is simple linear algebra to see that both are the same and for engineering simplicity. The *Further reading* section has a link to a Stack Overflow answer that explains the equivalence.

We have included both implementations in src/dl/attention.py under ConcatAttention and AdditiveAttention.

For AdditiveAttention, the key lines calculating the score are these:

```
q = q.repeat(1, v.size(1), 1)  # [batch_size, seq_length,
decoder_dim]
scores = self.W_q(q) + self.W_v(v)  # [batch_size, seq_length,
decoder_dim]
torch.tanh(scores) @ self.v  # [batch_size, seq_length]
```

The first line repeats the query vector to the sequence length. This is just a linear algebra trick to calculate the score for all the encoder hidden states in a single operation rather than looping through them. *Line 2* projects both query and value into the same dimension using self.W_q and self.W_v, and *line 3* applies the tanh activation function and uses matrix multiplication with self.v to produce the final scores. self.W_q, self.W_v, and self.v are learnable matrices, defined as follows:

```
self.W_q = torch.nn.Linear(self.decoder_dim, self.decoder_dim)
self.W_v = torch.nn.Linear(self.encoder_dim, self.decoder_dim)
self.v = torch.nn.Parameter(torch.FloatTensor(self.decoder_dim)
```

The only difference in `ConcatAttention` is that instead of two separate weights—`self.W_q` and `self.W_v`—we just have a single weight—`self.W`—defined as follows:

```
self.W = torch.nn.Linear(self.decoder_dim + self.encoder_dim,
self.decoder_dim)
```

And instead of adding the projections (*line 2*), we use the following line:

```
scores = self.W(
            torch.cat([q, v], dim=-1)
        )   # [batch_size, seq_length, decoder_dim]
```

Therefore, we can think of `AdditiveAttention` and `ConcatAttention` doing the same operation, but `AdditiveAttention` is adapted to handle different encoder and decoder dimensions.

Reference check

The research papers by Luong et al., Badahnau et al., and Vaswani et al. are cited in the *References* section under *2*, *1*, and *5* respectively.

Now that we have learned about a few popular alignment functions, let's turn our attention toward the distribution function of the attention model.

The distribution function

The primary goal of the distribution function is to convert the learned scores from the alignment function into a set of weights that add up to 1. The *softmax* function is the most popular choice as a distribution function. It converts the score into a set of weights that sum up to one. This also gives us the freedom to interpret the learned weights as probabilities—the probability that the corresponding element is the most relevant.

Although *softmax* is the most popular choice, it is not without its drawbacks. The *softmax* weights are typically *dense*. What that means is that there will be some probability mass (some weight) assigned to every element in the sequence over which we calculated the attention. The weights can be low, but still not 0. There are situations where sparsity in the distribution function is desirable. Maybe we want to make sure we don't give any weights some implausible options. Maybe we want to make the attention mechanism more interpretable.

There are alternate distribution functions such as *sparsemax* (Martins et al. 2016) and *entmax* (Peters et al. 2019) that are capable of assigning probability mass to a select few relevant elements and assigning zero to the rest of them. When we know that the output is only dependent on a few timesteps in the encoder, we can use such distribution functions to encode that knowledge into the model.

> **Reference check**
>
> The research papers by Martins et al. and Peters et al. are cited in the *References* section under 3 and 4 respectively.

Now that we have learned about a few attention mechanisms, it's time to put them into practice.

Forecasting with sequence-to-sequence models and attention

Let's pick up the thread from *Chapter 13, Common Modeling Patterns for Time Series*, where we used Seq2Seq models to forecast a sample household (if you have not read the previous chapter, I strongly suggest you do it now) and modify the `Seq2SeqModel` class to also include an attention mechanism.

> **Notebook alert**
>
> To follow along with the complete code, use the notebook named `01-Seq2Seq RNN with Attention.ipynb` in the `Chapter14` folder and the code in the `src` folder.

We are still going to inherit the `BaseModel` class we have defined in `src/dl/models.py`, and the overall structure is going to be very similar to the `Seq2SeqModel` class. The key difference will be that in our new model, with attention, we do not accept a fully connected layer as the decoder. It is not because it is not possible, but for convenience and brevity of the implementation. In fact, implementing a Seq2Seq model with a fully connected decoder can be some homework you can take up to really internalize the concept.

Similar to the `Seq2SeqConfig` class, we define a very similar `Seq2SeqwAttnConfig` class that has the exact same set of parameters, but with some additional validation checks. One of the validation checks is disallowing a fully connected decoder. Another validation check would be making sure the decoder input size allows for the attention mechanism as well. We will see those requirements in detail shortly.

In addition to `Seq2SeqwAttnConfig`, we also define a `Seq2SeqwAttnModel` class to enable attention-enabled decoding. The only additional parameter here is `attention_type`, which is a string parameter that takes the following values:

- `dot`—Dot product attention
- `scaled dot`—Scaled dot product attention
- `general`—General attention
- `additive`—Additive attention
- `concat`—Concat attention

The entire code is available in `src/dl/models.py`. We will be covering only the `forward` function in detail in the book because that is the only place where there is a key difference. The rest of the class is about defining the right attention model based on input parameters and so on.

The encoder part is exactly the same as `SeqSeqModel`, which we saw in the last chapter. The only difference is in the decoding where we will be using attention.

Now, let's talk about how we are going to use the attention output in decoding.

As I mentioned before, there are two schools of thought on how to use attention while decoding. Using the same terminology we have been using for attention, let's see the difference.

Luong et al. use the decoder hidden state at step j, s_j, to calculate the similarity between itself and all the encoder hidden states, H, to calculate the context vector, c_j. This context vector, c_j, is then concatenated with the decoder hidden state, s_j, and this combined tensor is used as the input to the linear layer that generates the output.

Bahdanau et al. use attention in another way. They use the decoder hidden state from the previous timestep, s_{j-1}, and calculate the similarity with all the encoder hidden states, H, to calculate the context vector, c_j. And now, this context vector, c_j, is concatenated with the input to decoding step j, x_j. It is this concatenated input that is used in the decoding step that uses an RNN.

We can see the differences visually in *Figure 14.3*. The *Further reading* section also has another brilliant animation of attention under *Attn: Illustrated Attention*. That can also help you understand the mechanism well:

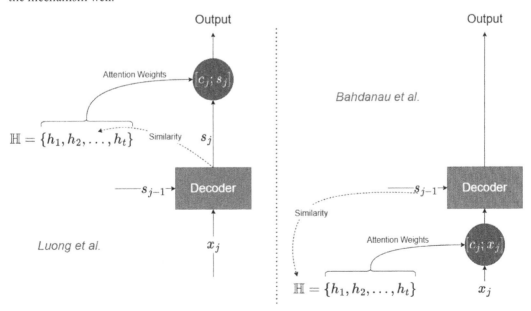

Figure 14.3 – Attention-based decoding: Bahdanau versus Luong

In our implementation, we have chosen the Bahdanau way of decoding, where we use the concatenated context vector and input as the input for decoding. And because of that, there is a condition the decoder must satisfy: the `input_size` parameter of the decoder should be equal to the sum of the `input_size` parameter of the encoder and the `hidden_size` parameter of the encoder. This validation is inbuilt into `Seq2SeqwAttnConfig`.

The following code block has all the code necessary for decoding with attention and has line numbers so that we can go line by line and explain what we are doing:

```
01          y_hat = torch.zeros_like(y, device=y.device)
02          dec_input = x[:, -1:, :]
03          for i in range(y.size(1)):
04              top_h = self._get_top_layer_hidden_state(h)
05              context = self.attention(
06                  top_h.unsqueeze(1), o
07              )
08              dec_input = torch.cat((dec_input, context.
unsqueeze(1)), dim=-1)
09              out, h = self.decoder(dec_input, h)
10              out = self.fc(out)
11              y_hat[:, i, :] = out.squeeze(1)
12              teacher_force = random.random() < self.hparams.
teacher_forcing_ratio
13              if teacher_force:
14                  dec_input = y[:, i, :].unsqueeze(1)
15              else:
16                  dec_input = out
```

Lines 1 and *2* are the same as in the `Seq2SeqModel` class where we set up the variable to store the prediction and extract the starting input to be passed to the decoder, and *line 3* starts the loop for decoding step by step.

Now, in each step, we need to use the hidden state from the previous timestep to calculate the context vector. If you remember the output shapes of an RNN (*Chapter 12, Building Blocks of Deep Learning for Time Series*), we know that it is (*number of layers, batch size, hidden size*). But we need our query hidden state to be of the dimension (*batch size, hidden size*). Luong et al. suggested using the hidden states from the top layer of a stacked RNN model as the query, and we are doing just that here:

```
hidden_state[-1, :, :]
```

If the RNN is bi-directional, we would need to slightly alter the retrieval because now, the last two rows of the tensor would be the output from the last layer (one forward and one backward). There are many ways we can combine these into a single tensor—we can concatenate them, we can sum them, or we can even mix them using a linear layer. Here, we just concatenate them:

```
torch.cat((hidden_state[-1, :, :], hidden_state[-2, :, :]),
dim=-1)
```

And now that we have the hidden state, we use it as the query in the attention layer (*line 5*). In *line 8*, we concatenate the context with the input. Lines *9* to *16* do the rest of the decoding similar to `Seq2SeqModel`.

The notebook trains a multi-step Seq2Seq model (the best-performing variant with teacher forcing) with all the different types of attention we covered in the chapter using the same setup we developed in the last chapter. The results are summarized in the following table:

Algorithm	MAE	MSE	MASE	Forecast Bias
MultiStep LSTM_LSTM_teacher_forcing_0.0	0.2058	0.1241	1.6039	15.32%
MultiStep LSTM_LSTM_teacher_forcing_1	0.1754	0.0912	1.3671	12.93%
MultiStep_Seq2Seq_dot_Attn_teacher_forcing_1	0.1536	0.0717	1.1967	8.25%
MultiStep_Seq2Seq_scaled_dot_Attn_teacher_forcing_1	0.1772	0.0878	1.3812	6.00%
MultiStep_Seq2Seq_general_Attn_teacher_forcing_1	0.1665	0.0818	1.2977	8.97%
MultiStep_Seq2Seq_concat_Attn_teacher_forcing_1	0.1632	0.0778	1.2717	6.65%
MultiStep_Seq2Seq_additive_Attn_teacher_forcing_1	0.1561	0.0734	1.2168	10.40%

Figure 14.4 – Summary table for Seq2Seq models with attention

We can see that it is showing considerable improvements in **MAE**, **MSE**, and **MASE** by including attention, and out of all the variants of attention, the simple dot product attention performed the best, closely followed by additive attention. At this point, some of you might have a question in your mind—*Why didn't the scaled dot product work better than dot product attention?* Scaling was supposed to make the dot product work better, wasn't it?

There is a lesson to be learned here (which applies to all **machine learning** (**ML**)). No matter how much better a particular technique is in theory, you can always find examples in which it performs worse. And here, we saw just one household, and it is not surprising that we saw that scaled dot product attention didn't work better than the normal dot product attention. But if we had evaluated at scale and realized that this is a pattern across multiple datasets, then it would be concerning.

So, we have seen that attention does make the models better. There was a lot of research done on using attention in various forms to enhance the performance of **neural network** (**NN**) models. Most of that research was carried out in **natural language processing** (**NLP**), specifically in language translation and language modeling. Soon, researchers stumbled upon a surprising result that changed the course of DL progress drastically.

Transformers – Attention is all you need

While the introduction of attention was a shot in the arm for RNNs and Seq2Seq models, they still had one problem. The RNNs were recurrent, and that meant it needed to process each word in a sentence in a sequential manner. And for popular Seq2Seq model applications such as language translation, it meant processing long sequences of words became really time-consuming. In short, it was difficult to scale them to a large corpus of data. In 2017, Vaswani et al. authored a seminal paper titled *Attention Is All You Need*. Just as the title of the paper implies, they explored an architecture that used attention (scaled dot product attention) and threw away recurrent networks altogether. And to the surprise of NLP researchers around the world, these models (which were dubbed Transformers) outperformed the then state-of-the-art Seq2Seq models in language translation.

This spurred a flurry of research activity around this new class of models, and pretty soon, in 2018, Devlin et al. from Google developed a bi-directional version of Transformers and trained the now famous language model, **BERT** (which stands for **Bidirectional Encoder Representations from Transformers**), and broke many state-of-the-art results across multiple tasks. This is considered to be the moment when Transformers as a model class really *arrived*. Fast-forward to 2022—Transformer models are ubiquitous. They are used in almost all tasks in NLP, and in many other sequence-based tasks such as time series forecasting, **reinforcement learning** (**RL**), and so on. They have also been successfully used in **computer vision** (**CV**) tasks as well.

There have been numerous modifications and adaptations to the vanilla Transformer model to make it more suitable for time series forecasting. But let's understand the vanilla Transformer architecture that Vaswani et al. proposed in 2017 first.

Attention is all you need

The model Vaswani et al. proposed (hereby referred to as the vanilla Transformer) is also an encoder-decoder model, but both the encoder and decoder are non-recurrent. They are entirely comprised of attention mechanisms and feed-forward networks. Since the Transformer model was developed first for text sequences, let's use the same example to understand and then adapt to the time series context.

There are a few key components of the model that need to be understood to put the whole thing together. Let's take them one by one.

Self-attention

We saw how scaled dot product attention works earlier in this chapter (in the *Alignment functions* section), but there, we were calculating attention between the encoder and decoder hidden states. Self-attention is when we have an input sequence, and we calculate the attention scores between that input sequence itself. Intuitively, we can think of this operation as enhancing the contextual information and enabling the downstream components to use this enhanced information for further processing.

We saw the `PyTorch` implementation for encoder-decoder attention earlier, but that implementation was more aligned toward the step-by-step decoding of an RNN. Computing the attention scores for each query-key pair in one shot is something very simple to achieve using standard matrix multiplication and is essential to computing efficiency.

> **Notebook alert**
>
> To follow along with the complete code, use the notebook named `02-Self-Attention and Multi-Headed Attention.ipynb` in the `Chapter14` folder.

In NLP, it is standard practice to represent each word as a learnable vector called an embedding. This is because text or strings have no place in a mathematical model. For our example's sake, let's assume we use an embedding vector of size 512 for each word, and let's assume that the attention mechanism has an internal dimension of 64. Let's elucidate the attention mechanism using a sentence with 10 words.

After embedding, the sentence would be a tensor with dimensions (10, 512). We need to have three learnable weight matrices, W_q, W_k, and W_v, to project the input embedding into the attention dimension (64). See *Figure 14.5*:

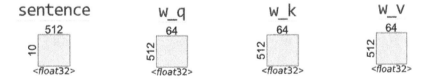

Figure 14.5 – Self-attention layer: input sentence and the learnable weights

The first operation projects the sentence tensor into a query, key, and value with dimensions equal to (*sequence length, attention dim*). This is done by using a matrix multiplication between the sentence tensor and learnable matrices. See *Figure 14.6*:

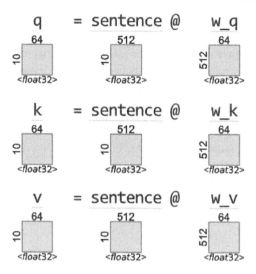

Figure 14.6 – Self-attention layer: query, key, and value projection

Now that we have the query, key, and value, we can calculate the attention weights of every query-key pair using matrix multiplication between the query and the transpose of the keys. The matrix multiplication is nothing but the dot product of each query with each of the values and gives us a square matrix of (*sequence length, sequence length*). See *Figure 14.7*:

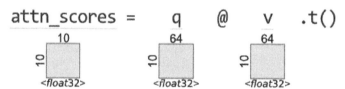

Figure 14.7 – Self-attention layer: attention scores between Q and K

Converting the attention scores to attention weights is just about scaling and applying the *softmax* function, as we discussed in the *Scaled dot product attention* section.

Now that we have the attention weights, we can use them to combine the value. The element-wise multiplication and then summing across the weights can be done efficiently using another matrix multiplication. See *Figure 14.8*:

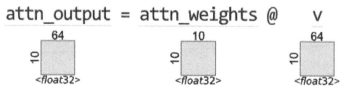

Figure 14.8 – Self-attention layer: combining V using the learned attention weights

Now, we have seen how attention is applied to all the query-key pairs in monolithic matrix operations rather than doing the same operation for each query in a sequential way. But *Attention is All you Need* proposed something even better.

Multi-headed attention

Since Transformers intended to take away the entire recurrent architecture, they needed to beef up the attention mechanism because that was the workhorse of the model. So, instead of using a single attention head, the authors of the paper proposed multiple attention heads acting together in different subspaces. We know that attention helps the model focus on a few elements from the many. **Multi-headed attention** (**MHA**) does the same thing but focuses on different aspects or different sets of elements, thereby increasing the capacity of the model. If we want to draw an analogy to the human mind, we consider many aspects of a situation before we take a decision.

For instance, if we decide to step out of the house, we will pay attention to the weather, we will pay attention to the time so that whatever we want to accomplish is still possible, we will pay attention to how punctual that friend you made a plan with has been in the past, and leave our house accordingly. Each of those aspects you can think of as one head of attention. Therefore, MHA enables Transformers to *attend* to multiple aspects at the same time.

Normally, if there are eight heads, we would assume that we would have to do the computation that we saw in the last section eight times. But thankfully, that is not the case. There are clever ways of accomplishing this MHA using the same kind of matrix multiplication, but now with larger matrices. Let's see how that is done.

We will continue the same example and see a case where we have eight attention heads. There is one condition that needs to be satisfied to do this efficient calculation of MHA—the attention dimension should be divisible by the number of heads we are using.

The initial steps are exactly the same. We take in the input sentence tensor and project it into the query, key, and value. Now, we split the query, key, and value into separate query, key, and value subspaces for each head by doing some basic tensor re-arrangement. See *Figure 14.9*:

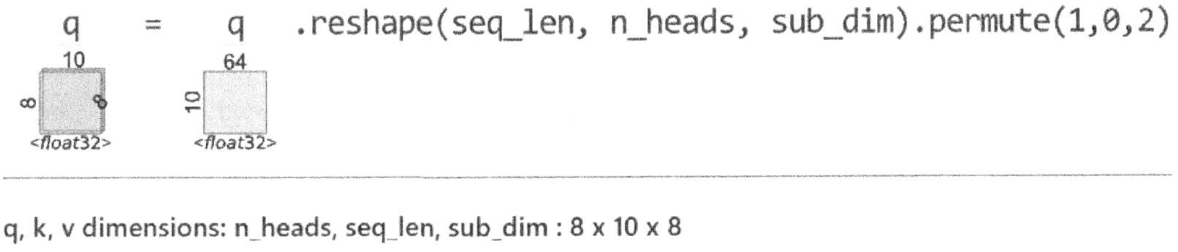

q, k, v dimensions: n_heads, seq_len, sub_dim : 8 x 10 x 8

Figure 14.9 – Multi-headed attention: reshaping Q, K, and V into subspaces for each head

Now, we calculate the attention scores for each head in a single operation and combine them with the value to get the attention output for each head. See *Figure 14.10*:

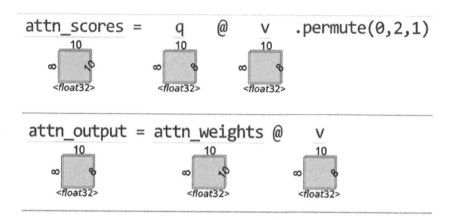

attn_output dimensions: n_heads, seq_len, sub_dim : 8 x 10 x 8

Figure 14.10 – Multi-headed attention: calculating attention weights and combining the value

We have the attention output of each head in the `attn_output` variable. Now, all we need to do is to reshape the array so that we stack the outputs from all the attention heads in a single dimension. See *Figure 14.11*:

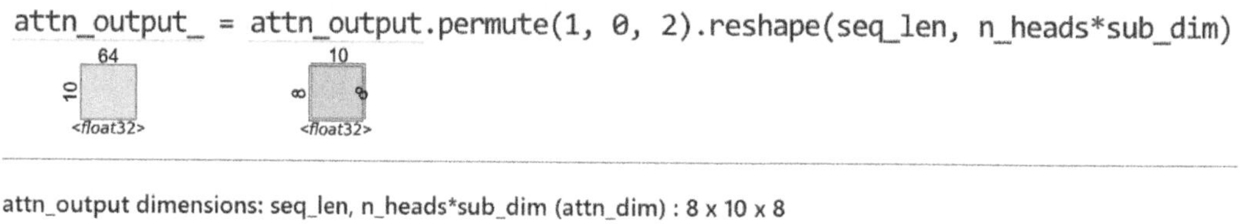

`attn_output_` = `attn_output.permute(1, 0, 2).reshape(seq_len, n_heads*sub_dim)`

attn_output dimensions: seq_len, n_heads*sub_dim (attn_dim) : 8 x 10 x 8

Figure 14.11 – Multi-headed attention: reshaping and stacking all the attention head outputs

In this way, we can do MHA in a fast and efficient manner. Now, let's look at another key innovation that makes Transformers work.

Positional encoding

Transformers successfully avoided the recurrence and unlocked a performance bottleneck of sequential operations. But now there is a problem. By processing all the positions in a sequence in parallel, the model also loses the ability to understand the relevance of the position. For the Transformer, each position is independent of the other, and hence one key aspect we would seek from a model that processes sequences is missing. The original authors did propose a way to make sure we do not lose this information—**positional encoding**.

There have been many variants of positional encoding that have come up in subsequent years of research, but the most common one is still the variant that is used in the vanilla Transformer.

The solution proposed by Vaswani et al. was to add a particular vector, which encodes the position mathematically using sine and cosine functions, to each of the input tokens before processing them through the self-attention layer. If the input, X, is a d_{model}-dimensional embedding for n tokens in a sequence, positional embeddings, P, is a matrix of the same size $(n \times d_{model})$. The element on the pos^{th} row and $2i^{th}$ or $(2i+1)^{th}$ column is defined as follows:

$$p_{pos,2i} = \sin \left(\frac{pos}{10000^{2i/d_{model}}} \right)$$

$$p_{pos,2i+1} = \cos \left(\frac{pos}{10000^{2i/d_{model}}} \right)$$

Although this looks a little complicated and counterintuitive, let's break this down to understand it better.

From 20,000 feet, we know that these positional encodings capture the positional information, and we add them to the input embeddings. But why do we add them to the input embeddings? Let's make that intuition clearer. Let's assume the embedding dimension is just 2 (this is for ease of visualization and grabbing the concept better), and we have a word, A, represented using this token. For our experiment, let's assume that we have the same word, A, repeated several times in our sequence. What happens if we add the positional encoding to it?

We know that the sine or cosine functions vary between 0 and 1. So, each of these encodings we add to the word embedding just perturbs the word embedding within a unit circle. As pos increases, we can see the position-encoded word embedding trace a unit circle around the original embedding (*Figure 14.12*):

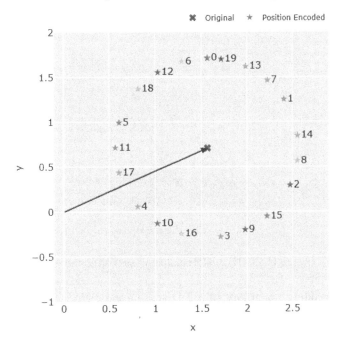

Figure 14.12 – Position encoding: intuition

In *Figure 14.12*, we have assumed a random embedding for a word, *A* (represented by the cross marker), and added position embedding assuming *A* is in different positions. And these position-encoded vectors are represented by star markers with the corresponding positions mentioned in numbers next to them. We can see how each position is a slightly perturbed point of the original vector, and it happens in a cyclical manner in a clockwise direction. We can see position 0 right at the top with 1, 2, 3, and so on in the clockwise direction. By having this representation, the model can figure out the word in different locations, and still retain the overall position in the semantic space.

Now that we know why we are adding the positional encodings to the input embeddings and have seen the intuition of why it works, let's get down into more details and see how the terms inside the sine and cosine are calculated. pos represents the position of the token in the sequence. If the maximum length of the sequence is 128, pos varies from 0 to 127. i represents the position along the embedding dimension, and because of the way the formula has been defined, for each value of i, we have two values—a sine and a cosine. Therefore, i will be half the number of dimensions, d_{model}, and will go from 0 to $d_{model}/2$.

With all this information, we know that the term inside the sine and cosine functions approaches 0 as we go toward the end of the embedding dimension. It also increases from 0 as we move along the sequence dimension. For each pair ($2i$ and $2i + 1$) of positions in the embedding dimension, we have a complementary sine and cosine wave, as *Figure 14.13* shows:

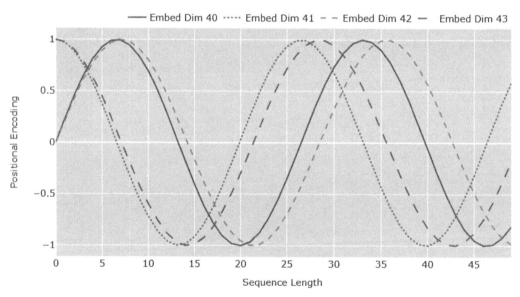

Figure 14.13 – Positional encoding: sine and cosine terms

We can see that embedding dimensions **40** and **41** are sine and cosine waves of the same frequency, and embedding dimensions **40** and **42** are sine waves with a slight increase in frequency. By using the combination of sine and cosine waves of varying frequencies, the positional encoding can encode rich positional information as a vector. If we plot a heatmap of the whole positional encoding vector (*Figure 14.14*), we can see how the values change and encode the positional information:

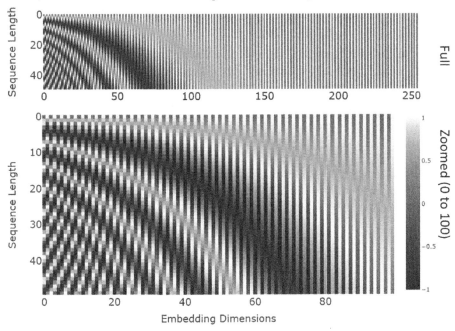

Figure 14.14 – Positional encoding: heatmap of the entire vector

Another interesting observation is that the positional encoding quickly shrinks to 0/1 as we move forward in the embedding dimension because the term inside the sine or cosine functions (angle in radians) quickly becomes zero on account of the large denominator. The zoomed plot shows the color differences more clearly.

Now for the last component in the Transformer model.

Position-wise feed-forward layer

We have already covered what feed-forward networks are in *Chapter 12, Building Blocks of Deep Learning for Time Series*. The only thing to be noted here is that the position-wise feed-forward layer is when we apply the same feed-forward layer in each position, independently. If we have 12 positions (or words), we will have a single feed-forward network to process each of these positions.

Vaswani et al. defined this as a two-layer feed-forward network where the transformations were defined in a way that the input dimensions get expanded to four times the input dimension, with a ReLU activation function applied at that stage, and then transformed back to the input dimension again. The exact operation can be written as a mathematical formula:

$$FFN(x) = max(0, W_1 x + b_1)W_2 + b_2$$

Here, W_1 is a matrix of dimensions (*input size, 4*input size*), W_2 is a matrix of dimensions (*4*input size, input size*), b_1 and b_2 are corresponding biases, and $max(0, x)$ is the standard ReLU operator.

There have been studies where researchers have tried replacing ReLU with other activation functions, more specifically **Gated Linear Units** (**GLUs**), which have shown promise. Noam Shazeer from Google has a paper on the topic, and if you want to know more about these new activation functions, I recommend checking out his paper in the *Further reading* section.

Now that we know all the necessary components of a Transformer model, let's see how they are put together.

Encoder

The vanilla Transformer model is an encoder-decoder model. There are N blocks of encoders, and each block contains an MHA layer and a position-wise feed-forward layer with residual connections in between (*Figure 14.15*):

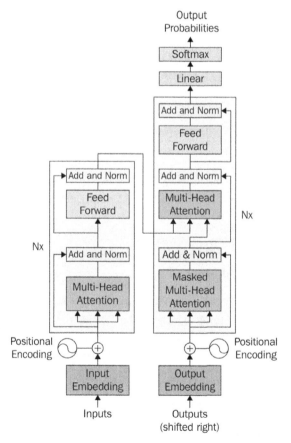

Figure 14.15 – Transformer model from Attention is All you Need by Vaswani et al.

For now, let's focus on the left side of *Figure 14.15*, which is the encoder. The encoder takes in the input embeddings, with the positional encoding vector added to it, as the input. The three-pronged arrow that goes into MHA denotes the query, key, and value split. The output from the MHA goes into a block named *Add & Norm*. Let's quickly see what that does.

There are two key operations that happen here—**residual connections** and **layer normalization**.

Residual connections

Residual connections (or skip connections) are a family of techniques that were introduced to DL to make learning deep networks easier. The primary benefit of the technique is that it makes the gradient flow through the network better and thereby encourages learning in all parts of the network. They incorporate a pass-through memory highway in the network. We have already seen one instance where a skip connection (although not an apparent one) resolved gradient flow issues—**long short-term memory networks** (**LSTMs**). The cell state in the LSTM serves as this highway to let gradients flow through the network without getting into vanishing gradient issues.

But nowadays, when we say residual connections, we typically think of *ResNets*, which made a splash in the history of DL through a **convolutional NN** (**CNN**) architecture that won major image classification challenges, including ImageNet in 2015. They introduced residual connections to train much deeper architectures than those prevalent at the time. The concept is deceptively simple. Let's look at it visually:

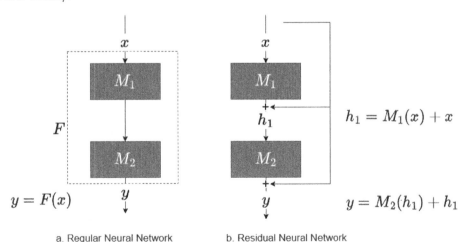

a. Regular Neural Network   b. Residual Neural Network

Figure 14.16 – Residual networks

Let's assume a DL model with two layers with functions, M_1 and M_2. In a regular NN, the input, x, passes through the two layers to give us the output, y. These two individual functions can be considered as a single function that converts x to y: $y = F(x)$.

In residual networks, we change this paradigm into saying that each individual function (or layer) only learns the difference between the input to the function and the expected output. That is where the name residual connections came from. So, if h_1 is the desired output and x is the input, then $M_1(x) = h_1 - x$. Rewriting that, we get $h_1 = M_1(x) + x$. And this is what is most used as residual connections.

Among many benefits such as better gradient flows, residual connections also make the loss surface smooth (Li et al. 2018) and more amenable to gradient-based optimization. For more details and intuition around residual networks, I urge you to check out the blog linked in the *Further reading* section.

So, the *Add* in the *Add & Norm* block in the Transformer is actually the residual connection.

Layer normalization

Normalization in **deep NNs (DNNs)** has been an active field of research. Among many benefits, normalization leads to faster training, higher learning rates, and even a bit of regularization. Batch normalization is the most common normalization technique in use, typically in CV, which makes the input have approximately zero mean and unit variance by subtracting the input mean in the current batch and dividing it by the standard deviation.

But in NLP, researchers prefer layer normalization, where the normalization is happening across each feature. The difference can be seen in *Figure 14.17*:

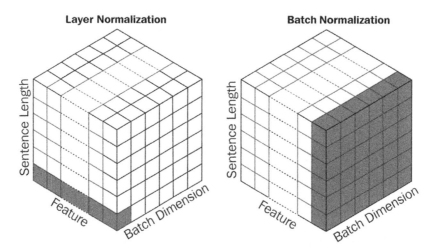

Figure 14.17 – Batch normalization versus layer normalization

This preference for layer normalization emerged empirically, but there have been studies and intuitions around the reason for this preference. NLP data usually has a higher variance as opposed to CV data, and this variance causes some problems for batch normalization. Layer normalization, on the other hand, is immune to this because it doesn't rely on batch-level variance.

Either way, Vaswani et al. decided to use layer normalization in their *Add & Norm* block.

Now, we know the *Add & Norm* block is nothing but a residual connection that is then passed through a layer normalization. So, we can see that the position-encoded inputs are first used in the MHA layer, and the output from the MHA is added with the position-encoded inputs again and passed through a layer normalization. And now, this output is passed through the position-wise feed-forward network and another *Add & Norm* layer, and this becomes one block of the encoder. An important point to keep in mind is that the architecture of all the elements in the encoder is designed in such a way that the dimension of the input at each position is preserved throughout. In other words, if the embedding vector is of dimension 100, the output from the encoder will also have a dimension of 100. This is a convenient way to make it possible to have residual connections and stack as many layers on top of each other as possible. Now, there are multiple such encoder blocks stacked on top of each other to form the encoder of the Transformer.

Decoder

The decoder block is also very similar to the encoder block, but with one key addition. Instead of a single self-attention layer, the decoder block has a self-attention layer, which operates on the decoder input, and an encoder-decoder attention layer. The encoder-decoder attention layer takes the query from the decoder at each stage and the key and values from the top encoder block.

There is something peculiar to the self-attention that is applied in the decoder block. Let's see what that is.

Masked self-attention

We talked about how the Transformer can process sequences in parallel and be computationally efficient. But the decoding paradigm poses another challenge. Suppose we have an input sequence, $X = \{x_1, x_2, ..., x_n\}$, and the task is to predict the next step. So, in the decoder, if we give the sequence, X, because of the parallel-processing architecture, each sequence is processed at once using self-attention. And we know self-attention is agnostic to sequence order. If left unrestricted, the model will cheat by using information from the future timesteps to predict the current timestep. This is where masked attention becomes important.

We saw earlier in the *Self-attention* section how calculate a square matrix (if the query and key have the same length) of attention weights, and it is with these weights that we combine the information from the value vector. This self-attention has no concept of temporality, and all the tokens will attend to all other tokens irrespective of their position. Let's see *Figure 14.18* to solidify our intuition:

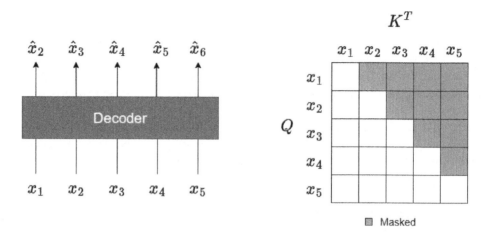

Figure 14.18 – Masked self-attention

We have the sequence, $X = \{x_1, x_2, \ldots, x_5\}$, and we are still trying to predict one step ahead. So, the expected output from the decoder would be $\hat{X} = \{\widehat{x_2}, \widehat{x_3}, \ldots, \widehat{x_6}\}$. When we use self-attention, the attention weights that will be learned will be a square matrix of $5x5$ dimension. But if we look at the upper triangle of the square matrix (the part that is shaded in *Figure 14.18*), those combinations of tokens violate the temporal sanctity.

We can take care of this simply by adding a pre-generated mask that has zeros in all the white cells and *-inf* in all the shaded cells to the generated attention energies (the stage before applying softmax). This makes sure the attention weights for the shaded region will be zero, and this in turn ensures that no future information is used while calculating the weighted sum of the value vector.

Now, to wrap everything up, the output from the decoder is passed to a standard task-specific head to generate the output we desire.

We discussed the Transformer in the context of NLP, but it is a very small leap to adapt it to time series data.

Transformers in time series

Time series have a lot of similarities with NLP because of the fact that both deal with information in sequences. This can be further evidenced by the phenomenon that most of the popular techniques that are used in NLP are promptly adapted to a time series context. Transformers are no exception to that.

Instead of looking at tokens at each position, we have real numbers in each position. And instead of talking about input embeddings, we can talk in terms of input features. The vector of features at each timestep can be considered the equivalent of an embedding vector in NLP. And instead of making causal decoding an optional step (in NLP, that really depends on the task at hand), we have a strict requirement for causal decoding. There, it is trivial to adapt Transformers to time series, although in practice, there are many challenges because in time series we typically encounter sequences that are much longer than the ones in NLP, and this creates a problem because the complexity of self-attention is scaled quadratically with respect to the input sequence length. There have been many alternate proposals for self-attention that make it feasible to use it for long sequences as well, and we will be covering a few of them in *Chapter 16, Specialized Deep Learning Architectures for Forecasting*.

Now, let's try to put everything we have learned about Transformers into practice.

Forecasting with Transformers

For some continuity, we will continue with the same household we were forecasting with RNNs and RNNs with attention.

> **Notebook alert**
>
> To follow along with the complete code, use the notebook named `03-Transformers.ipynb` in the `Chapter14` folder and the code in the `src` folder.

Although we learned about the vanilla Transformer as a model with an encoder-decoder architecture, it was really designed for language translation tasks. In language translation, the source sequence and target sequence are quite different, and therefore the encoder-decoder architecture made sense. But soon after, researchers figured out that using the decoder part of the Transformer alone does well. It is called a decoder-only Transformer in literature. The naming is a bit confusing because if you think about it, the decoder is different from the encoder in two things—masked self-attention and encoder-decoder attention. So, in a decoder-only Transformer, how do we have the encoder-decoder attention? The short answer is that we don't. The architecture of the decoder-only Transformer resembles the encoder block more, but we call it decoder-only because we use masked self-attention to make our model respect the temporal sanctity of our sequences.

We are also going to implement a decoder-only Transformer. The first thing we need to do is to define a config class, `TransformerConfig`, with the following parameters:

- `input_size`—This parameter defines the number of features the Transformer is expecting.
- `d_model`—This parameter defines the hidden dimension of the Transformer or the dimension over which all the attention calculation and subsequent operations happen.
- `n_heads`—This parameter defines how many heads we have in the MHA mechanism.
- `n_layers`—This parameter defines how many blocks of encoders we are going to stack on top of each other.

- ff_multiplier—This parameter defines the scale of expansion within the position-wise feed-forward layers.

- activation—This parameter lets us define which activation we need to use in the position-wise feed-forward layers. It can be either relu or gelu.

- multi_step_horizon—This parameter lets us define how many timesteps into the future we should be forecasting.

- dropout—This parameter lets us define the magnitude of dropout regularization to be applied in the Transformer model.

- learning_rate—This defines the learning rate of the optimization procedure.

- optimizer_params, lr_scheduler, lr_scheduler_params—These are parameters that let us tweak the optimization procedure. Let's not worry about these for now because all of them have been set to intelligent defaults.

Now, we are going to inherit the BaseModel class we defined in src/dl/models.py and define a TransformerModel class.

The first method we need to implement is _build_network. The entire model can be found in src/dl/models.py, but we will be covering the important aspects here as well.

The first module we need to define is a linear projection layer that takes in the input_size parameter and projects it into d_model:

```
self.input_projection = nn.Linear(
            self.hparams.input_size, self.hparams.d_model,
    bias=False
        )
```

This is an additional step we have introduced to adapt the Transformers to the time series forecasting paradigm. In the vanilla Transformer, this is not needed because each word is represented by an embedding vector that typically has dimensions such as 200 or 500. But while doing time series forecasting, we might have to do the forecasting with just one feature (which is the history), and this seriously restricts our ability to provide capacity to the model because, without the projection layer, d_model can only be equal to input_size. Therefore, we have introduced a linear projection layer that decouples the number of features available and d_model.

Now, we need to have a module that adds positional encoding. We have packaged the same code we saw earlier into a PyTorch module and added it to src/dl/models.py. We just use that module and define our positional encoding operator, like so:

```
self.pos_encoder = PositionalEncoding(self.hparams.d_model)
```

We said earlier that we are going to use a decoder-only approach to building the model, and for that, we are using the `TransformerEncoderLayer` and `TransformerEncoder` modules defined in `PyTorch`. Just keep in mind that when using these layers, we will be using masked self-attention, and that makes it a decoder-only Transformer. The code is presented here:

```
self.encoder_layer = nn.TransformerEncoderLayer(
            d_model=self.hparams.d_model,
            nhead=self.hparams.n_heads,
            dropout=self.hparams.dropout,
            dim_feedforward=self.hparams.d_model * self.
hparams.ff_multiplier,
            activation=self.hparams.activation,
            batch_first=True,
        )
        self.transformer_encoder = nn.TransformerEncoder(
            self.encoder_layer, num_layers=self.hparams.n_
layers
        )
```

The last module we need to define is a linear layer that converts the output from the Transformer into the number of timesteps we are forecasting:

```
self.decoder = nn.Sequential(nn.Linear(self.hparams.d_model,
100),
            nn.ReLU(),
            nn.Linear(100, self.hparams.multi_step_horizon)
        )
```

That concludes the definition of the model. Now, let's define a forward pass in the `forward` method.

The first step is to generate a mask we need to apply masked self-attention:

```
mask = self._generate_square_subsequent_mask(x.shape[1]).to(x.
device)
```

We define the mask to have the same length as the input sequence. `_generate_square_subsequent_mask` is a method we have defined that generates a mask. Assuming the sequence length is 5, we can look at the two steps in preparing the mask:

```
mask = (torch.triu(torch.ones(5, 5)) == 1).transpose(0, 1)
```

`torch.ones(sz,sz)` creates a square matrix with all ones, and `torch.triu(torch.ones(sz,sz))` makes the matrix with a top triangle (including the diagonal) as ones and the rest as zeros. And by using an equality operator with one condition and transposing it, we get a mask that has `True` in all the bottom triangles, including the diagonal, and `False` everywhere else. The output of the previous statement will be this:

```
tensor([[ True, False, False, False, False],
        [ True,  True, False, False, False],
        [ True,  True,  True, False, False],
        [ True,  True,  True,  True, False],
        [ True,  True,  True,  True,  True]])
```

We can see that this matrix has `False` at all the places where we need to mask attention. Now, all we need to do is to fill all `True` instances with `0` and all `False` instances with `-inf`:

```
mask = (
            mask.float()
            .masked_fill(mask == 0, float("-inf"))
            .masked_fill(mask == 1, float(0.0))
        )
```

These two lines of code are packaged into the `_generate_square_subsequent_mask` method, which we can use while training the model.

Now that we have created the mask for masked self-attention, let's start processing the input, x:

```
# Projecting input dimension to d_model
x_ = self.input_projection(x)
# Adding positional encoding
x_ = self.pos_encoder(x_)
# Encoding the input
x_ = self.transformer_encoder(x_, mask)
# Decoding the input
y_hat = self.decoder(x_)
```

In these four lines of code, we project the input to `d_model` dimensions, add positional encoding, pass it through the Transformer model, and lastly use the linear layer to convert the output to the predictions we want.

Now we have `y_hat`, which is the prediction from the model. All we need to think of now is how to train this output to be the desired output.

We know that the Transformer model processes all tokens in one shot, and if we have N elements in the sequence, we will have N predictions as well (each prediction corresponding to the next timestep). And if each prediction is of the next H timesteps, the shape of y_hat would be (B, N, H), where B is the batch size. There are a few ways we can use this output to compare with the target. The most simple and naïve way is to just take the prediction from the last position (which will have H timesteps) and compare it with y (which also has H timesteps).

But this is not the most efficient way of using all the information we have, is it? We are discarding *N-1* predictions and not giving any signal to the model on all those *N-1* predictions. So, while training, it makes sense to use all these *N-1* predictions also so that the model has a much richer signal feeding back while learning.

We can do that by using the original input sequence, x, but offsetting it by one. When *H=1*, we can think of this as a simple task where each position's prediction is compared with the target for the next position (one step ahead). We can easily accomplish this by concatenating x[:,1:,:] (the input sequence offset by 1) with y (the original target) and treating this as the target. But when *H>1*, this becomes slightly complicated, but we can still do it by using a helpful function from PyTorch called unfold:

```
y = torch.cat([x[:, 1:, :], y], dim=1).squeeze(-1).unfold(1,
y.size(1), 1)
```

We first concatenate the input sequence (offset by one) with y and then use unfold to create siding windows of *size=H*. This gives us a target of the same shape, *(B,N,H)*.

But during inference (when we are predicting using a trained model), we do not need the output of all the other positions, and hence we discard them, as seen here:

```
y_hat = y_hat[:, -1, :].unsqueeze(1)
```

Our BaseModel class that we defined also lets us define a slightly different prediction step by using a predict method. You can look over the complete model in src/dl/models.py once again to solidify your understanding now.

Now that we have defined the model, we can use the same framework we have been using to train TransformerModel. The full code is available in the notebook, but we will just look at a summary table with the results:

Algorithm	MAE	MSE	MASE	Forecast Bias
MultiStep LSTM_LSTM_teacher_forcing_1	0.1754	0.0912	1.3671	12.93%
MultiStep_Seq2Seq_dot_Attn_teacher_forcing_1	0.1536	0.0717	1.1967	8.25%
MultiStep_Transformer_Multi_Step_FF_decoder	0.1949	0.1104	1.5188	16.24%

Figure 14.19 – Metrics for Transformer model on MAC000193 household

We can see that the model is not doing as well as its RNN cousins. There can be many reasons for this, but the most probable one is that Transformers are really data-hungry. Transformers have far fewer inductive biases and therefore only shine where there is lots of data available to learn from. When forecasting just one household alone, our model has access to far less data and may not work very well. This is true, to an extent, for all the DL models we have seen so far. In *Chapter 10, Global Forecasting Models*, we talked about how we can train a single model for multiple households together, but that discussion was limited to classical ML models. DL is also perfectly capable of global forecasting models and that is exactly what we will be talking about in the next chapter—*Chapter 15, Strategies for Global Deep Learning Forecasting Models*.

For now, congratulations on getting through another concept-heavy and information-packed chapter. The concept of attention, which has taken the field by storm, should be clearer in your mind now than when you started the chapter. I urge you to take a second stab at the chapter, read through the *Further reading* section, and do some of your own googling if it's not clear because the future chapters assume you have this understanding.

Summary

We have been storming through the world of DL in the last few chapters. We started off with the basic premise of DL, what it is, and why it became so popular. Then, we saw a few common building blocks that are typically used in time series forecasting and got our hands dirty, learning how we can put what we have learned into practice using PyTorch. Although we talked about RNNs, LSTMs, GRUs, and so on, we purposefully left out attention and Transformers because they deserved a separate chapter.

We started the chapter by learning about the generalized attention model, helping you put a framework around all the different schemes of attention out there, and then went into detail on a few common attention schemes, such as scaled dot product, additive, and general attention. Right after incorporating attention into the Seq2Seq models we were playing with in *Chapter 12, Building Blocks of Deep Learning for Time Series*, we started with the Transformer. We went into detail on all the building blocks and architecture decisions involved in the original Transformer from the point of view of NLP, and after understanding the architecture, we adapted it to a time-series setting.

And finally, we capped it off by training a Transformer model for forecasting on a sample household. And now, by finishing this chapter, we have all the basic ingredients to really start using DL for time series forecasting.

In the next chapter, we are going to elevate what we have been doing and move on to the global forecasting model paradigm.

References

Following is the list of the references used in this chapter:

1. Dzmitry Bahdanau, KyungHyun Cho, and Yoshua Bengio (2015). *Neural Machine Translation by Jointly Learning to Align and Translate.* In *3rd International Conference on Learning Representations.* `https://arxiv.org/pdf/1409.0473.pdf`

2. Thang Luong, Hieu Pham, and Christopher D. Manning (2015). *Effective Approaches to Attention-based Neural Machine Translation.* In *Proceedings of the 2015 Conference on Empirical Methods in Natural Language Processing.* `https://aclanthology.org/D15-1166/`

3. André F. T. Martins, Ramón Fernandez Astudillo (2016). *From Softmax to Sparsemax: A Sparse Model of Attention and Multi-Label Classification.* In *Proceedings of the 33rd International Conference on Machine Learning.* `http://proceedings.mlr.press/v48/martins16.html`

4. Ben Peters, Vlad Niculae, André F. T. Martins (2019). *Sparse Sequence-to-Sequence Models.* In *Proceedings of the 57th Annual Meeting of the Association for Computational Linguistics.* `https://aclanthology.org/P19-1146/`

5. Ashish Vaswani, Noam Shazeer, Niki Parmar, Jakob Uszkoreit, Llion Jones, Aidan N. Gomez, Lukasz Kaiser, and Illia Polosukhin (2017). *Attention is All you Need.* In *Advances in Neural Information Processing Systems.* `https://papers.nips.cc/paper/2017/hash/3f5ee243547dee91fbd053c1c4a845aa-Abstract.html`

6. Jacob Devlin, Ming-Wei Chang, Kenton Lee, and Kristina Toutanova (2019). *BERT: Pre-training of Deep Bidirectional Transformers for Language Understanding.* In *Proceedings of the 2019 Conference of the North American Chapter of the Association for Computational Linguistics: Human Language Technologies, Volume 1 (Long and Short Papers).* `https://aclanthology.org/N19-1423/`

7. Hao Li, Zheng Xu, Gavin Taylor, Christoph Studer, and Tom Goldstein (2018). *Visualizing the Loss Landscape of Neural Nets.* In *Advances in Neural Information Processing Systems.* `https://proceedings.neurips.cc/paper/2018/file/a41b3bb3e6b050b6c9067c67f663b915-Paper.pdf`

8. Sneha Chaudhari, Varun Mithal, Gungor Polatkan, and Rohan Ramanath (2021). *An Attentive Survey of Attention Models. ACM Trans. Intell. Syst. Technol. 12, 5, Article 53 (October 2021).* `https://doi.org/10.1145/3465055`

Further reading

Here are a few resources for further reading:

- *The Illustrated Transformer* by *Jay Alammar*: `https://jalammar.github.io/illustrated-transformer/`

- *Transformer Networks: A mathematical explanation why scaling the dot products leads to more stable gradients*: `https://towardsdatascience.com/transformer-networks-a-mathematical-explanation-why-scaling-the-dot-products-leads-to-more-stable-414f87391500`

- *Why is Bahdanau's attention sometimes called concat attention?*: `https://stats.stackexchange.com/a/524729`

- *Noam Shazeer* (2020). *GLU Variants Improve Transformer.* arXiv preprint: *Arxiv-2002.05202.* `https://arxiv.org/abs/2002.05202`

- *What is Residual Connection?* by *Wanshun Wong*: `https://towardsdatascience.com/what-is-residual-connection-efb07cab0d55`

- *Attn: Illustrated Attention* by *Raimi Karim*: `https://towardsdatascience.com/attn-illustrated-attention-5ec4ad276ee3`

15

Strategies for Global Deep Learning Forecasting Models

All through the last few chapters, we have been building up deep learning for time series forecasting. We started with the basics of deep learning, saw the different building blocks, practically used some of those building blocks to generate forecasts on a sample household, and finally, talked about attention and transformers. Now, let's slightly alter our trajectory and take a look at global models for deep learning. In *Chapter 10*, *Global Forecasting Models*, we saw why global models make sense and also saw how we can use such a model in the machine learning context. We even got good results in our experiments. In this chapter, we will look at how we can apply similar concepts, but from a deep learning context. We will look at different strategies that we can use to make global deep learning models work better.

In this chapter, we will be covering these main topics:

- Creating global deep learning forecasting models
- Using time-varying information
- Using static/meta information
- Using the scale of the time series
- Balancing the sampling procedure

Technical requirements

You will need to set up the Anaconda environment following the instructions in the *Preface* of the book to get a working environment with all the packages and datasets required for the code in this book.

You will need to run these notebooks:

- `02 - Preprocessing London Smart Meter Dataset.ipynb` in Chapter02
- `01-Setting up Experiment Harness.ipynb` in Chapter04
- `01-Feature Engineering.ipynb` in Chapter06

The associated code for the chapter can be found at `https://github.com/PacktPublishing/ Modern-Time-Series-Forecasting-with-Python-/tree/main/notebooks/ Chapter15`.

Creating global deep learning forecasting models

In *Chapter 10, Global Forecasting Models*, we talked in detail about why a global model makes sense. We talked about the benefits regarding increased *sample size, cross-learning, multi-task learning* and the regularization effect that comes with it, and reduced *engineering complexity*. All of these are relevant for a deep learning model as well. Engineering complexity and sample size become even more important because deep learning models are data-hungry and take quite a bit more engineering effort and training time than other machine learning models. I would go to the extent to say that in the deep learning context, in most practical cases where we have to forecast at scale, global models are the only deep learning paradigm that makes sense.

So, why did we spend all that time looking at individual models? Well, it's easier to grasp the concept at that level, and the skills and knowledge we gained at that level are very easily transferred to a global modeling paradigm. In *Chapter 13, Common Modeling Patterns for Time Series*, we saw how we use a data loader to sample windows from a single time series to train the model. To make the model a global model, all we need to do is to change the data loader so that instead of sampling windows from a single time series, we sample from many time series. The sampling process can be thought of as a two-step process (although in practice, we do it in a single step, it is intuitive to think of it as two) – first, sample the time series we need to pick the window from, and then, sample the window from that time series. And by doing that, we are training a single deep learning model to forecast all the time series together.

To make our lives easier, we are going to use an open source library called `PyTorch Forecasting` to handle the data loading for us. `PyTorch Forecasting` aims to make time series forecasting with deep learning easy for both research and real-world cases alike. `PyTorch Forecasting` also has implementations for many state-of-the-art forecasting architectures, and we will come back to those in *Chapter 16, Specialized Deep Learning Architectures for Forecasting*. But now, let's use the high-level API in `PyTorch Forecasting`. This will significantly reduce our work in preparing `PyTorch` datasets. The `TimeSeriesDataset` class in `PyTorch Forecasting` takes care of a lot of boilerplate code dealing with different transformations, missing values, padding, and so on. We will be using this framework in this chapter when we look at different strategies to implement global deep learning forecasting models.

> **Notebook alert**
>
> To follow along with the complete code, use the notebook named `01-Global Deep Learning Models.ipynb` in the `Chapter15` folder. There are two variables in the notebook that act as a switch – `TRAIN_SUBSAMPLE = True` makes the notebook run for a subset of 10 households. `train_model = True` makes the notebook train different models (warning: training models on the full data takes upward of 3 hours each). `train_model = False` loads the trained model weights and predicts on them.

Preprocessing the data

We start by loading the necessary libraries and the dataset. We are using the preprocessed and feature-engineered dataset we created in *Chapter 6, Feature Engineering for Time Series Forecasting*. There are different kinds of features in the dataset and to make our feature assignment standardized, we use `namedtuple`. `namedtuple()` is a factory method in collections that lets you create subclasses of `tuple` with named fields. These named fields can be accessed using dot notation. We define `namedtuple` like this:

```
from collections import namedtuple
FeatureConfig = namedtuple(
    "FeatureConfig",
    [
        "target",
        "index_cols",
        "static_categoricals",
        "static_reals",
        "time_varying_known_categoricals",
        "time_varying_known_reals",
        "time_varying_unknown_reals",
        "group_ids"
    ],
)
```

Let's also quickly establish what these names mean:

- `target` – The column name of what we are trying to forecast.

- `index_cols` – The columns that we need to make as an index for quick access to data.

- `static_categoricals` – These are columns that are categorical in nature and do not change with time. They are specific to each time series. For instance, the *Acorn group* in our dataset is `static_categorical` because it is categorical in nature and is a value pertaining to a household.

- `static_reals` – These are columns that are numeric in nature and do not change with time. They are specific to each time series. For instance, the average energy consumption in our dataset is numeric in nature and pertains to a single household.

- `time_varying_known_categoricals` – These are columns that are categorical in nature and change with time and we know the future values. They can be seen as quantities that keep varying with time. A prime example would be holidays, which are categorical, vary with time, and we know the future holidays.

- `time_varying_known_reals` – These are columns that are numeric in nature and change with time and we know the future values. A prime example would be temperature, which is numeric, varies with time, and we know the future values (provided the source we are getting the weather from allows for forecasted weather data as well).

- `time_varying_unknown_reals` – These are columns that are numeric in nature and change with time and we don't know the future values. The target we are trying to forecast is an excellent example.

- `group_ids` – These columns uniquely identify each time series in the dataframe.

Once defined, we can assign different values to each of these names, as follows:

```
feat_config = FeatureConfig(
    target="energy_consumption",
    index_cols=["LCLid", "timestamp"],
    static_categoricals=[
        "LCLid",
        "stdorToU",
        "Acorn",
        "Acorn_grouped",
        "file",
    ],
    static_reals=[],
    time_varying_known_categoricals=[
        "holidays",
        "timestamp_Dayofweek",
    ],
    time_varying_known_reals=["apparentTemperature"],
    time_varying_unknown_reals=["energy_consumption"],
    group_ids=["LCLid"],
)
```

We can see that we are not using all the features as we did with machine learning models (*Chapter 10, Global Forecasting Models*). There are two reasons for that:

- Since we are using sequential deep learning models, a lot of the information we are trying to capture using rolling features and so on is already available to the model.

- Unlike robust gradient-boosted decision tree models, deep learning models aren't that robust to noise. So, irrelevant features would make the model worse.

There are a few preprocessing steps that are needed to make the dataset we have compatible with `PyTorch Forecasting`. `PyTorch Forecasting` needs a continuous time index as a proxy for time. Although we have a `timestamp` column, it has datetimes. So, we need to convert it to a new column, `time_idx`. The complete code is in the notebook, but the essence of the code is simple. We combine the train and test dataframes and use a formula using the `timestamp` column to derive a new `time_idx` column. The formula is such that it increments every successive timestamp by one and is consistent between `train` and `test`. For instance, `time_idx` of the last timestep in `train` is `256`, and `time_idx` of the first timesteps in `test` would be `257`. In addition to that, we also need to convert the categorical columns into `object` data types to play nicely with `TimeSeriesDataset` from `PyTorch Forecasting`.

For our experiments, we have chosen to have 2 days (96 timesteps) as the window and predict one single step ahead. And to enable early stopping, we would need a validation set as well. **Early stopping** is a way of regularization where we keep monitoring the validation loss and stop training when the validation loss starts to increase. We have selected the last day of training (48 timesteps) as the validation data and 1 whole month as the final test data. But when we prepare these dataframes, we need to take care of something: we have chosen 2 days as our history, and to forecast the first timestep in the validation or test set, we need the last 2 days of history along with it. So, we split our dataframes as shown in the following diagram (the exact code is in the notebook):

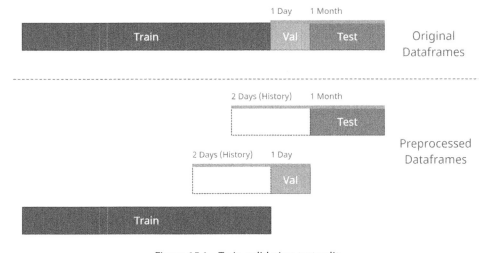

Figure 15.1 – Train-validation-test split

Now, before using `TimeSeriesDataset` on our data, let's try to understand what it does and what the different parameters involved are.

Understanding TimeSeriesDataset from PyTorch Forecasting

`TimeSeriesDataset` automates the following tasks and more:

- Scaling numeric features and encoding categorical features:

  - Scaling the numeric features to have the same mean and variance helps gradient descent-based optimization to converge faster and better.

  - Categorical features need to be encoded as numbers so that we can handle them the right way inside the deep learning models.

- Normalizing the target variable:

  - In a global model context, the target variable can have different scales for different time series. For instance, a particular household typically has higher energy consumption, and some other households may be vacant and have little to no energy consumption. Scaling the target variable to a single scale helps the deep learning model to focus on learning the patterns rather than capturing the variance in scale.

- Efficiently converting the dataframe into a dictionary of PyTorch tensors:

  - The dataset also takes in the information about different columns and converts the dataframe into a dictionary of PyTorch tensors, separately handling the static and time-varying information.

These are the major parameters of `TimeSeriesDataset`:

- `data` – This is the pandas DataFrame holding all the data such that each row is uniquely identified with `time_idx` and `group_ids`.

- `time_idx` – This refers to the column name with the continuous time index we created earlier.

- `target`, `group_ids`, `static_categoricals`, `static_reals`, `time_varying_known_categoricals`, `time_varying_known_reals`, `time_varying_unknown_categoricals`, and `time_varying_unknown_reals` – We already discussed all these parameters in the *Preprocessing the data* section. These hold the same meaning.

- `max_encoder_length` – This sets the maximum window length given to the encoder.

- `min_decoder_length` – This sets the minimum window given in the decoding context.

- `target_normalizer` – This takes in a transformer that normalizes the targets. There are a few normalizers built into `PyTorch Forecasting` – `TorchNormalizer`, `GroupNormalizer`, and `EncoderNormalizer`. `TorchNormalizer` does standard and robust scaling of the targets as a whole, whereas `GroupNormalizer` does the same but with each group separately (a group is defined by `group_ids`). `EncoderNormalizer` does the scaling at runtime by normalizing using the values in each window.

- `categorical_encoders` – This parameter takes in a dictionary of scikit-learn transformers as a category encoder. By default, the category encoding is similar to `LabelEncoder`, which replaces each unique categorical value with a number, adding an additional category for unknown and NaN values.

For the full documentation, please refer to `https://pytorch-forecasting.readthedocs.io/en/stable/data.html#time-series-data-set`.

Initializing TimeSeriesDataset

Now that we know the major parameters, let's initialize a time series dataset using our data:

```
training = TimeSeriesDataSet(
    train_df,
    time_idx="time_idx",
    target=feat_config.target,
    group_ids=feat_config.group_ids,
    max_encoder_length=max_encoder_length,
    max_prediction_length=max_prediction_length,
    time_varying_unknown_reals=[
        "energy_consumption",
    ],
    target_normalizer=GroupNormalizer(
        groups=feat_config.group_ids, transformation=None
    )
)
```

Note that we have used `GroupNormalizer` so that each household is scaled separately using its own mean and standard deviation using the following well-known formula:

$$\frac{x - mean}{standard\ deviation}$$

TimeSeriesDataset also makes it easy to declare validation and test datasets as well using a factory method, from_dataset. It takes in another time series dataset as an argument and uses the same parameters, scalers, and so on, and creates new datasets:

```
# Defining the validation dataset with the same parameters as
training
validation = TimeSeriesDataSet.from_dataset(training,
pd.concat([val_history,val_df]).reset_index(drop=True), stop_
randomization=True)
# Defining the test dataset with the same parameters as
training
test = TimeSeriesDataSet.from_dataset(training,
pd.concat([hist_df, test_df]).reset_index(drop=True), stop_
randomization=True)
```

Notice that we concatenate the history to both val_df and test_df to make sure we can predict on the entire validation and test period.

Creating the dataloader

All that is left to do is to create the dataloader from TimeSeriesDataset:

```
train_dataloader = training.to_dataloader(train=True, batch_
size=batch_size, num_workers=0)
val_dataloader = validation.to_dataloader(train=False, batch_
size=batch_size, num_workers=0)
```

Before we proceed, let's solidify our understanding of the dataloader with the help of an example. The train dataloader we just created has split the dataframe into a dictionary of PyTorch tensors. We have chosen 512 as a batch size and can inspect the dataloader using the following code:

```
# Testing the dataloader
x, y = next(iter(train_dataloader))
print("\nsizes of x =")
for key, value in x.items():
    print(f"\t{key} = {value.size()}")
print("\nsize of y =")
print(f"\ty = {y[0].size()}")
```

We will get an output as follows:

```
sizes of x =
        encoder_cat = torch.Size([512, 96, 0])
        encoder_cont = torch.Size([512, 96, 1])
        encoder_target = torch.Size([512, 96])
        encoder_lengths = torch.Size([512])
        decoder_cat = torch.Size([512, 1, 0])
        decoder_cont = torch.Size([512, 1, 1])
        decoder_target = torch.Size([512, 1])
        decoder_lengths = torch.Size([512])
        decoder_time_idx = torch.Size([512, 1])
        groups = torch.Size([512, 1])
        target_scale = torch.Size([512, 2])

size of y =
        y = torch.Size([512, 1])
```

Figure 15.2 – Shapes of tensors in a batch of a train dataloader

We can see that the dataloader and `TimeSeriesDataset` have split the dataframe into PyTorch tensors and packed them into a dictionary with the encoder and decoder sequences separate. We can also see that the categorical and continuous features are also separated. The main *keys* we will be using from this dictionary are `encoder_cat`, `encoder_cont`, `decoder_cat`, and `decoder_cont`. The `encoder_cat` and `decoder_cat` keys have zero dimensions because we haven't declared any categorical features.

Visualizing how the dataloader works

Let's try to unpeel what happened here one level deeper and understand what `TimeSeriesDataset` has done visually:

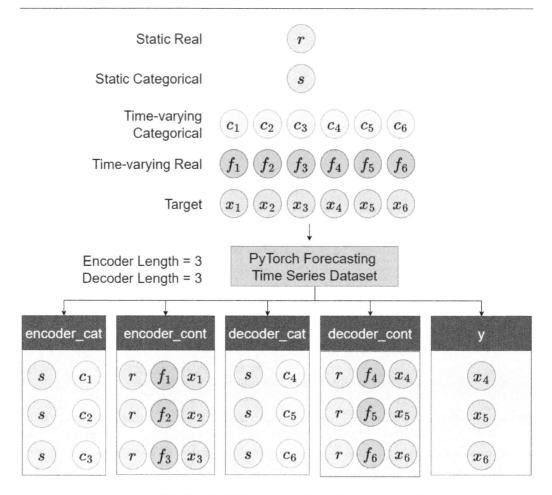

Figure 15.3 – TimeSeriesDataset – an illustration of how it works

Let's assume we have a time series, x_1 to x_6 (this would be the target as well as `time_varying_unknown` in the `TimeSeriesDataset` terminology). We have a time-varying real, f_1 to f_6, and a time-varying categorical, c_1 to c_2. In addition to that, we also have a static real, r, and a static categorical, s. If we chose the encoder and decoder length as 3, we will have the tensors constructed as shown in *Figure 15.3*. Notice how the static categorical and real are repeated for all timesteps. These different tensors are constructed so that the model encoder can be trained using the encoder tensors and the decoder tensors are used in the decoding process.

Now, let's proceed with building our first global model.

Building the first global deep learning forecasting model

`PyTorch Forecasting` uses PyTorch and PyTorch Lightning in the backend to define and train deep learning models. The models that can be used seamlessly with `PyTorch Forecasting` are essentially PyTorch Lightning models. But the recommended approach is to inherit `BaseModel` from `PyTorch Forecasting`. The developer of `PyTorch Forecasting` has excellent documentation and tutorials to help new users use it the way they want. One tutorial worth mentioning here is titled *How to use custom data and implement custom models and metrics* (link in the *Further reading* section).

I have slightly modified the basic model from the tutorial to make it more flexible. The implementation can be found in `src/dl/ptf_models.py` under the name `SingleStepRNNModel`. The class takes in two parameters:

- `network_callable` – This is a callable that, when initialized, becomes a PyTorch model (inheriting `nn.Module`).

- `model_params` – This is a dictionary containing all the parameters necessary to initialize `network_callable`.

The structure is pretty simple. The `__init__` function initializes `network_callable` into a PyTorch model under the `network` attribute. And the `forward` function sends the input to the network, formats the returned output the way `PyTorch Forecasting` wants, and returns it. It is a very short model because the bulk of the heavy lifting is done by `BaseModel`, which handles the loss calculation, logging, gradient descent, and so on. The benefit we get by defining a model this way is that we can now define standard PyTorch models and pass it to this model to make it work well with `PyTorch Forecasting`.

In addition to this, we also define an abstract class called `SingleStepRNN`, which takes in a set of parameters and initializes the corresponding network that is specified by the parameters. If the parameter specifies an LSTM, with two layers, then it will be initialized and saved under the `rnn` attribute. It also defines a fully connected layer under the `fc` attribute, which turns the output of the RNN into the prediction. The `forward` method is an abstract method that needs to be overwritten in any class subclassing this class.

Defining our first RNN model

Now that we have the necessary setup, let's define our first model inheriting the `SingleStepRNN` class we defined:

```
class SimpleRNNModel(SingleStepRNN):
    def __init__(
        self,
        rnn_type: str,
        input_size: int,
```

```
        hidden_size: int,
        num_layers: int,
        bidirectional: bool,
    ):
        super().__init__(rnn_type, input_size, hidden_size,
num_layers, bidirectional)


    def forward(self, x: Dict):
        # Using the encoder continuous which has the history
window
        x = x["encoder_cont"] # x --> (batch_size, seq_len,
input_size)
        # Processing through the RNN
        x, _ = self.rnn(x)  # --> (batch_size, seq_len, hidden_
size)
        # Using a FC layer on last hidden state
        x = self.fc(x[:,-1,:])  # --> (batch_size, seq_len, 1)
        return x
```

This is the most straightforward implementation. We take `encoder_cont` from the dictionary and pass it through the RNN, and then use a fully connected layer on the last hidden state from the RNN to generate the prediction. If we take the example in *Figure 15.3*, we used x_1 to x_3 as the history and trained the model to predict x_4 (because we are using `min_decoder_length=1`, there will be just one timestep in the decoder and target).

Initializing the RNN model

Now let's initialize the model using some parameters. I have defined two dictionaries for parameters:

- `model_params` – This has all the parameters necessary for the `SingleStepRNN` model to be initialized.

- `other_params` – These are all the parameters such as `learning_rate`, `loss`, and so on, which we pass on to `SingleStepRNNModel`.

Now we can initialize the `PyTorch Forecasting` model using a factory method it supports – `from_dataset`. This factory method lets us pass a dataset and infer some parameters from the dataset instead of us filling everything in all the time:

```
model = SingleStepRNNModel.from_dataset(
    training,
    network_callable=SimpleRNNModel,
```

```
    model_params=model_params,
    **other_params
)
```

Training the RNN model

Training the model is just like we have been doing in previous chapters because this is a PyTorch Lightning model. We can follow these steps:

1. Initialize the trainer with early stopping and model checkpoints:

```
trainer = pl.Trainer(
    auto_select_gpus=True,
    gpus=-1,
    min_epochs=1,
    max_epochs=20,
    callbacks=[
        pl.callbacks.EarlyStopping(monitor="val_loss",
patience=4*3),
        pl.callbacks.ModelCheckpoint(
            monitor="val_loss", save_last=True,
mode="min", auto_insert_metric_name=True
        ),
    ],
    val_check_interval=2000,
    log_every_n_steps=2000,
)
```

2. Fit the model:

```
trainer.fit(
    model,
    train_dataloaders=train_dataloader,
    val_dataloaders=val_dataloader,
)
```

3. Load the best model after training:

```
best_model_path = trainer.checkpoint_callback.best_model_
path
best_model = SingleStepRNNModel.load_from_
checkpoint(best_model_path)
```

The training can run for some time. To save you some time, I have included the trained weights for each of the models we are using, and if the `train_model` flag is `False`, it will skip training and load the saved weights.

Forecasting with the trained model

Now, after training, we can predict on the test dataset as follows:

```
pred, index = best_model.predict(test, return_index=True, show_
progress_bar=True)
```

We store the predictions in a dataframe and evaluate them using our standard metrics: **MAE**, **MSE**, **meanMASE**, and **Forecast Bias**. Let's see the results:

Algorithm	MAE	MSE	meanMASE	Forecast Bias
simple	0.085441	0.030798	1.078673	1.410458

Figure 15.4 – Aggregate results using the baseline global model

This is not a very good model because we know from *Chapter 10, Global Forecasting Models,* that the baseline global model using LightGBM was as follows:

- MAE = 0.079581

- MSE = 0.027326

- meanMASE = 1.013393

- Forecast Bias = 28.718087

Apart from Forecast Bias, our global model is nowhere close to the best. Let's refer to the **global machine learning model** as **GFM(ML)** and the current model as **GFM(DL)** for the rest of our discussion. Now, let's start looking at some strategies to make the global model better.

Using time-varying information

The GFM(ML) used all the available features. So obviously, that model had access to a lot more information than the GFM(DL) we have built till now. The GFM(DL) we just built only takes in the history and nothing else. Let's change that by including time-varying information. We will just use time-varying real features this time because dealing with categorical features is a topic I want to leave for the next section.

We initialize the training dataset the same way as before, but we add `time_varying_known_reals=feat_config.time_varying_known_reals` to the initialization parameters. Now that we have all the datasets created, let's move on to setting up the model.

To set up the model, we need to understand one concept. We are now using the history of the target and time-varying known features. In *Figure 15.3*, we saw how `TimeSeriesDataset` arranges the different kinds of variables in PyTorch tensors. In the previous section, we used only `encoder_cont` because there were no other variables to worry about. But now, we have time-varying variables along with it, which brings an added complication. If we take a step back and think about it, in the single-step-ahead forecasting context, we can see that the time-varying variables and the history of the target cannot be of the same timestep. Let's use a visual example to elucidate:

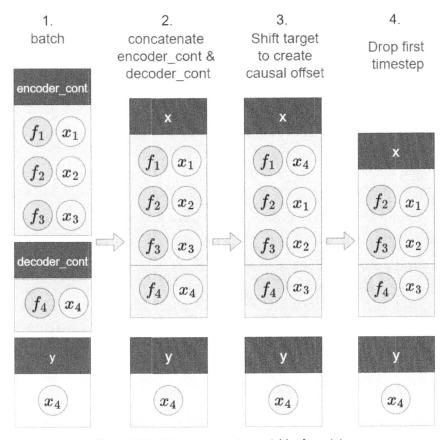

Figure 15.5 – Using time-varying variables for training

Following the same spirit of the example from *Figure 15.3*, but reducing it to fit our context here, we have a time series, x_1 to x_4, and time-varying real variable, f_1 to f_4. So, for `max_encoder_length=3` and `min_decoder_length=1`, we would have `TimeSeriesDataset` make the tensors as shown in *Step 1* in *Figure 15.5*.

Now, for each timestep, we have the time-varying variable, f, and the history, x, in `encoder_cont`. The time-varying variable, f, is a variable for which we know the future values as well and therefore, there is no causal constraint on that variable. That means that for predicting the timestep, t, we can use f_t because it is known. But the history of the target variable is not. We do not know the future because it is the very quantity we are trying to forecast. That means that there is a causal constraint on x and, because of this, we cannot use x_t to predict timestep t. But the way the tensors are formed right now, we have f and x aligned on timesteps and if we passed them through a model, we would be essentially cheating because we would be using x_t to predict timestep t. Ideally, there should be an offset between the history, x, and the time-varying feature, f, such that at timestep t, the model sees x_{t-1} and then sees f_t and then predicts x_t.

To achieve that, we do the following:

1. Concatenate `encoder_cont` and `decoder_cont` because we need to use f_4 to predict timestep $t = 4$ (*Step 2* in *Figure 15.5*).

2. Shift the target history, x, forward by one timestep so that f_t and x_{t-1} are aligned (*Step 3* in *Figure 15.5*).

3. Drop the first timestep because we don't have the history to go with the first timestep (*Step 4* in *Figure 15.5*).

This is exactly what we need to implement in our `forward` method in the new model we defined, `DynamicFeatureRNNModel`, as well:

```
Def forward(self, x: Dict):
    # Step 2 in Figure 15.5
    x_cont = torch.cat([x["encoder_cont"],x["decoder_cont"]],
dim=1)
    # Step 3 in Figure 15.5
    x_cont[:,:,-1] = torch.roll(x_cont[:,:,-1], 1, dims=1)
    x = x_cont
    # Step 4 in Figure 15.5
    x = x[:,1:,:] # x -> (batch_size, seq_len, input_size)
    # Processing through the RNN
    x, _ = self.rnn(x)  # --> (batch_size, seq_len, hidden_
size)
    # Using a FC layer on last hidden state
    x = self.fc(x[:,-1,:])  # --> (batch_size, seq_len, 1)
    return x
```

Now, let's train this new model and see how it performs. The exact code is in the notebook and is exactly the same as before:

Algorithm	MAE	MSE	meanMASE	Forecast Bias
simple	0.0854	0.0308	1.0787	1.41%
simple+time_varying	0.0851	0.0310	1.0764	0.73%

Figure 15.6 – Aggregate results using the time-varying features

It looks like having temperature as a feature did make the model slightly better, but there's still a long way to go. Not to worry, we have other features to use.

Using static/meta information

There are some features such as the Acorn group, whether dynamic pricing is enabled, and so on, that are specific to a household, which will help the model learn patterns specific to these groups. Naturally, including that information makes intuitive sense. But as we discussed in *Chapter 10*, *Global Forecasting Models*, categorical features do not play well with machine learning models because they aren't numerical. In that chapter, we discussed a few ways of encoding categorical features into numerical representations. We can use any of those in a deep learning model as well. But there is one way of handling categorical features that is unique to deep learning models – **embedding vectors**.

One-hot encoding and why it is not ideal

One of the ways of converting categorical features to numerical representation is one-hot encoding. It encodes the categorical features in a higher dimension, placing the categorical values equally distant in that space. The size of the dimension it requires to encode the categorical values is equal to the cardinality of the categorical variable. For a more detailed discussion on one-hot encoding, refer to *Chapter 10*, *Global Forecasting Models*.

The representation that we would get after one-hot encoding of a categorical feature is what we call a **sparse representation**. If the cardinality of the categorical feature (number of unique values) is C, each row representing a value of the categorical feature would have $C - 1$ zeros. So, the representation is predominantly zeros and hence is called a sparse representation. This causes the overall dimension required to effectively encode a categorical feature to be equal to the cardinality of the vector. Therefore, one-hot encoding of a categorical feature with 5,000 unique values instantly adds 5,000 dimensions to the problem you are solving.

In addition to that, one-hot encoding is also completely uninformed. It places each categorical value equidistant from each other without any regard for the possible similarity between those values. For instance, if we are encoding the days in a week, one-hot encoding would place each day in a completely different dimension, making them equidistant from each other. But if we think about it, Saturday and Sunday should be closer together than the other weekdays on account of them being the weekend, right? This kind of information is not captured through one-hot encoding.

Embedding vectors and dense representations

An embedding vector is a similar representation, but instead of a sparse representation, it strives to give us a dense representation of a categorical feature. We can achieve this by using an embedding layer. The embedding layer can be thought of as a mapping between each categorical value and a numerical vector, and this vector can have a much lower dimension than the cardinality of the categorical feature. The only question that remains is *"How do we know what vector to choose for each categorical value?"*

The good news is that we need not because the embedding layer is trained along with the rest of the network. So, while training a model for some task, the model itself figures out what the best vector representation is for each categorical value. This approach is really popular in natural language processing, where thousands of words are embedded into dimensions as small as 200 or 300. In PyTorch, we can accomplish this by using nn.Embedding, which is a module that is a simple lookup table that stores the embeddings of fixed discrete values and size. There are two mandatory parameters while initializing:

- num_embeddings – This is the size of the dictionary of embeddings. In other words, this is the cardinality of the categorical feature.

- embedding_dim – This is the size of each embedding vector.

Now, let's come back to global modeling. Let's first introduce the static categorical features. Please note that we are also including the time-varying categorical because now we know how to deal with categorical features in a deep learning model. The code to initialize the dataset is the same, with the addition of the following two parameters to the initialization:

- static_categoricals=feat_config.static_categoricals

- time_varying_known_categoricals=feat_config.time_varying_known_categoricals

Defining a model with categorical features

Now that we have the datasets, let's look at how we can define the __init__ function in our new model, StaticDynamicFeatureRNNModel. In addition to invoking the parent model, which sets up the standard RNN and fully connected layer, we also set up the embedding layers using an input, embedding_sizes. embedding_sizes is a list of tuples (*cardinality and embedding size*) for each categorical feature:

```
def __init__(
    self,
    rnn_type: str,
    input_size: int,
    hidden_size: int,
```

```
    num_layers: int,
    bidirectional: bool,
    embedding_sizes = []
):
    super().__init__(rnn_type, input_size, hidden_size, num_
layers, bidirectional)
    self.embeddings = torch.nn.ModuleList(
        [torch.nn.Embedding(card, size) for card, size in
embedding_sizes]
    )
```

We used nn.ModuleList to store a list of nn.Embedding modules, one for each categorical feature. While initializing this model, we will need to give embedding_sizes as input. The embedding size required for each categorical feature is technically a hyperparameter that we can tune. But there are a few rules of thumb to get you started. The idea behind these thumb rules is that the bigger the cardinality of the categorical feature, the larger the embedding size required to encode the information in them. And also, the embedding size can be much smaller than the cardinality of the categorical feature. The rule of thumb that we have adopted is as follows:

$$ \min\left(50, round\left(\frac{c+1}{2} \right) \right) $$

Therefore, we create the embedding_sizes list of tuples using the following code:

```
# Finding the cardinality using the categorical encoders in the
dataset
cardinality = [len(training.categorical_encoders[c].classes_)
for c in training.categoricals]
# using the cardinality list to create embedding sizes
embedding_sizes = [
    (x, min(50, (x + 1) // 2))
    for x in cardinality
]
```

And now, turning our attention toward the forward method, it is going to be similar to the previous model, but with an additional part to handle the categorical features. We essentially use the embedding layers to convert the categorical features into embeddings and concatenate them with the continuous features:

```
def forward(self, x: Dict):
    # Using the encoder and decoder sequence
    x_cont = torch.cat([x["encoder_cont"],x["decoder_cont"]],
```

```
dim=1)
    # Roll target by 1
    x_cont[:,:,-1] = torch.roll(x_cont[:,:,-1], 1, dims=1)
    # Combine the encoder and decoder categoricals
    cat = torch.cat([x["encoder_cat"],x["decoder_cat"]], dim=1)
    # if there are categorical features
    if cat.size(-1)>0:
        # concatenating all the embedding vectors
        x_cat = torch.cat([emb(cat[:,:,i]) for i, emb in
enumerate(self.embeddings)], dim=-1)
        # concatenating continuous and categorical
        x = torch.cat([x_cont, x_cat], dim=-1)
    else:
        x = x_cont
    # dropping first timestep
    x = x[:,1:,:] # x --> (batch_size, seq_len, input_size)
    # Processing through the RNN
    x, _ = self.rnn(x)  # --> (batch_size, seq_len, hidden_
size)
    # Using a FC layer on last hidden state
    x = self.fc(x[:,-1,:])  # --> (batch_size, seq_len, 1)
    return x
```

Now, let's train this new model with static features and see how it performs:

Algorithm	MAE	MSE	meanMASE	Forecast Bias
simple	0.0854	0.0308	1.0787	1.41%
simple+time_varying	0.0851	0.0310	1.0764	0.73%
simple+static+time_varying	0.0843	0.0297	1.0685	0.94%

Figure 15.7 – Aggregate results using the static and time-varying features

Adding the static variables also improved our model. Now let's look at another strategy.

Using the scale of the time series

We used `GroupNormlizer` in `TimeSeriesDataset` to scale each household using its own mean and standard deviation. We did this because we wanted to make the target zero mean and unit variance so that the model does not waste effort trying to change its parameters to capture the scale of individual household consumption. Although this is a good strategy, we do have some information loss here. There may be patterns that are specific to households whose consumption is on the larger side and some other patterns that are specific to households that consume much less. But now, they are both lumped in together and the model tries to learn common patterns. In such a scenario, these unique patterns seem like noise to the model because there is no variable to explain those.

The bottom line is that there is information in the scale that we removed, and adding that information back would be beneficial. So, how do we add it back? Definitely not by including the unscaled targets, which brings back the disadvantage that we were trying to get away from in the first place. A way to do it is to add the scale information as static-real features to the model. We would have kept track of the mean and standard deviation of each household when we scaled them in the first place (because we need them to do the inverse transformation and get back the original targets). All we need to do is make sure we include them as a static real variable so that the model has access to the scale information while learning the patterns in the time series dataset.

`PyTorch Forecasting` makes this easier for us by having a handy parameter in `TimeSeriesDataset` called `add_target_scales`. If you make it `True`, then `encoder_cont` and `decoder_cont` will also have the mean and standard deviation of individual time series as.

Nothing changes in our existing model; all we need to do is add this parameter to `TimeSeriesDataset` while initializing it and train and predict using the model. Let's see how that worked out for us:

Algorithm	MAE	MSE	meanMASE	Forecast Bias
simple	0.0854	0.0308	1.0787	1.41%
simple+time_varying	0.0851	0.0310	1.0764	0.73%
simple+static+time_varying	0.0843	0.0297	1.0685	0.94%
simple+static+time_varying+scale	0.0822	0.0298	1.0395	-3.20%

Figure 15.8 – Aggregate results using the static, time-varying, and scale features

The scale information has improved the model yet again. And with that, let's look at one of the last strategies we will be covering in this book.

Balancing the sampling procedure

We saw a few strategies for improving a global deep learning model by adding new types of features. Now, let's look at a different aspect that is relevant in a global modeling context. In an earlier section, when we were talking about global deep learning models, we talked about how the process by which we sample a window of sequence to feed to our model can be thought of as a two-step process:

1. Sampling a time series out of a set of time series

2. Sampling a window out of that time series

Let's use an analogy to make the concept clearer. Imagine we have a large bowl that we have filled with N balls. Each ball in the bowl represents a time series in the dataset (a household in our dataset). Now, each ball, i, has M_i chits of paper representing all the different windows of samples we can draw from it.

In the batch sampling we use by default, we open all the balls and dump all the chits into the bowl and discard the balls. Now, with our eyes closed, we pick B chits out of this bowl and set them aside. This is a batch that we sample from our dataset. We do not have any information that separates the chits from each other and so the probability of picking any chit is equal, which can be formulated as:

$$\frac{1}{\sum_{i=0}^{N} M_i}$$

Now, let's add something to our analogy to the data. We know that we have different kinds of time series – different lengths, different levels of consumption, and so on. Let's pick one aspect, the length of the series, for our example (although it applies to other aspects as well). So, if we discretize the length of our time series, we end up with different bins; let's assign a color for each bin. So, now we have C different colored balls in the bowl and the chits of paper also are colored accordingly.

In our current sampling strategy (where we dump all the chits of paper, now colored, and pick B chits at random), we would end up replicating the probability distribution of our bowl in a batch. It is not a stretch to understand that if the bowl has more of the longer time series than shorter ones, the chits we draw will also have that bias. And consequently, the batch will also be biased toward a long time series. What happens because of that?

In mini-batch stochastic gradient descent (we saw this in *Chapter 11, Introduction to Deep Learning*), we do a gradient update every mini-batch, and we use this gradient update to move closer to our minima in the optimization process. Therefore, if a mini-batch is biased toward a particular type of case, then the gradient updates would be biased toward a solution that works better for them. There are good parallels to be drawn here to imbalanced learning. Longer time series and shorter time series may have different patterns, and having this sampling imbalance causes the model to learn patterns that work well for the longer time series and not so well for the shorter ones.

Visualizing the data distribution

We calculated the length of each household (`LCLid`) and binned them into 10 bins – `bin_0` for the shortest bin and `bin_9` for the longest bin:

```
n_bins= 10
# Calculating the length of each LCLid
counts = train_df.groupby("LCLid")['timestamp'].count()
# Binning the counts and renaming
out, bins = pd.cut(counts, bins=n_bins, retbins=True)
out = out.cat.rename_categories({
    c:f"bin_{i}" for i, c in enumerate(out.cat.categories)
})
```

Let's visualize the distribution of the bins in the original data:

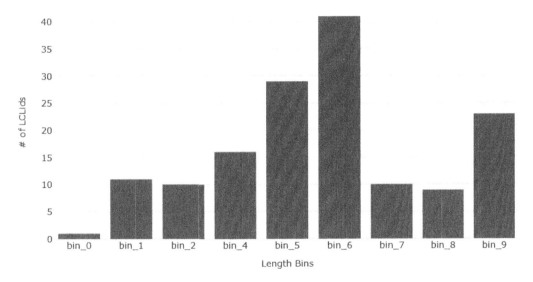

Figure 15.9 – Distribution of length of time series

We can see that `bin_5` and `bin_6` are the most common lengths while `bin_0` is the least common. Now, let's get the first 50 batches from the dataloader and plot them as a stacked bar chart to check the distribution in each batch:

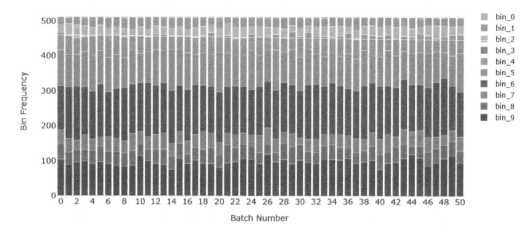

Figure 15.10 – Stacked bar chart of batch distribution

We can see that the same distribution you saw in *Figure 15.9* is replicated in the batch distributions as well with `bin_5` and `bin_6` leading the pack. `bin_0` is barely making an appearance and LCLids that are in `bin_0` would not have been learned that well.

Tweaking the sampling procedure

Now, what do we do? Let's step into the analogy of bowls with chits inside for a bit. We were picking a ball at random, and we saw that the resulting distribution is identical to the original distribution of colors. Therefore, to get a more balanced distribution of colors in a batch, we need to sample different colored chits at different probabilities. In other words, we should be sampling more from colors that have low representation in the original distribution and less from colors that dominate the original representation.

Let's look at the process by which we are selecting the chits from the bowl from another perspective. We know that the probability of selecting each chit in the bowl is equal. So, another way to select chits from the bowl is by using a uniform random number generator. We pick a chit from the bowl, generate a random number between 0 and 1 (p), and select the chit if the random number is less than 0.5 ($p < 0.5$). So, it is equally likely that we select or reject the chit. We continue this until we get B samples. Although a bit more inefficient than the previous procedure, this sampling process approximates the original procedure closely. The advantage here is that we have a threshold now with which we can tweak our sampling to suit our needs. Having a lower threshold makes the chit harder to accept under this sampling procedure, and having a higher threshold makes it easier to accept.

Now that we have a threshold with which we can tweak the sampling procedure, all we need to do is find out the right thresholds for each of the chits so that the resulting batch has a uniform representation of all the colors. In other words, we need to find and assign the right weight to each LCLid such that the resulting batch will have an even distribution of all length bins.

How do we do that? There is a very simple strategy for that. We want the weights to be lower for length bins that have a lot of samples, and higher for length bins that have fewer samples. We can get this kind of weight by taking the inverse of the count of each bin. If there are C LCLids in a bin, the weight of the bin can be $\frac{1}{C}$. The *Further reading* section has a link where you can read more about weighted random sampling and the different algorithms used for the purpose.

`TimeSeriesDataset` has an internal index, which is a dataframe with all the samples it can draw from the dataset. We can use that to construct our array of weights:

```
# TimeSeriesDataset stores a df as the index over which it
samples
df = training.index.copy()
# Adding a bin column to it to represent the bins we have
created
df['bins'] = [f"bin_{i}" for i in np.digitize(df["count"].
values, bins)]
# Calculate Weights as inverse counts of the bins
weights = 1/df['bins'].value_counts(normalize=True)
# Assigning the weights back to the df so that we have an array
of
# weights in the same shape as the index over which we are
going to sample
weights = weights.reset_index().rename(columns={"index":"bins",
"bins":"weight"})
df = df.merge(weights, on='bins', how='left')
probabilities = df.weight.values
```

This way ensures that the `probabilities` array has the same length as the internal index over which `TimeSeriesDataset` samples, and that is a mandatory requirement when using this technique – each possible window should have a corresponding weight attached to it.

Now that we have this weight, there is an easy way to put this into practice. We can use `WeightedRandomSampler` from PyTorch, which has been created specifically for this purpose:

```
from torch.utils.data import WeightedRandomSampler
sampler = WeightedRandomSampler(probabilities,
len(probabilities))
```

Using and visualizing the dataloader with WeightedRandomSampler

Now, we can use this sampler in the dataloaders we create from `TimeSeriesDataset`:

```
train_dataloader = training.to_dataloader(train=True, batch_
size=batch_size, num_workers=0, sampler=sampler)
```

Let's visualize the first 50 batches like before and see the difference:

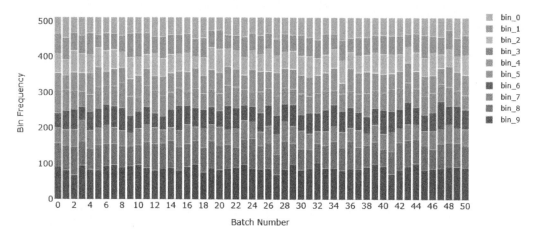

Figure 15.11 – Stacked bar chart of batch distribution with weighted random sampling

Now we can see a more uniform distribution of bins in each batch. Let's also see the results after training the model using this new data loader:

Algorithm	MAE	MSE	meanMASE	Forecast Bias
simple	0.0854	0.0308	1.0787	1.41%
simple+time_varying	0.0851	0.0310	1.0764	0.73%
simple+static+time_varying	0.0843	0.0297	1.0685	0.94%
simple+static+time_varying+scale	0.0822	0.0298	1.0395	-3.20%
simple+static+time_varying+num_sampler	0.0815	0.0297	1.0372	-4.06%

Figure 15.12 – Aggregate results using the static, time-varying,
and scale features along with batch samplers

Looks like the sampler also made a good improvement in the model in all metrics, except `Forecast Bias`. Although we have not achieved better results than the GFM(ML) (which had an MAE of 0.079581), we are close enough. Maybe with some hyperparameter tuning, partitioning, or stronger models, we might reach closer to that number, or we may not. We used a custom sampling option to make the length of the time series balanced in a batch. We can use the same techniques to balance it on other aspects such as the level of consumption, region, or any other aspect that seems relevant. As always in machine learning, we will need to go with our experiments to say anything for sure, and all we need to do is form our hypothesis about the problem statement and construct experiments to validate those hypotheses.

And with that, we have come to the end of yet another practical-heavy (and compute-heavy) chapter. Congratulations on making it through the chapter; feel free to go back and refer to any points that didn't quite land yet.

Summary

After having built a strong foundation on deep learning models in the last few chapters, we started to look at a new paradigm of global models in the context of deep learning models. We learned how to use `PyTorch Forecasting`, an open source library for forecasting using deep learning, and used the feature-filled `TimeSeriesDataset` to start developing our own models.

We started off with a very simple LSTM in the global context and saw how we can add time-varying information, static information, and the scale of individual time series to the features to make models better. We closed by looking at an alternating sampling procedure for mini-batches that helps us present a more balanced view of the problem in each batch. This chapter is by no means an exhaustive list of all such techniques to make the forecasting models better. Instead, this chapter aims to build the right kind of thinking that is necessary to work on your own models and make them work better than before.

And now that we have a strong foundation in deep learning and global models, it is time to take a look at a few specialized deep learning architectures that have been proposed over the years for time series forecasting in the next chapter.

Further reading

You can check out the following sources for further reading:

- *How to use custom data and implement custom models and metrics* (PyTorch Forecasting): `https://pytorch-forecasting.readthedocs.io/en/stable/tutorials/building.html`

- *Random Sampling from Databases* by Frank Olken, Page 22-23: `https://dsf.berkeley.edu/papers/UCB-PhD-olken.pdf`

16
Specialized Deep Learning Architectures for Forecasting

Our journey through the world of **deep learning** (**DL**) is coming to an end. In the previous chapter, we were introduced to the global paradigm of forecasting and saw how we can make a simple model such as a **Recurrent Neural Network** (**RNN**) perform close to the high benchmark set by global machine learning models. In this chapter, we are going to review a few popular DL architectures that were designed specifically for time series forecasting. With these more sophisticated model architectures, we will be better equipped at handling problems in the wild that call for more powerful models than vanilla RNNs and LSTMs.

In this chapter, we will be covering these main topics:

- The need for specialized architectures
- Neural Basis Expansion Analysis for Interpretable Time Series Forecasting (N-BEATS)
- Neural Basis Expansion Analysis for Interpretable Time Series Forecasting with Exogenous Variables (N-BEATSx)
- Neural Hierarchical Interpolation for Time Series Forecasting (N-HiTS)
- Informer
- Autoformer
- Temporal Fusion Transformer (TFT)
- Interpretability
- Probabilistic forecasting

Technical requirements

You will need to set up an Anaconda environment by following the instructions in the *Preface* to get a working environment with all the packages and datasets required for the code in this book.

The code associated with this chapter can be found at `https://github.com/PacktPublishing/Modern-Time-Series-Forecasting-with-Python/tree/main/notebooks/Chapter16`.

You will need to run the following notebooks for this chapter:

- `02-Preprocessing London Smart Meter Dataset.ipynb` in `Chapter02`
- `01-Setting up Experiment Harness.ipynb` in `Chapter04`
- `01-Feature Engineering.ipynb` in `Chapter06`

The need for specialized architectures

Inductive bias, or learning bias, refers to a set of assumptions a learning algorithm makes to generalize the function it learns on training data to unseen data. Deep learning is thought to be a completely data-driven approach where the feature engineering and final task are learned end-to-end, thus avoiding the inductive bias that the modelers bake in while designing the features. But that view is not entirely correct. These inductive biases, which used to be put in through the features, now make their way through the design of architecture. Every DL architecture has its own inductive biases, which is why some types of models perform better on some types of data. For instance, a **Convolutional Neural Network (CNN)** works well on images, but not as much on sequences because the spatial inductive bias and translational equivariance that the CNN brings to the table are most effective on images.

In an ideal world, we would have an infinite supply of good, annotated data and we would be able to learn entirely data-driven networks with no strong inductive biases. But sadly, in the real world, we will never have enough data to learn such complex functions. This is where designing the right kind of inductive biases makes or breaks the DL system. We used to heavily rely on RNNs for sequences and they had a strong auto-regressive inductive bias baked into them. But later, Transformers, which have a much weaker inductive bias for sequences, came in and with large amounts of data, they were able to learn better functions for sequences. Therefore, this decision about how strong an inductive bias we bake into models is an important question in designing DL architectures.

Over the years, many DL architectures have been proposed specifically for time series forecasting and each of them has its own inductive biases attached to it. We'll not be able to review every single one of those models, but we will cover the major ones that made a lasting impact on the field. We will also look at how we can use a few open source libraries to train those models on our data. We will exclusively focus on models that can handle the global modeling paradigm, directly or indirectly. This is because of the infeasibility of training separate models for each time series when we are forecasting at scale.

We are going to look at a few popular architectures developed for time series forecasting. One of the major factors influencing the inclusion of a model is also the availability of stable open source frameworks that support these models. This is in no way a complete list because there are many architectures we are not covering here. I'll try and share a few links in the *Further reading* section to get you started on your journey of exploration.

Now, without further ado, let's get started on the first model on the list.

Neural Basis Expansion Analysis for Interpretable Time Series Forecasting (N-BEATS)

The first model that used some components from DL (we can't call it DL because it is essentially a mix of DL and classical statistics) and made a splash in the field was a model that won the M4 competition (univariate) in 2018. This was a model by *Slawek Smyl* from Uber (at the time) and was a Frankenstein-style mix of exponential smoothing and an RNN, dubbed **ES-RNN** (*Further reading* has links to a newer and faster implementation of the model that uses GPU acceleration). This led to Makridakis et al. putting forward an argument that "*hybrid approaches and combinations of methods are the way forward.*" The creators of the **N-BEATS** model aspired to challenge this conclusion by designing a pure DL architecture for time series forecasting. They succeeded in this when they created a model that beat all other methods in the M4 competition (although they didn't publish it in time to participate in the competition). It is a very unique architecture, taking a lot of inspiration from signal processing. Let's take a deeper look and understand the architecture.

> **Reference check**
>
> The research paper by Makridakis et al. and the blog post by Slawek Smyl are cited in the *References* section as *1* and *2*, respectively.

We need to establish a bit of context and terminology before moving ahead with the explanation. The core problem that they are solving is univariate forecasting, which means it is similar to classical methods such as exponential smoothing and ARIMA in the sense that it takes only the history of the time series to generate a forecast. There is no provision to include other covariates in the model. The model is shown a window from the history and is asked to predict the next few timesteps. The window of history is referred to as the **lookback period** and the future timesteps are the **forecast period**.

The architecture of N-BEATS

The N-BEATS architecture is different from the existing architectures (at the time) in a few aspects:

- Instead of the common encoder-decoder (or sequence-to-sequence) formulation, N-BEATS formulates the problem as a multivariate regression problem.

- Most of the other architectures at the time were relatively shallow (~5 LSTM layers). However, N-BEATS used the residual principle to stack many basic blocks (we will explain this shortly) and the paper has shown that we can stack up to 150 layers and still facilitate efficient learning.

- The model lets us extend it to human interpretable output, still in a principled way.

Let's look at the architecture and go deeper:

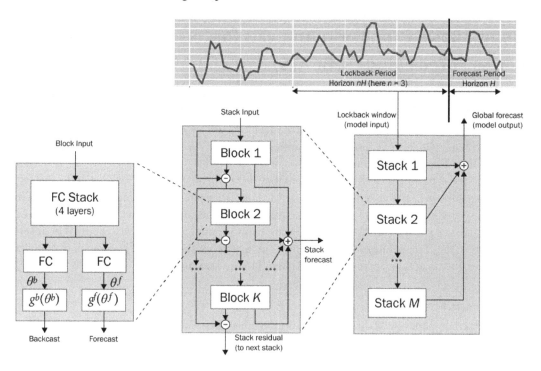

Figure 16.1 – N-BEATS architecture

We can see three columns of *rectangular blocks*, each one an exploded view of another. Let's start at the left most (which is the most granular view) and then go up step by step, building up to the architecture. At the top, there is a representative time series, which has a lookback window and a forecast period.

Blocks

The fundamental learning unit in N-BEATS is a **block**. Each block, l, takes in an input, (x_l), of the size of the lookback period and generates two outputs: a forecast, $(\hat{y}_l)$, and a backcast, $(\hat{x}_l)$. The backcast is the block's own best prediction of the lookback period. It is synonymous with fitted values in the classical sense; they tell us how the stack would have predicted the lookback window using the function it has learned. The block input is first processed by a stack of four standard fully connected layers (complete with a bias term and non-linear activation), transforming the input into a hidden representation, h_l. Now, this hidden representation is transformed by two separate linear layers (no bias or non-linear activation) to something the paper calls expansion coefficients for the backcast and forecast, θ_l^b and θ_l^f, respectively. The last part of the block takes these expansion coefficients and maps them to the output using a set of basis layers (g_l^b and g_l^f). We will talk about the basis layers in a bit more detail later, but for now, just understand that they take the expansion coefficients and transform them into the desired outputs ($\widehat{y}_l$ and $\widehat{x}_l$).

Stacks

Now, let's move one layer up the abstraction to the middle column of *Figure 16.1*. It shows how different blocks are arranged in a **stack**, s. All the blocks in a stack share the same kind of basis layers and therefore are grouped as a stack. As we saw earlier, each block has two outputs, $\widehat{y}_l$ and $\widehat{x}_l$. The blocks are arranged in a residual manner, each block processing and cleaning the time series step by step. The input to a block, l, is $x_l = x_{l-1} - \widehat{x_{l-1}}$. At each step, the backcast generated by the block is subtracted from the input to that block before it's passed on to the next layer. And all the forecast outputs of all the blocks in a stack are added up to make the *stack forecast*:

$$\widehat{y^s} = \sum_l \widehat{y_l^s}$$

The residual backcast from the last block in a stack is the *stack residual* (x^s).

The overall architecture

With that, we can move to the rightmost column of *Figure 16.1*, which shows the top-level view of the architecture. We saw that each stack has two outputs – a stack forecast (y^s) and stack residual (x^s). There can be N stacks that make up the N-BEATS model. Each stack is chained together so that for any stack (s), the stack residual out of the previous stack (x^{s-1}) is the input and the stack generates two outputs: the stack forecast (y^s) and the stack residual (x^s). Finally, the N-BEATS forecast, $\widehat{y}$, is the additive sum of all the stack forecasts:

$$\widehat{y} = \sum_{s=1}^{N} \widehat{y^s}$$

Now that we have understood what the model is doing, we need to come back to one point that we left for later – **basis functions**.

> **Disclaimer**
>
> The explanation here is to mostly aid intuition, so we might be hand-waving over a few mathematical concepts. For a more rigorous treatment of the subject, you should refer to mathematical books/articles that cover the topic. For example, *Functions as Vector Spaces* from the *Further reading* section and *Function Spaces* (`https://cns.gatech.edu/~predrag/courses/PHYS-6124-12/StGoChap2.pdf`).

Basis functions and interpretability

To understand what basis functions are, we need to understand a concept from linear algebra. We talked about vector spaces in *Chapter 11, Introduction to Deep Learning*, and gave you a geometric interpretation of vectors and vector spaces. We talked about how a vector is a point in the n-dimensional vector space. We had that discussion regarding regular Euclidean space (R^n), which is intended to represent physical space. Euclidean spaces are defined with an origin and an orthonormal basis. An orthonormal basis is a unit vector (magnitude=1) and they are orthogonal (in simple intuition, at 90 degrees) to each other. Therefore, a vector, $A = \begin{bmatrix} 5 \\ 2 \end{bmatrix}$, can be written as $5\hat{\imath} + 2\hat{\jmath}$, where $\hat{\imath}$ and $\hat{\jmath}$ are the orthonormal basis. You may remember this from high school.

Now, there is a branch of mathematics that views a function as a point in a vector space (at which point we call it a functional space). This comes from the fact that all the mathematical conditions that need to be satisfied for a vector space (things such as additivity, associativity, and so on) are valid if we consider functions instead of points. To better drive that intuition, let's consider a function, $f(x) = 2x + 4x^2$. We can consider this function as a vector in the function space with basis x and x^2. Now, the coefficients, 2 and 4, can be changed to give us different functions; this can be any real number from -∞ to +∞. This space of all functions that can have a basis of x and x^2 is the functional space, and every function in the function space can be defined as a linear combination of the basis functions. We can have the basis of any arbitrary function, which gives us a lot of flexibility. From a machine learning perspective, searching for the best function in this functional space automatically means that we are restricting the function search so that we have some properties defined by the basis functions.

Coming back to N-BEATS, we talked about the expansion coefficients, θ^b and θ^f, which are mapped to the output using a set of basis layers (g_l^b and g_l^f). A basis layer can also be thought of as a basis function because we know that a layer is nothing but a function that maps its inputs to its outputs. Therefore, by learning the expansion coefficients, we are essentially searching for the best function that can represent the output but is constrained by the basis functions we choose.

There are two modes in which N-BEATS operates: *generic* and *interpretable*. The N-BEATS paper shows that under both modes, N-BEATS managed to beat the best in the M4 competition. Generic mode is where we do not have any basis function constraining the function search. We can also think of this as setting the basis function to be the identity function. So, in this mode, we are leaving the function completely learned by the model through a linear projection of the basis coefficients. This mode lacks human interpretability because we don't have any idea how the different functions are learned and what each stack signifies.

But if we have fixed basis functions that constrain the function space, we can bring in more interpretability. For instance, if we have a basis function that constrains the output to represent the trends for all the blocks in a stack, we can say that the forecast output of that stack represents the trend component. Similarly, if we have another basis function that constrains the output to represent the seasonality for all the blocks in a stack, we can say that the forecast output of the stack represents seasonality.

This is exactly what the paper has proposed as well. They have defined specific basis functions that capture trend and seasonality, and including such blocks makes the final forecast more interpretable by giving us a decomposition. The trend basis function is a polynomial of a small degree, p. So, as long as p is low, such as 1, 2, or 3, it forces the forecast output to mimic the trend component. And for the seasonality basis function, the authors chose a Fourier basis (similar to the one we saw in *Chapter 6, Feature Engineering for Time Series Forecasting*). This forces the forecast output to be functions of these sinusoidal basis functions that mimic seasonality. In other words, the model learns to combine these sinusoidal waves with different coefficients to reconstruct the seasonality pattern as best as possible.

For a deeper understanding of these basis functions and how they are structured, I have linked to a *Kaggle notebook* in the *Further reading* section that provides a clear explanation of the trend and seasonality basis functions. The associated notebook also has an additional section that visualizes the first few basis functions of seasonality. Along with the original paper, these additional readings will help you solidify your understanding.

N-BEATS wasn't designed to be a global model, but it does well in the global setting. The M4 competition was a collection of unrelated time series and the N-BEATS model was trained so that the model was exposed to all those series and learned a common function to forecast each time series in the dataset. This, along with ensembling multiple N-BEATS models with different lookback windows, was the success formula for the M4 competition.

> **Reference check**
>
> The research paper by Boris Oreshkin et al (N-BEATS) is cited in the *References* section as *3*.

Forecasting with N-BEATS

N-BEATS is implemented in PyTorch Forecasting. We can use the same framework we worked with in *Chapter 15, Strategies for Global Deep Learning Forecasting Models*, and extend it to train N-BEATS on our data. First, let's look at the initialization parameters of the implementation.

The `Nbeats` class in PyTorch Forecasting has the following parameters:

- `stack_types`: This defines the number of stacks that we need to have in the N-BEATS model. This should be a list of strings (*generic*, *trend*, or *seasonality*) denoting the number and type of stacks. Examples include `["trend", "seasonality"]`, `["trend", "seasonality", "generic"]`, `["generic", "generic", "generic"]`, and so on. However, if the entire network is generic, we can just have a single generic stack with more blocks as well.

- `num_blocks`: This is a list of integers signifying the number of blocks in each stack that we have defined. If we had defined `stack_types` as `["trend", "seasonality"]`, and we want three blocks each, we can set `num_blocks` to `[3,3]`.

- `num_block_layers`: This is a list of integers signifying the number of FC layers with ReLU activation in each block. The recommended value is 4 and the length of the list should be equal to the number of stacks we have defined.

- `width`: This sets the width or the number of units in the FC layers in each block. This is also a list of integers with lengths equal to the number of stacks defined.

- `sharing`: This is a list of Booleans signifying whether the weights generating the expansion coefficients are shared with other blocks in a stack. It is recommended to share the weights in the interpretable stacks and not share them in the generic stacks.

- `expansion_coefficient_length`: This represents the size of the expansion coefficients (θ). Depending on the kind of block, the intuitive meaning of this parameter changes. For the trend block, this means the number of polynomials we are using in our basis functions. And for the seasonality, this lets us control how quickly the underlying Fourier basis functions vary. The Fourier basis functions are sinusoidal basis functions with different frequencies; if they have a large `expansion_coefficient_length`, this means that subsequent basis functions will have a larger frequency than if you had a smaller `expansion_coefficient_length`. This is a parameter that we can tune as a hyperparameter. A typical range can be between 2 and 10.

There are a few other parameters, but these are not as important. A full list of parameters and their descriptions can be found at `https://pytorch-forecasting.readthedocs.io/en/stable/api/pytorch_forecasting.models.nbeats.NBeats.html`.

Since the strength of the model is in forecasting slightly longer durations, we move from one-step ahead to one-day ahead (48 steps) forecasting. The only change we have to implement is changing the `max_prediction_length` parameter to `48` instead of `1` while initializing `TimeSeriesDataset`.

> **Notebook alert**
>
> The complete code for training N-BEATS can be found in the `01-N-BEATS.ipynb` notebook in the `Chapter16` folder. There are two variables in the notebook that act as switches: `TRAIN_SUBSAMPLE = True` makes the notebook run for a subset of 10 households, while `train_model = True` makes the notebook train different models (warning: training the model on full data takes hours). `train_model = False` loads the trained model weights (not included in the repository but saved every time you run training) and predicts on them.

Interpreting N-BEATS forecasting

N-BEATS, if we are running it in the interpretable model, also gives us more interpretability by separating the forecast into trend and seasonality. To get the interpretable output, we only need to make a small change in the `predict` function – we must change `mode="prediction"` to `mode="raw"` in the parameters:

```
best_model.predict(val_dataloader, mode="raw")
```

This will return us a `namedtuple` from which trend can be accessed using the *trend* key, seasonality from the *seasonality* key, and total predictions from the *prediction* key. Let's see how one of the household predictions decomposed:

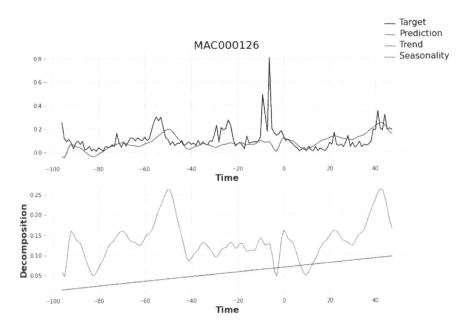

Figure 16.2 – Decomposed predictions from N-BEATS (interpretable)

With all its success, N-BEATS was still a univariate model. It was not able to take in any external information, apart from its history. This was fine for the M4 competition, where all the time series in question were also univariate. But many real-world time series problems come with additional explanatory variables (or exogenous variables). Let's look at a slight modification that was made to N-BEATS that enabled exogenous variables.

Neural Basis Expansion Analysis for Interpretable Time Series Forecasting with Exogenous Variables (N-BEATSx)

Olivares et al. proposed an extension of the N-BEATS model by making it compatible with exogenous variables. The overall structure is the same (with blocks, stacks, and residual connections) as N-BEATS (*Figure 16.1*), so we will only be focusing on the key differences and additions that the **N-BEATSx** model puts forward.

> **Reference check**
>
> The research paper by Olivares et al. (N-BEATSx) is cited in the *References* section as *4*.

Handling exogenous variables

In N-BEATS, the input to a block was the lookback window, y^b. But here, the input to a block is both the lookback window, y^b, and the array of exogenous variables, X. These exogenous variables can be of two types: time-varying and static. The static variables are encoded using a static feature encoder. This is nothing but a single-layer FC that encodes the static information into a dimension specified by the user. Now, the encoded static information, the time-varying exogenous variables, and the lookback window are concatenated to form the input for a block so that the hidden state representation, h_l, of block l is not $FC(y^b)$ like in N-BEATS, but $FC([y^b; X])$, where $[;]$ represents concatenation. This way, the exogenous information is part of the input to every block as it is concatenated with the residual at each step.

Exogenous blocks

In addition to this, the paper also proposes a new kind of block – an *exogenous block*. The exogenous block takes in the concatenated lookback window and exogenous variables (just like any other block) as input and produces a backcast and forecast:

$$\overline{y_l^{exog}} = \sum_{i=0}^{N_x} X_\ell^i \theta_l^{exog}$$

Here, N_x is the number of exogenous features.

Here, we can see that the exogenous forecast is the linear combination of the exogenous variables and that the weights for this linear combination are learned by the expansion coefficients, θ^{exog}. The paper refers to this configuration as the interpretable exogenous block because by using the expansion weights, we can define the importance of each exogenous variable and even figure out the exact part of the forecast, which is because of a particular exogenous variable.

N-BEATSx also has a generic version (which is not interpretable) of the exogenous block. In this block, the exogenous variables are passed through an encoder that learns a context vector, C_l, and the forecast is generated using the following formula:

$$\overline{y_l^{exog}} = \sum_{i=0}^{N_x} C_\ell^i \theta_l^{exog}$$

They proposed two encoders: a **Temporal Convolutional Network** (TCN) and **WaveNet** (a network similar to the TCN, but with dilation to expand the receptive field). The *Further reading* section contains resources if you wish to learn more about WaveNet, an architecture that originated in the sound domain.

> **Additional information**
>
> N-BEATSx is not implemented in PyTorch Forecasting, but we can find it in another library for forecasting using DL – `neuralforecast` by Nixtla. One feature that `neuralforecast` lacks (which is kind of a deal breaker to me) is that it doesn't support categorical features. So, we will have to encode the categorical features into numerical representations (like we did in *Chapter 10, Global Forecasting Models*) before using `neuralforecast`. Also, the documentation of the library isn't great, which means we need to dive into the code base and hack it to make it work.

The research paper also showed that N-BEATSx outperformed N-BEATS, ES-RNN, and other benchmarks on electricity price forecasting considerably.

Continuing with the legacy of N-BEATS, we will now talk about another modification to the architecture that makes it suitable for long-term forecasting.

Neural Hierarchical Interpolation for Time Series Forecasting (N-HiTS)

Although there has been a good amount of work from DL to tackle time series forecasting, very little focus has been on long-horizon forecasting. Despite recent progress, long-horizon forecasting remains a challenge because of two reasons:

- The expressiveness required to truly capture the variation
- The computational complexity

Attention-based methods (Transformers) and N-BEATS-like methods scale quadratically in memory and the computational cost concerning the forecasting horizon.

The authors claim that N-HiTS drastically cuts long-forecasting compute costs while simultaneously showing 25% accuracy improvements compared to existing Transformer-based architectures across a large array of multi-variate forecasting datasets.

> **Reference check**
>
> The research paper by Challu et al. on N-HiTS is cited in the *References* section as 5.

The Architecture of N-HiTS

N-HiTS can be considered as an alteration to N-BEATS because the two share a large part of their architectures. *Figure 16.1*, which shows the N-BEATS architecture, is still valid for N-HiTS. N-HiTS also has stacks of blocks arranged in a residual manner; it differs only in the kind of blocks it uses. For instance, there is no provision for interpretable blocks. All the blocks in N-HiTS are generic. While

N-BEATS tries to decompose the signal into different patterns (trend, seasonality, and so on), N-HiTS tries to decompose the signal into multiple frequencies and forecast them separately. To enable this, a few key improvements have been proposed:

- Multi-rate data sampling

- Hierarchical interpolation

- Synchronizing the rate of input sampling with a scale of output interpolation across the blocks

Multi-rate data sampling

N-HiTS incorporates sub-sampling layers before the fully connected blocks so that the resolution of the input to each block is different. This is similar to smoothing the signal with different resolutions so that each block is looking at a pattern that occurs at different resolutions – for instance, if one block looks at the input every day, another block looks at the output every week, and so on. This way, when arranged with different blocks looking at different resolutions, the model will be able to predict patterns that occur in those resolutions. This significantly reduces the memory footprint and the computation required as well, because instead of looking at all H steps of the lookback window, we are looking at smaller series (such as H/2, H/4, and so on).

N-HiTS accomplishes this using a Max Pooling or Average Pooling layer of kernel size k_l on the lookback window. A pooling operation is similar to a convolution operation, but the function that is used is non-learnable. In *Chapter 12, Building Blocks of Deep Learning for Time Series*, we learned about convolutions, kernels, stride, and so on. While a convolution uses weights that are learned from data while training, a pooling operation uses a non-learnable and fixed function to aggregate the data in the receptive field of a kernel. Common examples of these functions are the maximum, average, sum, and so on. N-HiTS uses MaxPool1d or AvgPool1d (in PyTorch terminology) with different kernel sizes for different blocks. Each pooling operation also has a stride equal to the kernel, resulting in non-overlapping windows over which we do the aggregation operation. To refresh our memory, let's see what max pooling with kernel=2 and stride=2 looks like:

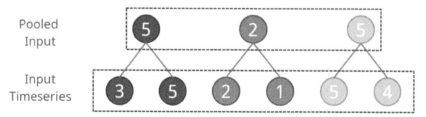

Figure 16.3 – Max pooling on one dimension – kernel=2, stride=2

Therefore, a larger kernel size will tend to cut more high-frequency (or small-timescale) components from the input. This way, the block is forced to focus on larger-scale patterns. The paper calls this **multi-rate signal sampling**.

Hierarchical interpolation

In a standard multi-step forecasting setting, the model must forecast H timesteps. And as H becomes larger, the compute requirements increase and lead to an explosion of expressive power the model needs to have. Training a model with such a large expressive power, without overfitting, is a challenge in itself. To combat these issues, N-HiTS proposes a technique called **temporal interpolation**.

The pooled input (which we saw in the previous section) goes into the block along with the usual mechanism to generate expansion coefficients and finally gets converted into forecast output. But here, instead of setting the dimension of the expansion coefficients as H, N-HiTS sets them as $r_l \times H$, where r_l is the **expressiveness ratio**. This parameter essentially reduces the forecast output dimension and thus controls the issues we discussed in the previous paragraph. To recover the original sampling rate and predict all the H points in the forecast horizon, we can use an interpolation function. There are many options for the interpolation functions – linear, nearest neighbor, cubic, and so on. All these options can easily be implemented in `PyTorch` using the `interpolate` function.

Synchronizing the input sampling and output interpolation

In addition to proposing the input sampling through pooling and output interpolation, N-HiTS also proposes to arrange them in different blocks in a particular way. The authors argue that hierarchical interpolation can only happen the right way if the expressiveness ratios are distributed across blocks in a manner that is synchronized with the multi-rate sampling. Blocks closer to the input should have a smaller expressiveness ratio, r_l, and larger kernel sizes, k_l. This means that the blocks closer to the input will generate larger resolution patterns (because of aggressive interpolation) while being forced to look at aggressively subsampled input signals. The paper proposes exponentially increasing expressiveness ratios as we move from the initial block to the last block to handle a wide range of frequency bands. The official N-HiTS implementation uses the following formula to set the expressiveness ratios and pooling kernels:

```
pooling_sizes = np.exp2(
    np.round(np.linspace(0.49, np.log2(prediction_length / 2),
n_stacks))
)
pooling_sizes = [int(x) for x in pooling_sizes[::-1]]
downsample_frequencies = [
    min(prediction_length, int(np.power(x, 1.5))) for x in
pooling_sizes
]
```

We can also provide explicit `pooling_sizes` and `downsampling_fequences` to reflect known cycles of the time series (weekly seasonality, monthly seasonality, and so on). The core principle of N-BEATS (one block removing the effect it captures from the signal and passing it on to the next block) is used here as well so that, at each level, the patterns or frequencies that a block captures are removed from the input signal before being passed on to the next block. In the end, the final forecast is the sum of all such individual block forecasts.

Forecasting with N-HiTS

N-HiTS is implemented in PyTorch Forecasting. We can use the same framework we were working with in *Chapter 15, Strategies for Global Deep Learning Forecasting Models,* and extend it to train *N-HiTS* on our data. What's even better is that the implementation supports exogenous variables, the same way N-BEATSx handles exogenous variables (although without the exogenous block). First, let's look at the initialization parameters of the implementation.

The `NHiTS` class in PyTorch Forecasting has the following parameters:

- `n_blocks`: This is a list of integers signifying the number of blocks to be used in each stack. For instance, `[1,1,1]` means there will be three stacks with one block each.

- `n_layers`: This is either a list of integers or a single integer signifying the number of FC layers with a ReLU activation in each block. The recommended value is 2.

- `hidden_size`: This sets the width or the number of units in the FC layers in each block.

- `static_hidden_size`: The static features are encoded using an FC encoder into a dimension that is set by this parameter. We covered this in detail in the *Neural Basis Expansion Analysis for Interpretable Time Series Forecasting with Exogenous Variables (N-BEATSx)* section.

- `shared_weights`: This signifies whether the weights generating the expansion coefficients are shared with other blocks in a stack. It is recommended to share the weights in the interpretable stacks and not share them in the generic stacks.

- `pooling_sizes`: This is a list of integers that defines the pooling size (k_l) for each stack. This is an optional parameter, and if provided, we can have more control over how the pooling happens in the different stacks. Using an ordering of higher to lower improves results.

- `pooling_mode`: This defines the kind of pooling to be used. It should be either `'max'` or `'average'`.

- `downsample_frequencies`: This is a list of integers that defines the expressiveness ratios (r_l) for each stack. This is an optional parameter, and if provided, we can have more control over how the interpolation happens in the different stacks.

> **Notebook alert**
>
> The complete code for training N-HiTS can be found in the `02-N-HiTS.ipynb` notebook in the `Chapter16` folder. There are two variables in the notebook that act as switches – `TRAIN_SUBSAMPLE = True` makes the notebook run for a subset of 10 households, while `train_model = True` makes the notebook train different models (warning: training the model on full data takes hours). `train_model = False` loads the trained model weights (not included in the repository but saved every time you run training) and predicts on them.

Now, let's shift our focus and look at a few modifications of the Transformer model to make it better for time series forecasting.

Informer

Recently, Transformer models have shown superior performance in capturing long-term patterns than standard RNNs. One of the major factors of that is the fact that self-attention, which powers Transformers, can reduce the length that the relevant sequence information has to be held on to before it can be used for prediction. In other words, in an RNN, if the timestep 12 steps before holds important information, that information has to be stored in the RNN through 12 updates before it can be used for prediction. But with self-attention in Transformers, the model is free to create a shortcut between lag 12 and the current step directly because of the lack of recurrence in the structure.

But the same self-attention is also the reason why we can't scale vanilla Transformers to long sequences. In the previous section, we discussed how long-term forecasting is a challenge because of two reasons: the expressiveness required to truly capture the variation and computational complexity. Self-attention, with its quadratic computational complexity, contributes to the second reason. Scaling Transformers on very long sequences will require us to pour computation into the model using multi-GPU setups, which makes real-world deployment a challenge, especially when good alternative models such as ARIMA, LightGBM, and N-BEATS exist.

The research community has recognized this challenge and has put a lot of effort into devising efficient transformers through many techniques such as downsampling, low-rank approximations, sparse attention, and so on. For a detailed account of such techniques, refer to the link for *Efficient Transformers: A Survey* in the *Further reading* section.

> **Reference check**
>
> The research paper by Zhou et al. on the Informer model is cited in the *References* section as *8*.

The architecture of the Informer model

The Informer model is a modification of Transformers. The following are its major contributions:

- **Uniform Input Representation**: A methodical way to include the history of the series along with other information, which will help in capturing long-term signals such as the week, month, holidays, and so on

- **ProbSparse**: An efficient attention mechanism based on information theory

- **Attention distillation**: A mechanism to provide dominating attention scores while stacking multiple layers and also reduce computational complexity

- **Generative-style decoder**: Used to generate the long-term horizon in a single forward pass instead of via dynamic recurrence

Let's take a look at the overall architecture (*Figure 16.4*) to see how they fit together, and then look at them in more detail:

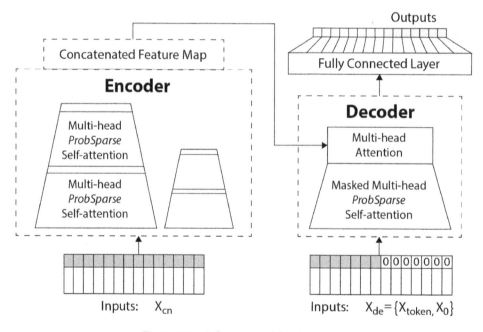

Figure 16.4 – Informer model architecture

The overall architecture is akin to a standard encoder-decoder transformer model. The encoder takes in the inputs and uses multi-headed attention to generate features that are passed to the decoder, which, in turn, uses these features to generate the forecast. Special modifications are made to the architecture in each of these steps. Let's review them in detail.

Uniform Input Representation

RNNs capture time series patterns with their recurrent structure, so they only need the sequence; they don't need information about the timestamp to extract the patterns. However, the self-attention in Transformers is done via point-wise operations that are performed in sets (the order doesn't matter in a set). Typically, we include positional encodings to capture the order of the sequence. Instead of using positional encodings, we can use richer information, such as hierarchical timestamp information (such as weeks, months, years, and so on). This is what the authors proposed through **Uniform Input Representation**.

Uniform Input Representation uses three types of embeddings to capture the history of the time series, the sequence of values in the time series, and the global timestamp information. The sequence of values in the time series is captured by the standard positional embedding of the **d_model** dimension.

Uniform Input Representation uses a one-dimensional convolutional layer with `kernel=3` and `stride=1` to project the history (which is scalar or one-dimensional) into an embedding of d_model dimensions. This is referred to as **value embedding**.

The global timestamp information is embedded by a learnable embedding of d_model dimensions with limited vocabulary in a mechanism that is identical to embedding categorical variables into fixed-size vectors (*Chapter 15, Strategies for Global Deep Learning Forecasting Models*). This is referred to as **temporal embedding**.

Now that we have three embeddings of the same dimension, d_model, all we need to do is add them together to get the Uniform Input Representation.

ProbSparse attention

In *Chapter 14, Attention and Transformers for Time Series*, we defined a generalized attention model as follows:

$$\mathcal{A}(q, K, V) = \sum_i p\big(a(k_i, q)\big) \times v_i$$

Here, a is an **alignment function** that calculates a similarity or a notion of similarity between the queries and keys, p is a **distribution function** that converts this score into attention weights that sum up to 1, and q, k, and v are the query, key, and values of the attention mechanism, respectively.

Additional information

The original Transformer uses scaled dot product attention, along with different projection matrices for the query, key, and values. The formula can be written like so:

$$\mathcal{A}(q, K, V) = softmax\left(\frac{qW_q(kW_k)^T}{\sqrt{d_k}}\right)vW_v$$

Here, W_q, W_k, and W_v are learnable projection matrices for the query, key, and values, respectively, and d_k is the attention dimension. We know that $softmax(z_i)$ is defined as follows:

$$\frac{e^{z_i}}{\sum_{j=1}^{K} e^{z_j}}$$

Let's denote qW_q as q^* and kW_k as k^*. So, using the *softmax* expansion, we can write the previous formula like so:

$$\mathcal{A}(q_i, K, V) = \sum_j \frac{e^{\langle q_i^*, k_j^* \rangle / d_k}}{\sum_l e^{\langle q_i^*, k_l^* \rangle / d_k}} v_j^*$$

Here, $\langle \cdot \rangle$ denotes the inner product. In 2019, Tsai et al. proposed an alternate view of the attention mechanism using kernels. The math and history behind kernels are quite extensive and are outside the scope of this book. Just know that a kernel is a special kind of function, similar to a similarity function. In this case, if we define $e^{\langle q_i^*, k_j^* \rangle / d_k}$ as $k(q_i^*, k_j^*)$ (which is an asymmetric exponential kernel), the attention equation becomes like this:

$$\mathcal{A}(q_i, K, V) = \sum_j \frac{k(q_i^*, k_j^*)}{\sum_l k(q_i^*, k_l^*)} v_j^*$$

This interpretation leads to a probabilistic view of attention where the first term is:

$$\sum_j \frac{k(q_i^*, k_j^*)}{\sum_l k(q_i^*, k_l^*)})$$

Which can be interpreted as the probability of k^*, given q^*, $P(k_j^* | q_i^*)$.

The attention equation can also be written as follows:

$$\mathcal{A}(q_i, K, V) = \mathbb{E}_{P(k_j^* | q_i^*)} v_j$$

Here, $E_{P(k_j^* | q_i^*)}$ is the expectation of the probability of k^*, given q^*. The quadratic computational complexity stems from the calculation of this expectation. We will have to use all the elements in the query and the key to calculate a matrix of probabilities.

Previous studies had revealed that this distribution of self-attention probability has potential sparsity. The authors of the paper also reaffirmed this through their experiments. The essence of this sparsity is that there are only a few query-key pairs that absorb the majority of the probability mass. In other words, there will be a few query-key pairs that will have a high probability; the others will be closer to zero. But the key question is to identify which query-key pairs contribute to major attention without doing the actual calculation.

From the re-written attention equation, the i-th query's attention on all the keys is defined as a probability $P(k_j^*|q_i^*)$ and the output is its composition with values, v. If $P(k_j^*|q_i^*)$ is close to a uniform distribution, $P(k_j^*|q_i^*)$ will be $\frac{1}{L_q}$. This means that self-attention becomes a simple sum of all values. The dominant dot-product query-key pairs encourage the corresponding query's probability distribution to deviate away from the uniform distribution. So, we can measure how *different* the attention distribution $P(k_j^*|q_i^*)$ is from the uniform distribution to measure how dominant a query-key pair is. We can use **Kullback-Liebler (KL) Divergence** to measure this *difference*. KL Divergence is based on information theory and is defined as the information loss that happens when one distribution is approximated using the other. Therefore, the more different the two distributions are, the larger the loss, and thereby KL Divergence. In this manner, it measures how much one distribution diverges from another.

The formula for calculating KL Divergence with the uniform distribution works out to be as follows:

$$ln \sum_{i=1}^{L_K} e^{\frac{q_i k_l^\top}{\sqrt{d}}} - \frac{1}{L_k} \frac{q_i k_j^\top}{\sqrt{d}} - ln L_k$$

The first term here is the **Log-Sum-Exp (LSE)** of `q_i`, on all the keys. LSE is known to have numerical stability issues, so the authors proposed an empirical approximation. The complete proof is in the paper for those who are interested. So, after the approximation, the measure of divergence, $M(q_k, K)$, becomes as follows:

$$M(q_k, K) = max_j \left[\frac{q_i k_l^\top}{\sqrt{d}} \right] - \frac{1}{L_k} \frac{q_i k_j^\top}{\sqrt{d}}$$

This still doesn't absolve us of the quadratic calculation of the dot product of all query-key pairs. But the authors further prove that to approximate this measure of divergence, we only need to randomly sample $U = L_K ln L_Q$ query-key pairs, where L_Q is the length of the query and L_K is the length of the keys. We only calculate the dot product on these sampled pairs and fill zero for the rest of it. Furthermore, we select a sparse *Top-u* from the calculated probabilities as $\overline{Q}$. It is on this $\overline{Q}$, for which we already have the dot products, we calculate the attention distribution. This considerably reduces the computational load on the self-attention calculation.

Attention distillation

One of the consequences of using ProbSparse attention is that we end up with redundant combinations of values. This is mainly because we might keep sampling the same dominant query-key pairs. The authors propose using a distilling operation to privilege the superior ones with dominating features and make the self-attention feature maps more focused layer after layer. They do this by using a mechanism similar to dilated convolutions. The attention output from each layer is passed through a `Conv1d` filter with `kernel = 3` on the time dimension, an activation (the paper suggests ELU), and a `MaxPool1d` with `kernel = 3` and `stride = 2`. More formally, the output of a layer j+1 is as follows:

$$X_{j+1}^t = MaxPool\left(ELU\left(Conv1d\left(\left[X_j^t \right]_{AB} \right) \right) \right)$$

Here, $[\cdot]_{AB}$ represents the attention block.

Generative-style decoder

The standard way of inferencing a Transformer model is by decoding one token at a time. This autoregressive process is time-consuming and repeats a lot of calculations for each step. To alleviate this problem, the Informer model adopts a more generative fashion where the entire forecasting horizon is generated in a single forward pass.

In NLP, it is a popular technique to use a special token (START) to start the dynamic decoding process. Instead of choosing a special token for this purpose, the Informer model chooses a sample from the input sequence, such as an earlier slice before the output window. For instance, if we say the input window is t_1 to t_W, we will sample a sequence of length C from the input, t_{W-C} to t_W, and include this sequence as the starting sequence of the decoder. And to make the model predict the entire horizon in a single forward pass, we can extend the decoder input tensor so that its length is $C + H$, where H is the length of the prediction horizon. The initial C tokens are filled with the sample sequence from the input, and the rest is filled as zeros – that is, $X_{de}^t = Concat(X_{token}^t, X_0^t)$. This is just the target. Although X_0^t has zeros filled in for the prediction horizon, this is just for the target. The other information, such as the global timestamps, is included in X_0^t. Sufficient masking of the attention matrix is also employed so that each position does not attend to future positions, thus maintaining the autoregressive nature of the prediction.

Forecasting with the Informer model

Unfortunately, the **Informer** model has not been implemented in PyTorch Forecasting. However, we have adapted the original implementation by the authors of the paper so that it can work with PyTorch Forecasting; it can be found in `src/dl/ptf_models.py` in a class named `InformerModel`. We can use the same framework we worked with in *Chapter 15, Strategies for Global Deep Learning Forecasting Models*, with this implementation.

> **Important note**
>
> We have to keep in mind that the Informer model does not support exogenous variables. The only additional information it officially supports is global timestamp information such as the week, month, and so on, along with holiday information. We can technically extend this to use any categorical feature (static or dynamic), but no real-valued information is currently supported.

Let's look at the initialization parameters of the implementation.

The `InformerModel` class has the following major parameters:

- `label_len`: This is an integer representing the number of timesteps from the input sequence to sample as a START token while decoding.

- `distil`: This is a Boolean flag for turning the attention distillation off and on.

- `e_layers`: This is an integer representing the number of encoder layers.

- `d_layers`: This is an integer representing the number of decoder layers.

- `n_heads`: This is an integer representing the number of attention heads.

- `d_ff`: This is an integer representing the number of kernels in the one-dimensional convolutional layers used in the encoder and decoder layers.

- `activation`: This is a string that takes in one of two values – `relu` or `gelu`. This is the activation to be used in the encoder and decoder layers.

- `factor`: This is a float value that controls the sparsity of the attention calculation. For a value less than 1, it reduces the number of query-value pairs to calculate the divergence measure and reduces the number of Top-u samples taken than the standard formula for these quantities.

- `dropout`: This is a float between 0 and 1, which determines the strength of the dropout in the network.

> **Notebook alert**
>
> The complete code for training the Informer model can be found in the `03-Informer.ipynb` notebook in the `Chapter16` folder. There are two variables in the notebook that act as switches – `TRAIN_SUBSAMPLE = True` makes the notebook run for a subset of 10 households, while `train_model = True` makes the notebook train different models (warning: training the model on the full data takes hours). `train_model = False` loads the trained model weights (not included in the repository but saved every time you run training) and predicts on them.

Now, let's look at another modification of the Transformer architecture that uses autocorrelation and time series decomposition more effectively.

Autoformer

Autoformer is another model that is designed for long-term forecasting. While the Informer model focuses on making the attention computation more efficient, Autoformer invents a new kind of attention and couples it with aspects from time series decomposition.

The architecture of the Autoformer model

Autoformer has a lot of similarities with the Informer model, so much so that it can be thought of as an extension of the Informer model. Uniform Input Representation and the generative-style decoder have been reused in Autoformer. But instead of ProbSparse attention, Autoformer has an AutoCorrelation mechanism. And instead of attention distillation, Autoformer has a time series decomposition-inspired encoder-decoder setup.

> **Reference check**
>
> The research paper by Wu et al. on Autoformer is cited in the *References* section as 9.

Let's look at the time series decomposition architecture first.

Decomposition architecture

We saw this idea of decomposition back in *Chapter 3, Analyzing and Visualizing Time Series Data*, and even in this chapter (N-BEATS). Autoformer successfully renovated the Transformer architecture into a deep-decomposition architecture:

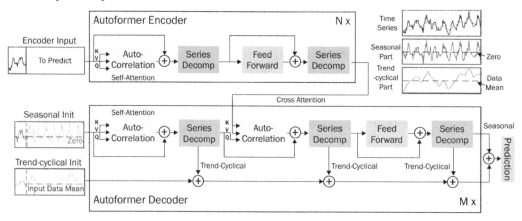

Figure 16.5 – Autoformer architecture

It is easier to understand the overall architecture first and then dive deeper into the details. In *Figure 16.5*, there are boxes labeled **Auto-Correlation** and **Series Decomp**. For now, just know that auto-correlation is a type of attention and that series decomposition is a particular block that decomposes the signal into trend-cyclical and seasonal components.

Encoder

With the level of abstraction discussed in the preceding section, let's understand what is happening in the encoder:

1. The uniform representation of the time series, $\mathcal{X}_{en}$, is the input to the encoder. The input is passed through an **Auto-Correlation** block (for self-attention) whose output is $\mathcal{X}_{ac}$.

2. The uniform representation, $\mathcal{X}_{en}$, is added back to $\mathcal{X}_{ac}$ as a residual connection, $\mathcal{X}_{ac} = \mathcal{X}_{ac} + \mathcal{X}_{en}$.

3. Now, $\mathcal{X}_{ac}$ is passed through a **Series Decomp** block, which decomposes the signal into a trend-cyclical component ($\mathcal{X}_T$) and a seasonal component, $\mathcal{X}_{seas}$.

4. We discard $\mathcal{X}_T$ and pass $\mathcal{X}_{seas}$ to a **Feed Forward** network, which gives $\mathcal{X}_{FF}$ as an output.

5. $\mathcal{X}_{seas}$ is again added to $\mathcal{X}_{FF}$ as a residual connection, $\mathcal{X}_{seas} = \mathcal{X}_{FF} + \mathcal{X}_{seas}$.

6. Finally, this $\mathcal{X}_{seas}$ is passed through another **Series Decomp** layer, which again decomposes the signal into the trend, $\mathcal{X}_{\tilde{T}}$, and a seasonal component, $\mathcal{X}_{\overline{seas}}$.

7. We discard $\mathcal{X}_{\tilde{T}}$, and pass on $\mathcal{X}_{\overline{seas}}$ as the final output from one block of the encoder.

8. There may be N blocks of encoders stacked together, one taking in the output of the previous encoder as input.

Now, let's shift our attention to the decoder block.

Decoder

Like the Informer model, the Autoformer model uses a START token-like mechanism by including a sampled window from the input sequence. But instead of just taking the sequence, Autoformer does a bit of special processing on it. Autoformer uses the bulk of its learning power to learn seasonality. The output of the transformer is also just the seasonality. Therefore, instead of including the complete window from the input sequence, Autoformer decomposes the signal and only includes the seasonal component in the START token. Let's look at this process step by step:

1. If the input (the context window) is $\mathcal{X}$, we decompose it with the **Series Decomp** block into $\mathcal{X}_T^{init}$ and $\mathcal{X}_{seas}^{init}$.

2. Now, we sample C timesteps from the end of $\mathcal{X}_{seas}^{init}$ and append H zeros, where H is the forecast horizon, and construct $\mathcal{X}_{ds}$.

3. This $\mathcal{X}_{ds}$ is then used to create a uniform representation, $\mathcal{X}_{dec}$.

4. Meanwhile, we sample C timesteps from the end of $\mathcal{X}_T^{init}$ and append H timesteps with the series mean ($mean(\mathcal{X})$), where H is the forecast horizon, and construct $\mathcal{X}_{dt}$.

This $\mathcal{X}_{dec}$ is then used as the input for the decoder. This is what happens in the decoder:

1. The input, $\mathcal{X}_{dec}$, is first passed through an **Auto-Correlation** (for self-attention) block whose output is $\mathcal{X}_{dac}$.

2. The uniform representation, X_{dec}, is added back to X_{dac} as a residual connection, $X_{dac} = X_{dac} + X_{dec}$

3. Now, X_{dac} is passed through a **Series Decomp** block that decomposes the signal into a trend-cyclical component (X_{dT1}) and a seasonal component, X_{dseas}.

4. In the decoder, we do not discard the trend component; instead, we save it. This is because we will be adding all the trend components with the trend in it (X_{dt}) to come up with the overall trend part ($\mathcal{T}$).

5. The seasonal output from the **Series Decomp** block (X_{dseas}), along with the output from the encoder ($X_{\overline{seas}}$), is then passed into another **Auto-Correlation** block where cross-attention between the decoder sequence and encoder sequence is calculated. Let the output of this block be X_{cross}.

6. Now, X_{dseas} is added back to X_{cross} as a residual connection, $X_{cross} = X_{cross} + X_{dseas}$.

7. X_{cross} is again passed through a **Series Decomp** block, which splits X_{cross} into two components – X_{dT2} and X_{dseas2}.

8. X_{dseas} is then transformed using a **Feed Forward** network into X_{dff} and X_{dseas} is added to it in a residual connection, $X_{dff} = X_{dff} + X_{dseas}$.

9. Finally, X_{dff} is passed through yet another **Series Decomp** block, which decomposes it into two components – X_{dT3} and X_{dseas3}. X_{dseas3} is the final output of the decoder, which captures seasonality.

10. Another output is the residual trend, $X_{\overline{trend}}$, which is a projection of the summation of all the trend components extracted in the decoder's **Series Decomp** blocks. The projection layer is a **Conv1d** layer, which projects the extracted trend to the desired output dimension:

$$X_{\overline{trend}} = Conv1d(X_{dT1} + X_{dT2} + X_{dT3})$$

11. M such decoder layers are stacked on top of each other, each one feeding its output as the input to the next one.

12. The residual trend, $X_{\overline{trend}}$, of each decoder layer gets added to the trend init, X_{dt}, to model the overall trend component ($\mathcal{T}$).

13. The X_{dseas3} of the final decoder layer is considered to be the overall seasonality component and is projected to the desired output dimension (S) using a linear layer.

14. Finally, the prediction or the forecast $X_{out} = \mathcal{T} + S$.

The whole architecture is cleverly designed so that the relatively stable and easy-to-predict part of the time series (the trend-cyclical) is removed and the difficult-to-capture seasonality can be modeled well.

Now, how does the **Series Decomp** block decompose the series? The mechanism may be familiar to you already: `AvgPool1d` with some padding so that it maintains the same size as the input. This acts like a moving average over the specified kernel width.

We have been talking about the **Auto-Correlation** block throughout this explanation. Now, let's understand the ingenuity of the **Auto-Correlation** block.

Auto-correlation mechanism

Autoformer uses an auto-correlation mechanism in place of standard scaled dot product attention. This discovers sub-series similarity based on periodicity and uses this similarity to aggregate similar sub-series. This clever mechanism breaks the information bottleneck by expanding the point-wise operation of the scaled dot product attention to a sub-series level operation. The initial part of the overall mechanism is similar to the standard attention procedure, where we project the query, key, and values into the same dimension using weight matrices. The key difference is the attention weight calculation and how they are used to calculate the values. This mechanism achieves this by using two salient sub-mechanisms: discovering period-based dependencies and time delay aggregation.

Period-based dependencies

Autoformer uses autocorrelation as the key measure of similarity. Auto-correlation, as we know, represents the similarity between a given time series, X_t, and its lagged series. For instance, $\mathcal{R}_{xx}(\tau)$ is the autocorrelation between the time series X_t and $X_{t-\tau}$. Autoformer considers this autocorrelation as the unnormalized confidence of the particular lag. Therefore, from the list of all τ, we choose k most possible lags and use *softmax* to convert these unnormalized confidences into probabilities. We use these probabilities as weights to aggregate relevant sub-series (we will talk about this in the next section).

The autocorrelation calculation is not the most efficient operation and Autoformer suggests an alternative to make the calculation faster. Based on the **Wiener–Khinchin theorem** in **Stochastic Processes** (this is outside the scope of the book, but for those who are interested, I have included a link in the *Further reading* section), autocorrelation can also be calculated using **Fast Fourier Transforms** (**FFTs**). The process can be seen as follows:

$$\mathcal{S}_{xx}(\tau) = \mathcal{F}(X_t)\mathcal{F}^*(X_t)$$

Here, $\mathcal{F}$ denotes the FFT and $\mathcal{F}^*$ denotes the conjugate operation (the conjugate of a complex number is the number with the same real part and an imaginary part, which is equal in magnitude but with the sign reversed. The mathematics around this is outside the scope of this book). This can easily be written in PyTorch as follows:

```
# calculating the FFT of Query and Key
q_fft = torch.fft.rfft(queries.permute(0, 2, 3,
1).contiguous(), dim=-1)
k_fft = torch.fft.rfft(keys.permute(0, 2, 3, 1).contiguous(),
dim=-1)
# Multiplying the FFT of Query with Conjugate FFT of Key
res = q_fft * torch.conj(k_fft)
```

Now, $\mathcal{S}_{xx}(\tau)$ is in the spectral domain. To bring it back to the real domain, we need to do an inverse FFT:

$$\mathcal{R}_{xx}(\tau) = \mathcal{F}^{-1}\big(\mathcal{S}_{xx}(\tau)\big)$$

Here, $\mathcal{F}^{-1}$ denotes the inverse FFT. In PyTorch, we can do this easily:

```
corr = torch.fft.irfft(res, dim=-1)
```

When the query and key are the same, this calculates self-attention; when they are different, they calculate cross-attention.

Now, all we need to do is take the top-k values from `corr` and use them to aggregate the sub-series.

Time delay aggregation

We have identified the major lags that are auto-correlated using the FFT and inverse-FFT. For a more concrete example, the dataset we have been working on (*London Smart Meter Dataset*) has a half-hourly frequency and has strong daily and weekly seasonality. Therefore, the auto-correlation identification may have picked out 48 and 48*7 as the two most important lags. In the standard attention mechanism, we use the calculated probability as weights to aggregate the value. Autoformer also does something similar, but instead of applying the weights to points, it applies them to sub-series.

Autoformer does this by shifting the time series by the lag, τ, and then using the lag's weight to aggregate them:

$$Auto - Correlation(Q, K, V) = \sum_{i=1}^{k} Roll(V, \tau_i)\widehat{R_{Q,K}}(\tau_i)$$

Here, $\widehat{R_{Q,K}}(\tau_i)$ is the *softmax*-ed probabilities on the *top-k* autocorrelations.

In our example, we can think of this as shifting the series by 48 timesteps so that the previous day's timesteps are aligned with the current day and then using the weight of the 48 lag to scale it. Then, we can move on to the 48*7 lag and align the previous week's timesteps with the current week, and then use the weight of the 48*7 lag to scale it. So, in the end, we will get a weighted mixture of the seasonality patterns that we can observe daily and weekly. Since these weights are learned by the model, we can hypothesize that different blocks learn to focus on different seasonalities, and thus as a whole, the blocks learn the overall pattern in the time series.

Forecasting with Autoformer

Similar to the Informer model, the Autoformer model has also not been implemented in PyTorch Forecasting. However, we have adapted the original implementation by the authors of the paper so that it works with PyTorch Forecasting; this can be found in `src/dl/ptf_models.py` in a class named `AutoformerModel`. We can use the same framework we worked with in *Chapter 15, Strategies for Global Deep Learning Forecasting Models*, with this implementation.

> **Important note**
>
> We have to keep in mind that the Autoformer model does not support exogenous variables. The only additional information it officially supports is global timestamp information such as the week, month, and so on, along with holiday information. We can technically extend this to any categorical feature (static or dynamic), but no real-valued information is currently supported. The Autoformer model is also more memory hungry, probably because of its sub-series aggregation.

Let's look at the initialization parameters of the implementation.

The `AutoformerModel` class has the following major parameters:

- `label_len`: This is an integer representing the number of timesteps from the input sequence to sample as a START token while decoding.

- `moving_avg`: This is an *odd* integer that determines the kernel size to be used in the **Series Decomp** block.

- `e_layers`: This is an integer representing the number of encoder layers.

- `d_layers`: This is an integer representing the number of decoder layers.

- `n_heads`: This is an integer representing the number of attention heads.

- `d_ff`: This is an integer representing the number of kernels in the **Conv1d** layers used in the encoder and decoder layers.

- `activation`: This is a string that takes in one of two values – `relu` or `gelu`. This is the activation to be used in the encoder and decoder layers.

- `factor`: This is a float value that controls the top-k selection of autocorrelations. For a factor of 1, the top-k is calculated as *log(length of window)*. For a value less than 1, it selects a smaller top-k.

- `dropout`: This is a float between 0 and 1 that determines the strength of the dropout in the network.

> **Notebook alert**
>
> The complete code for training the Autoformer model can be found in the `04-Autoformer. ipynb` notebook in the `Chapter16` folder. There are two variables in the notebook that act as switches – `TRAIN_SUBSAMPLE = True` makes the notebook run for a subset of 10 households, while `train_model = True` makes the notebook train different models (warning: training the model on full data takes hours). `train_model = False` loads the trained model weights (not included in the repository but saved every time you run training) and predicts on them.

Now, let's look at one more, very successful, architecture that is well-designed to utilize all kinds of information in a global context.

Temporal Fusion Transformer (TFT)

TFT is a model that is thoughtfully designed from the ground up to make the most efficient use of all the different kinds of information in a global modeling context – static and dynamic variables. TFT also has interpretability at the heart of all design decisions. The result is a high-performing, interpretable, and global DL model.

> **Reference check**
>
> The research paper by Lim et al. on TFT is cited in the *References* section as *10*.

At first glance, the model architecture looks complicated and daunting. But once you peel the onion, it is quite simple and ingenious. We will take this one level of abstraction at a time to ease you into the full model. Along the way, there will be many black boxes I'm going to ask you to take for granted, but don't worry – we will open every one of them as we dive deeper.

The Architecture of TFT

Let's establish some notations and a setting before we start. We have a dataset with I unique time series and each entity, i, has some static variables (S_i). The collection of all static variables of all entities can be represented by S. We also have the context window of length k. Along with this, we have the time-varying variables, which have one distinction – for some variables, we do not have the future data (unknown), and for other variables, we know the future (known). Let's denote all the time-varying information (the context window, known, and unknown time-varying variables) from the context window's input, $X_{t-k} \dots X_t$. The known time-varying variables for the future are denoted using $X_{t+1} \dots X_{t+\tau}$, where τ is the forecast horizon. With these notations, we are ready to look at the first level of abstraction:

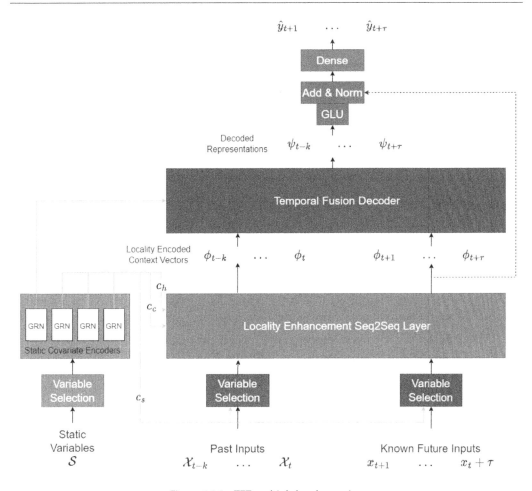

Figure 16.6 – TFT – a high-level overview

There is a lot to unpack here. Let's start with the static variables, S. First, the static variables are passed through a **Variable Selection Network** (**VSN**). The VSN does instance-wise feature selection and performs some non-linear processing on the inputs. This processed input is fed into a bunch of **Static Covariate Encoders** (**SEs**). The SE block is designed to integrate the static metadata in a principled way.

If you follow the arrows from the SE block in *Figure 16.6*, you will see that the static covariates are used in three (four distinct outputs) different places in the architecture. We will see how these are used in each of these places when we talk about them. But all these different places may be looking at different aspects of the static information. To allow the model this flexibility, the processed and variable-selected output is fed into four different **Gated Residual Networks** (**GRNs**), which, in turn, generate four outputs – c_s, c_e, c_c, and c_h. We will explain what a GRN is later, but for now, just understand that it is a block capable of non-linear processing, along with a residual connection, which enables it to bypass the non-linear processing if needed.

The past inputs, $X_{t-k} \dots X_b$ and the future known inputs, $X_{t+1} \dots X_{t+\tau}$, are also passed through separate VSNs and these processed outputs are fed into a **Locality Enhancement** (**LE**) Seq2Seq layer. We can think of LE as a way to encode the local context and temporal ordering into the embeddings of each timestep. This is similar to the positional embeddings in vanilla Transformers. We can also see similar attempts in the **Conv1d** layers that were used to encode the history in the uniform representation in the Informer and Autoformer models. We will see what is happening inside the LE later, but for now, just understand it captures the local context conditioned on other observed variables and static information. Let's call the output of the block **Locality Encoded Context Vectors** ($\phi_{t-k} \dots \phi t$, and $\phi_{t+1} \dots \phi_{t+\tau}$).

> **Important note**
>
> The terminology, notation, and grouping of major blocks are not the same as in the original paper. I have changed these to make them more accessible and understandable.

Now, these LE context vectors are fed into a **Temporal Fusion Decoder** (**TD**). The TD applies a slight variation of multi-headed self-attention in a Transformer model-like manner and produces the **Decoded Representation** ($\psi_{t-k} \dots \psi t + \tau$). Finally, this Decoded Representation is passed through a **Gated Linear Unit** (**GLU**) and an **Add and Norm** block that adds the LE context vectors as a residual connection.

A GLU is a unit that helps the model decide how much information it needs to allow to flow through. We can think of it as a learned information throttle that is widely used in **Natural Language Processing** (**NLP**) architectures. The formula is really simple:

$$GLU(X) = (X * W + b) \otimes \sigma(X * V + c)$$

Here, W and V are learnable weight matrices, b and c are learnable biases, σ is an activation function, and $\otimes$ is the Hadamard product operator (element-wise multiplication).

The **Add & Norm** block is the same as in the vanilla Transformer; we discussed this back in *Chapter 14, Attention and Transformers for Time Series*.

Now, to top it all off, we have a **Dense** layer (linear layer with bias) that projects the output of the **Add & Norm** block to the desired output dimensions.

And with that, it is time for us to step one level down in our abstraction.

Locality Enhancement Seq2Seq layer

Let's peel back the onion and see what's happening inside the LE Seq2Seq layer. Let's start with a figure:

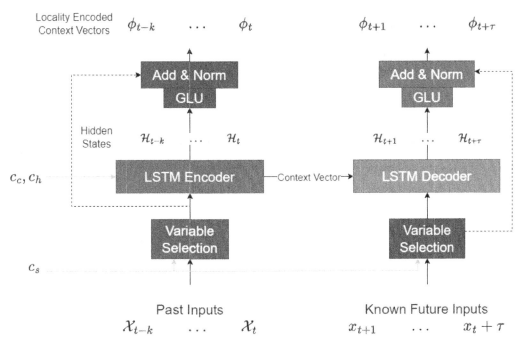

Figure 16.7 – TFT – LE Seq2Seq layer

The LE uses a Seq2Seq architecture to capture the local context. The process starts with the processed past inputs. The LSTM encoder takes in these past inputs, $\mathcal{X}_{t-k} \dots \mathcal{X}_t$. c_h; c_c from the static covariate encoder acts as the initial hidden states of the LSTM. The encoder processes each timestep at a time, producing hidden states at each time step, $\mathcal{H}_{t-k} \dots \mathcal{H}_t$. The last hidden states (context vector) are now passed on to the LSTM decoder, which processes the known future inputs, $x_{t+1} \dots x_{t+\tau}$, and produces the hidden states at each of the future timesteps, $\mathcal{H}_{t+1} \dots \mathcal{H}_{t+\tau}$. Finally, all these hidden states are passed through a **GLU + AddNorm** block with the residual connection from before the LSTM processing. The outputs are the LE context vectors ($\phi_{t-k} \dots \phi_t$, and $\phi_{t+1} \dots \phi_{t+\tau}$).

Now, let's look at the next block: the TFD.

Temporal fusion decoder

Let's start this discussion with another figure:

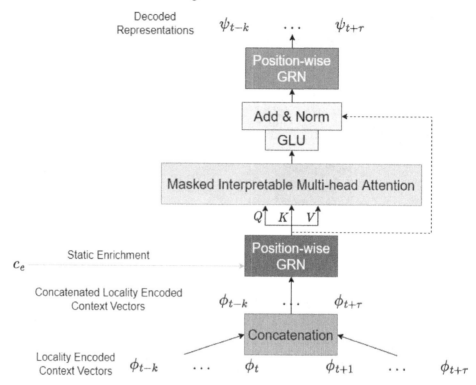

Figure 16.8 – Temporal Fusion Transformer – Temporal Fusion Decoder

The LE context vectors from both the past input and known future input are concatenated into a single LE context vector. Now, this can be thought of as the position-encoded tokens in the Transformer paradigm. The first thing the TFD does is enrich these encodings with static information, c_e, that was created from the static covariate encoder. This was concatenated with the embeddings. A position-wise GRN is used to enrich the embeddings. These enriched embeddings are now used as the query, key, and values for the **Masked Interpretable Multi-Head Attention** block.

The paper posits that the **Masked Interpretable Multi-Head Attention** block learns long-term dependencies across time steps. The local dependencies are already captured by the LE Seq2Seq layer in the embeddings, but the point-wise long-term dependencies are captured by **Masked Interpretable Multi-Head Attention**. This block also enhances the interpretability of the architecture. The attention weights that are generated in the process give us some indication of the major timesteps involved in the process. But the multi-head attention has one drawback from the interpretability perspective. In vanilla multi-head attention, we use separate projection weights for the values, which means that the values for each head are different and hence the attention weights are not straightforward to interpret.

TFT gets over this limitation by employing a *single shared weight matrix* for projecting the values into the attention dimension. Even with the shared value projection weights, because of the individual query and key projection weights, each head can learn different temporal patterns. In addition to this, TFT also employs masking to make sure information from the future is not used in operations. We discussed this type of causal masking in *Chapter 14, Attention and Transformers for Time Series*. With these two modifications, TFT names this layer **Masked Interpretable Multi-Head Attention**.

And with that, it's time to open the last and most granular level of abstraction we have been using.

Gated Residual Network

We have been talking about GRNs for some time now; so far, we have just taken them at face value. Let's understand what is happening inside a GRN – one of the most basic building blocks of a TFT.

Let's look at a schematic diagram of a GRN to understand it better:

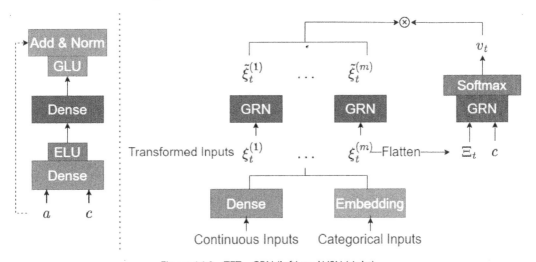

Figure 16.9 – TFT – GRN (left) and VSN (right)

The GRN takes in two inputs: the primary input, a, and the external context, c. The context, c, is an optional input and is treated as zero if it's not present. First, both the inputs, a and c, are transformed by separate dense layers and a subsequent activation function – the **Exponential Linear Unit** (**ELU**) (https://pytorch.org/docs/stable/generated/torch.nn.ELU.html).

Now, the transformed a and c inputs are added together and then transformed again using another **Dense** layer. Finally, this is passed through a **GLU+Add & Norm** layer with residual connections from the original a. This structure bakes in enough non-linearity to learn complex interactions between the inputs, but at the same time lets the model ignore those non-linearities through a residual connection. Therefore, such a block allows the model to scale the computation required up or down based on the data.

Variable Selection Network

The last building block of the TFT is the VSN. VSNs enable TFT to do instance-wise variable selection. Most real-world time series datasets have many variables that do not have a lot of predictive power, so being able to select the ones that do have predictive power automatically will help the model pick out relevant patterns. *Figure 16.9* (right) shows this VSN.

These additional variables can be categorical or continuous. TFT uses Entity Embeddings to convert the categorical features into numerical vectors of the dimension that we desire (d_{model}). We talked about this in *Chapter 15, Strategies for Global Deep Learning Forecasting Models*. The continuous features are linearly transformed (independently) into the same dimension, d_{model}. This gives us the Transformed inputs, $\xi_t^{(1)} \dots \xi_t^{(m)}$, where m is the number of features and t is the timestep. We can concatenate all these embeddings (flatten them) and that flattened representation can be represented as Ξ_t.

Now, there are two parallel streams in which these embeddings are processed – one for non-linear processing of the embeddings and another to do feature selection. Each of these embeddings is processed by separate GRNs (but shared for all timesteps) to give us the non-linearly processed ones, $\widetilde{\xi}_t^{(1)} \dots \widetilde{\xi}_t^{(m)}$. In another stream, the VSN processes the flattened representation, Ξ_t, along with optional context information, c, and processes it through a GRN with a softmax activation. This gives us a weight, v_t, which is a vector of length m. This v_t is now used in a weighted sum of all the non-linearly processed feature embeddings, $\widetilde{\xi}_t^{(1)} \dots \widetilde{\xi}_t^{(m)}$, which is calculated as follows:

$$\widetilde{\xi}_t = \sum_{j=1}^{m} v_t^{(j)} \widetilde{\xi}_t^{(j)}$$

Forecasting with TFT

TFT is implemented in PyTorch Forecasting. We can use the same framework we worked with in *Chapter 15, Strategies for Global Deep Learning Forecasting Models*, and extend it to train TFT on our data.

The `TemporalFusionTransformer` class in PyTorch Forecasting has the following major parameters:

- `hidden_size`: This is an integer representing the hidden dimension across the model. This is the dimension in which all the GRNs work, the VSN, the LSTM hidden sizes, the self-attention hidden sizes, and so on. Arguably, this is the most important hyperparameter in the model.

- `lstm_layers`: This is an integer that determines the number of layers in the LSTMs we use in the LE Seq2Seq block.

- `attention_head_size`: This is an integer representing the number of attention heads.

- `embedding_sizes`: This is a dictionary of categorical feature names to a tuple of (`cardinality`, `embedding size`). Although the original paper suggests projecting all categorical and continuous variables to a single dimension, the PyTorch Forecasting implementation allows the flexibility to have separate dimensions for each variable.

- `hidden_continuous_size`: This is an integer that is the default embedding size for continuous features.

- `hidden_continuous_sizes`: This is a dictionary of continuous feature names to a hidden size for variable selection. This lets us override `hidden_continuous_size` for specific features.

- `dropout`: This is a float between 0 and 1, which determines the strength of the dropout in the network.

> **Notebook alert**
>
> The complete code for training TFT can be found in the `05-TFT.ipynb` notebook in the `Chapter16` folder. There are two variables in the notebook that act as switches – `TRAIN_SUBSAMPLE = True` makes the notebook run for a subset of 10 households, while `train_model = True` makes the notebook train different models (warning: training the model on the full data takes hours). `train_model = False` loads the trained model weights (not included in the repository but saved every time you run training) and predicts on them.

Interpreting TFT

TFT approaches interpretability from a slightly different perspective than N-BEATS. While N-BEATS gives us a decomposed output for interpretability, TFT gives us visibility into how the model has interpreted the variables it has used. On account of the VSNs, we have ready access to feature weights. Like the feature importance we get from tree-based models, TFT gives us access to similar scores. And because of the self-attention layer, the attention weights can also be interpreted to help us understand which time steps hold a large enough weightage in the attention mechanism.

PyTorch Forecasting makes this possible by performing a few steps. First, we get the **raw predictions** using `mode="raw"` in the `predict` function. Then, we use those raw predictions in the `interpret_output` function. There is a parameter called `reduction` in the `interpret_output` function that decides how to aggregate the weights across different instances. We know that TFT does instance-wise feature selection in VSNs and attention is also done instance-wise. `'mean'` is a good option for looking at the global interpretability:

```
raw_predictions, x = best_model.predict(val_dataloader,
mode="raw", return_x=True)
interpretation = best_model.interpret_output(raw_predictions,
reduction="sum")
```

This `interpretation` variable is a dictionary with weights for different aspects of the model, such as `attention`, `static_variables`, `encoder_variables`, and `decoder_variables`. PyTorch Forecasting also provides us with an easy way to visualize this importance:

```
best_model.plot_interpretation(interpretation)
```

This generates four plots:

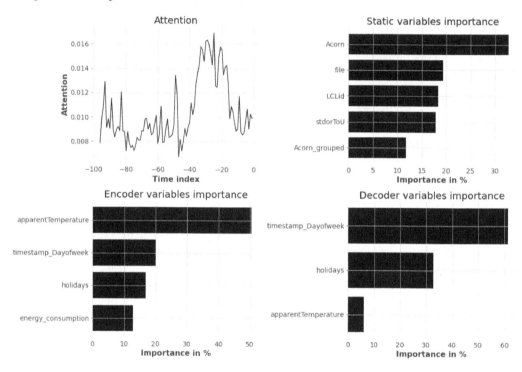

Figure 16.10 – Interpreting TFT

We can also look at each instance and plot similar visualizations for each prediction we make. All we need to do is use `reduction="none"` and then plot it ourselves. The accompanying notebook explores how to do that and more.

We have covered a few popular specialized architectures for time series forecasting, but this is in no way a complete list. There are so many model architectures and techniques out there. I have included a few in the *Further reading* section to get you started.

Interpretability

I directed you toward a few interpretability techniques for machine learning models back in *Chapter 10, Global Forecasting Models*. While some of those, such as SHAP and LIME, can still be applied to deep learning models, none of them considers the temporal aspect by design. This is because all those techniques were developed for more general purposes, such as classification and regression. That being said, there has been some work in interpretability for DL models and time series models. Here, I'll list a few promising papers that tackle the temporal aspect head-on:

- *TimeSHAP*: This is a model-agnostic recurrent explainer that builds upon *KernelSHAP* and extends it to the time series domain. *Research paper*: `https://dl.acm.org/doi/10.1145/3447548.3467166`. *GitHub*: `https://github.com/feedzai/timeshap`.

- *Instance-wise Feature Importance in Time (FIT)*: This is an interpretability technique that relies on the distribution shift between the predictive distribution and a counterfactual where all but the feature under inspection are unobserved. *Research paper*: `https://proceedings.neurips.cc/paper/2020/file/08fa43588c2571ade19bc0fa5936e028-Paper.pdf`. *GitHub*: `https://github.com/sanatonek/time_series_explainability`.

- *Dynamask - Explaining Time Series Predictions with Dynamic Masks*: A technique that produces instance-wise importance scores for each feature at each time step by fitting a perturbation mask to the input sequence. *Research paper*: `http://proceedings.mlr.press/v139/crabbe21a.html`. *GitHub*: `https://github.com/JonathanCrabbe/Dynamask`.

While this is not an exhaustive list, these are a few works that I feel are important and promising. This is an area of active research and new techniques will come up as time goes on.

Now, let's take a look at another aspect, although not a specialized architecture, but a key component that can elevate the forecasts you generate to another dimension.

Probabilistic forecasting

So far, we have been talking about the forecast as a single number. We have been projecting our DL models to a single dimension and training the model using a loss such as mean squared loss. This paradigm is what we call a **point forecast**. A probabilistic forecast is when the forecast, instead of having a single-point prediction, captures the uncertainty of that forecast as well. This means that the model doesn't output a single number, but an output that reflects the probabilities associated with all possible future outcomes.

In the econometrics and classical time series world, the prediction intervals were already baked into the formulation. The statistical grounding of those methods made sure that the output of those models was readily interpreted in a probabilistic way as well (so long as you could satisfy the assumptions that were stipulated by those models). But in the modern machine/DL world, probabilistic forecasting is not an afterthought. A combination of factors such as less rigid assumptions and the way we train the models leads to this predicament.

From a probabilistic point of view, a forecast at position t, $\hat{y}_t$, can be seen as the realization of a probability distribution, $p(y_t)$. And instead of estimating $\hat{y}_t$, the model estimates $p(y_t)$. There are a few popular ways in DL to estimate $p(y_t)$. Let's look at them one by one.

Probability Density Function (PDF)

This is the most common way of representing probability distribution in forecasting. Standard parametric probability distributions have a few parameters that define the full distribution. For instance, the Gaussian distribution can be fully parameterized by the mean and the standard deviation. So, if we assume that the forecast is from one of these parametric distributions, we can tweak the model so that it outputs the parameters of the distribution, rather than a single-point estimate. For instance, the final projection to the output space of a DL model can be tweaked to output two parameters – the mean, μ_t, and the standard deviation, σ_t, at time t. There are specific constraints to these outputs that are typically handled by the right activation function. For instance, σ_t should be a positive number because a negative standard deviation doesn't make sense. So, we can apply an activation function, such as a **ReLU** or a **SoftPlus** function, to make sure those considerations are met.

Now that the model has two outputs, the mean and standard deviation, we also need to change the loss function. It is not as if the target that we are training the model with is in PDF form. In other words, the targets are still real numbers and not means and standard deviations. So, instead of a loss function such as mean squared error, we need to use something such as a **negative log-likelihood** (**NLL**). Let's understand this a bit more.

For instance, let's say you have a set of iid observations (in our case, the target), $y_1, \dots, y_n$. With PDF, we will be able to tell the probability of each of those observations, $p(y_x)$. From high school probability, we know that when two independent events occur, to get the joint probability, we can just multiply them together. Using the same logic, to calculate the joint probability of all n iid observations (the probability that all of them occur), we can just multiply all of them together:

$$\prod_{i=1}^{n} p(y_i)$$

However, this operation is not numerically stable – if you start multiplying numbers less than zero, it gets smaller and smaller and eventually leads to numerical underflow. Therefore, a more stable version of the same likelihood is used – log-likelihood. Optimizing a function and a log of the same function is synonymous. By using the log, the series of multiplications becomes an addition and instantly more stable:

$$\sum_{i=1}^{n} ln(p(y_i))$$

So, all we need is $p(y_i)$ to plug into the NLL loss. This comes from our assumption regarding the distribution the output will be in and the estimated parameters of the model. This allows the model to compute the likelihood that a particular point (the target) is under the predicted distribution and then minimize the NLL (or maximize the likelihood) by changing the model parameters.

Apart from the Gaussian assumption, several differentiable parametric distributions have been used by different researchers for forecasting problems – student-t distribution, Tweedie distribution, negative binomial distribution, and so on. **DeepAR** by Salinas et al. is a prominent example where this approach has been used to great success.

Reference check

The research paper by Salinas et al. on DeepAR is cited in the *References* section as *11*.

Quantile functions

Another way $p(y_t)$ can be represented is by using quantile functions. Before talking about the quantile function, let's spend a minute on the **Cumulative Distribution Function** (**CDF**). This, again, is high school probability. In simple words, a CDF returns the probability of some random variable, X, being less than or equal to some value, x:

$$F(x) = P(X \leq x)$$

Here, F is the CDF. This function takes in an input, x, and returns a value between 0 and 1. Let's call this value p.

A quantile function is an inverse of the CDF. This function tells you the value of x, which would make F(x) return a particular value, p:

$$F^{-1}(p) = x$$

This function, F^{-1}, is the quantile function. Similar to the PDF, the quantile function also provides a complete description of the distribution. Therefore, repurposing the model to learn the quantile function for specific quantiles that are of interest to us also gives us probabilistic forecasts.

From an implementation perspective, we would have to choose q quantiles we want to estimate (0.1, 0.5, and 0.9 are popular choices) and tweak the last layer that projects to the output space so that there are q outputs. In this case, the most common choice for a loss function is the Quantile Loss or the Pinball Loss.

The Quantile Loss can be defined as follows:

$$L_q(y_t, y_t^q) = \begin{cases} (y_t - y_t^q)q, \text{ if } y_t \geq y_t^q \\ (y_t^q - y_t)(1-q), \text{ if } y_t < y_t^q \end{cases}$$

Here, y_t is the target value at time t, y_t^q is the quantile forecast, and q is the quantile we are forecasting. While implementing this, we can easily replace the branched equation with a maximum operation:

```
def quantile_loss(q, y, y_hat_q):
    # q: Quantile to be evaluated, e.g., 0.5 for median.
    # y: Target Value
    # y_hat_q: Quantile Forecast.
    e = y - f
    return np.maximum(q * e, (q - 1) * e)
```

Typically, we train with multiple quantiles. In this case, the loss the model optimizes for will be the sum of all the quantile loss for each of the quantiles we are training for.

TFTs are a great example where uncertainty quantification is done using a quantile function. The paper originally proposed TFT as a probabilistic forecasting option. For a more detailed explanation of quantile loss, head over to the *Further reading* section.

Other approaches

Apart from PDF and quantile functions, there are a lot of other approaches to probabilistic forecasting. We will not be able to cover all of them here, but I will still try to mention the major ones and give you references so that you can read more about the technique:

- **Monte Carlo dropout**: This trick only works for networks with dropout. Dropouts are generally turned off while inferencing. However, in Monte Carlo dropout, we keep the dropout on and predict multiple times. This approximates Bayesian computation and estimates model uncertainty. A popular research paper implementing this idea for time series is *Deep and Confident Prediction for Time Series at Uber* by Zhu et al. at https://doi.org/10.1109/ICDMW.2017.19.

- **Normalizing flows**: Normalizing flows are a method for learning complex data distributions by transforming a simple distribution into a complex distribution. They do this by learning a series of invertible and differentiable functions, such that we have a one-to-one correspondence between points in the simple distribution to points in the complex distribution. Therefore, we can have a bijective function (a function mapping between domain A to domain B such that for every element, b, in B, there is exactly one element, a, in A) that maps the data distribution (complex) to a simple distribution (such as a Gaussian distribution). A recent paper that applies normalizing flows to multivariate time series forecasting is *Multivariate Probabilistic Time Series Forecasting via Conditioned Normalizing Flows* by Rasul et al. This was presented in ICLR 2021 and can be accessed at https://openreview.net/forum?id=WiGQBFuVRv.

- **Conformal prediction**: Conformal prediction is an increasingly popular way to create distribution-free prediction intervals. It uses a trained model's experience in past data (calibration data) to recalibrate the confidence in new predictions. There is a large body of work and it is a very rapidly advancing field. I'm citing an example where the authors apply conformal predictions to a time series setting. For more information, you can refer to *Conformal Time-series Forecasting* by Stankeviciute et al., which was presented at NeurIPS 2021 and is accessible at `https://proceedings.neurips.cc/paper/2021/hash/312f1ba2a72318edaaa995a67835fad5-Abstract.html`.

Congratulations on making it through probably, one of the toughest and densest chapters in this book. Give yourself a pat on the back, sit back, and relax.

Summary

Our journey with deep learning for time series has finally reached a conclusion with us reviewing a few specialized architectures for time series forecasting. We now understand how different models such as N-BEATS, N-BEATSx, N-HiTS, Informer, Autoformer, and TFT work.

We also looked at how we can apply those models using PyTorch Forecasting. For the models such as *Informer* and *Autoformer* that were not implemented in PyTorch Forecasting, we saw how we can port normal `PyTorch` models into a form that can be used with PyTorch Forecasting. Models such as N-BEATS and TFT also offer interpretability and we explored those use cases as well.

To top this off, we covered probabilistic forecasting at a high level and provided references so that you can start your journey of looking at them. This brings this part of this book to a close. At this point, you should be much more comfortable with using DL for time series forecasting problems.

In the next part of this book, we will look at a few mechanics of forecasting, such as multi-step forecasting, cross-validation, and evaluation.

References

The following is a list of the references that we used throughout this chapter:

1. Spyros Makridakis, Evangelos Spiliotis, and Vassilios Assimakopoulos. (2020). *The M4 Competition: 100,000 time series and 61 forecasting methods*. International Journal of Forecasting, Volume 36, Issue 1. Pages 54-74. `https://doi.org/10.1016/j.ijforecast.2019.04.014`.

2. Slawek Smyl. (2018). *M4 Forecasting Competition: Introducing a New Hybrid ES-RNN Model*. `https://www.uber.com/blog/m4-forecasting-competition/`.

3. Boris N. Oreshkin, Dmitri Carpov, Nicolas Chapados, and Yoshua Bengio. (2020). *N-BEATS: Neural basis expansion analysis for interpretable time series forecasting*. 8th International Conference on Learning Representations, (ICLR). `https://openreview.net/forum?id=r1ecqn4YwB`.

4. Kin G. Olivares and Cristian Challu and Grzegorz Marcjasz and R. Weron and A. Dubrawski. (2022). *Neural basis expansion analysis with exogenous variables: Forecasting electricity prices with NBEATSx*. International Journal of Forecasting, 2022. https://www.sciencedirect.com/science/article/pii/S0169207022000413.

5. Cristian Challu and Kin G. Olivares and Boris N. Oreshkin and Federico Garza and Max Mergenthaler-Canseco and Artur Dubrawski. (2022). *N-HiTS: Neural Hierarchical Interpolation for Time Series Forecasting*. arXiv preprint arXiv: Arxiv-2201.12886. https://arxiv.org/abs/2201.12886.

6. Vaswani, Ashish, Shazeer, Noam, Parmar, Niki, Uszkoreit, Jakob, Jones, Llion, Gomez, Aidan N, Kaiser, Lukasz, and Polosukhin, Illia. (2017). *Attention is All you Need*. Advances in Neural Information Processing Systems. https://papers.nips.cc/paper/2017/hash/3f5ee243547dee91fbd053c1c4a845aa-Abstract.html.

7. Yao-Hung Hubert Tsai, Shaojie Bai, Makoto Yamada, Louis-Philippe Morency, and Ruslan Salakhutdinov. (2019). *Transformer Dissection: An Unified Understanding for Transformer's Attention via the Lens of Kernel*. N Proceedings of the 2019 Conference on Empirical Methods in Natural Language Processing and the 9th International Joint Conference on Natural Language Processing (EMNLP-IJCNLP), pages 4,344–4,353. https://aclanthology.org/D19-1443/.

8. Haoyi Zhou, Shanghang Zhang, Jieqi Peng, Shuai Zhang, Jianxin Li, Hui Xiong, and Wancai Zhang. (2021). *Informer: Beyond Efficient Transformer for Long Sequence Time-Series Forecasting*. Thirty-Fifth {AAAI} Conference on Artificial Intelligence, {AAAI} 2021. https://ojs.aaai.org/index.php/AAAI/article/view/17325.

9. Haixu Wu, Jiehui Xu, Jianmin Wang, and Mingsheng Long. (2021). *Autoformer: Decomposition Transformers with Auto-Correlation for Long-Term Series Forecasting*. Advances in Neural Information Processing Systems 34: Annual Conference on Neural Information Processing Systems 2021, NeurIPS 2021, December 6-14, 2021. https://proceedings.neurips.cc/paper/2021/hash/bcc0d400288793e8bdcd7c19a8ac0c2b-Abstract.html.

10. Bryan Lim, Sercan Ö. Arik, Nicolas Loeff, and Tomas Pfister. (2019). *Temporal Fusion Transformers for Interpretable Multi-horizon Time Series Forecasting*. International Journal of Forecasting, Volume 37, Issue 4, 2021, Pages 1,748-1,764. https://www.sciencedirect.com/science/article/pii/S0169207021000637.

11. David Salinas, Valentin Flunkert, and Jan Gasthaus. (2017). *DeepAR: Probabilistic Forecasting with Autoregressive Recurrent Networks*. International Journal of Forecasting, 2017. https://www.sciencedirect.com/science/article/pii/S0169207019301888.

Further reading

You can check out the following resources for further reading:

- *Fast ES-RNN: A GPU Implementation of the ES-RNN Algorithm*: https://arxiv.org/abs/1907.03329 and https://github.com/damitkwr/ESRNN-GPU

- *Functions as Vector Spaces*: https://www.youtube.com/watch?v=NvEZo12Q8rs

- *Forecast with N-BEATS*, by Gaetan Dubuc: https://www.kaggle.com/code/gatandubuc/forecast-with-n-beats-interpretable-model/notebook

- *WaveNet: A Generative Model for Audio*, by DeepMind: https://www.deepmind.com/blog/wavenet-a-generative-model-for-raw-audio

- *What is Residual Connection?*, by Wanshun Wong: https://towardsdatascience.com/what-is-residual-connection-efb07cab0d55

- *Efficient Transformers: A Survey*, by Tay et al.: https://arxiv.org/abs/2009.06732

- *Autocorrelation and the Wiener-Khinchin theorem*: https://www.itp.tu-berlin.de/fileadmin/a3233/grk/pototskyLectures2012/pototsky_lectures_part1.pdf

- *Modelling Long- and Short-Term Temporal Patterns with Deep Neural Networks*, by Lai et al.: https://dl.acm.org/doi/10.1145/3209978.3210006 and https://github.com/cure-lab/SCINet.

- *Think Globally, Act Locally: A Deep Neural Network Approach to High-Dimensional Time Series Forecasting*, by Sen et al.: https://proceedings.neurips.cc/paper/2019/hash/3a0844cee4fcf57de0c71e9ad3035478-Abstract.html and https://github.com/rajatsen91/deepglo

- *Enhancing the Locality and Breaking the Memory Bottleneck of Transformer on Time Series Forecasting*, by Li et al.: https://proceedings.neurips.cc/paper/2019/hash/6775a0635c302542da2c32aa19d86be0-Abstract.html

- *Quantile loss function for machine learning*, by Evergreen Innovations: https://www.evergreeninnovations.co/blog-quantile-loss-function-for-machine-learning/

Part 4 –
Mechanics of Forecasting

In this last part, we cover a few concepts that are essential for creating an industry-ready forecasting system. We discuss rarely talked about concepts such as multi-step forecasting and delve into the details of evaluating a forecast.

This part comprises the following chapters:

17
Multi-Step Forecasting

In the previous parts, we covered some basics of forecasting and different types of modeling techniques for time series forecasting. But a complete forecasting system is not just the model. There are a few mechanics of time series forecasting that make a lot of difference. These topics cannot be called *basics* because they require a nuanced understanding of the forecasting paradigm, and that is why we didn't cover these upfront.

Now that you have worked on some forecasting models and are familiar with time series, it's time to get more nuanced in our approach. Most of the forecasting exercises we have done throughout the book focus on forecasting the next timestep.

In this chapter, we will look at strategies to generate multi-step forecasting. In other words, how to forecast the next H timesteps.

In this chapter, we will be covering these main topics:

- Why multi-step forecasting?
- Recursive strategy
- Direct strategy
- Joint strategy
- Hybrid strategies
- How to choose a multi-step forecasting strategy

Why multi-step forecasting?

A multi-step forecasting task consists of forecasting the next H timesteps, $y_{t+1}, ..., y_{t+H}$, of a time series, $y_1, ... y_t$, where $H > 1$. Most real-world applications of time series forecasting demand multi-step forecasting, whether it is the energy consumption of a household or the sales of a product. This is because forecasts are never created to know what will happen in the future, but to take some action using the visibility we get. To effectively take any action, we would want to know the forecast a little ahead of time. For instance, the dataset we have been using throughout the book is about the energy consumption of households, logged every half an hour. If the energy provider wants to plan its energy production to meet customer demand, the next half an hour doesn't help at all. Similarly, if we look at the retail scenario, where we want to forecast the sales of a product, we will want to forecast a few days ahead so that we can purchase necessary goods, ship them to the store, and so on, in time for the demand.

Despite a more prevalent use case, multi-step forecasting has not received the attention it deserves. One of the reasons for that is the existence of classical statistical models or econometrics models such as the *ARIMA* and *exponential smoothing* methods, which include the multi-step strategy bundled within what we call a model; because of that, these models can generate multiple timesteps without breaking a sweat (although, as we will see in the chapter, they rely on one specific multi-step strategy to generate their forecast). Because these models were the most popular models used, practitioners need not have worried about multi-step forecasting strategies. But the advent of **machine learning (ML)** and **deep learning (DL)** methods for time series forecasting has opened up the need for a more focused study of multi-step forecasting strategies once again.

Another reason for the lower popularity of multi-step forecasting is that it is simply harder than single-step forecasting. This is because the more steps we extrapolate into the future, the more uncertainty in the predictions due to complex interactions between the different steps ahead.

There are many strategies that can be used to generate multi-step forecasting, and the following figure summarizes them neatly:

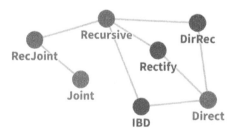

Figure 17.1 – Multi-step forecasting strategies

Each node of the graph in *Figure 17.1* is a strategy, and different strategies that have common elements have been linked together with edges in the graph. In the rest of the chapter, we will be covering each of these nodes (strategies) and explaining them in detail.

Let's establish a few basic notations to help us understand these strategies. We have a time series, $\mathbb{Y}_T$, of T timesteps, $y_1, \ldots, y_T$. $\mathbb{Y}_t$ denotes the same series, but ending at timestep t. We also consider a function, $\mathcal{W}$, which generates a window of size $k > 0$ from a time series. This function is a proxy for how we prepare the inputs for the different models we have seen throughout the book. So, if we see $\mathcal{W}(\mathbb{Y}_t)$, it means the function would draw a window from $\mathbb{Y}_t$ that ends at timestep t. We will also consider H to be the forecast horizon, where $H > 1$. We will also be using $;$ as an operator, which denotes concatenation.

Now, let's look at the different strategies (#1 in *References* is a good survey paper for different strategies). The discussion about merits and where we can use each of them is bundled in another upcoming section.

Recursive strategy

The recursive strategy is the oldest, most intuitive, and most popular technique to generate multi-step forecasts. To understand a strategy, there are two major regimes we have to understand:

- How is the training of the models done?

- How are the trained models used to generate forecasts?

Let's take the help of a diagram to understand the recursive strategy:

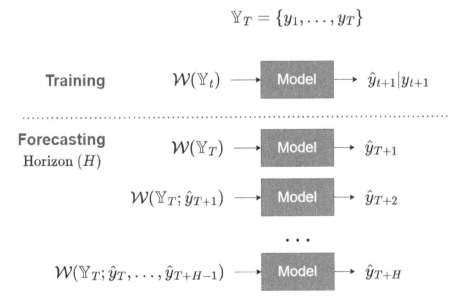

Figure 17.2 – Recursive strategy for multi-step forecasting

Let's discuss these regimes in detail.

Training regime

The recursive strategy involves training a single model to perform a *one-step-ahead* forecast. We can see in *Figure 17.1* that we use the window function, $\mathcal{W}(\mathbb{Y}_t)$, to draw a window from $\mathbb{Y}_t$ and train the model to predict y_{t+1}. And during training, a loss function (which measures the divergence between the output of the model, $\widehat{y_{t+1}}$, and the actual value, y_{t+1}) is used to optimize the parameters of the model.

Forecasting regime

We have trained a model to do *one-step-ahead* predictions. Now, we use this model in a recursive fashion to generate forecasts H timesteps ahead. For the first step, we use $\mathcal{W}(\mathbb{Y}_T)$, the window using the latest timestamp in training data, and generate the forecast one step ahead, $\widehat{y_{T+1}}$. Now, this generated forecast is added to the history and a new window is drawn from this history, $\mathcal{W}(\mathbb{Y}_T; \widehat{y_{T+1}})$. This window is given as the input to the same *one-step-ahead* model, and the forecast for the next timestep, $\widehat{y_{T+2}}$, is generated. This process is repeated until we get forecasts for all H timesteps.

This is the strategy that classical models that have stood the test of time (such as *ARIMA* and *Exponential Smoothing*) use internally when they generate multi-step forecasts. In the ML context, this means that we will train a model to predict one step ahead (as we have done all through this book), and then do a recursive operation where we forecast one step ahead, use the new forecast to recalculate all the features such as lags, rolling windows, and so on, and forecast the next step. In the context of the DL models, we can think of this as adding the forecast into the context window and using the trained model to generate the next step.

Direct strategy

The direct strategy, also called the independent strategy, is a popular strategy in forecasting using ML. This involves forecasting each horizon independently of each other. Let's look at the diagram first:

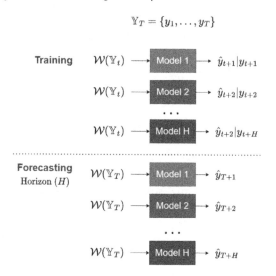

Figure 17.3 – Direct strategy for multi-step forecasting

Next, let's discuss the regimes in detail.

Training regime

Under the direct strategy, we train H different models, which take in the same window function but are trained to predict different timesteps in the forecast horizon. Therefore, we are learning a separate set of parameters, one for each timestep in the horizon, such that all the models combined learn a direct and independent mapping from the window, $\mathcal{W}(\mathbb{Y}_t)$, to the forecast horizon, H.

This strategy has gained ground along with the popularity of ML-based time series forecasting. From the ML context, we can practically implement it in two ways:

- **Shifting targets** – Each model in the horizon is trained by shifting the target by that many steps as the horizon we are training the model to forecast.

- **Eliminating features** – Each model in the horizon is trained by using only the features that are allowable to use according to the rules. For instance, when predicting $H = 2$, we can't use lag 1 (because to predict $H = 2$, we will not have actuals for $H = 1$).

> **Important note**
> The two ways mentioned in the preceding list work nicely if we only have lags as features. For instance, for eliminating features, we can just drop the offending lags and train the model. But in cases where we are using rolling features and other more sophisticated features, simple dropping doesn't work because lag 1 is already used in calculating the rolling features. This leads to data leakage. In such scenarios, we can make a dynamic function that calculates these features taking in a parameter to specify the horizon we are creating these features for. All the helper methods we used in *Chapter 6, Feature Engineering for Time Series Forecasting*, (add_rolling_features, add_seasonal_rolling_features, and add_ewma) have a parameter called n_shift, which handles this condition. If we are training a model for $H = 2$, we need to pass n_shift=2 and the method will take care of the rest. Now, while training the models, we use this dynamic method to recalculate these features for each horizon separately.

Forecasting regime

The forecasting regime is also fairly straightforward. We have the H trained models, one for each timestep in the horizon, and we use $\mathcal{W}(\mathbb{Y}_T)$ to forecast each of them independently.

Joint strategy

The previous two strategies consider the model to have a single output. This is the case with most ML models; we formulate the model to predict a single scalar value as the prediction after taking in an array of inputs: **multiple input, single output** (**MISO**). But there are some models, such as the DL models, which can be configured to give us multiple outputs. Therefore, the joint strategy, also called **multiple input, multiple output** (**MIMO**), aims to learn a single model that produces the entire forecasting horizon as an output:

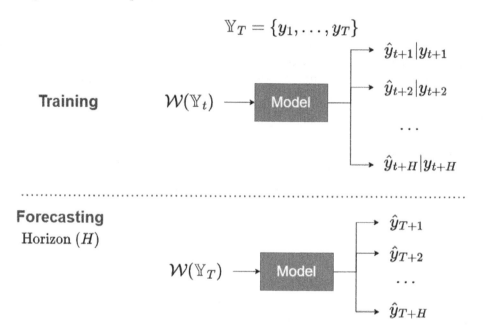

Figure 17.4 – Joint strategy for multi-step forecasting

Let's see how these regimes work.

Training regime

The joint strategy involves training a single multi-output model to forecast all the timesteps in the horizon at once. We can see in *Figure 17.1* that we use the window function, $\mathcal{W}(\mathbb{Y}_t)$, to draw a window from $\mathbb{Y}_t$ and train the model to predict $y_{t+1}, \ldots, y_{t+H}$. And during training, a loss function that measures the divergence between all the outputs of the model, $\widehat{y_{t+1}}, \ldots, \widehat{y_{t+H}}$, and the actual values, $y_{t+1}, \ldots, y_{t+H}$, is used to optimize the parameters of the model.

Forecasting regime

The forecasting regime is also very simple. We have a trained model that is able to forecast all the timesteps in the horizon and we use $\mathcal{W}(\mathbb{Y}_T)$ to forecast them at once.

This strategy is typically used in DL models where we configure the last layer to output H scalars instead of 1.

We have already seen this strategy in action at multiple places in the book:

- The Tabular Regression (*Chapter 13, Common Modeling Patterns for Time Series*) paradigm can easily be extended to output the whole horizon.

- We have seen *Sequence-to-Sequence* models with a *fully connected* decoder (*Chapter 13, Common Modeling Patterns for Time Series*) using this strategy for multi-step forecasting.

- In *Chapter 14, Attention and Transformers for Time Series*, we used this strategy to forecast using transformers.

- In *Chapter 16, Specialized Deep Learning Architectures for Forecasting*, we saw models such as *N-BEATS*, *N-HiTS*, and *Temporal Fusion Transformer*, which used this strategy to generate multi-step forecasts.

Hybrid strategies

The three strategies we have already covered are the three basic strategies for multi-step forecasting, each with its own merits and demerits. Over the years, researchers have tried to combine these into hybrid strategies that try to capture the good parts of all these strategies. Let's go through a few of them here. This will not be a comprehensive list because there is none. Anyone with enough creativity can come up with alternate strategies, but we will just cover a few that have received some attention and deep study from the forecasting community.

DirRec Strategy

As the name suggests, the **DirRec** strategy is the combination of *direct* and *recursive* strategies for multi-step forecasting. First, let's look at the following diagram:

$$\mathbb{Y}_T = \{y_1, \ldots, y_T\}$$

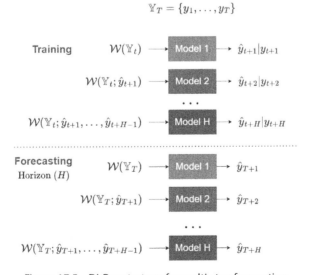

Figure 17.5 – DirRec strategy for multi-step forecasting

Now, let's see how these regimes work for the DirRec strategy.

Training regime

Similar to the direct strategy, the DirRec strategy also has H models for a forecasting horizon of H, but with a twist. We start the process by using $\mathcal{W}(\mathbb{Y}_t)$ and train a model to predict one step ahead. In the recursive strategy, we used this forecasted timestep in the same model to predict the next timestep. But in DirRec, we train a separate model for $H = 2$, but using the forecast we generated in $H = 1$. To generalize at timestep $h < H$, in addition to $\mathcal{W}(\mathbb{Y}_t)$, we include all the forecasts generated by different models at timesteps 1 to h.

Forecasting regime

The forecasting regime is just like the training regime, but instead of training the models, we use the H trained models to generate the forecasts in a recursive manner.

Iterative block-wise direct strategy

The **iterative block-wise direct** (**IBD**) strategy is also called the **iterative multi-SVR strategy**, paying homage to the research paper that suggested this (*#2* in *References*). The direct strategy requires H different models to train, and that makes it difficult to scale for long-horizon forecasting. The IBD strategy tries to tackle that shortcoming by using a block-wise iterative style of forecasting:

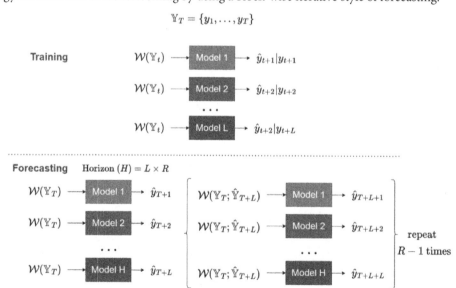

Figure 17.6 – IBD strategy for multi-step forecasting

Let's understand the training and forecasting regimes for this strategy.

Training regime

In the IBD strategy, we split the forecast horizon, H, into R blocks of length L, such that $H = L \times R$. And instead of training H direct models, we train L direct models.

Forecasting regime

While forecasting, we use the L trained models to generate the forecast for the first L timesteps ($T + 1$ to $T + L$) in H using the window $\mathcal{W}(\mathbb{Y}_T)$. Let's denote this L forecast as $\mathbb{Y}_{T+L}$. Now, we will use $\mathbb{Y}_{T+L}$, along with $\mathbb{Y}_T$, in the window function to draw a new window, $\mathcal{W}(\mathbb{Y}_T; \mathbb{Y}_{T+L})$. This new window is used to generate the forecast for the next L timesteps ($T + L$ to $T + 2L$). This process is repeated many times to complete the full horizon forecast.

Rectify strategy

The rectify strategy is another way we can combine direct and recursive strategies. It strikes a middle ground between the two by forming a two-stage training and inferencing methodology. We can see this as a model stacking approach (*Chapter 9, Ensembling and Stacking*) but between different multi-step forecasting strategies:

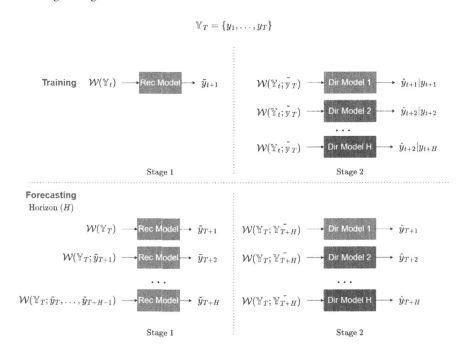

Figure 17.7 – Rectify strategy for multi-step forecasting

Let's understand how this strategy works.

Training regime

The training happens in two steps. The recursive strategy is applied to the horizon and the forecast for all H timesteps is generated. Let's call this $\widetilde{\mathbb{Y}_{t+H}}$. Now, we train direct models for each horizon using the original history, $\mathbb{Y}_t$, and the recursive forecasts, $\widetilde{\mathbb{Y}_{t+H}}$, as inputs.

Forecasting regime

The forecasting regime is similar to the training, where the recursive forecasts are generated first and they, along with the original history, are used to generate the final forecasts.

RecJoint

True to its name, RecJoint is a mashup between the recursive and joint strategies, but applicable for single-output models:

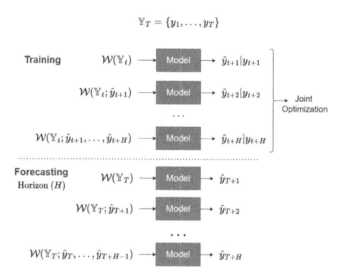

Figure 17.8 – RecJoint strategy for multi-step forecasting

The following sections detail the working of this strategy.

Training regime

The training in the RecJoint strategy is very similar to the recursive strategy in the way it trains a single model and recursively uses prediction at $t + 1$ as an input to train $t + 2$, and so on. But the recursive strategy trains the model on just the next timestep. RecJoint generates the predictions for the entire horizon, and jointly optimizes the entire horizon forecasts while training. This forces the model to look at the next H timesteps and jointly optimize the entire horizon instead of the myopic one-step-ahead objective. We saw this strategy at play when we trained Seq2Seq models using an RNN encoder and decoder (*Chapter 13, Common Modeling Patterns for Time Series*).

Forecasting regime

The forecasting regime for RecJoint is exactly the same as for the recursive strategy.

Now that we have understood a few strategies, let's also discuss the merits and demerits of these strategies.

How to choose a multi-step forecasting strategy?

Let's summarize all the different strategies that we learned now in a table:

Strategy	# of Models	Type	Output Size	Training Time	Prediction Time
Recursive	1	S.O	1	$1 \times T_{so}$	$H \times I_{so}$
Direct	H	S.O	1	$H \times T_{so}$	$H \times I_{so}$
DirRec	H	S.O	1	$H \times T_{so}$	$H \times I_{so}$
IBD	L	S.O	1	$L \times T_{so}$	$H \times I_{so}$
Rectify	H+1	S.O	1	$(H+1) \times T_{so}$	$2 \times H \times I_{so}$
Joint	1	M.O	H	$1 \times T_{mo}$	$1 \times I_{mo}$
RecJoint	1	M.O	1	$1 \times (T_{mo} + \delta)$	$H \times I_{mo}$

Figure 17.9 – Multi-step forecasting strategies – a summary

Here, the following applies:

- **S.O**: Single output
- **M.O**: Multi-output
- T_{so} and I_{so}: Training and inferencing time of a single output model
- T_{mo} and I_{mo}: Training and inferencing time of a multi-output model (practically, T_{mo} is larger than T_{so} mostly because multi-output models are typically DL models and their training time is higher than standard ML models)
- H: The horizon
- $L = \dfrac{H}{R}$, where R is the number of blocks in the IBD strategy
- δ is some positive real number

The table will help us understand and decide which strategy is better from multiple perspectives:

- **Engineering complexity**: *Recursive, Joint, RecJoint << IBD << Direct, DirRec << Rectify*

- **Training time**: *Recursive << Joint* (typically $T_{mo} > T_{so}$) *<< RecJoint << IBD << Direct, DirRec << Rectify*

- **Inference time**: *Joint << Direct, Recursive, DirRec, IBD, RecJoint << Rectify*

It also helps us to decide the kind of model we can use for each strategy. For instance, a joint strategy can only be implemented with a model that supports multi-output, such as a DL model. But we are yet to discuss how these strategies affect accuracies.

Although in ML, the final word goes to empirical evidence, there are ways we can analyze the different methods to provide us with some guidelines. *Taieb et al.* analyzed the bias and variance of these multi-step forecasting strategies, both theoretically and using simulated data. With this analysis, along with other empirical findings over the years, we do have an understanding of the strengths and weaknesses of these strategies, and some guidelines from these findings.

> **Reference check**
>
> The research paper by *Taieb et al.* is cited in *References* under *3*.

Taieb et al. point out several disadvantages of the recursive strategy, contrasting with the direct strategy, based on the bias and variance components of error analysis. They further corroborated these observations through an empirical study as well.

The key points that elucidate the difference in performance are as follows:

- For the recursive strategy, the bias and variance components of error in step $h = 1$ affect step $h = 2$. Because of this phenomenon, the errors that a recursive model makes tend to accumulate as we move further in the forecast horizon. But for the direct strategy, this dependence is not explicit and therefore doesn't suffer the same deterioration that we see in the recursive strategy. This was also seen in the empirical study where the recursive strategy was very erratic and had the highest variance, which increased significantly as we moved further in the horizon.

- For the direct strategy, the bias and variance components of error in step $h = 1$ do not affect $h = 2$. This is because each horizon, h, is forecasted in isolation. Intuitively, a downside of this approach is the fact that this strategy can produce completely unrelated forecasts across the horizon leading to unrealistic forecasts. The complex dependencies that may exist between the forecast in the horizon are not captured in the direct strategy. For instance, a direct strategy on a time series with a non-linear trend may result in a broken curve because of the independence of each timestep in the horizon.

- Practically, in most cases, a direct strategy produces coherent forecasts.

- The bias for the recursive strategy was also amplified when the forecasting model produces forecasts that have large variations. Highly complex models are known to have low bias but a high amount of variations, and these high variations seem to amplify the bias for recursive strategy models.

- When we have very large datasets, the bias term of the direct strategy becomes zero, but the recursive strategy bias was still non-zero. This was further demonstrated in experiments – for long time series, the direct strategy almost always outperformed the recursive strategy. From the learning theory perspective, we are learning H functions using the data for the direct strategy, whereas for recursive, we are just learning 1. So, with the same amount of data, it is harder to learn H true functions than 1. This is amplified in low-data situations.

- Although the recursive strategy seems inferior to the direct strategy theoretically and empirically, it is not without some advantages:

  - For highly non-linear and noisy time series, learning direct functions for all the horizons can be hard. And in such situations, recursive can work better.

  - If the underlying **data-generating process** (**DGP**) is very smooth and can be easily approximated, the recursive strategy can work better.

  - When the time series is shorter, the recursive strategy can work better.

- We talked about the direct strategy generating possible unrelated forecasts for the horizon, but this is exactly the part that the joint strategy takes care of. The joint strategy can be thought of as an extension of the direct strategy, but instead of having H different models, we have a single model produce H outputs. We are learning a single function instead of H functions from the given data. Therefore, the joint strategy doesn't have the same weakness as the direct strategy in short time series.

- One of the weaknesses of the joint strategy (and RecJoint) is the high bias on very short horizons (such as $H = 2, H = 3,$ and so on). We are learning a model that optimizes across all the H timesteps in the horizon using a standard loss function such as the mean squared error. But these errors are at different scales. The errors that can occur further down the horizon are larger than the ones close by, and this implicitly puts more weight on the longer horizons, and the model learns a function that is skewed toward getting the longer horizons right.

- The joint and RecJoint strategies are comparable from the variance perspective. But the joint strategy can give us a lower bias because the RecJoint strategy learns a recursive function and it may not be flexible enough to capture the pattern. But the joint strategy uses the full power of the forecasting model to directly forecast the horizon.

Hybrid strategies, such as DirRec, IBD, and so on, try to balance the merits and demerits of fundamental strategies such as direct, recursive, and joint. With these merits and demerits, we can make an informed experimentation framework to come up with the best strategy for the problem at hand.

Summary

We touched upon a particular aspect of forecasting that is highly relevant for real-world use cases, but rarely talked about and studied. We saw why we needed multi-step forecasting and then went on to review a few popular strategies we can use. We understood the popular and fundamental strategies such as direct, recursive, and joint, and then went on to look at a few hybrid strategies such as DirRec, rectify, and so on. To top it off, we looked at the merits and demerits of these strategies and discussed a few guidelines for selecting the right strategy for your problem.

In the next chapter, we will be looking at another important aspect of forecasting – evaluation.

References

The following is the list of the references that we used throughout the chapter:

1. Taieb, S.B., Bontempi, G., Atiya, A.F., and Sorjamaa, A. (2012). *A review and comparison of strategies for multi-step ahead time series forecasting based on the NN5 forecasting competition.* Expert Syst. Appl., 39, 7067-7083: `https://arxiv.org/pdf/1108.3259.pdf`

2. Li Zhang, Wei-Da Zhou, Pei-Chann Chang, Ji-Wen Yang, Fan-Zhang Li. (2013). *Iterated time series prediction with multiple support vector regression models.* Neurocomputing, Volume 99, 2013: `https://www.sciencedirect.com/science/article/pii/S0925231212005863`

3. Taieb, S.B. and Atiya, A.F. (2016). *A Bias and Variance Analysis for Multistep-Ahead Time Series Forecasting.* in IEEE Transactions on Neural Networks and Learning Systems, vol. 27, no. 1, pp. 62-76, Jan. 2016: `https://ieeexplore.ieee.org/document/7064712`

18

Evaluating Forecasts – Forecast Metrics

We started getting into the nuances of forecasting in the previous chapter where we saw how to generate multi-step forecasts. While that covers one of the aspects, there is another aspect of forecasting that is as important as it is confusing – *how to evaluate forecasts*.

In the real world, we generate forecasts to enable some downstream processes to plan better and take relevant actions. For instance, the operations manager at a bike rental company should decide how many bikes he should make available at the metro station the next day at 4 p.m. However, instead of using the forecasts blindly, he may want to know which forecasts he should trust and which ones he shouldn't. This can only be done by measuring how good a forecast is.

We have been using a few metrics throughout the book and it is now time to get down into the details to understand those metrics, when to use them, and when to not use some metrics. We will also elucidate a few aspects of these metrics experimentally.

In this chapter, we will be covering these main topics:

- Taxonomy of forecast error measures
- Investigating the error measures
- Experimental study of the error measures
- Guidelines for choosing a metric

Technical requirements

You will need to set up the Anaconda environment following the instructions in the *Preface* of the book to get a working environment with all packages and datasets required for the code in this book.

The associated code for the chapter can be found here: `https://github.com/PacktPublishing/ Modern-Time-Series-Forecasting-with-Python/tree/main/notebooks/ Chapter18`.

For this chapter, you need to run the notebooks in the `Chapters02` and `Chapter04` folders from the book's GitHub repository.

Taxonomy of forecast error measures

Measurement is the first step that leads to control and eventually improvement.

–H. James Harrington

Traditionally, in regression problems, we have very few, general loss functions such as the mean squared error or the mean absolute error, but when you step into the world of time series forecasting, you will be hit with a myriad of different metrics.

> **Important note**
> Since the focus of the book is on point predictions (and not probabilistic predictions), we will stick to reviewing point forecast metrics.

There are a few key factors that distinguish the metrics in time series forecasting:

- **Temporal relevance**: The temporal aspect of the prediction we make is an essential aspect of a forecasting paradigm. Metrics such as forecast bias and the tracking signal take this aspect into account.

- **Aggregate metrics**: In most business use cases, we would not be forecasting a single time series, but rather a set of time series, related or unrelated. In these situations, looking at the metrics of individual time series becomes infeasible. Therefore, there should be metrics that capture the idiosyncrasies of this mix of time series.

- **Over- or under-forecasting**: Another key concept in time series forecasting is over- and under-forecasting. In a traditional regression problem, we do not really worry whether the predictions are more than or less than expected, but in the forecasting paradigm, we must be careful about structural biases that always over- or under-forecast. This, when combined with the temporal aspect of time series, accumulates errors and leads to problems in downstream planning.

These aforementioned factors, along with a few others, have led to an explosion in the number of forecast metrics. In a recent survey paper by *Hewamalage et al.* (#1 in *References*), the number of metrics that was covered stands at *38*. Let's try and unify these metrics under some structure. *Figure 18.1* depicts a taxonomy of forecast error measures:

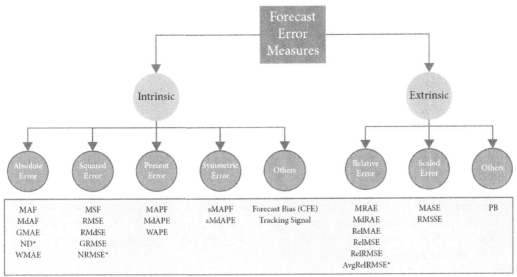

Figure 18.1 – Taxonomy of forecast error measures

We can semantically separate the different forecast metrics into two buckets – **intrinsic** and **extrinsic**. *Intrinsic* metrics measure the generated forecast using nothing but the generated forecast and the corresponding actuals. As the name suggests, it is a very inward-looking metric. *Extrinsic* metrics, on the other hand, use an external reference or benchmark in addition to the generated forecast and ground truth to measure the quality of the forecast.

Before we start with the metrics, let's establish a notation to help us understand. y_t and $\hat{y}_t$ are the actual observation and the forecast at time t. The forecast horizon is denoted by H. In cases where we have a dataset of time series, we assume there are M time series, indexed by m, and finally, $e_t = y_t - \hat{y}_t$ denotes the error at timestep t. Now, let's start with the intrinsic metrics.

Intrinsic metrics

There are four major base errors – absolute error, squared error, percent error, and symmetric error – that are aggregated or summarized in different ways in a variety of metrics. Therefore, any property of these base errors also applies to the aggregate ones, so let's look at these base errors first.

Absolute error

The error, e_t, can be positive or negative, depending on whether $y_t < \hat{y}_t$ or not, but then when we are calculating and adding this error over the horizon, the positive and negative errors may cancel each other out and that paints a rosier picture. Therefore, we include a function on top of e_t to ensure that the errors do not cancel each other out.

The absolute function is one of these functions: $Absolute\ Error(AE) = |e_t|$. The absolute error is a scale-dependent error. This means that the magnitude of the error depends on the scale of the time series. For instance, if you have an AE of 10, it doesn't mean anything until you put it in context. For a time series with values of around 500 to 1,000, an AE of 10 may be a very good number, but if the time series has values around 50 to 70, then it is bad.

> **Important note**
>
> Scale dependence is not a deal breaker when we are looking at individual time series, but when we are aggregating or comparing across multiple time series, scale-dependent errors skew the metric in favor of the large-scale time series. The interesting thing to note here is that this is not necessarily bad. Sometimes, the scale in the time series is meaningful and it makes sense from the business perspective to focus more on the large-scale time series than the smaller ones. For instance, in a retail scenario, one would be more interested in getting the high-selling product forecast right than those of the low-selling ones. In these cases, using a scale-dependent error automatically favors the high-selling products.
>
> You can see this by carrying out an experiment on your own. Generate a random time series, A. Now, similarly, generate a random forecast for the time series, F. Now, we multiply the forecast, F, and time series, A, by 100 to get two new time series and their forecasts, A_{scaled} and F_{scaled}. If we calculate the forecast metric for both these sets of time series and forecasts, the scaled-dependent metrics will give very different values, whereas the scale-independent ones will give the same values.

Many metrics are based on this error:

- **Mean Absolute Error (MAE)**: $MAE = \dfrac{1}{H}\sum_{t=1}^{H}|e_t|$

- **Median Absolute Error**: $MdAE = median(|e_t|)$

- **Geometric Mean Absolute Error**: $GMAE = \sqrt[H]{\prod_{t=1}^{H}|e_t|}$

- **Weighted Mean Absolute Error**: This is a more esoteric method that lets you put more weight on a particular timestep in the horizon:

$$WMAE = \frac{\sum_{t=1}^{H} w_t |e_t|}{\sum_{t=1}^{H} w_t}$$

Here, w_t is the weight of a particular timestep. This can be used to assign more weight to special days (such as weekends or promotion days).

- **Normalized Deviation (ND)**: This is a metric that is strictly used to calculate aggregate measures across a dataset of time series. This is also one of the popular metrics used in the industry to measure aggregate performance across different time series. This is not scale-free and will be skewed toward large-scale time series. This metric has strong connections with another metric called the **Weighted Average Percent Error (WAPE)**. We will discuss these connections when we talk about the WAPE in the following sections.

To calculate ND, we just sum all the absolute errors across the horizons and time series and scale it by the actual observations across the horizons and time series:

$$ND = \frac{\sum_{m=1}^{M} \sum_{t=1}^{H} |e_{(t,m)}|}{\sum_{m=1}^{M} \sum_{t=1}^{H} |y_{t,m}|}$$

Squared error

Squaring is another function that makes the error positive and thereby prevents the errors from canceling each other out:

$$Squared\ Error(SE) = e_t^2$$

There are many metrics that are based on this error:

- **Mean Squared Error**: $MSE = \frac{1}{H} \sum_{t=1}^{H} (e_t^2)$

- **Root Mean Squared Error (RMSE)**: $RMSE = \sqrt{\frac{1}{H} \sum_{t=1}^{H} (e_t^2)}$

- **Root Median Squared Error**: $RMdSE = median\left(\sqrt{e_t^2}\right)$

- **Geometric Root Mean Squared Error**: $GRMSE = \sqrt[2n]{\prod_{t=1}^{H}(e_t^2)}$

- **Normalized Root Mean Squared Error** (**NRMSE**): This is a metric that is very similar to ND in spirit. The only difference is that we take the square root of the squared errors in the numerator rather than the absolute error:

$$NRMSE = \frac{\sqrt{\frac{1}{MH} \sum_{m=1}^{M} \sum_{t=1}^{H} \left(e_{(t,m)}^2\right)}}{\frac{1}{MH} \sum_{m=1}^{M} \sum_{t=1}^{H} |y_{t,m}|}$$

Percent error

While absolute error and squared error are scale-dependent, percent error is a scale-free error measure. In percent error, we scale the error using the actual time series observations: $Percent\ Error(PE) = \frac{100e_t}{y_t}$. Some of the metrics that use percent error are as follows:

- **Mean Absolute Percent Error (MAPE)** – $MAPE = \sum_{t=1}^{H} \frac{100|e_t|}{y_t}$

- **Median Absolute Percent Error** – $MdAPE = median\left(\frac{100|e_t|}{y_t}\right)$

- **WAPE** – WAPE is a metric that embraces scale dependency and explicitly weights the errors with the scale of the timestep. If we want to give more focus to high values in the horizon, we can weigh those timesteps more than the others. Instead of taking a simple mean, we use a weighted mean on the absolute percent error. We can choose the weight to be anything but more often than not, it is chosen as the quantity of the observation itself. And in that special case, the math (with some assumptions) works out to be a simple formula which reminds us of ND. The difference is that ND is a metric which aggregates across multiple time series, and WAPE is a metric which weights across timestep:

$$WAPE = \frac{\sum_{t=1}^{H}|e_t|}{\sum_{t=1}^{H}|y_t|}$$

Symmetric error

Percent error has a few problems – it is asymmetrical (we will see this in detail later in the chapter), and it breaks down when the actual observation is zero (due to division by zero). Symmetric error was proposed as an alternative to avoid this asymmetry, but as it turns out, symmetric error is itself asymmetric – more on that later, but for now, let's see what symmetric error is:

$$Symmetric\ Error(SE) = \frac{200|e_t|}{|y_t| + |\hat{y}_t|}$$

There are only two metrics that are popularly used under this base error:

- **Symmetric Mean Absolute Percent Error (sMAPE):**

$$sMAPE = \frac{1}{H}\sum_{t=1}^{H}\frac{200|e_t|}{|y_t| + |\hat{y}_t|}$$

- **Symmetric Median Absolute Percent Error:**

$$sMdAPE = median\left(\frac{200|e_t|}{|y_t| + |\hat{y}_t|}\right)$$

Other intrinsic metrics

There are a few other metrics that are intrinsic in nature but don't conform to the other metrics. Notable among those are three metrics that measure the over- or under-forecasting aspect of forecasts:

- **Cumulative Forecast Error (CFE)** – CFE is simply the sum of all the errors, including the sign of the error. Here, we want the positives and negatives to cancel each other out so that we understand whether a forecast is consistently over- or under-forecasting in a given horizon. A CFE close to zero means the forecasting model is neither over- nor under-forecasting:

$$CFE = \sum_{t=1}^{H} e_t$$

- **Forecast Bias** – While CFE measures the degree of over- and under-forecasting, it is still scale-dependent. When we want to compare across time series or have an intuitive understanding of the degree of over- or under-forecasting, we can scale CFE by the actual observations. This is called Forecast Bias:

$$Forecast\ Bias = \frac{\sum_{t=1}^{H} e_t}{\sum_{t=1}^{H} y_t}$$

- **Tracking Signal** – The Tracking Signal is another metric that is used to measure the same over- and under-forecasting in forecasts. While CFE and Forecast Bias are used more offline, the Tracking Signal finds its place in an online setting where we are tracking over- and under-forecasting over periodic time intervals, such as every hour or every week. It helps us detect structural biases in the forecasting model. Typically, the Tracking Signal is used along with a threshold value so that going above or below it throws a warning. Although a thumb rule is to use ± 3.75, it is totally up to you to decide the right threshold for your problem:

$$TS_w = \frac{\sum_{t=0}^{w} e_t}{\frac{1}{w} \sum_{t=0}^{w} |e_t|}$$

Here, w is the past window over which TS is calculated.

Now, let's turn our attention to a few extrinsic metrics.

Extrinsic metrics

There are two major buckets of metrics under the extrinsic umbrella – relative error and scaled error.

Relative error

One of the problems of intrinsic metrics is that they don't mean a lot unless a benchmark score exists. For instance, if we hear that the MAPE is 5%, it doesn't mean a lot because we don't know how forecastable that time series is. Maybe 5% is a bad error rate. Relative error solves this by including a benchmark forecast in the calculation so that the errors of the forecast we are measuring are measured against the benchmark and thus show the relative gains of the forecast. Therefore, in addition to the notation that we have established, we need to add a few more.

Let y_t^* be the forecast from the benchmark and $e_t^* = y_t - y_t^*$ be the benchmark error. There are two ways we can include the benchmark in the metric:

- Using errors from the benchmark forecast to scale the error of the forecast

- Using forecast measures from the benchmark forecast to scale the forecast measure of the forecast we are measuring

Let's look at a few metrics which follow these:

- **Mean Relative Absolute Error (MRAE):** $MRAE = \frac{1}{H}\sum_{t=1}^{H}\frac{|e_t|}{|e_t^*|}$

- **Median Relative Absolute Error:** $MdRAE = median\left(\frac{|e_t|}{|e_t^*|}\right)$

- **Geometric Mean Relative Absolute Error:** $GMRAE = \sqrt[H]{\prod_{t=1}^{H}\frac{|e_t|}{|e_t^*|}}$

- **Relative Mean Absolute Error (RelMAE):** $RelMAE = \frac{MAE}{MAE^*}$, where MAE^* is the MAE of the benchmark forecast

- **Relative Root Mean Squared Error (RelRMSE):** $RelRMSE = \frac{RMSE}{RMSE^*}$, where $RMSE^*$ is the RMSE of the benchmark forecast

- **Average Relative Root Mean Squared Error:** Davydenko and Fildes (#2 in *References*) proposed another metric that is strictly for calculating aggregate scores across time series. They argued that using a geometric mean over the RelMAEs of individual time series is better than an arithmetic mean, so they defined the Average Relative Root Mean Squared Error as follows:

$$AvgRelMAE = \sqrt[\Sigma_{m=1}^{M}h_m]{\prod_{m=1}^{M}\left(\frac{MAE_m}{MAE_m^*}\right)^{h_m}}$$

Scaled error

Hyndman and Koehler introduced the idea of scaled error in 2006. This was an alternative to relative error and measures and tries to get over some of the drawbacks and subjectivity of choosing the benchmark forecast. Scaled error scales the forecast error using an in-sample MAE of a benchmark method such as naïve forecasting. Let the entire training history be of T timesteps, indexed by i.

So, the scaled error is defined as follows:

$$SE = \frac{|e_t|}{\frac{1}{T-1}\sum_{i=2}^{T}|y_t - y_{t-1}|}$$

There are a couple of metrics that adopt this principle:

- **Mean Absolute Scaled Error (MASE):** $MASE = \frac{1}{H}\sum_{t=1}^{H}|SE|$

- **Root Mean Squared Scaled Error (RMSSE):** A similar scaled error was developed for the squared error and was used in the M5 Forecasting Competition in 2020:

$$RMSSE = \frac{1}{H}\sum_{t=1}^{H}\frac{e_t^2}{\frac{1}{T-1}\sum_{i=2}^{T}(y_t - y_{t-1})^2}$$

Other extrinsic metrics

There are other extrinsic metrics that don't fall into the categorization of errors we have made. One such error measure is the following:

Percent Better (**PB**) is a method that is based on counts and can be applied to individual time series as well as a dataset of time series. The idea here is to use a benchmark method and count how many times a given method is better than the benchmark and report it as a percentage. Formally, we can define it using MAE as the reference error as follows:

$$PB_{MAE} = 100 \ mean(\mathbb{I}\{MAE < MAE^*\})$$

Here, $\mathbb{I}$ is an indicator function that returns 1 if the condition is true and 0 otherwise.

We have seen a lot of metrics in the previous sections, but now it's time to understand a bit more about the way they work and what they are suited for.

Investigating the error measures

It's not enough to know the different metrics since we also need to understand how these work, what are they good for, and what they are not good for. We can start with the basic errors and work our way up because understanding the properties of basic errors such as *absolute error*, *squared error*, *percent error*, and *symmetric error* will help us understand the others as well because most of the other metrics are derivatives of these primary errors; either aggregating them or using relative benchmarks.

Let's do this investigation using a few experiments and understand them through the results.

> **Notebook alert**
>
> The notebook for running these experiments on your own is `01-Loss Curves and Symmetry.ipynb` in the `Chapter18` folder.

Loss curves and complementarity

All these base errors depend on two factors – forecasts and actual observations. We can examine the behavior of these several metrics if we fix one and alter the other in a symmetric range of potential errors. The expectation is that the metric will behave the same way on both sides because deviation from the actual observation on either side should be equally penalized in an unbiased metric. We can also swap the forecasts and actual observations and that also should not affect the metric.

In the notebook, we did exactly these experiments – loss curves and complementary pairs.

Absolute error

When we plot these for absolute error, we get *Figure 18.2*:

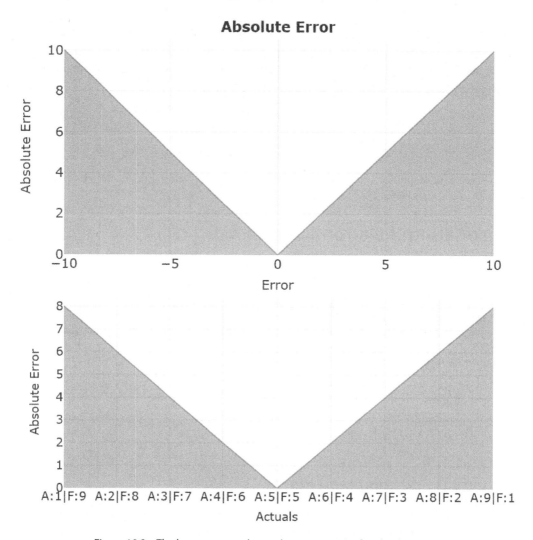

Figure 18.2 – The loss curves and complementary pairs for absolute error

The first chart plots the signed error against the absolute error and the second one plots the absolute error with all the combinations of actuals and forecast, which add up to 10. The two charts are obviously symmetrical, which means that an equal deviation from the actual observed on either side is penalized equally, and if we swap the actual observation and the forecast, the metric remains unchanged.

Squared error

Now, let's look at squared error:

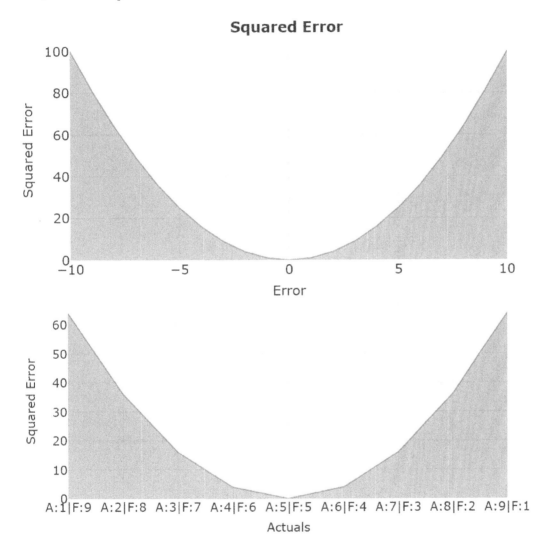

Figure 18.3 – The loss curves and complementary pairs for squared error

These charts also look symmetrical, so the squared error also doesn't have an issue with asymmetric error distribution – but we can notice one thing here. The squared error increases exponentially as the error increases. This points to a property of the squared error – it gives undue weightage to outliers. If there are a few timesteps for which the forecast is really bad and excellent at all other points, the squared error inflates the impact of those outlying errors.

Percent error

Now, let's look at percent error:

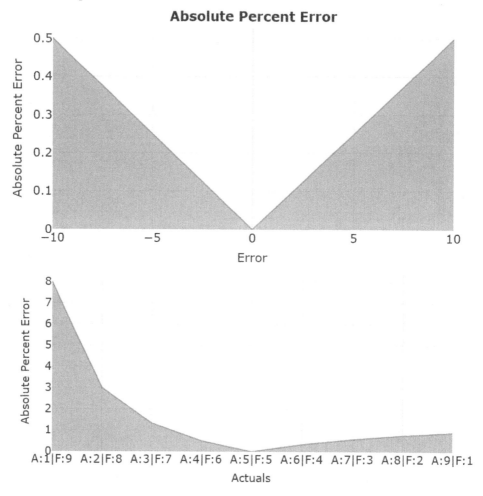

Figure 18.4 – The loss curves and complementary pairs for percent error

There goes our symmetry. The percent error is symmetrical when you move away from the actuals on both sides (mostly because we are keeping the actuals constant), but the complementary pairs tell us a whole different story. When the actual is 1 and the forecast is 9, the percent error is 8, but when we swap them, the percent error drops to 1. This kind of asymmetry can cause the metric to favor under-forecasting. The right half of the second chart in *Figure 18.4* are all cases where we are under-forecasting and we can see that the error is very low there when compared to the left half.

We will look at under- and over-forecasting in detail in another experiment.

Symmetric error

For now, let's move on and look at the last error we had – symmetric error:

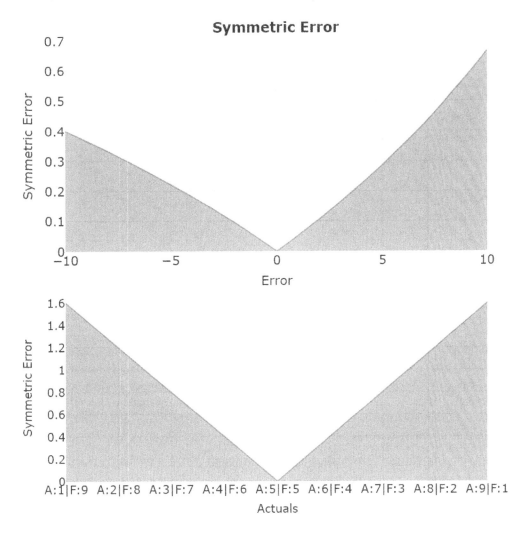

Figure 18.5 – The loss curves and complementary pairs for symmetric error

Symmetric error was proposed mainly because of the asymmetry we saw in the percent error. MAPE, which uses percent error, is one of the most popular metrics used and sMAPE was proposed to directly challenge and replace MAPE – true to its claim, it did resolve the asymmetry that was present in percent error. However, it introduced its own asymmetry. In the first chart, we can see that for a particular actual value, if the forecast moves on either side, it is penalized differently, so in effect, this metric favors over-forecasting (which is in direct contrast to percent error, which favors under-forecasting).

Extrinsic errors

With all the intrinsic measures done, we can also take a look at the extrinsic ones. With extrinsic measures, plotting the loss curves and checking symmetry is not as easy. Instead of two variables, we now have three – the actual observation, the forecast, and the reference forecast; the value of the measure can vary with any of these. We can use a contour plot for this as shown in *Figure 18.6*:

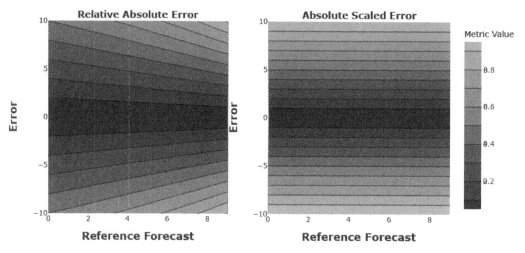

Figure 18.6 – Contour plot of the loss surface – relative absolute error and absolute scaled error

The contour plot enables us to plot three dimensions in a 2D plot. The two dimensions (error and reference forecast) are on the *x*- and *y*-axes. The third dimension (the relative absolute error and absolute scaled error values) is represented as color, with contour lines bordering same-colored areas. The errors are symmetric around the error (horizontal) axis. This means that if we keep the reference forecast constant and vary the error, both measures vary equally on both sides of the errors. This is not surprising since both these errors have their base in absolute error, which we know was symmetric.

The interesting observation is the dependency on the reference forecast. We can see that for the same error, *relative absolute error* has different values for different reference forecasts, but *scaled error* doesn't have this problem. This is because it is not directly dependent on the reference forecast and rather uses the MAE of a naïve forecast. This value is fixed for a time series and eliminates the task of choosing a reference forecast. Therefore, scaled error has good symmetry for absolute error and very little or fixed dependency on the reference forecast.

Bias towards over- or under-forecasting

We have seen indications of bias toward over- or under-forecasting in a few metrics that we saw. In fact, it looked like the popular metric, MAPE, favors under-forecasting. To finally put that to test, we can perform another experiment with synthetically generated time series and we included a lot more metrics in this experiment so that we know which are safe to use and which need to be looked at carefully.

Notebook alert

The notebook to run these experiments on your own is `02-Over and Under Forecasting.ipynb` in the `Chapter18` folder.

The experiment is simple and detailed as follows:

1. We randomly sample a count time series of integers with a length of 100 from a uniform distribution between 2 and 5:

    ```
    np.random.randint(2,5,n)
    ```

2. We use the same process to generate a forecast, which is also drawn from a uniform distribution between 2 and 5:

    ```
    np.random.randint(2,5,n)
    ```

3. Now, we generate two additional forecasts, one from the uniform distribution between 0 to 4 and another between 3 and 7. The former predominantly under-forecasts and the latter over-forecasts:

    ```
    np.random.randint(0,4,n) # Underforecast
    np.random.randint(3,7,n)  # Overforecast
    ```

4. We calculate all the measures we want to investigate using all three forecasts.

5. We repeat it 10,000 times to average out the effect of random draws.

After the experiment is done, we can plot a box plot of different metrics so that it shows the distribution of each metric for each of those three forecasts over these 10,000 runs of the experiment. Let's see the box plot in *Figure 18.7*:

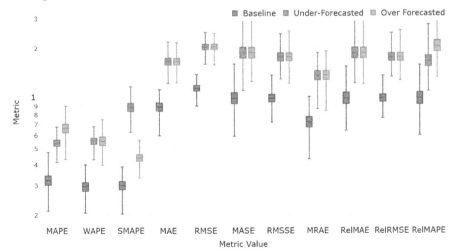

Figure 18.7 – Over- and under-forecasting experiment

Let's go over what we would expect from this experiment first. The over- (green) and under- (red) forecasted forecasts would have a higher error than the baseline (blue). The over- and under-forecasted errors would be similar.

With that, let's summarize our major findings:

- MAPE clearly favors the under-forecasted with a lower MAPE than the over-forecasted.

- WAPE, although based on percent error, managed to get over the problem by having explicit weighting. This may be counteracting the bias that percent error has.

- sMAPE, in its attempt to fix MAPE, does a worse job in the opposite direction. sMAPE highly favors over-forecasting.

- Metrics such as MAE and RMSE, which are based on absolute error and squared error respectively, don't show any preference for either over- or under-forecasting.

- MASE and RMSSE (both using versions of scaled error) are also fine.

- MRAE, in spite of some asymmetry regarding the reference forecast, turns out to be unbiased from the over- and under-forecasting perspective.

- The relative measures with absolute and squared error bases (RelMAE and RelRMSE) also do not have any bias toward over- or under-forecasting.

- The relative measure of mean absolute percentage error, RelMAPE, carries MAPE's bias toward under-forecasting.

We have investigated a few properties of different error measures and understood the basic properties of some of them. To further that understanding and move closer to helping us select the right measure for our problem, let's do one more experiment using the London Smart Meters dataset we have been using through this book.

Experimental study of the error measures

As we discussed earlier, there are a lot of metrics for forecasting that people have come up with over the years. Although there are many different formulations of these metrics, there can be similarities in what they are measuring. Therefore, if we are going to choose a primary and secondary metric while modeling, we should pick some metrics that are diverse and measure different aspects of the forecast.

Through this experiment, we are going to try and figure out which of these metrics are similar to each other. We are going to use the subset of the *London Smart Meters* dataset we have been using all through the book and generate some forecasts for each household. I have chosen to do this exercise with the darts library because I wanted multi-step forecasting. I've used five different forecasting methods – *seasonal naïve, exponential smoothing, Theta, FFT,* and *LightGBM (local)* – and generated forecasts. On top of that, I have also calculated the following metrics on all of these forecasts – *MAPE,*

WAPE, sMAPE, MAE, MdAE, MSE, RMSE, MRAE, MASE, RMSSE, RelMAE, RelRMSE, RelMAPE, CFE, Forecast Bias, and *PB(MAE)*. In addition to this, we also calculated a few aggregate metrics – *meanMASE, meanRMSSE, meanWAPE, meanMRAE, AvgRelRMSE, ND,* and *NRMSE*.

Using Spearman's rank correlation

The basis of the experiment is that if different metrics measure the same underlying factor, then they will also rank forecasts on different households similarly. For instance, if we say that MAE and MASE are measuring one latent property of the forecast, then those two metrics would give similar rankings to different households. At the aggregated level, there are five different models and aggregate metrics that measure the same underlying latent factor and should also rank them in similar ways.

Let's look at the aggregate metrics first. We ranked the different forecast methods at the aggregate level using each of the metrics and then we calculated the Pearson correlation of the ranks. This gives us Spearman's rank correlation between the forecasting methods and metrics. The heatmap of the correlation matrix is in *Figure 18.8*:

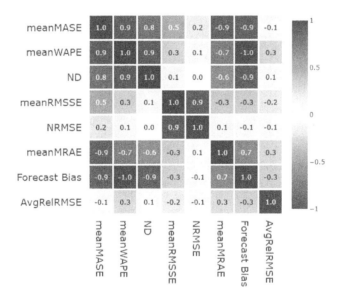

Figure 18.8 – Spearman's rank correlation between the forecast methods and aggregate metrics

These are the major observations:

- We can see that *meanMASE, meanWAPE,* and *ND* (all based on absolute error) are highly correlated, indicating that they might be measuring similar latent factors of the forecast.

- The other pair that is highly correlated is *meanRMSSE* and *NRMSE*, which are both based on squared error.

- There is a weak correlation between *meanMASE* and *meanRMSSE*, maybe because they are both using scaled error.

- *meanMRAE* and *Forecast Bias* seem to be highly correlated, although there is no strong basis for that shared behavior. Some correlations can be because of chance and this needs to be validated further on more datasets.

- *meanMRAE* and *AvgRelRMSE* seem to be measuring very different latent factors from the rest of the metrics and each other.

Similarly, we calculated Spearman's rank correlation between the forecast methods and metrics across all the households (*Figure 18.9*). This enables us to have the same kind of comparison as before at the item level:

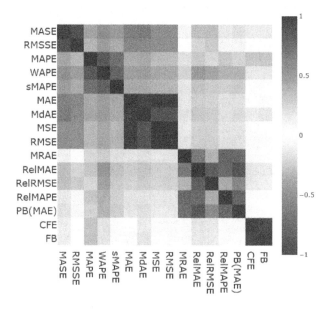

Figure 18.9 – Spearman's rank correlation between the forecast methods and item-level metrics

The major observations are as follows:

- We can see there are five clusters of highly correlated metrics (the five green boxes).

- The first group is *MASE* and *RMSSE*, which are highly correlated. This can be because of the scaled error formulation of both metrics.

- *WAPE*, *MAPE*, and *sMAPE* are the second group. Frankly, this is a bit confusing because I would have expected *MAPE* and *sMAPE* to have less correlated results. They do behave in the opposite way from an over- and under-forecasting perspective. Maybe all the forecasts we have used to check this correlation don't over- or under-forecast and therefore the similarity came out through the shared percent error base. This needs to be investigated further.

- *MAE, MdAE, MSE*, and *RMSE* form the third group of highly similar metrics. *MAE* and *MdAE* are both absolute error metrics and *MSE* and *RMSE* are both squared error metrics. The similarity between these two can be because of the lack of outlying errors in the forecasts. The only difference between these two base errors is that squared error puts a much greater weight on outlying errors.

- The next group of similar metrics is the motley crew of relative measures – *MRAE, RelMAE, RelRMSE, RelMAPE*, and *PB(MAE)*, but the intercorrelation among this group is not as strong as the other groups. The pairs of metrics that stand out in terms of having low inter-correlations are *MRAE* and *RelRMSE* and *RelMAPE* and *RelRMSE*.

- The last group that stands totally apart with much less correlation with any other metric but a higher correlation with each other is *Forecast Bias* and *CFE*. Both are calculated on unsigned errors and measure the amount of over- or under-forecasting.

- If we look at intergroup similarities, the only thing that stands out is the similarity between the scaled error group and absolute error and squared error group.

> **Important note**
> Spearman's rank correlation on aggregate metrics is done using a single dataset and has to be taken with a grain of salt. The item-level correlation has a bit more significance because it is made across many households, but there are still a few things in there that warrant further investigation. I urge you to repeat this experiment on some other datasets and check whether we see the same patterns repeated before adopting them as rules.

Now that we have explored the different metrics, it is time to summarize and probably leave you with a few guidelines for choosing a metric.

Guidelines for choosing a metric

Throughout this chapter, we have come to understand that it is difficult to choose one forecast metric and apply it universally. There are advantages and disadvantages for each metric and being cognizant of these while selecting a metric is the only rational way to go about it.

Let's summarize and note a few points we have seen through different experiments in the chapter:

- Absolute error and squared error are both symmetric losses and are unbiased from the under- or over-forecasting perspective.

- Squared error does have a tendency to magnify the outlying error because of the square term in it. Therefore, if we use a squared-error-based metric, we will be penalizing high errors much more than small errors.

- RMSE is generally preferred over MSE because RMSE is on the same scale as the original input and therefore is a bit more interpretable.

- Percent error and symmetric error are not symmetric in the complete sense and favor under-forecasting and over-forecasting, respectively. MAPE, which is a very popular metric, is plagued by this shortcoming. For instance, if we are forecasting demand, optimizing for MAPE will lead you to select a forecast that is conservative and therefore under-forecast. This will lead to an inventory shortage and out-of-stock situations. sMAPE, with all its shortcomings, has fallen out of favor with practitioners.

- Relative measures are a good alternative to percent-error-based metrics because they are also inherently interpretable, but relative measures depend on the quality of the benchmark method. If the benchmark method performs poorly, the relative measures will tend to dampen the impact of errors from the model under evaluation. On the other hand, if the benchmark forecast is close to an oracle forecast with close to zero errors, the relative measure will exaggerate the errors of the model. Therefore, you have to be careful when choosing the benchmark forecast, which is an additional thing to worry about.

- Although a geometric mean offers a few advantages over an arithmetic mean (such as resistance to outliers and better approximation when there is high variation in data), it is not without its own problems. Geometric mean-based measures mean that even if a single series (when aggregating across time series) or a single timestep (when aggregating across timesteps) performs really well, it will make the overall error come down drastically due to the multiplication.

- PB, although an intuitive metric, has one disadvantage. We are simply counting the instances in which we perform better. However, it doesn't assess how well or poorly we are doing. The effect on the PB score is the same whether our error is 50% less than the reference error or 1% less.

Hewamalage et al. (#1 in *References*) have proposed a very detailed flowchart to aid in decision-making, but that is also more of a guideline as to what not to use. The selection of a single metric is a very debatable task. There are a lot of conflicting opinions out there and I'm just adding another to that noise. Here are a few guidelines I propose to help you pick a forecasting metric:

- Avoid *MAPE*. In any situation, there is always a better metric to measure what you want. At the very least, stick to *WAPE* for single time series datasets.

- For a single time series dataset, the best metrics to choose are *MAE* or *RMSE* (depending on whether you want to penalize large errors more or not).

- For multiple time series datasets, use *ND* or *NRMSSE* (depending on whether you want to penalize large errors more or not). As a second choice, *meanMASE* or *meanRMSSE* can also be used.

- If there are large changes in the time series (in the horizon we are measuring, there is a huge shift in time series levels), then something such as *PB* or *MRAE* can be used.

- Whichever metric you choose, always make sure to use *Forecast Bias*, *CFE*, or Tracking Signal to keep an eye on structural over- or under-forecasting problems.

- If the time series you are forecasting is intermittent (as in, has a lot of time steps with zero values), use *RMSE* and avoid *MAE*. *MAE* favors forecasts that generate all zeros. Avoid all percent-error-based metrics because intermittency brings to light another one of their shortcomings – it is undefined when actual observations are zero (*Further reading* has a link to a blog that explores other metrics for intermittent series).

Congratulations on finishing a chapter full of new terms and metrics and I hope you have gained the necessary intuition to intelligently select the metric to focus on for your next forecasting assignment!

Summary

In this chapter, we looked at the thickly populated and highly controversial area of forecast metrics. We started with a basic taxonomy of forecast measures to help you categorize and organize all the metrics in the field.

Then, we launched a few experiments through which we learned about the different properties of these metrics, slowly approaching a better understanding of what these metrics are measuring, but looking at synthetic time series experiments, we learned how *MAPE* and *sMAPE* favor under- and over-forecasting, respectively.

We also analyzed the rank correlations between these metrics on real data to see how similar the different metrics are and finally, rounded off by laying out a few guidelines that can help you pick a forecasting metric for your problem.

In the next chapter, we will look at cross-validation strategies for time series.

References

The following are the references that we used throughout the chapter:

1. Hewamalage, Hansika; Ackermann, Klaus; and Bergmeir, Christoph. (2022). *Forecast Evaluation for Data Scientists: Common Pitfalls and Best Practices.* arXiv preprint arXiv: Arxiv-2203.10716: `https://arxiv.org/abs/2203.10716v2`

2. Davydenko, Andrey and Fildes, Robert. (2013). *Measuring forecasting accuracy: the case of judgmental adjustments to SKU-level demand forecasts.* In *International Journal of Forecasting.* Vol. 29, No. 3., 2013, pp. 510-522: `https://doi.org/10.1016/j.ijforecast.2012.09.002`

3. Hyndman, Rob J. and Koehler, Anne B.. (2006). *Another look at measures of forecast accuracy.* In *International Journal of Forecasting*, Vol. 22, Issue 4, 2006, pp. 679-688: `https://robjhyndman.com/publications/another-look-at-measures-of-forecast-accuracy/`

Further reading

If you wish to read further about forecast metrics, you can check out the blog post *Forecast Error Measures: Intermittent Demand* by Manu Joseph – `https://deep-and-shallow.com/2020/10/07/forecast-error-measures-intermittent-demand/`.

19

Evaluating Forecasts – Validation Strategies

Throughout the last few chapters, we have been looking at a few relevant, but seldom discussed, aspects of time series forecasting. While we learned about different forecasting metrics in the previous chapter, we now move on to the final piece of the puzzle – validation strategies. This is another integral part of evaluating forecasts.

In this chapter, we try to answer the question *How do we choose the validation strategy to evaluate models from a time series forecasting perspective?* We will look at different strategies and their merits and demerits so that by the end of the chapter, you can make an informed decision to set up the validation strategy for your time series problem.

In this chapter, we will be covering these main topics:

- Model validation
- Holdout strategies
- Cross-validation strategies
- Choosing a validation strategy
- Validation strategies for datasets with multiple time series

Technical requirements

You will need to set up the Anaconda environment following the instructions in the *Preface* of the book to get a working environment with all the packages and datasets required for the code in this book.

The associated code for the chapter can be found at `https://github.com/PacktPublishing/Modern-Time-Series-Forecasting-with-Python-/tree/main/notebooks/Chapter19`.

Model validation

In *Chapter 18, Evaluating Forecasts – Forecast Metrics*, we learned about different forecast metrics that can be used to measure the quality of a forecast. One of the main uses for this is to measure how well our forecast is doing on test data (new and unseen data), but this comes after we train a model, tweak it, and tinker with it until we are happy with it. How do we know whether a model we are training or tweaking is good enough?

Model validation is the process of evaluating a trained model using data to assess how good the model is. We use the metrics we learned about in *Chapter 18, Evaluating Forecasts – Forecast Metrics*, to calculate the goodness of the forecast. But, there is one question we haven't answered. Which part of the data do we use to evaluate? In a standard machine learning setup (classification or regression), we randomly sample a portion of the training data and call it validation data, and it is based on this data that all the modeling decisions are taken. The best practice in the field is to use cross-validation. **Cross-validation** is a resampling procedure where we sample different portions of the training dataset to train and test in multiple iterations. In addition to repeated evaluation, cross-validation also makes the most efficient use of the data.

But, in the field of time series forecasting, such a consensus on best practice does not exist. This is mainly because of the temporal nature and the sheer variety of ways we can go about it. Different time series might have different lengths of history and we may choose different ways to model it, or there might be different horizons to forecast for, and so on. Because of the temporal dependence in the data, standard assumptions of i.i.d. don't hold true, therefore techniques such as cross-validation have their own complications. When randomly chosen, the validation and training datasets may not be independent, which will lead to an optimistic and misleading estimate of error.

There are two main paradigms of validation:

- **In-sample validation** – As the name suggests, the model is evaluated on the same or a subset of the same data that was used to train it.

- **Out-of-sample validation** – Under this paradigm, the data we use to evaluate the model has no intersection with the data used to train the model.

In-sample validation helps you understand how well your model has fit the data you have. This was very popular in the era of statistics, where the models were meticulously designed and primarily used for inferencing and not predicting. In such cases, the in-sample error shows how well the specified model fits the data and how valid the inferences we make from that model are. But in a predictive paradigm, like most of machine learning, the in-sample error is not the right measure of the *goodness* of a model. Complex models can easily fit the training data, memorize it, and not work well on new and unseen data. Therefore, out-of-sample validations are almost exclusively used in today's predictive model evaluations. Since this book is solely concerned with forecasting, which is a predictive task, we will be sticking to out-of-sample evaluations only.

As discussed earlier, deciding on a validation strategy for forecasting problems is not as trivial as standard machine learning. There are two major schools of thought here:

- Holdout-based strategies, which respect the temporal integrity of the problem
- Cross-validation-based strategies, which sample validation splits with a very loose or no sense of temporal ordering

Let's discuss the major ones in each category. What we have to keep in mind is that all the validation strategies that we discuss in the book are not exhaustive. They are merely a few popular ones. In the explanations that follow, the length of the validation period is L_v and the length of the training period is L_t.

Now, let's look at the first school of thought.

Holdout strategies

There are three aspects of a holdout strategy, and they can be mixed and matched to create many variations of the strategy. The three aspects are as follows:

- **Sampling strategy** – A sampling strategy is how we sample the validation split(s) from training data.
- **Window strategy** – A window strategy decides how we sample the window of training split(s) from training data.
- **Calibration strategy** – A calibration strategy decides whether a model should be recalibrated or not.

That said, designing a holdout validation strategy for a time series problem includes making decisions on these three aspects.

Sampling strategies are ways to pick one or more origins in the training data. These **origins** are point(s) in time that determine the starting point of the validation split and the ending point of the training split. The exact length of the validation split is governed by a parameter L_v, which is the horizon chosen for validation. The length of the training split depends on the window strategy.

Window strategy

There are two ways we can draw the windows of training split – expanding window and rolling window. *Figure 19.1* shows the difference between the two setups:

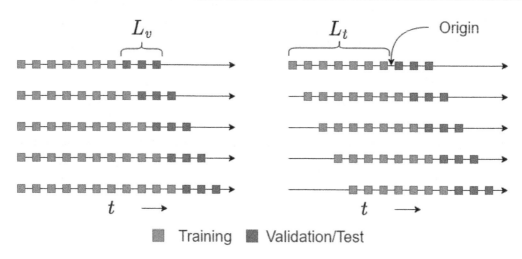

Figure 19.1 – Expanding (left) versus rolling (right) strategy

Under the expanding window strategy, the training split expands as the origin moves forward in time. In other words, under the expanding window strategy, we choose all the data that is available before the origin as the training split. This effectively increases the training length every time the origin moves forward in time.

In the rolling window strategy, we keep the length of the training split constant (L_t). Therefore, when we move the origin forward by three timesteps, the training split drops three timesteps from the start of the time series.

> **Important note**
>
> Although the expanding and rolling window concept may remind you of the window we use for feature engineering or use as the context in deep learning models, this window is not the same. The window we talk about in this chapter is the window of training data that we chose to train our model. For instance, the features of a machine learning model may only extend to the 5 days before, and we can have the training split use the last 5 years of data.

There are merits and demerits to both of these window strategies. Let's summarize them in a few key points:

- Expanding window is a good setup for a short time series, where the expanding window leads to more data being available for the models.

- Rolling window removes the oldest data from training. If the time series is non-stationary and the behavior is bound to change as time passes, having a rolling window will be beneficial to keep the model up to date.

- When we use the expanding window strategy for repeated evaluation, such as in cross-validation, the increase in time series length used for training can introduce some bias toward windows with a longer history. The rolling window strategy takes care of that bias by maintaining the same length of the series.

Calibration strategy

The calibration strategy is only valid in cases where we do multiple evaluations with different origins. There are two ways we can do evaluations with different origins – recalibrate every origin, or update every origin (terminology from Tashman, #1 in *References*).

Under the *recalibrate* strategy, the model is retrained with the new training split for every origin. This retrained model is used to evaluate the validation split. But, for the *update* strategy, we do not retrain the model, but use the trained model to evaluate the new validation split.

Let's summarize a few key points to be considered for choosing a strategy here:

- The golden standard is to recalibrate every new origin, but many times this may not be feasible. In the econometrics/classical statistical models, the norm was to recalibrate every origin. That was feasible because those models are relatively less compute-intensive and the datasets at the time were also small. So, one could refit a model in a very short time. Nowadays, the datasets have grown in size, and so have the models. Retraining a deep learning model every time we move the origin may not be as easy.

  Therefore, if you are using modern, complex models with long training times, an update strategy might be better.

- For classical models that run fast, we can explore the recalibration strategy.

  But, if the time series you are forecasting is so dynamic that the behavior changes very frequently, then the recalibration strategy might be the way to go.

Now let's get on to the third part of the validation strategy.

Sampling strategy

In the holdout strategy, we sample a point (*origin*) on the time series, preferably toward the end, such that the portion of the time series after the origin is shorter than the portion of the time series before. From this origin, we can use either the *expanding* or *rolling window* strategy to generate training and validation splits. The model is trained on the training split and tested on the held-out validation split. This strategy is simply called the **holdout** strategy. The calibration strategy is fixed at *recalibrate* because we are only testing and evaluating the model once.

The simple holdout strategy has one disadvantage – the forecast measure we have calculated on the held-out data may not be robust enough because of the single evaluation paradigm. We are relying on a single split of data to calculate the predictive performance of the model. For non-stationary series, this can be a problem because we might be selecting a model that captures the idiosyncrasies of the split that we have chosen.

We can get over this problem by repeating the holdout evaluation multiple times. We can either hand-tailor the different origins using business domain knowledge, such as taking into account seasonality, or some other factor. Or we could sample the origin points randomly. If we repeat this n times, there will be n validation splits, and they may or may not overlap with each other. The performance metric from these repeated trials can be aggregated using a function such as the mean, maximum, and minimum. This is called the **repeated holdout (Rep-Holdout)** strategy.

> **Note on implementation**
>
> The simple holdout strategy is very simple to implement because we decide the size of the validation split, and keep that much from the end of the time series aside as the validation. The *Rep-Holdout* strategy involves sampling multiple windows at random or using predefined windows as validation splits. We can make use of the `PredefinedSplit` class from scikit-learn to this effect.

Figure 19.2 shows the two holdout strategies using an expanding window approach:

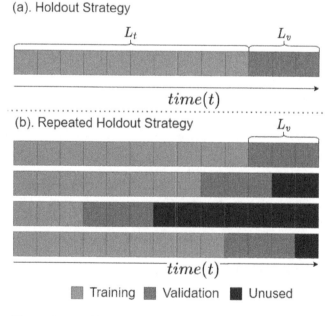

Figure 19.2 – Holdout strategy (a) and Rep-Holdout strategy (b)

The Rep-Holdout strategy has a few more variants. The vanilla *Rep-Holdout* strategy evaluates multiple validation datasets, is mostly hand-crafted, and can have overlapping validation datasets. A variation of the Rep-Holdout strategy that insists that multiple validation splits should have no overlap is a more popular option. We call this **Repeated Holdout (No Overlap) (Rep-Holdout-O)**. This has some properties from the cross-validation family and tries to use more data systematically. *Figure 19.3(a)* shows this strategy:

(a). Rep Hold-out (No Overlap)(Rep-Holdout-O)

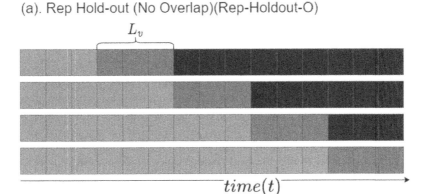

(b). Rep Hold-out (No Overlap) with Gaps (Rep-Holdout-O(G))

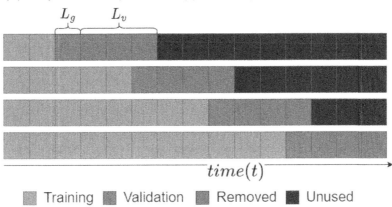

Figure 19.3 – Variations of Rep-Holdout strategy

The *Rep-Holdout-O* strategy is easy to implement in scikit-learn using the `TimeSeriesSplit` class for single time series datasets.

> **Notebook alert**
>
> The associated notebook that shows how to implement different validation strategies can be found in the `Chapter19` folder under the name `01-Validation Strategies.ipynb`.

The `TimeSeriesSplit` class from `sklearn.model_selection` implements the Rep-Holdout validation strategy and even supports expanding or rolling window variants. The main parameter is `n_splits`. This determines how many splits you want from the data, and the validation split size is decided automatically, according to this formula:

$$round\left(\frac{n\_samples}{n\_splits + 1}\right)$$

In the default configuration, this implements an expanding window Rep-Holdout-O strategy. But, there is a parameter, `max_train_size`. If we set this parameter, then it will use a window of `max_train_size` in a rolling window manner.

Yet another variant of the Rep-Holdout strategy introduces a gap of length L_g between the train and validation splits. This is to increase the independence between the train and validation splits, hence getting a better error estimate through the procedure. We call this strategy **Repeated Holdout (No Overlap) with Gaps (Rep-Holdout-O(G))**. This strategy is depicted in *Figure 19.3(b)*.

We can implement this using the `TimeSeriesSplit` class as well. All we need to do is use a parameter called `gap`. By default, the gap is set to 0. But if we change to a non-zero number, it inserts that much timestep gap between the end of the training and the beginning of validation.

Before we move on to the next set of strategies, let's summarize and discuss some key points about the holdout strategies:

- Holdout strategies respect the temporal integrity of the problem and have been the preferred way of evaluating forecasting models for a long time.

  But, it does have a weakness in the inefficient use of available data. For short time series, holdout or Rep-Holdout may not have enough training data to train a model.

- A simple holdout depends on a single evaluation, and the error estimate is not robust. Even in a stationary series, this procedure does not guarantee a good estimate of the error. In non-stationary time series, such as a seasonal time series, this problem exacerbates. But the Rep-Holdout and its variants take care of that issue.

Now let's look at the other major school of thought.

Cross-validation strategies

Cross-validation is one of the most important tools when evaluating standard regression and classification methods. This is because of two reasons:

- A simple holdout approach doesn't use all the data available and in cases where data is scarce, cross-validation makes the best use of the available data.

- Theoretically, the time series we have observed is one realization of a stochastic process, and so the acquired error measure of the data is also a stochastic variable. Therefore, it is essential to sample multiple error estimates to get an idea about the distribution of the stochastic variable. Intuitively, we can think of this as a "lack of reliability" on the error measure derived from a single slice of data.

The most common strategy that is used in standard machine learning is called **k-fold cross-validation**. Under this strategy, we randomly shuffle and partition the training data into k equal parts. Now, the whole training of the model and calculating the error is repeated k times, such that every k subset we have kept aside is used as a test set once, and only once. When we use a particular subset as testing data, we use all the other subsets as the training data. After we acquire k different estimates of the error measure, we aggregate it using a function such as an average. This mean will typically be more robust than a single error measure.

But, there is one assumption that is central to the validity procedure: *i.i.d samples*. This is one assumption that is invalid in time series problems because, by definition, the different samples in time series are dependent on each other through autocorrelation.

> **Additional information**
>
> Some argue that when we use time delay embedding to convert time series to a regression problem, we can start to use k-fold cross-validation on time series problems. While there are obvious theoretical problems, *Bergmeir et al.* (#2 in *References*) showed that empirically, the k-fold cross-validation is not a bad option. But, the caveat is that the time series needs to be stationary. We will talk more about this in the next section, where we will discuss the merits and demerits of these strategies.

But there have been modifications to the k-fold strategy, specifically aimed at sequential data.

Snijders et al. (#4 in *References*) proposed a modification we call the **Blocked Cross-Validation (Bl-CV)** strategy. It is similar to the standard *k-fold* strategy, but we do not randomly shuffle the dataset before partitioning into k subsets of length L_v. So, this partitioning strategy results in k contiguous blocks of observations. Then, like a standard k-fold strategy, we train and test each of these k blocks and aggregate the error measure over these multiple evaluations. So, the temporal integrity of the problem is satisfied partially. In other words, temporal integrity is maintained within each of the blocks, but not between the blocks. *Figure 19.4(a)* shows this strategy:

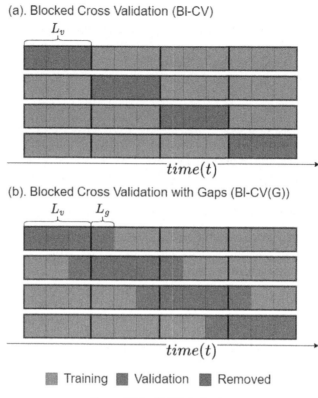

Figure 19.4 – BI-CV strategies

To implement the **BI-CV strategy**, we can use the same Kfold class from scikit-learn. As we saw earlier, the main parameter the cross-validation classes in scikit-learn takes in is n_splits. Here, n_splits also defines the number of equally sized folds it selects. There is another parameter, shuffle, which is set to True by default. If we make sure our data is sorted according to time, then use the Kfold class with shuffle=False, it will imitate the *BI-CV* strategy. The associated notebook shows this usage. I urge you to check the notebook for a better understanding of how this is implemented.

In the previous section, we talked about introducing gaps between train and validation splits, to increase independence between them. Another variant of the BI-CV is a version that uses these gaps. We call it **Blocked Cross-Validation with Gaps (BI-CV(G))**. We can see this in action in *Figure 19.4(b)*.

Unfortunately, the Kfold implementation in scikit-learn does not support this variant. But, it's simple to extend the Kfold implementation to include gaps as well. The associated notebook has an implementation of this. It has an additional parameter, gap, that lets us set the gap between the train and validation splits.

We saw many different strategies for validation; now let's try and lay down a few points that will help you in deciding the right strategy for your problem.

Choosing a validation strategy

Choosing the right validation strategy is one of the most important, but overlooked tasks in the machine learning workflow. A good validation setup will go a long way in all the different steps in the modeling process, such as feature engineering, feature selection, model selection, and hyperparameter tuning. Although there are no hard and fast rules in setting up a validation strategy, there are a few guidelines we can follow. Some of them are from experience (both mine and others) and some of them are from empirical and theoretical studies that have been published as research papers:

- One guiding principle in the design is that we try to make the validation strategy replicate the real use of the model as much as possible. For instance, if the model is going to be used to predict the next 24 timesteps, we make the length of the validation split 24 timesteps. Of course, it's not as simple as that, because other practical constraints such as the availability of enough data, time, and computers have to be kept in mind while designing a validation strategy.

- Rep-Holdout strategies that respect the temporal order of the time series problem are the preferred option, especially in cases where there is sufficient data available.

- For purely autoregressive formulations of stationary time series, regular Kfold can also be used and *Bergmeir et al.* (#2 in *References*) empirically show that they perform better than holdout strategies. But, Blocked Cross Validation is a better alternative among cross-validated strategies. *Cerqueira et al.* (#3 in *References*) corroborated the findings in their empirical study for stationary time series.

- If the time series is non-stationary, then *Cerqueira et al.* showed empirically that the holdout strategies (especially Rep-Holdout strategies) are the best ones to choose.

- If the time series is short, using Bl-CV after making the time series stationary is a good strategy for autoregressive formulations, such as time delay embedding. But, for models that use some kind of memory of the history to forecast, such as exponential smoothing or deep learning models such as RNN, cross-validation strategies may not be safe to use.

- If we have exogenous variables, in addition to the autoregressive part, it may not be safe to use cross-validation strategies. It is best to stick to holdout-based strategies.

- For a strongly seasonal time series, it is beneficial to use validation periods that mimic the forecast horizon. For instance, if we are forecasting for October, November, and December, it is beneficial to check the performance of the model in October, November, and December of last year.

Up until now, we were talking about validation strategies for a single time series. But in the context of global models, we are at a point where we need to think about validation strategies for such cases as well.

Validation strategies for datasets with multiple time series

All the strategies we have seen till now are perfectly valid for datasets with multiple time series, such as the London Smart Meters dataset we have been working with in this book. The insights we discussed in the last section are also valid. The implementation of such strategies can be slightly tricky because the scikit learn classes we discussed work for single time series. Those implementations assume that we have a single time series, sorted according to the temporal order. If there are multiple time series, the splits will be haphazard and messy.

There are a couple of options we can adopt for datasets with multiple time series:

- We can loop over the different time series and use the methods we discussed to do the train-validation split, and then concatenate the resulting sets across all the time series. But, that is not going to be so efficient.

- We can write some code and design the validation strategies to use datetime or a time index (such as the one we saw in PyTorch forecasting in *Chapter 15, Strategies for Global Deep Learning Forecasting Models*). I have linked to a brilliant notebook from *Konrad Banachewicz* in the *Further reading* section of this chapter, where he uses a custom `GroupSplit` class that uses the time index as the group. This is one way to use Rep-Holdout strategies on a dataset with multiple time series.

There are a few points that we need to keep in mind for datasets with multiple time series:

- Do not use different time windows for different time series. This is because different windows in time would have different errors, and that would skew the aggregate error metric we are tracking.

- If different time series have different lengths, align the length of the validation period across all the series. Training length can be different, but validation windows should be the same so that every time series equally contributes to the aggregate error metric.

- It is easy to get carried away by complicated validation schemes, but always keep the technical debt you incur by choosing a specific technique in mind.

With that, we have come to the end of a short but important chapter.

Summary

We have come to the end of our journey through the world of time series forecasting. In the last couple of chapters, we addressed a few mechanics of forecasting, such as how to do multi-step forecasting, and how to evaluate forecasts. Different validation strategies for evaluating forecasts and forecasting models were the topics of the current chapter. We started by enlightening you as to why model validation is an important task. Then, we looked at a few different validation strategies, such as the holdout strategies, and navigated the controversial use of cross-validation for time series. We spent some time summarizing and laying down a few guidelines to be used to select a validation strategy. To top it all off, we looked at how these validation strategies are applicable to datasets with multiple time series and talked about how to adapt them to such scenarios.

With that, we have come to the end of the book. Congratulations on making it all the way through, and I hope you have gained enough skills from the book to tackle the next time series problem that comes your way. I strongly urge you to start putting into practice the skills that you have gained from the book because, as Richard Feynman rightly put it, *"You do not know anything until you have practiced."*

References

The following are the references used in this chapter:

1. Tashman, Len. (2000). *Out-of-sample tests of forecasting accuracy: An analysis and review.* International Journal of Forecasting. 16. 437-450. 10.1016/S0169-2070(00)00065-0: `https://www.researchgate.net/publication/223319987_Out-of-sample_tests_of_forecasting_accuracy_An_analysis_and_review`

2. Bergmeir, Christoph and Benítez, José M. (2012). *On the use of cross-validation for time series predictor evaluation.* In Information Sciences, Volume 191, 2012, Pages 192-213: `https://www.sciencedirect.com/science/article/abs/pii/S0020025511006773`

3. Cerqueira, V., Torgo, L., and Mozetič, I. (2020). *Evaluating time series forecasting models: an empirical study on performance estimation methods.* Mach Learn 109, 1997–2028 (2020): `https://doi.org/10.1007/s10994-020-05910-7`

4. Snijders, T.A.B. (1988). *On Cross-Validation for Predictor Evaluation in Time Series.* In: *Dijkstra, T.K.* (eds) *On Model Uncertainty and its Statistical Implications.* Lecture Notes in Economics and Mathematical Systems, vol 307. Springer, Berlin, Heidelberg. `https://doi.org/10.1007/978-3-642-61564-1_4`

Further reading

TS-10: *Validation methods for time series* by *Konrad Banachewicz* – `https://www.kaggle.com/code/konradb/ts-10-validation-methods-for-time-series`

Index

Packt.com

Subscribe to our online digital library for full access to over 7,000 books and videos, as well as industry leading tools to help you plan your personal development and advance your career. For more information, please visit our website.

Why subscribe?

- Spend less time learning and more time coding with practical eBooks and Videos from over 4,000 industry professionals

- Improve your learning with Skill Plans built especially for you

- Get a free eBook or video every month

- Fully searchable for easy access to vital information

- Copy and paste, print, and bookmark content

Did you know that Packt offers eBook versions of every book published, with PDF and ePub files available? You can upgrade to the eBook version at packt.com and as a print book customer, you are entitled to a discount on the eBook copy. Get in touch with us at customercare@packtpub.com for more details.

At www.packt.com, you can also read a collection of free technical articles, sign up for a range of free newsletters, and receive exclusive discounts and offers on Packt books and eBooks.

Other Books You May Enjoy

If you enjoyed this book, you may be interested in these other books by Packt:

Intelligent Document Processing with AWS AI/ML

Sonali Sahu

ISBN: 9781801810562

- Understand the requirements and challenges in deriving insights from a document
- Explore common stages in the intelligent document processing pipeline
- Discover how AWS AI/ML can successfully automate IDP pipelines
- Find out how to write clean and elegant Python code by leveraging AI
- Get to grips with the concepts and functionalities of AWS AI services
- Explore IDP across industries such as insurance, healthcare, finance, and the public sector
- Determine how to apply business rules in IDP
- Build, train, and deploy models with serverless architecture for IDP

Practical Deep Learning at Scale with MLflow

Yong Liu

ISBN: 9781803241333

- Understand MLOps and deep learning life cycle development
- Track deep learning models, code, data, parameters, and metrics
- Build, deploy, and run deep learning model pipelines anywhere
- Run hyperparameter optimization at scale to tune deep learning models
- Build production-grade multi-step deep learning inference pipelines
- Implement scalable deep learning explainability as a service
- Deploy deep learning batch and streaming inference services
- Ship practical NLP solutions from experimentation to production

Packt is searching for authors like you

If you're interested in becoming an author for Packt, please visit `authors.packtpub.com` and apply today. We have worked with thousands of developers and tech professionals, just like you, to help them share their insight with the global tech community. You can make a general application, apply for a specific hot topic that we are recruiting an author for, or submit your own idea.

Share Your Thoughts

Now you've finished *Modern Time Series Forecasting with Python*, we'd love to hear your thoughts! Scan the QR code below to go straight to the Amazon review page for this book and share your feedback or leave a review on the site that you purchased it from.

https://packt.link/r/1-803-24680-4

Your review is important to us and the tech community and will help us make sure we're delivering excellent quality content.

Download a free PDF copy of this book

Thanks for purchasing this book!

Do you like to read on the go but are unable to carry your print books everywhere?

Is your eBook purchase not compatible with the device of your choice?

Don't worry, now with every Packt book you get a DRM-free PDF version of that book at no cost.

Read anywhere, any place, on any device. Search, copy, and paste code from your favorite technical books directly into your application.

The perks don't stop there, you can get exclusive access to discounts, newsletters, and great free content in your inbox daily

Follow these simple steps to get the benefits:

1. Scan the QR code or visit the link below

https://packt.link/free-ebook/9781803246802

2. Submit your proof of purchase
3. That's it! We'll send your free PDF and other benefits to your email directly

Made in the USA
Coppell, TX
08 January 2023

10693511R00306